Bricklin on Technology

Bricklin on Technology

Dan Bricklin

WILEY

Wiley Publishing, Inc.

Bricklin on Technology

Published by
Wiley Publishing, Inc.
10475 Crosspoint Boulevard
Indianapolis, IN 46256
www.wiley.com

Published by Wiley Publishing, Inc., Indianapolis, Indiana

Published simultaneously in Canada

ISBN: 978-0-470-40237-5

Manufactured in the United States of America

10 9 8 7 6 5 4 3 2 1

Library of Congress Cataloging-in-Publication Data
Bricklin, Dan, 1951–
  Bricklin on technology / Dan Bricklin.
     p. cm.
  Includes index.
  ISBN 978-0-470-40237-5 (paper/website)
  1. Computers and civilization. 2. Information technology. 3. System design. 4. Technological
innovations. I. Title.
  QA76.9.C66B75 2009
  303.48'34—dc22

                              2009004137

To my father and mother, Baruch and Ruth Bricklin

About the Author

Daniel Bricklin, a software developer and entrepreneur, is best known as the cocreator of VisiCalc, the first electronic spreadsheet.

Dan was born in 1951 and started programming while still in high school in the mid-1960s. He attended college at the Massachusetts Institute of Technology and received a B.S. in Electrical Engineering/Computer Science in 1973. While attending school, he also worked at MIT's Laboratory for Computer Science, programming various interactive systems. It was there that he met Bob Frankston.

After MIT, Dan worked at Digital Equipment Corporation (DEC), where he was involved in computerized typesetting and some editing hardware. He was project leader of the initial WPS-8 word processing software (later sold as part of the DECmate system), helping to specify and develop one of the first stand-alone screen-based word processing systems. In 1976, he left DEC and worked at FasFax Corporation, a small maker of microprocessor-based electronic cash registers. He returned to school in 1977, this time receiving an M.B.A. from Harvard in 1979.

It was during his tenure as a graduate student that he conceived of the idea and design for the electronic spreadsheet, teaming up with his friend Bob Frankston to do the programming. Together, they founded Software Arts, Inc., in 1979, where Dan served as chairman from 1979 to 1985.

His next venture was as president of Software Garden, Inc., a small company with headquarters in his home. There Dan developed a product called "Dan Bricklin's Demo Program," a program for prototyping and simulating other pieces of software, which won the 1986 Software Publishers Association Award for "Best Programming Tool." A new version of the product, "Dan Bricklin's Demo II Program," was announced in December of 1987 and won the 1987 award. In 1989 he released "Dan Bricklin's PageGarden Program" for facilitating repetitive printing on laser printers.

In early 1990, Dan cofounded a venture-capital-funded software development company, Slate Corporation, along with other personal computer industry veterans. Slate's mission was to develop applications software for pen computers. With the lackluster sale of pen computers, Slate closed its doors after four years, and Dan returned to Software Garden.

Upon returning to Software Garden, Dan developed "Dan Bricklin's OverAll Viewer," a tool for displaying data visually, published by Software Garden, and "Dan Bricklin's demo-it!," a new program for demonstrating software on Microsoft Windows, published by Lifeboat Publishing.

In late 1995, Dan founded another company, Trellix Corporation, which became the leading provider of private-label web site publishing technology and managed hosting services to top online providers for small-business and personal web sites. Its main product was Trellix Web Express, a server-based web site authoring system private labeled by web communities and hosting services. Previously it produced Trellix Web, a PC-based web site creation tool bundled on over 35 million devices from companies like HP, Dell, and Kodak.

In early 2003, Trellix was acquired by Interland, Inc., a supplier of business-class web hosting solutions for small and medium-sized businesses. Dan served as Chief Technology Officer of Interland, working out of Interland's Trellix office in Concord, Massachusetts.

In early 2004, Dan returned to Software Garden where as president he has been doing software development, speaking, expert witness engagements, and consulting for a variety of companies. Software development projects include the Open Source ListGarden and wikiCalc programs, and, in conjunction with Socialtext, Inc., the SocialCalc system.

Dan is a founding trustee of the Massachusetts Technology Leadership Council and has served on the boards of the Software Publishers Association and the Boston Computer Society. He has received many honors for his contributions to the computer industry, including the IEEE Computer Society Computer Entrepreneur Award and a Lifetime Achievement Award from the Software Publishers Association. Along with VisiCalc cocreator Bob Frankston, he received the 2001 Washington Award from the Western Society of Engineers. He has received numerous other awards, from organizations such as the Association for Computer Machinery, the Boston Jaycees, and MIT, and from publications such as *Computer Reseller News* and *PC Magazine*. He is a member of the National Academy of Engineering.

Credits

Executive Editor
Carol Long

Senior Development Editor
Kevin Kent

Production Editor
Liz Britten

Copy Editor
C.M. Jones

Editorial Manager
Mary Beth Wakefield

Production Manager
Tim Tate

Vice President and Executive Group Publisher
Richard Swadley

Vice President and Executive Publisher
Barry Pruett

Associate Publisher
Jim Minatel

Project Coordinator, Cover
Lynsey Stanford

Compositor
Maureen Forys,
Happenstance Type-O-Rama

Proofreader
Justin Neely, Word One

Indexer
Jack Lewis

Cover Images
Author photo. ©Louis Fabian Bachrach
(From the 1997 "Wizards and Their
Wonders" historical series for the
Computer Museum and ACM)

Background images:
Computer: © Creatas/Jupiter
Diagram: © Dan Bricklin

Cover Designer
Michael Trent

Acknowledgments

I'd like to thank all of the people who helped make this book possible. I can't possibly list them all here, though I will list some. I apologize for any that I leave out inadvertently.

Since this is based on my web site, I need to thank Dave Winer, whose examples have influenced the path that I, and many others, have followed online. Thank you, Bob Frankston, for starting me on Dave's DaveNet, helping make VisiCalc a reality, being such a good friend all these years, and for countless other things.

Thank you, Julianne Chatelain, for all the help and encouragement during the first two years of my web site.[1] Thank you, Ed Blachman, Peter Levin, and the others at Trellix, who were quick to comment on my posts, and thank you, Don Bulens, for being so supportive of my blogging. Thank you to all of my readers for encouraging me to continue, either with an email, a link, or even just clicking to read what I wrote and thereby leaving a line in the server log file.

This book owes a big debt to my personal editors. My cousin Tova Zeff read and corrected every chapter and spent endless time giving me advice and encouragement. Chris Daly took time off from working on his own book to help me clean up several of the chapters. Adina Bricklin helped me get a clear handle on early drafts of parts of the book. Jonathan Bricklin, who has been a great supporter and source of insight throughout my career, went over most of the final draft. Carol Singer also used her red pen to the readers' benefit.

I'd also like to thank the people who took the time to look over a late draft and then were willing to go on the record with the comments that appear on the cover.

At Wiley, Kevin Kent guided me through the editorial process and had his hand in improving every chapter. Tim Tate worked with me to develop a new template to meet my needs. Angela Smith, Liz Britten, and others at Wiley are working on this manuscript after I write this. I am sure they are turning it into a real book and are making me look like a much better writer than I really am. Thank you to all of you.

---

[1] http://www.bricklin.com/log/2001_03_01.htm#julianne,
http://www.juliannechatelain.com/

This book happened because Joe Wikert started the ball rolling at Wiley when he first approached me in late 2007. Executive Acquisitions Editor Carol Long did what was necessary to get both me and Wiley to commit to really doing it and has been with the project the rest of the way. Thank you both.

There are many people and entities quoted in this book in some way or another. I contacted most of them, and I thank them for the help they so kindly gave that made this book possible. I especially want to thank A K M Adam, Dan Ariely, Charles Arthur, Bernard Bailyn, Mark Bernstein, Congregation Beth El of the Sudbury River Valley, Ed Blachman, Don Bulens, Bill Buxton, Eric Clemons, Frank Clines, Charles Cooper, Bob Cringely, Ward Cunningham, Donna Dubinsky, Jørn Eriksen, Gary Eskow, Louis Fabian Bachrach, Claude Fischer, Everett Fox, Bob Frankston, Dan Fylstra, Jean-Louis Gassée, Dan Gillmor, Malcolm Gladwell, Helen Greiner, Mathew Gross, Carl Hewitt, Meg Hourihan, Judith Hurwitz, Sherry Israel, Peter Jennings, Scott Kirsner, Trevor Kletz, Larry Kushner, Julian Lange, Peter Levin, Tom Matrullo, John Morgan, Jakob Nielsen, Don Norman, Tim O'Reilly, Andrew Odlyzko, John Palmer, Charles Perrow, Jim Raycroft, David Reed, Ben Rosen, Larry Schwartz, Clay Shirky, Jean-Yves Stervinou, Jesse Taylor, David Weinberger, Kevin Werbach, Evan Williams, Mike Wilson, Dave Winer, and Amy Wohl.

Finally, I'd like to thank my immediate family, my parents and grandparents, and other family and friends who inspired and taught me, and encouraged me throughout my career and during the creation of this book.

Dan Bricklin
March 2009

Contents

1 Introduction: Case Studies and Details

The goal of this book is to help you better understand the juncture between computer technology and people, the process of creating that technology, and the evolution of those innovations. It does this through the use of essays and annotated case studies of people using technologies such as cell phones, blogs, and personal computer productivity tools. This book takes advantage of writings and recordings I have made over the past ten years as source material from which we can learn.

Computer Technology in Everyday Life

When I was a child, my grandfather showed me a punched card sorter at the newspaper where he worked. Ever since, I have loved computer technology and strived to find ways to exploit its potential. However, until the 1990s, people's use of computer technology in their everyday lives was seemingly limited to a small group of people like me. It was uncommon to have your own personal computer—that was a "hobbyist" thing or something only businesses did. Other than using automated bank machines and perhaps "programming" a microwave oven, most people felt they had no daily interaction with computers, especially as an obvious integral part of their personal lives. (The flashing 12:00 on a VCR was a common reminder that many people wouldn't go to the trouble to even learn how to do something as simple as "program" that machine.) Cameras had film, and you shared copies of pictures by getting "doubles" when the film was developed and mailing the copies in an envelope. To talk with someone at a distance, you had to go to a particular place inside a building or a special booth where a fixed device using 100-year-old technology was wired into the phone system. You had to know which specific such device the other person was near at that moment to talk to them. The fact that a few disparate computer systems around the world could be networked together and may have been used for academic sharing had no meaning to most people. People would probably have guessed that the "Internet" was a sports term.

I remember in the early 1980s when Jim Finke, then head of the company that made Commodore computers, reminded us at trade conferences that the personal computer market was about the size of the potato chip market and would hopefully get as big as the pantyhose market. We in the personal computer industry were focused on our wonderful products and their potential and reveled in the glow of each little mention in the popular press or exotic bit part in the plot of a movie. By comparing us to such mundane, minor parts of everyday life, he helped show how insignificant we were in the scheme of things at the time.

I also remember going to an industry conference in Palm Springs, California, in the early 1980s. Personal computer luminaries were there, including the heads of major companies: Bill Gates, Steve Jobs, Mitch Kapor, and others. We heard that a boxer was training at the same hotel for an upcoming championship fight. And then, as some of us went outside to go from one building to another, a visitor passed by on his way to observe the training—the visitor was the great boxer Muhammad Ali. As he walked by, I felt us all just stop and stand there staring, with our jaws dropped. Here was one of the most famous people on the planet—and he probably didn't have a clue who we were. Suddenly our "greatest" seemed so much less.

Things have changed. Some of our industry's most influential people are now as well known as famous sports stars. People now make up jokes and stories involving Bill Gates the same way they used to with the Rockefellers and Rothschilds in the olden days. Television news treats new product introductions, Internet service interruptions, and computer virus outbreaks as major general news.

Today, computer-based technology is rapidly affecting all of society. Word processing is the expected way to write. An email address is often the only contact information you ask for. Carrying a cell phone is more important than a watch or wallet for many people around the world. Apple is the largest reseller of recorded music in the USA, and it doesn't ship any of it on vinyl or CD, the old dominant formats. Digital cameras have replaced film cameras, with iconic names like Nikon abandoning film cameras. New uses of the Internet and computing power are appearing constantly, with many of them catching on and, like YouTube and Facebook, having major impacts on areas such as politics and courtship, which are seemingly unrelated to technology.

Insight into the forces that govern computer technology, and how that technology affects and is affected by a society made up of people, used to be of concern to just a few insiders. With the new, prominent role that computer technology plays supporting all of society, this insight is now something of interest to a much wider range of people. This book brings a unique perspective to help gain that insight.

I believe that it is important for people to at least try to understand these forces. We are all involved in using technology and making decisions that can affect its evolution, and its evolution in turn affects our lives. Some of us are building new technology and some of us are deciding what and when to adopt or discourage. We make decisions based upon our belief in the value of what we see now and how we think things will play out in the future.

About Me and My Book

I view myself as a tool maker. I create "tools" that make use of computer technology to help people do things they couldn't do before, or to do them better than they could without the tools. The most famous tool I helped create is VisiCalc, the early personal computer spreadsheet program, but I've worked on many others before and after, from word processors to accounting systems. In a way, this book is another type of tool that people can use.

I am a mixture of techie geek engineer, entrepreneur, and general business executive. As a teenager, I was a photographer, selling photos of children to their parents to make money so I could buy hobbyist parts like transistors and capacitors, and electronic kits from Heathkit. I learned to program computers in the 1960s, and from that time on, doing programming helped pay for cameras and film. I went to MIT for a bachelor's degree, which prepared me for programming jobs at Digital Equipment Corporation and elsewhere, but then I went off to the Harvard Business School for an MBA, which helped prepare me to found four companies since.

I've created products that have had great impact, like VisiCalc for businesspeople and others, and Dan Bricklin's Demo Program for programmers, software designers, and trainers. I've been in companies that failed. I've met and sat across the dinner table from people who are household names. I've watched firsthand as the computer industry evolved over the past five decades.

After VisiCalc came out in 1979, I started giving talks about computer software at conferences, and reporters started seeking me out as a source to comment on technology and the computer industry in general. When posting on web sites was starting to become a popular method to provide commentary and analysis in the late 1990s, I created some web sites focusing on particular topics and then eventually started my own personal web site, www.bricklin.com.

On that new web site I initially put background material about me for reporters and others so that my discussions with them could start without the preliminaries, and I put answers to common questions I received by email from people doing homework in their computer courses. I continued building the web site, adding essays and reports on events I attended, complete with many photos (which was something unusual in those days), mixing in my old love of photography.

In October of 1999, I added an ongoing blog to the web site. The blog has shorter entries than the essays and is organized in reverse chronological order. At the time, many blogs were mainly lists of links to recent articles on the Web with just a bit of commentary or were very personal diaries about daily life. My entries were focused on topics related to the computer industry and on trying to use blogs to communicate my observations to others. I made frequent use of photos, a rarity on most blogs I was reading in those days related to my topics.

Since then, I have been chronicling on the Web many of my experiences through written words, photos, and more recently audio and video recordings. I've also posted many of my thoughts at the time about different issues, trying to use my unique perspective to provide insight to others. This was a time when much of that acceptance of computer technology and Internet communication came about, and that is what I was following.

Now, after a decade of periodic essays on topics of interest to me at the moment—blogging, and documenting things chronologically—it's time to step back and try to clarify, organize, and make use of that raw material.

On the Web, I've covered many areas, from theories about computer network architecture to the joy of walking through crunchy multicolored leaves in the New England fall. Two important themes, though, were **the human aspect of the development and use of technology, and the evolution of that use. This book is the result of extracting those themes, reordering and regrouping the material from its original chronological progression, and embellishing the raw material with commentary and new observations.** The result is, hopefully, a presentation in a more coherent and useful fashion.

Web Posts as Case Material

One of the theories behind the teaching at the Harvard Business School is that business, like law and other topics, can be well taught by the case method. Cases consist of a number of pages of prose and figures describing a situation.

Exposure to cases based on real-world events and situations helps you understand the intricate world of business. It is like the immersion method of teaching a foreign language, where the students are surrounded by the second language as everything from math to meals is conducted in the new language. Principles that are difficult to articulate become second nature as you follow a multitude of complete situations and listen to "natives" speaking and follow them as they go about their activities. My web posts included here serve as case material.

In many of those business school case studies what is presented is not a lean, coherent, clean story tuned to the one pedagogic issue. There are lots of pieces and lots of extra material in a narrative. You'll find that here, too.

Much of my material was originally written to stand on its own without regard to flowing cleanly into the next piece, which is one of the important properties of a blog and web site like mine. Things are presented as chunks: single web pages, blog entries (posts), or recordings. They are linked to each other and to other pages and posts on the Web, but the order of reading was never fixed, except perhaps chronologically in the order in which they were written. On the Web, most people would read only one piece at a time, either because they were following my writings on a daily or weekly basis, or, more commonly, because they were directed to that particular piece by a link on somebody else's web writing, through an email, or as the result of using a search engine. Everybody reads a different set of pieces of the material and in a different order.

A book is different. It has a definite preferred order, and you expect people to go from one page directly to the next with few pauses. In this book, I found an order that follows the major theme of each piece and strings them together into a logical whole. I add footnotes and other material to fill in gaps and put the material in context.

In this book, I also include some of the material to which some of my writings are a reaction and also some of the reactions that are in response to my writings. In addition to putting what I write in a fuller context, it will also give you a better feel for the give and take that a blog writer gets with the community made up of readers.

Hopefully, the essays, anecdotes, interviews, and first-hand observations, and the narrative I try to build around them in this book, will help you get a better feel for that important interface between people and machines, and their evolution. Computers and the technologies that make use of them are tools that people use, just as ploughs and pen and paper have always been used. How tools become an extension of your person matters to how well they leverage what you can do. What they leverage helps drive what you can accomplish. How tools come about matters because we want to foster the continued development of new and better tools.

In any case, I think reading all this should be interesting and illuminating to people curious about the technology-infused world we live in.

The Structure of This Book

I start this book in Chapter 1 with some discussion about why I like to go into great detail looking at various ways to understand things.

In Chapter 2 I examine some of the emotional and sociological forces that affect what people are willing to pay for in technology-assisted personal communication (such as cell phones and photographs). I follow that in Chapter 3 with a look at the recording industry as a case study about some of these forces and relate them to a business situation being impacted by changing technology.

In Chapters 4 and 5 I expand from looking at the behavior of individuals to looking at using the enhanced connectivity made possible by the Internet to leverage larger groups of people. This includes the role of people who volunteer. I also include transcripts of two interviews I conducted with a senior person from the United States Navy about cooperation and use of technology at the national and international level. As a case study, in Chapter 6 I look at a portion of the evolution of blogging and podcasting, with a detailed look at the role of bloggers during the Democratic National Convention in Boston in 2004.

In the second part of the book I change focus a bit more to the technology side and look at the nature of tools themselves. I cover in detail in Chapter 7 my view that, as human beings, we need tools and not "assistants." In Chapter 8 I look at some aspects of mobile and hand-operated computer technology-based tools, an area that is now flourishing with our ability to build products like the Apple iPhone. This way of having a person control computing power is much more intimate than the older deskbound and keyboard-controlled computers of the 1980s and 1990s and is becoming a dominant means for controlling computer power. I look at the very real issue of usability through an examination of the Palm Beach, Florida, ballot situation, which I covered in detail at the time in the fall of 2000 on my blog.

Usability is concerned with operation on a second-by-second basis and human errors that occur in an instant. Another issue is long-term usefulness and dealing with unexpected changes and events over time. As computer technology, driven by software, becomes the fabric through which we run society and conduct much of our commerce, its robustness and durability are crucial. In Chapter 9 I cover that extensively in a discussion of both copy-protection and the long-term maintenance of the software that helps run our world, looking to noncomputer fields for guidance.

In Chapter 10 I look at an important product that has so far successfully evolved over three decades, the personal computer, especially the IBM PC and its descendents, including source material from its introduction. Too often we think of tools as static entities, born fully formed and staying unchanged, with their use and potential fully understood at the outset. Looking at the evolution of important products can help you get a better feel for the true nature of the process through which they change.

To look at the development of other tools, in Chapter 11 I cover the creation of the wiki, an Internet-based tool used by groups of individuals to leverage the group, through an interview with its inventor. In Chapter 12, I chronicle the early development of VisiCalc, a tool mainly used by individuals to leverage themselves. These stories show how inventors react to common needs to produce a solution and how those products end up in the hands of others.

Essays, Blog Posts, Quotes, and Footnotes

In addition to this new, main narrative, you will find a large number of other elements in this book that are set off typographically:

- **Essays** are writings that originally appeared on my web site, usually in my site's "Writings" section. These have a title, often followed by a summary, and include the date they were originally published to help you put them in perspective. When written, they were meant to stand by themselves like a magazine article or white paper.
- **Blog posts** are usually much shorter pieces than the essays. They were originally written with an implicit assumption that they are to be read as part of an ongoing series or in the context of following a link from another web site. They often relate to a particular recent event or writing on the Web and are more conversational than an essay. They are presented here with day and date along with the title, as they would in a blog entry.
- **Quotes** from the writings of other people are listed with attribution.

- **Footnotes** are used to present additional new commentary, background information, and reference details such as URLs.[1] The notes are meant to be read along with the main text and form an important part of this book.

Some of the essays and blog posts have been edited a bit from the original to improve readability and understanding.

I put in many headings and other section breaks to make it easier to keep your bearings as you read. In many cases the essays and posts are like short stories, and you should feel free to skip one.

As I go over my essays, I find that many of the links no longer point to the original web pages. Many give "not found" errors, or default to the home page of a publication. In some cases I was able to use Archive.org's "Wayback Machine" (a massive online database constructed by repeatedly going from web site to web site and storing what it finds) to find a copy archived by that wonderful service years ago, but in some cases I was not.[2]

One thing I am doing to make sure that my material is still available in the future is turning many of my writings into another form—this published, printed book. This gives them another path to follow through the years, and anybody who wants to refer to them another means. I discuss the issue of permanence further in Chapter 9.

Why Delve Into Details?

As you read this book, you'll see that one of the goals of my writing has been to point out ways that people or systems behave that are not obvious or generally acknowledged. I believe that this is very important for improving decision making. It is important to tool makers like myself who need to understand

---

[1] Many people find the URL web page addresses helpful for giving more information about a reference. For example, the domain name (the first part of the web address, usually ending in ".com") sometimes serves as a simple publication name, and at that address you may be able to find out more information about the publication or author.

[2] This points out one of the dilemmas when you quote someone on the Web. The "right" way to do things is to link and not present a copy of what you are commenting on, except perhaps a very short, "fair use" excerpt that directly applies. After all, one of the beauties of the Web is being able to link to provide access to source material. Unfortunately, you are at the mercy of the target of that link to maintain it permanently. In many cases, even with large commercial endeavors, "permanently" seems to mean a few years at most, not decades or more. This is an issue that we need to solve. Archive.org is a good start, and the people who support it are to be commended.

which facilities or "levers" to provide to people and what those levers move. For example, if you were designing a type of screwdriver, you would want to know what shape the tip needed to be to best connect to the type of screw it would be used with, which grip would be best for the type of turning the person would be doing, etc. With computer tools used in expression or communication, you need to know what type of communication people need to do, in which circumstances, and with which constraints on time, training, etc.

When you try to figure out why something is happening or what will happen in the future—for example, to predict the success or failure of a particular company's endeavor—you usually base your prediction on some sort of model that you construct of how the components behave. For example, we assume customers behave a certain way given the choice between different prices: if two companies are selling the same product, the less expensive will be preferred. This model may be explicitly written in a document or kept in our head, often without even thinking that we are creating a model. We often think of it as "reality" even though it is a simplification, a tool for use in thinking.

In constructing these models, people seem to have a tendency to view relationships between things in two ways. The most simple is sometimes called "binary": Something is either on or off. You do "this," and it causes "that." "Natural foods appeal to health-conscious people." Something is either "good" or "bad." "Company A's products are good, and Company B's are bad."

Another view is linear. "The more you do A, the more B you get." In mathematical terms, as we are taught in grade school, "y equals m times x plus b." Change a little of the input, and you get a certain change in the output. Change twice as much in, and you get twice as much of a change out.

A graph of a linear relationship is shown in Figure 1-1.

Linearizing the description of the relationship between two items makes it much easier to calculate different values than when you need to have a table of all possible inputs with their resulting outputs. What we often do is take a few sample inputs and their corresponding outputs and from that extrapolate out a linear relationship that covers all other inputs. For many things, the linear relationship seems to predict what happens quite well, such as in describing the operation of many mechanical objects.

Unfortunately, the world is not made of simple levers and gears with no friction or wear (the traditional simplifications used in introductory physics). We forget that we are thinking about models and start thinking that the bunch of linear relationships are what is really going on. We often ignore elements that don't fit into our models, that are hard to measure, or that don't

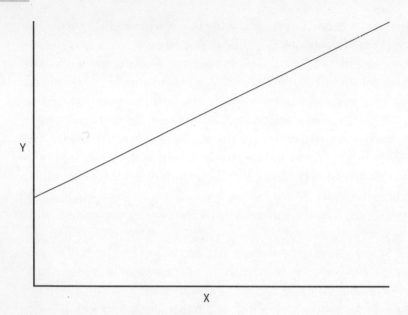

Figure 1-1 Graph of a linear function

lend themselves to easy linearization. While many things behave in a simple linear fashion in a narrow range of inputs, they often behave quite differently out of that range. For example, when blowing up a balloon, more air makes it grow larger—until it bursts. Many companies model their businesses assuming simple linear variations in sales and costs, ignoring nonlinear effects such as the loss of a market or entry of a disruptive competitor. They assume that each year will always be a minor change from the year before.

Many things of interest in the world are nonlinear, and there are often discontinuities (conditions where there is a sudden, big change in the result given a supposedly trivial change in input). For example, the more you heat water, the hotter it gets, but it is still a liquid. Past a certain point, though, it suddenly turns to steam, which behaves quite differently from a liquid.

This brings up a classic story.

A policeman is walking down the street one night and encounters a man down on his hands and knees next to a lamppost searching for something on the sidewalk and the ground around it. The policeman asks the man what he is doing. He replies, "I lost my keys at 6th and Vine Street and I'm looking for them." The policeman says, "But this is 7th and Walnut Street. Why are you looking here when you lost your keys two blocks away?" The man replies, "The lights are out over there and I can't see anything. The light is much better over here, so that's where I'm looking."

While this seems like an absurd story about a very foolish person (so much so that the person is usually described as drunk to explain why this would not be something a normal person would do), it is really a very important lesson to remember. It is often called the "Lamppost Problem" or "Lamppost Story." People often search for answers where it's easy to get results, even if those results may have little to do with what they are really looking for.

Combining the lesson of the Lamppost Story with problems of linearizing things brings up an issue. Many of the explanations that we give for why something works may be merely oversimplifications that we use because they, or the data to use them, were easy to obtain.

As a child I went to a school where, in addition to the traditional subjects, we studied the Jewish scripture in the original Hebrew as well as some Talmud (1,700-year-old books with Jewish laws and the discussions and reasoning behind them, laid out on the printed page in a very hypertext-y way, some of which I emulate in this book). Early on, I learned to examine things very carefully, looking at alternative interpretations, looking at related writings, and going well below the surface.

When I went to engineering school at MIT, I learned in great detail how things worked, down to the hardware behind the computers, the electronic circuits that made up the computers, and the properties of the materials that made up the transistors that made up the circuits. I worked with people who invented some of the things we took for granted.

As an MBA student at Harvard, I was exposed to many of the intricacies of business, from accounting to finance to production planning to workforce management and marketing. We looked at situations with many different options balancing many competing needs.

All this gives me a tendency to want to understand the details, even when I might feel that we have a model that's "good enough" and that I should just go with the common wisdom. Often what I find is something that is not much different than the obvious answer, but at least I have some material behind it, and at least I say it explicitly. Other times, though, I find different, and more realistic, answers. When you dig very deeply into something, you often find surprising nuggets that turn out to be keys to understanding. Often, you need to look at both forests and trees, leaves and roots.

Weighting Factors

Simple linear or binary models are often not sufficient for understanding the areas we care about here. More complex models that take into account multiple factors make more sense for understanding these areas.

In the book *The Tipping Point*,[3] author Malcolm Gladwell deals with the problem of linearization. The term *tipping point* itself drives home the idea that many things are not linear. In his book, Malcolm writes about the popular adoption of an idea or desire for a product where things seem to suddenly take off.

In 2004, after the release of *The Tipping Point* but before his later book *Blink*,[4] Malcolm was interviewed by Boston reporter (and now book author) Scott Kirsner at an event in Cambridge, Massachusetts. I wrote up a report of the interview in a blog post along with my thoughts about it.

Malcolm talked about some of the ideas that ended up in *Blink*. He wondered why sometimes having more information about a situation does not help you make better decisions than your first impression or a much simpler piece of information. I tried to come up with a short, more-technical explanation of the situations he talked about that would be more generally applicable than just saying "trust your instinct."

Here's the blog post:

- -

Tuesday, May 25, 2004
MITX FIRESIDE CHAT WITH *TIPPING POINT* AUTHOR
MALCOLM GLADWELL

Last night I attended yet another MITX Fireside Chat. The speaker was Malcolm Gladwell, best known as the author of the book *The Tipping Point*. Since 1996, he has been a staff writer for *The New Yorker* magazine. As usual, the interviewer was journalist Scott Kirsner.

The questioning started by covering Malcolm's career, starting with his childhood. He said that his father told him one thing not to be: a journalist (not very lucrative). He tried getting a job in advertising (being rejected by 21 places) and, after all else failed, took a job with the *American Spectator*, a publication

---

[3] *The Tipping Point: How Little Things Can Make a Big Difference*, Gladwell, 2002, Back Bay Books, ISBN: 0316346624

[4] *Blink: The Power of Thinking Without Thinking*, Gladwell, 2007, Back Bay Books, ISBN: 0316010669

May 25, 2004

he knew nothing about at the time but that was willing to hire him. He eventually ended up at the *Washington Post* and from there, like many others, ended up at *The New Yorker*.

Scott starts the questioning of Malcolm Gladwell.

Scott asked him: "What's a typical 'Malcolm Gladwell' article?" He said that he's interested in how systems work. He likes to write about "dumb obvious" things, like SUVs, malls, and ketchup. He says that anybody can make a good $300,000 car; it's making a good $12,000 one that's hard. The GAP is interesting; Oscar de la Renta is not. "The fringes are not interesting."[5]

He talked about an upcoming article on ketchup.[6] There are more fortunes lost on going after Heinz than in most anything else in food, he said. There is no gourmet high-end nor bargain low-end. In mustard there used to be just the brown and the yellow. Then Grey Poupon came in and sold a fraction as much mustard for three times the price. They had turned a commodity product into a high-margin item. "Ah ha!" went the market. That's it, we'll broaden the lines of everything, so now we have lots of different types of tomato sauce, etc. But not ketchup. He has ideas why that's true. (Wait for the article. It has to do with the mechanics of taste.)

Scott asked him to discuss his famous book, *The Tipping Point*. He talked about the difference between the rides of William Dawes and Paul Revere. They both had the same idea, telling people the British were coming, but Dawes'

---

[5] To me, though, the fringes are often quite interesting, especially when they are leading indicators that we can learn from. Of course, in my blog I often write for an audience of people who are trying to predict or create the future, not the general audience that he addresses.

[6] http://www.gladwell.com/2004/2004_09_06_a_ketchup.html

ride produced no outpouring of volunteers while Revere's did. It seemed that the way the message was carried mattered, not just the idea itself. (Revere was a well-known citizen, Dawes was little known; and Revere knew who the influential people were to tell in each city, Dawes did not. As one person said, "Better Rolodex.") There are the concepts of "Mavens, Connectors, and Salesmen" in his book.

He then went on to talk about the fall of the Hummer SUV. In 2000-2001 every car company had to say they were working on something like it. Not now. Not all new ideas have strong roots in society to keep them going. He also talked about French Fries and the oil that makes them taste good and why we switch to worse-tasting oils for reasons that don't seem reasonable.

Scott then asked about technology, etc., including weblogs. Malcolm said that he reads several, including the New York-centric Gawker and one oriented to pharmaceutical houses. He sees blogs as a "wonderful form," but that we have to sort the information.

Technology, he says, raises questions it can't answer. He talked about cancer. Mammography shows us a type of breast cancer that can only be found on x-rays. Because we see them, we treat them, but it's unclear if that is cutting down the number of bad cases of breast cancer the little ones are supposed to be a precursor to. The diagnostic tools become the definition of the disease. Full-body MRI of normal people he sees as a bad idea. Most cancers don't progress—better to learn how to fix things after they progress.

He had a new book coming out. It's about when is there too much information. He compares rapid cognition (e.g., quick first impressions) to having lots of data. Patterns appear much more rapidly than we think.

Asked from the audience about where he gets his sources, he said the psychology literature, but mainly when someone told him. "If you mingle with interesting people long enough they'll tell you something interesting."[7]

Asked about job interviews, he said that it's better to use darts. There are implicit prejudices in addition to the conscious ones. Those come out in body language, etc., and the interviewee responds and there is a feedback loop that affects the results. The situation doesn't measure most jobs. "Who you end up choosing is a function of how you choose."

Asked about reactions to his famous book, he talked about missing the issues that might lead to the suicide bombings in the Middle East, and the roles of an abundance of young males. He was too pessimistic about curbing smoking. He got the term "tipping point" from Thomas Schelling of Harvard.

He was asked by someone in the audience how to help move the Web from silent to sound as a medium (not technically but in acceptance of the idea). He talked about "reframing." He talked about how the broadcast in 1921 of the Dempsey-Carpentier fight reframed the view of radio. It changed from reporting of the news, just like a newspaper and other media, to bringing the event "into your living room." Atkins moved it from figuring out complicated fat content to easy carbohydrates. Seat belt usage was very low in the early 1980s. Then child restraint laws came in and usage jumped to the majority by 1986. Your strapped-in kids asked why you weren't wearing them. It went from the government telling you to buckle up to your kids asking.

Finally, he says that the bias should be in editing information, and not in adding more information.

My take on his claim that less information is better? I think it has merit if understood in the context he presents it. As I see it, people are very bad appliers of weighting factors[8] when evaluating lots of criteria. There ends up being a compression of ranges, and some items are given heavy weight because we have them (or because they were expensive to obtain) and others ignored because

---

[7] I think, looking back on this today, you could say, "If you read the blogs and Twitter posts of interesting people long enough they'll tell you something interesting." Blogs and Twitter are covered later in this book.

[8] Let me explain what I mean by weighting factors. It is a metaphor based on using a formula to describe a model. The formula is often in the form of: *total = measurement 1 × factor 1 + measurement 2 × factor 2 + . . .* The factors represent how much weight you give to the importance of each element that you are measuring. For example, in evaluating a potential racing car design you might give a large factor to speed and a low factor to visual appearance and noise. In evaluating a luxury car you might use the opposite.

we don't have them. Using a simpler method for making decisions, based upon fewer factors that we know are relevant, may work better than having many for which we assign incorrect weightings. In those cases, less is better.

Here's a visual example. I've taken a picture of Scott and rendered it with just a simple brightness curve that just splits dark and light as well a complex curve that misapplies the dark and light but is generally correct. The simple curve works fine for identifying the picture while the complex one does not even though it takes into account more information.

Original photo, simple curve that only makes every color either dark or light, complex curve that gives inappropriate factors to each brightness level

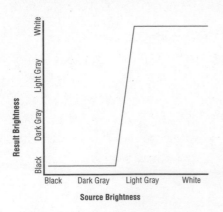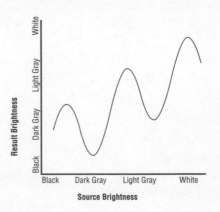

The curves used in Photoshop to transform the pictures, "simple" and "complex"

http://danbricklin.com/log/2004_05_19.htm

Applying This Here

How do we apply my theory that more information can be helpful, but only if you give each piece of information appropriate weight? We have to find as many independent variables that have a major influence on results as possible and then understand their impact. If you find only a few factors and ignore others that can have a larger influence, you may optimize against those unknown factors and end up with a worse result.

I believe that there is a "people factor" in the adoption of technology that is too often neglected. We carefully craft the usability of a product so that it is easy to use, or add functions so that it does well in comparison charts with the competition, often without looking at how its use fits in with real people's lives and their needs and how they interact with others. Product developers often are stuck in the thinking of their "silo" of expertise, such as programming or marketing.

The Mindset of an Engineer

To understand the writings in this book it helps to understand the mindset of the engineer, innovator, and entrepreneur.

Part of that mindset comes from what motivates me. Understanding some of the drives that I have will help you see why I focus on certain aspects of situations in my writings. Those drives are commonly found in other people in my field, and knowing about them can put what we choose to do and say in perspective.

People in different fields of endeavor are often motivated by different drives. They get great joy out of satisfying those drives. For example, teachers feel rewarded when they successfully help students who are struggling to discover the key to a new concept or when they introduce a child to a field that becomes their life's work. Some people are driven by wanting to "win" no matter what the field. Others are driven by wanting to help others who are in need, in pain, or suffering. Yet others are driven by wanting to express themselves in some medium, such as paint or song, and bring new beauty or understanding into the world.

Let's take a look at the drives that motivate an engineer.

One drive is the drive to build things, especially things that others will use. Engineers love to take components and put them together to create a greater whole. We build the world.

Engineers love to have their work actually used. There is beauty in something well designed, but there is also beauty in something that actually enhances someone else's life. Part of good design is solving the problems inherent in what existed before and thereby improving upon it.

This talk of "love," "beauty," and "building the world" brings up a spiritual side of being an engineer.

Here is an old parable that, as an engineer, always brings a smile to my face. It comes from the prayer book created by members of Congregation Beth El of the Sudbury River Valley[9] and is read by many of the congregants every Friday night at the time when they are celebrating the beginning of the Sabbath and the remembering of the end of the last day of Creation.[10] It is based upon something found in a book of parables and commentaries from over 1,500 years ago.

> When the world was created,
> God made everything a little bit incomplete.
> Rather than making bread grow out of the earth,
> God made wheat grow so that we might bake it into bread.
> Rather than making the earth of bricks,
> God made it of clay
> so that we might bake the clay into bricks. Why?
> So that we might become partners
> in completing the work of creation.
>
> Congregation Beth El prayer book, page 9

I see this as expressing a view of a sacred place for the engineer in the scheme of things.

---

[9] *Vetaher Libenu*, 1980, Congregation Beth El of the Sudbury River Valley, ISBN: B000EICUAG

[10] Periodically in my writings I make reference to a story from the Bible to illustrate the timelessness of a concept. I like to look at old teachings from religion to find values that have been passed down for many generations, withstanding the examination of many wise and experienced people, and are seen as somewhat timeless.

When Don Bulens joined me at Trellix[11] as CEO, he had been a senior manager more experienced in working with sales forces and marketing people than developers. He was looking for help in understanding engineers. He found that he had problems understanding how they chose what to concentrate on. Being connected to sales and the bottom line, he was very driven by types of success that he could easily understand and measure, but the engineers all seemed to march to a different drummer.

I told him an illustrative tale that I had heard that I thought would help him understand the mindset of many of us. This is how I remember the story:

Three men are brought to the guillotine to be executed: a lawyer, a doctor, and an engineer. The lawyer has his head placed in the device first. The executioner pulls the lever and the blade comes screaming down. Miraculously, the blade screeches to a halt just inches above his neck. As a lawyer, he quickly points out that the law states that they have but one chance at execution. He is led away a free man. Next, the doctor is brought up. Again, the blade starts its journey at full speed, only to get stuck and stop just in the nick of time. Having observed what happened with the lawyer, he demands that he, too, be freed, and he is.

Finally, it is the engineer's turn. As they push him into place, he turns his head and looks up. "Wait!" he cries. "I think I see the problem . . . "

The apparent absurdity of this story of being so much the engineer, trying to understand and fix the problem of the minute, even to your own detriment, really worked for Don. He could see that same story played out again and again in front of him. As an engineer, you feel the dilemma of that poor condemned man, dying to figure out an engineering problem and help others, even when there was a good reason not to.

Over the years, we'd make reference to that story ("remember the guillotine . . . "). It continued to be helpful to remind us of some of the motivations of engineers and the need to make sure that they understood the corporate problems (like meeting particular needs of customers) that might not be as obvious for them to consider.

Related to these drives is the interplay of value systems of different groups. "Values" in this case refers to the beliefs people hold about what is good and what is not good. These values, often unstated, help guide decision-making

---

[11]I founded Trellix Corporation in late 1995 to develop software tools for creating documents with linked pages. It evolved into a company making web site creation tools. I left the company in early 2004. Trellix is now part of Web.com. I still use one of Trellix's early tools to create my web site and blog.

and facilitate communication among people who share those beliefs. They are often taught to newcomers through stories, jokes, reverence of particular individuals, and other techniques well known to sociologists. While you usually hear them discussed in relation to culture at the level of societies, countries, and religions, they are also important within a business and in relation to professions.

An observation that I learned many years ago from a friend who was studying for an MBA soon after I did was about the importance of understanding the different value systems of people when they interact.

To me, the key observation was about the miscommunication that occurs when people with different value systems try to make decisions together. When one group makes a proposal and says that it has a particular attribute, thinking that means it's a good proposal, another group may think that the same attribute means it's a bad proposal. Each has no clue why the other doesn't understand the correctness of their opinion.

As an example, here is a simple view of some different parts of a company:

- Often people involved in **sales** are accustomed to making many attempts when trying to get new customers. Each potential sale has a low probability of success. Many factors unrelated to the product itself can affect success, such as interpersonal skills, luck, and persistence. The sales team may be made up of many individuals, each working independently, perhaps sharing tips on what seems to work and what doesn't. To them, a lost sale is a common occurrence, and particular successes may be unrelated to particular failures. What matters is to have lots of good leads and a good approach.

  In this culture, having lots of opportunities is a key. As in baseball, a 33% success rate can be a very good thing. Attitude matters. Caution and slow planning can be a bad thing, wasting time for something that will cut down the number of opportunities to have a chance with more potential customers for a small increase in likelihood of success.

- In **manufacturing**, the goal is often to reliably produce products as inexpensively as possible with as few undetected defects as possible. Product designs that help this are "good," and those that don't are "bad."

- In **bookkeeping and accounting**, constant accuracy is important. It is "bad" to ever have errors. Low risk is a "good" thing. Attention to process and details are "good" things. Each transaction matters: The books must be correct at all times. It is an ongoing process, with no real end.

- In **product development**, you are often working on a long-term project. There are many steps along the way, each building to a single goal that must be met successfully. Many aspects of a project start out ill defined and may only be worked out through experimentation. People are often doing things that they have never done before. Status within the profession is often based on the technical merit or novelty of certain parts of the final product.

You can see how a meeting involving these four groups could have problems. A proposed product design using a new technology would be "good" for the developers. For manufacturing, it would be "bad" if it increased the likelihood of defects or was expensive to manufacture on the current equipment. Sales people may like it if it could attract more potential customers or not like it if it would scare them off or delay shipment. The benefit of being in a project with higher risk and unknown components may not be attractive to the financial people.

You can just hear the conversation: A developer says, "But it's cutting edge!" meaning "it's good!" Some of the others hearing that as "but it's bad!" would respond, "So we shouldn't do it!" Others think it's good, but for different reasons, which may not play out when the product is finished being developed because the developers didn't know of those reasons.

You can see how it is important to understand the value systems for different parts of a business.

Some of my writings assume an understanding of the value systems of people in different professions. Sometimes, I address those value systems directly. In all cases, reading this book should give you insight into the mindset of engineers and innovators. Part of turning my raw writings into a book has been an effort to make these values more explicit and accessible to those with different backgrounds.

I have been involved in projects that had influence beyond my wildest dreams. My most famous creation, VisiCalc, and the products that followed and were influenced by it, have changed the way all sorts of business people do their jobs. (Some accountants thank me and say that "it made accounting fun.") In the old days, only accountants, bookkeepers, and planners dealt with spreadsheets, and it was mainly by using paper and pencil. Now "spreadsheeting," the personal computer way, is taught to everybody in many grade schools. Doing "what if?" analysis is available to all, not just big corporations with staffs of clerks and MBAs.

I have also been involved in many projects that had very little effect and that even I probably forget.

It is important to understand that much of the time while you are developing a new product the likelihood of success seems the same whether it eventually ends up an influential success or a forgotten failure. You need a strong belief in the project to spur you on. Many of the signs of ultimate failure are subtle, ambiguous, or not always present, and are, therefore, often ignored, which is appropriate. You might also be so caught up in the details that you find it hard to step back and take a wider view.

As an engineer, you are tempted to think that the reasons for success are related to how "good" one product's technology or internal craftsmanship is compared to another. As a business person, you are tempted to think that the reasons are related to the project management, marketing plan, sales strategy, or amount of money spent. Analysts and other observers look at industry trends, changes in the population of people using the products, and sociological forces. In reality, there are many components to product success, and they are often completely interrelated.

At this point, you should understand what I am trying to do here in this book and where I come from, including my feeling about the importance of looking at details and a variety of viewpoints. Next let us look at some of the personal uses of technology. We'll see how some of the simplistic business-oriented models of what can make money may not explain what really motivates people to pay for things or to create for others.

2 What Will People Pay For?

The writings included in this chapter all address the issues raised by trying to understand what people want so much that they are willing to pay for it and why. I look at communicating with others using cell phones, taking photographs, and various types of self-expression. I also examine the tough question, in the era of easy MP3 downloads, of how artists will get paid.

Cell Phone Use

I was first introduced to a mobile telephone when I was in college in the early 1970s. My father, back home in Philadelphia, was stuck in traffic and late for an appointment. All the cars near him were completely stopped. He looked around and saw that the person in the car next to him was chatting away on a telephone. My father got out of his car and asked that person if it was possible for him to make a call to a nearby town. The guy said, "Sure—I've been talking to another state." My father, who owned a small printing company and used a station wagon for deliveries, thought, "What a good idea—I'll order one of these, which will be useful in the heavy traffic downtown where I do most of the deliveries. It will be worth it because the delivery person won't have to keep asking customers to borrow use of their phone to see if there are any changes before returning to the shop." He told the family about this and announced that he had signed up for service but that there was a long waiting list. With this early technology, there were just a few "cells" in a city, so there was a limit to how many phones could be active at once, and mobile phones were therefore limited in number.[1] It sounded so futuristic.

---

[1] The name changed from "mobile phones" to "cell phones" when the technology improved to take advantage of multiple, closer transmitters.

Eventually, my father's name came up, and he had a mobile phone installed in the car. It had a big box in the back near the spare tire with the main electronics, and a phone unit near the driver with a corded handset and, as I recall, rotary dialing. I eventually learned the hard way one reason they said not to talk while you were driving: I made a turn while talking and the headset cord got tangled up around the steering wheel. When I was home visiting from college, I had fun driving up to a friend's house and calling to see if I could visit. I'd watch them run for the phone through the window. When they said yes, I'd quickly go up to the front door and ring the bell, much to their great surprise.

The mobile phone was very helpful to my father's business. For example, one night, as he was driving home from work, a major customer, the ballet, called. The programs my father had printed hadn't been delivered to the theater and the show was about to start. He quickly turned around and headed back to the print shop. With a lot of work he got everything together and delivered the programs in time for them to be handed out at intermission, averting a potential disaster for his business.

The big "aha!" moment for me, though, happened soon after he got the mobile phone. Visiting the Philadelphia area to attend the wedding of one of those surprised friends in 1974, I drove out far into the suburbs to pick up another attendee who was also in town just for the wedding. On the way to the wedding, I got horribly lost, it was dark, and the time of the wedding was fast approaching. Panic set in. What to do? I called my father at home from the mobile phone. He kept a fairly complete supply of local maps behind his desk. I asked for help. My friend read off street names as we passed them and my father gave us turn-by-turn directions. We made it to the wedding just in the nick of time. Without that help we would surely have been late. What a useful device! My father said he felt like he was at Mission Control directing a space flight. Little did I know that years later I'd be on the other end, using Keyhole's Earthviewer (now Google Earth) and then Google Maps to give family and friends directions as they called from their cell phones. As I taught people this use of a cell phone in the last few years (which was not obvious to most of them because until recently you didn't think that someone you could call had a detailed map of where you are in front of them), I always remembered that trip to the wedding.

I first used a modern cell phone by myself at an industry conference almost 20 years ago. My friend Bob Frankston,[2] always an early adopter, lent me one of his so we could find each other in the huge conference center and participate together in an important work-related conference call. It was the size and weight of a small brick.

I first got my own cell phone in the winter of 1990. My parents were in a horrible traffic accident (another car skidded across the road and hit them head on). I spent days and days at the hospital waiting room. Friends and relatives throughout the city and around the world wanted updates. People were coming and going to town to help out. I borrowed Bob's extra cell phone again at first to help me coordinate things. Within days I purchased my own (for about $1,000 for a Motorola flip-phone). After that, I continued using the cell phone, spending about $35–$70 a month for about a couple of hours of talk time. I kept calls as short as possible to save money.

In May of 1998, AT&T Wireless (the old AT&T) launched their One-Rate service. From the press release:

> *"AT&T Digital One Rate, available now, provides customers a single, all-inclusive rate for incoming or outgoing calls anytime, anywhere in the United States—eliminating separate roaming and long-distance charges."*
>
> AT&T[3]

For only about $90 a month, about the same amount I was spending for a few hours of regular cell service, you could get 600 minutes for talking anywhere in the country. Ten hours of talking in a month, about 20 minutes a day, seemed like a long time. Bob Frankston told me about it and said that it really changed things—you could talk on it without worrying about how long you took or where you were calling. It felt different. It also came with a new, very small phone, the Nokia 6160, that fit easily into your pocket and had long battery life.

I listened to Bob and signed up. This changed my use of cell phones. I'd call my mother just to say "Hi!" on the way home from work or when traveling.

---

[2] Bob Frankston, www.frankston.com, is a very close friend of mine. We developed VisiCalc together in the late 1970s, and collaborated on a variety of projects before and after. His name will come up repeatedly throughout this book, and he helped me in the original development of many of the ideas that I present.

[3] http://findarticles.com/p/articles/mi_m0EIN/is_1998_May_7/ai_n27527882

"Unused" time in my life, such as when driving alone, could be spent on the phone instead of listening to the radio or recorded music.

I started looking at other people's use of their cell phones, paying attention in taxis and noting the use by people on the street. They, too, were talking more. Maybe they had before, paying for bigger plans than I would, and I had thought it strange and extravagant. Now I saw the value. People would convince themselves to buy cell phones "for safety—in case I have a flat tire in a deserted area," but often ended up using them for the most mundane things.

Cell phone use has grown dramatically. In 1990, right before I got mine, there were about 5 million cell phone subscribers in the USA, paying an average of about $80 a month.[4] Calls averaged 2.2 minutes. By the beginning of 1998 when One-Rate started, there were about 55 million subscribers. By 2000, there were about 110 million. Average call length was 2.5 minutes. By 2006, there were over 230 million subscribers paying about $50 a month, and the average call length increased to over 3 minutes. Revenues totaled over $125 billion.[5]

In 2000, the press, though, seemed to be ignoring the mundane use. It seemed like they were concentrating on the phone moving to a commerce platform. This fit with the view that what regular people wrote or said was of little interest unless it involved making money. This view was also applied to blogging and other uses of the Internet. My observations, though, brought me to write this essay.

July 11, 2000

WHAT WILL PEOPLE PAY FOR?

> *Regular people are willing to pay money to interact with people they care about.*

You keep reading stories about how cell phones will be used for checking stock quotes and making trades, buying stuff, and other eCommerce. It seems business plans are based on people paying for such stuff. I think that eCommerce is not where things will go.

If you look at normal people's use of the Internet, cell phones, and other communications technologies that they pay for, they are not driven by wanting to buy things or track their money. Unlike the kings in children's rhymes,

---

[4] http://www.census.gov/prod/2002pubs/01statab/inforcomm.pdf

[5] http://www.census.gov/compendia/statab/tables/08s1120.pdf

most people don't "sit in their counting houses counting out their money." Most people don't buy and sell stocks so frequently and on such whim that they need to do it on a cell phone. "Oh, look! That trendy kid over there is wearing penny loafers! Quick, I must buy stock in a penny loafer company before it goes up this afternoon." Most people don't buy and sell many stocks at all. Some people do, but not this huge majority that will drive the "wireless Internet revolution."

Look at how regular people use cell phones, especially if the cost is low like it is in many countries outside the USA. Listen to cab drivers with their own cell phones, bus drivers, mothers, kids, etc. They mainly talk to their friends and loved ones for very personal, mundane things:

"I finally left the office, but traffic is light."
"Yes, I can pick up a pizza on the way home."
"I've got a free minute and thought I'd say hi."
"Did you find it yet?"
"Where are you?"
"No, I didn't do it, I thought you were going to do it."
"Well, tell him Daddy says no, too."
"What's up? Wanna do something tonight?"
Etc.

Look at what people do when they go to an Internet cafe when traveling and don't have their own access to the Internet. You don't find them surfing to buy things. They pay money to access their email to stay in touch with friends and loved ones. A huge percentage of AOL usage is Instant Messaging. They pay to say hi, flirt, chitchat about their day, etc., especially with their "buddies."

Also, people like interacting by giving little gifts to each other, saying, "I remembered you and what you might like." They send postcards (mainly the paper kind but also the e-kind). They spend a large amount of their valuable vacation time buying "I remembered you" gifts. They love spending money on friends and loved ones at special times like Christmas. ("It's better to give than to receive.") They forward jokes they've heard/read to people they care about.

People like to interact with people they care about. The interactions are often simple, but personally important. They are willing to pay money for this. That's why they pay for cell phones, for Internet access, for postcards and postage, and for souvenirs. It gives them emotional satisfaction. They pay money to travel to visit family and friends.[6]

I get an image in my head when I see people on the street having these simple interactions on the phone. It's the image of primates sitting next to each other grooming one another. Simple, kind interactions with the ones close to us are innate.

People also pay money for other forms of emotional satisfaction that aren't through other people directly: listening to music, watching movies, seeing something beautiful or interesting.

Buying isn't fun. Shopping is. Shopping is looking at things and imagining owning them or wearing them or using them. Shopping is looking for "just the right thing" out of many possibilities. Shopping is often around or with other people. People pay money to shop in interesting places, even if they don't buy much. For instance, they travel to New York City to walk down 5th Avenue and look in at Tiffany's, Steuben Glass (until they moved), and FAO Schwartz; they go to Italy to look at the stores with the designer clothes.

So, people will pay money for things that give them emotional satisfaction, especially those things that involve interacting with others, or have a high emotion content, like music.

Follow-up, May 10, 2001:

I found an interesting article that is well researched and shows how communication (especially for social reasons) commands more money than professionally produced content. "Content is Not King" by Andrew Odlyzko of AT&T Labs appeared in *First Monday*.[7] An example from the Introduction:

> *Content certainly has all the glamor. What content does not have is money. . . . The annual movie theater ticket sales in the U.S. are well under $10 billion. The telephone industry collects that much money*

---

[6] A few months before this essay was written, an extremely popular (and later award-winning) TV commercial was first aired. It was the Budweiser "Wazzup?" ad in their "True" series. It showed a bunch of friends calling each other on the phone and intercom, basically saying, "Wazzup? What'cha doin? Watching the game, havin' a Bud." That's about the extent of their conversation. While this may seem silly to many, to me it really was the key to what I write about here: Mundane interactions, but personal with in-jokes and part of an ongoing relationship with the person, are very much a part of being human, and are what we pay for. They matter to us. If you think the guys in the ad aren't like you, you may be missing a driving force in the market.

[7] http://firstmonday.org/issues/issue6_2/odlyzko/

every two weeks! Those "commodity pipelines" attract much more spending than the glamorous "content."

Andrew Odlyzko

http://www.bricklin.com/peoplepay.htm

A personal example

Cell phones have moved from playing a minor role in our interpersonal relationships to being internalized by many people as an integral part of maintaining those relationships. Here is a related blog post I wrote the following year:

Wednesday, November 6, 2002
WITH MY DAD AND THE CELL PHONE AS LIFELINE

I was visiting my Dad in the nursing home yesterday. I took him over to the auditorium to hear Cantor Louise Treitman sing some Hebrew songs. As we sat there, she announced her next song: the old pioneer farmer song *Shir Ha'Emek*. It's the song I still remember my Dad singing to my sister and me as a lullaby when I was four and younger. My Dad perked up, and the two of us sang along while I held his hand—probably two of a very few out of the 125 people in the room to do so since the song is not well known today. My eyes were filled with tears. Memories of a long time ago. I wanted to share the moment somehow. Holding his hand was one way, but what about my sister? I didn't have my camera with me, so I couldn't use its sound record function. I pulled out my cell phone and hit her name on speed dial, hoping to put some of the sound on her answering machine, but unfortunately it had problems connecting (the problems with cell phones . . .) and I was too busy singing to pay attention. I waited until the night to call her and tell her about it.

That moment with the cell phone brought up another image I saw earlier in the day: a woman getting out of the driver's seat in her car and opening up the back door to take her small child out of a car seat while still clutching an object in her hand that she obviously felt was important—her cell phone. I remember thinking: More and more I see people clutching their cell phones as a major source of comfort or something. It's like they are holding onto a railing when they walk down stairs; the cell phone gives them some sense of security. I feel that it represents a lifeline to the rest of our circle of important people, and we treat it as such. It's a space warp that connects us to others we need as we go through life. In today's complicated world, we can juggle our disconnected lives and make them connected by using technology like cell phones, email, IM, and digital cameras. I may be very busy and never be sure where I'll be at any given time, but that doesn't affect my being able to coordinate with others. ("I'm on my way and it looks like I'll get to the building around 8 p.m. When I get there I'll call you on your cell phone and we'll figure out where to meet.")

With all the talk about commerce and advertising, I still think that friend-to-friend relationships are a major driving force in our adoption of (and paying for) much of new technology. (If you haven't read it, you should take a look at my "What will people pay for?" essay. In my recording industry essay,[8] I also point out how the huge increases in use of cell phones may explain some of the drop in music sales—increasingly you see people walking or standing with cell phones pressed to their ears instead of wearing earphones from personal music systems. With email, can you imagine how unlikely it would have been 10 years ago to think that email would be so important that spam would be a problem that mattered to regular people?)

http://danbricklin.com/log/2002_11_06.htm#shir

Acceptance of Cell Phone Uses Similar to Landline's Acceptance

In the book *America Calling: A Social History of the Telephone to 1940*,[9] Claude S. Fischer shows how it took a long time for the landline telephone to move from a tool for "serious" business use only to one mainly used for social purposes. For many years, telephone companies thought that social use of the phone ("visiting," gossiping, and other personal uses) was an abuse of the service and discouraged such use. They thought in terms of their previous work with the telegraph, even referring to calls as "messages" and measuring use in "message units." He writes:

---

[8] Presented here in Chapter 3.

[9] *America Calling: A Social History of the Telephone to 1940*, Fischer, 1994, University of California Press, ISBN: 0520086473

... Alexander Graham Bell himself wrote his wife in 1878, "When people can ... chat comfortably with each other over some bit of gossip, every person will desire to put money in our pockets by having telephones." Yet, this remained a minority opinion during the first half-century of the telephone's existence.

Instead, early telephone men often fought their residential customers over social conversations, labeling such calls frivolous and unnecessary.

... the marketers of telephone service were slow to employ as a sales tool the use that was to dominate the home telephone's future, sociable conversation.

The story of how and why the telephone industry discovered sociability provides a few lessons in the nature of technological diffusion. It suggests that the promoters of a technology do not necessarily know or decide its final uses; that they seek problems or needs for which their technology is the answer, but that consumers themselves develop new uses and ultimately decide which will predominate. The story suggests that in promoting a technology, vendors are constrained not only by its technical and economic attributes but also by an interpretation of its uses that is shaped by its and their histories, a cultural constraint that can persist over many years. This insistence of consumers on "visiting" over the telephone and the eventual adoption of the sociability theme in the industry's campaigns to "educate the public" represents a case in which a use was found and propelled by the consumers of a technology.

America Calling: A Social History of the Telephone to 1940, pages 78 and 85

Photographs

The idea that land and mobile phones would evolve from being business tools to indispensable parts of relating to our friends and loved ones was not obvious at first to many people. Likewise, early photographers probably didn't see how personally taking pictures (as opposed to having professionals create them) would become such an integral part of life.

As an engineer, I often looked at photography in terms of creating the most realistic or aesthetically pleasing images. The unevenly lit and poorly composed photos created by everyday people appeared to me to be somehow lacking, yet they surprisingly seemed of great value to those people. Why take a poor picture when you could buy a professional image of the same scene? It seems related to how our mundane conversations on cell phones should pale in comparison to the professional fare on commercial radio, but instead we pay for the mundane and usually don't for the professional (which needs advertising to survive financially). This essay addresses the evolution of my thoughts on that.

October 21, 1999

OUR PHOTOS AS AN EDITED RECORD OF OUR LIVES

We take pictures for many reasons. Here is one very important one to understand.

With the advent of digital cameras and personal web sites, I've returned to my childhood hobby of amateur photography. Writing about different types of pictures for my Web Photo Journals web site[10] got me thinking more about the psychological aspects of our relationship with personal photography. Pictures aren't just for the sake of being an art object—they also have great personal meaning and are central to how we view our own lives.

This essay explores two items that gave me some insight.

Choosing photos

The first item was a few lines in a book that talked about personal photos. The book was written by Larry Kushner, a person I've known for over twenty years. He has been my Rabbi, and taught me how emotion and spirituality are an integral part of everyday life over which we have some control. In his wonderful book *Invisible Lines of Connection: Sacred Stories of the Ordinary*,[11] he writes:

> *I am in charge of the family albums in our house. I go through each roll of film and pick out the half dozen best shots . . . That's what history's all about: Saving photos of yourself that make you look good.*

---

[10]The Web Photo Journals site is now at http://www.bricklin.com/webphotojournals/default.htm

[11]*Invisible Lines of Connection: Sacred Stories of the Ordinary*, Kushner, 1998, Jewish Lights Publishing, ISBN: 1879045982

[Then one day, forced to look back at the ones he didn't pick, he commented:] *Here we were like archaeologists in our own basement, looking at all the pictures of the people we had been pretending we weren't . . . there we were, not quite as flawless as we were in the family albums up in the living room . . . All this time, I had been pretending that the people in my family looked the way they did in the carefully censored photos in the album. Now I realized that these only captured one moment of millions. And that at each one of those other moments, there were other expressions, other faces, other fears and other dreams, parallel universes.*

Invisible Lines of Connection, Kushner, pages 76–77

This idea of albums being an edited version of our lives as we want to remember them, not the "real thing" or just random, pretty *objets d'art*, struck me. The techie I am, I had always looked at pictures for their artistic value, not as a personal statement of who we want to be in a life as we want to remember it. I started looking more carefully at the process of this editing.

Taking photographs is a continual process of editing. Not only do we choose the pictures we put in albums, but we also choose when to bring a camera, when to take it out, when and what to take pictures of, and when and to whom to show the pictures. Through this process of choosing, we say to ourselves and others what we feel is important.

The *Mona Lisa*

The second item that struck me was an incident on my trip to Paris last summer. We were visiting the Louvre and went, of course, to see Leonardo da Vinci's painting of *Mona Lisa*. People crowded around the glass-encased painting to behold this most famous of all portraits in person. We had all seen photos of the painting, but here we could see the real thing and contemplate why it was so special and feel the presence of the actual work of the hand of a most remarkable individual. Approaching the room, I was remembering the feeling of awe I had the year before in Florence seeing the actual telescope handmade by Galileo that he used to discover the moons of Jupiter.

So what did people do? They took pictures. They viewed the painting in front of them through the viewfinder:

This all got me thinking. Is there a problem with these people? Surely their pictures will be nowhere near as "good" as those they could get on any postcard or book. Also, neither they nor their loved ones are in the picture for a "Don't I look cute next to . . ." type of shot.

No, they were fine. What they were doing was putting together the story of their lives, and they wanted to add something famous and beautiful to it. As they tell the story of their trip they can have that important stop that they have in common with so many others. Their photo shows that they, too, experienced something great.

The fact that we instinctively take out a camera to record "famous" scenes affects our use of the camera in other settings. Bringing a camera along says that we think this will be something worth remembering. Actually taking a snapshot of something or somebody is a way of saying, "At this moment, I think this is a part of my life that I want to put in my 'highlights reel.'" Taking a picture of someone is a way of paying them the compliment of saying, "You are important to me."

Dogs wag their tails. We take photographs.

Here's another shot I like:

Why did I take these pictures? What was going through my head? I like telling stories. I like showing people something special they may not have noticed. Seeing all these viewfinders just struck me as something you wouldn't think about. I had in my mind the image of art students standing with intent looks or sitting and sketching. Crowds with camcorders (Video! Motion! Sound!) was not what I expected. Ira Glass of NPR wrote that surprises make good stories.[12] This was a surprise and people to whom I showed these pictures expressed similar surprise. Voila! A story to share with you, my readers. The more I thought about it, though, I realized there is something more here. Hopefully this essay helps you (and me) understand the importance of individually choosing when to take pictures of our lives.

http://www.bricklin.com/editedlives.htm

A related blog post:

Sunday, November 14, 2004
ANOTHER SHARED EXPERIENCE ON THE PLANE

This morning on the 7 a.m. return flight to Boston I had another shared experience with others on the plane. As I was getting comfortable in my seat, taking out some reading material before taking off, someone a row or two behind, still in the aisle, yelled out something like, "Way to go, Johnny!" A few others made some approving sounds. I assumed it was a group and Johnny had made it on when they didn't expect him to. More cheer from a good time at Disney World or something. Then some others clapped. I looked forward to see who was getting on. Lo, and behold, it was Johnny Damon, center fielder of the (I love to say this) World Series Champion Red Sox. What a treat! (The gifts for the friends I had just visited were Red Sox hats bought in the Boston airport on the way down on Friday.) After several seconds of applause, people quieted down and left him alone for the flight (well, every time he stood up flashes went off, and one person handed his cell phone to the stewardess to take a picture of Johnny a few rows ahead, but people didn't walk up asking for autographs or anything). When we landed, he pulled down his carry-on and left to take

---

[12]http://www.current.org/people/p809i1.html

a cab. As I got off the plane, I passed by all these people who were waiting to get on the plane for their flight who were now on their cell phones: "You wouldn't believe . . .," "No, I couldn't get a picture with my cell phone, but I tried . . ." (We couldn't do this when we first saw him—who are you going to call at 6:50 in the morning for something like that? I sent an email from my Treo cell phone, though, and then am blogging now that I'm home . . .) The urge to share an experience is great.

I talked to another passenger at the baggage claim who told me that he had noticed this person who looked a lot like Johnny Damon in the security line. Remembering an article he had recently read in the Orlando paper he knew that Johnny had been in town to receive some award. So as the security line snaked back on itself and he passed by, he said, "Hi, Johnny!" He said that Johnny looked surprised that someone recognized him (obviously dozens who had seen him had not and many of us were going to Boston and would surely know who he is and what he looks like), and they talked a bit. I know that if I hadn't heard that person cry out at the back of the plane, I wouldn't have known he was on board, even though he looks just like he does on TV and I've watched his face intently many times when he was at bat. I wonder how many other people whose stories I know I pass by every day that I don't know about. The world is more connected than you think, and we know more as a group than we do as individuals.

http://danbricklin.com/log/2004_10_15.htm#damon

Getting Paid

There is a lot of controversy about digital media, copy protection, fair use, and the Internet. In most cases, from the viewpoint of legislators trying to react to lobbyists, as I understand it, it boils down to one question: How will the artists get paid? My answer is simple: Artists will get paid the same way artists have always gotten paid. I wrote an essay to examine that issue to see how it applies to today's world. As you'll see, it also addresses people's motivation.

HOW WILL THE ARTISTS GET PAID?

Throughout history there have been a variety of ways that artists have gotten paid so they can create their work: through an ecosystem that looks to a mixture of amateur, performance, patronage, and commission forms of payment. This essay explores that ecosystem.

Art

For as long as we know, humans have had art. We find paintings in caves. The Bible talks about the songs of leader Moses's sister Miriam celebrating national deliverance at the Red Sea and the artisan Betzalel who was "filled . . . with the spirit of God, in practical-wisdom, in discernment and in knowledge, and in all kinds of workmanship to design designs . . . to make carvings . . . jewel-cuttings . . . embroidery . . . and weaving . . ."[13] and led the building of the Tabernacle using materials donated by the Israelites. The songs of King David are still with us today, as is the melody of the medieval Greensleeves (with many different lyrics). (Coincidentally, as I write this flying on an airplane, I'm listening to a rendition of Greensleeves using an MP3 file I made from a CD I bought. Could the author of that piece have envisioned any of that?)

Art has many manifestations. I will define producing art (a dangerous thing, but helpful for this discussion) as manipulating something that can be sensed with human senses in a way that is not dictated purely for a utilitarian purpose but rather for some form of expression.

Some art is obvious, such as an oil painting. Other works, like the compilations made by a DJ, may not be (but you can tell a good one from a bad one).

Art usually involves using the results of some other artist. The musician uses an instrument crafted by an instrument maker and plays the music written by a composer. An illustrator may draw images, invoked by a song written about a love story recounted in a play, on handmade paper using an intricately carved pen.

---

[13]Based on Exodus 35:30-35, *The Five Books of Moses*, Everett Fox, 1995, Schocken, ISBN: 0805240616. Everett's translation strives to "echo the style of the original . . . This translation is guided by the principle that the Hebrew Bible, like much of literature of antiquity, was meant to be read out loud, and that consequently it must be translated with careful attention to rhythm and sound." I often use his translations, especially if they are not accompanied by a reading in the original Hebrew.

April 14, 2003

Motivation

What motivates artists? For some it is just expressing themselves, no matter what others think. For some it is the joy of practicing their craft. For some, it is the "high" that comes from playing in front of an audience. For some, it is having their work appreciated and continue on in the hands of others. Finally, for some it is a way to earn a living and pursue riches. For many it is a combination.

The USA was founded upon the principles of the right of all to life, liberty, and the pursuit of happiness. For the artist, that would be by letting them create their art and be able to reasonably make a living. The pursuit of happiness for all of us, in many respects, depends upon the artists being able to share their works with the rest of us, and us being able to use those works in ways that bring us happiness. The best benefit to society is when the most appreciated art is available for use by as much of society as possible. For the artists themselves, the best benefit is when they meet their personal goals of expression, practice, having an audience, appreciation, and material wealth. Since many forms of art and styles of practicing that art involve using the artistic works of others, the more that art can be used by others the better, too. To help the artists make their living, though, certain deals were struck with the public, such as the public allowing limited monopolies like copyrights.[14]

Most artists do not rely upon their art to provide them with a livelihood. They have other means to provide for that. For example, most photographers, singers, musicians, painters, etc., are "amateurs"—they do it for the love of doing it. (This is true of many pursuits of happiness, from sports to personal intimacy.) Some artists, though, make earning a living through their art a part, or all, of their career. Some types of art, especially if they require full-time devotion for proficiency, lend themselves to full-time careers if one wants to be at the highest level. However, making a living from creating art is not necessarily an indication that one's art is "better" than that from one who does not. Some amateur or part-time singers have as pleasing a sound as many full-time professionals. As in other fields, making more money than another is often an indication of business acumen and luck rather than "quality" of the art.

According to U.S. Census Bureau statistics, there are on the order of 500,000 people in the U.S. paying taxes for being an independent artist, writer, performer,

---

[14]"The Congress shall have Power . . . To promote the Progress of Science and useful Arts, by securing for limited Times to Authors and Inventors the exclusive Right to their respective Writings and Discoveries." *Constitution of the United States*, Article I, Section 8.

photographer, etc. Digital camera sales alone in 2002 were over 6 million units in the U.S. In the one year of 1999, over 100,000 pianos were sold, and over 1.3 million guitars. Compared to the number of "professionals," there are quite a few amateurs willing to spend money to practice their craft.

The means to getting paid

As I see it, there are a few common ways that artists get paid for doing their work:

- Performance: The artist gets paid by someone to have access (perhaps exclusive access, in the case of physical art like sculpture) to the art whose content the artist has chosen.
- Patronage: Someone provides money to meet the artist's needs without restriction on the content of the work they create.
- Commission: The artist does specific work using their skills at the request of another in return for payment.

Let's look at these a bit closer.

Performance has many variations. In the case of the work of a painter, the result of paying could be owning a particular painting and hanging it on the wall of one's home. In the case of a singer, it could be attending a concert and hearing the singer perform. In these cases, the physical nature of the art provides exclusivity—the painting can only hang on one wall, and only those in the limited space of the music hall can hear and see the singer live.

Through laws, we have added additional, nonphysical exclusivities to provide additional opportunities for performance payment, providing additional means to earn a living for a wider range of artists. For example, copyright laws let songwriters have a way to get paid for performance during a limited (but sufficiently long to have economic meaning) time. Basically, you, as a singer, must not perform that songwriter's work and receive performance payment yourself without also paying the song writer. This is a means for writers to get paid as one of the results of some of their work. (It's not turning their work into property. It is just a simple technique for monetizing one aspect of the result of their work in a way that society finds acceptable.)

Patronage has always been part of art. Without people paying more than their "fair share," the livelihood of many artists and forms of art would not be practical. Most people find particular art and artists that they especially like. People with "extra" means sometimes use those means to help those artists

April 14, 2003

carry on as they wish with their art without needing to have other types of jobs, or needing to meet the desires of a larger public. The "monetizing use" model described above does not always work in balance with the financial needs of the artist and art form. The benefit to the patrons comes in knowing they are helping to promote the art, or in bringing benefit to a larger community as a type of philanthropy. For those without the "gift" of being artistic but with the "gift" of business skill, luck, or rich family, it is a way of expression and sharing their gift with others. Sometimes, the patron is really us all when the government sponsors the art (a very important case).

A variant of patronage is when the patron pays for the privilege to get something related to the art work or artist, usually for a price much higher than the perceived value to others. Examples of these related performances are items of clothing with the artist's image, memorabilia such as items that belonged to the artist or autographed by them, ancillary items to the art like CD inserts with lyrics and essays, and presence at a reception attended by the artist with a chance to have a personal discussion with the artist. Sometimes the patronage is purchasing the art directly from the artist in a way that returns a larger amount of money to the artist than they would get through normal distribution.

A purchase of a CD at a concert is often a combination of types of patronage along with performance, where the price of the CD is high, there is an option for it to be autographed, and the artist is the one behind the table selling and listening politely to your comments as you express your appreciation of the work through the purchase.

Commission is a type of support for an artist that is often overlooked. Paying artists to perform their artistry for a particular purpose has always been important. Painters have always done portraits for the wealthy and others. Composers have written to celebrate the events in the life of a noble at the request of the noble who pays for the privilege. Illustrators have created logos for companies of all sizes. Commissioned work allows the artist to practice their art while bringing particular benefit to the one who does the commissioning. For those who get joy out of practicing their craft, or in the appreciation of their work, or in being paid, commissioned work is very important. Often, it allows the artist to hone his or her skills while earning a livelihood. Using that skill and savings, the artist may then be free to also create other art that is an expression of something more inner-directed. Sometimes the commissioned art is of value to a wider community, and it is a form of patronage from society's viewpoint.

As we've seen with desktop publishing and small-business web sites, a much wider range of companies are able, and required, to take advantage of professionally created content—the commissioned work of artists. Graphic design, illustration, photography, video, and other artistic skills are being used by everybody. The cost to produce this material, in terms of equipment, is constantly dropping, but the need for a "trained eye" and other skills is growing. We don't accept the homemade look in as many places as we used to. The smallest of businesses are insisting on "a professional look," according to the research I've been seeing. Big businesses are expected to use professionally created content in more and more places. All of this means more opportunities for commissioned work for the artist.

Throughout time, artists have put together for themselves a mixture of each of these ways to earn a living (funding themselves, performance, patronage, and commission). See my write-up[15] of Buskin and Batteau for a discussion of the mix one pair of singer-songwriters have put together. (Most people have never heard of them, but if you read the write-up, you'll see why they are an interesting example—you probably have heard their work.[16])

Free release

In many cases, artists' work ends up being appreciated and used by a wider range of people than those who gave them money in the first place. Artists whose work is too confined usually do not do as well from their own, nor society's, view. Unpaid or unplanned exposure to an artist's work is often the source that leads to a patron or other income. Without exposure, there is no audience, no appreciation, and no reuse where your work lives on (the "most sincere form of flattery," which is a motivator for many). Without free exposure, many people without means or who do not know of an art form or of an

---

[15]http://www.bricklin.com/buskinandbatteau.htm

[16]Two of my favorite performers are David Buskin and Robin Batteau. They are very talented singers and songwriters. I have heard them in concert many times over the years and own copies of their recordings. My write-up on Buskin and Batteau includes this:

Most people to whom I mention Buskin and Batteau have never heard their names. However, through commissioned work, according to the *Boston Globe* 4/3/2003: "[In] the 1980s, theirs were 'the most-heard voices in America, more than Michael Jackson, Mickey Mouse, and Ronald Reagan combined—a horrifying thought by itself' boasts one press release." Among others, Buskin wrote a short "logo" jingle for NBC, co-wrote "All Aboard America" for Amtrak, and did work for Burger King, JC Penney, and the U.S. Postal Service. For ". . . a new Tufts song, the gift of Overseer Rysia de Ravel, J71, P94, on the occasion of Tufts' 150th anniversary . . . De Ravel commissioned award-winning singer and songwriter David Buskin, whose previous clients have included Judy Collins, Tom Rush and Roberta Flack." Batteau wrote and sang Coca-Cola's "Can't Beat The Feeling" and Chevrolet's "Heartbeat of America," and wrote "Be All You Can Be" for the U.S. Army.

artist's work would not be inspired to become artists themselves. (How many stories do we hear of children repeatedly sneaking into theaters or concert halls, or hanging out in libraries and museums, later to become major artists in the field?)

There has always been lots of free release to society, where the artist is not paid for his or her work. Fair-use carve-outs in legislation and foreseeable difficulties in enforcement have made the copyright laws work for society. (Again, these laws do not make works property; they are just schemes that enhance exclusivity and scarcity that help bring in some money from performance where the physical nature of the art does not provide it. They are not mimics of physical exclusivity, which in any case themselves vary from art form to art form.) Built into many types of performing art is a way to not be paid, though sometimes for a "diminished" form of that performance. Copies of popular or important paintings or sculptures have always been made, for example.

The needs of the "commercial" or "professional" or "public" arena have helped balance out this free release. We can hum a new song we like for free, or even sing it along with friends around a campfire, but we can't use it in a TV commercial without paying the author. A photograph copied from a web site works fine for a child's term paper, but only the original high-resolution version may suffice for a magazine, which would have staff to arrange for payment.

For each art form and artist, there is a wide range of mixtures of payment and free-release nonpayment that works. Like many things in life, the particular mixture can be very free-form and change over time, tailored to the individual and the particular art form. The street musician plays for all who pass by and is funded by the few who are moved to give a donation. That same musician may have had his or her training paid by an uncle who wanted to help them and eventually make most of his or her money creating soundtracks for corporate videos. The proportions in the mixture of users and payers, of people who don't make any financial contribution to the artist, those that make a small amount, and those that make significant amounts, vary from artist to artist and art form to art form. The creator of large sculptures for public places, such as in parks and courtyards, needs but a few patrons or commissioners. Most of the people who will enjoy the art work will have no direct financial connection to the artist. The painter of family portraits, on the other hand, will need many people who commission work, most of whom, along with their families and friends, will be the only people to see the work.

This use of a mixture of payments is common in all of selling. A hamburger is usually sold for much closer to its actual cost than the drink or fries consumed with it. The child-friendly environment in the restaurant is provided free of charge.

Fans

Fan bases are an important element for many types of art. These are the people who know and appreciate the particular artist's work and seek it out. They are more likely to pay for "performances" of all sorts, to be patrons or sponsors, to decide to use that artist for commissioned work, etc. Knowing that they have a fan base, artists can plan for the future, creating new works without up-front payment. The fan base can provide the people that satisfy the need to have an audience and appreciation.

Crucial to this ecosystem of different types and needs for payment is the discovery of the artist by people who would be admirers of that artist's work, and perhaps become part of the fan base and payers for performance, patrons, and commissioners. Frequently, that discovery comes from free, serendipitous exposure to the artist's work. A caricaturist who sketches likenesses of people in a public square is also an entertainer (another form of artist), providing free entertainment to those who watch. The crowds that form help attract others, a few of whom may become customers. Many singers build their fan base by starting as the warm-up band to a more established act. Many people learn about new artists from friends who share what they have found and like. Performers learn of other performers with whom they pair up when they overhear each other playing at the same venue. The less expensive the act of introducing others to the art you like, the more likely you are to do it and they are to let you. The wider variety of art you are exposed to, the more likely you will find something that really resonates, much to the benefit of the artist.

The fact that there is free release is a key aspect of the ecosystem of art. The free release results not only in discovery, but also in use by other artists, resulting in yet more art. Free release is not the only source of discovery and other art, but it is a component that must not be ignored or eliminated. It is as important as variations are to biological evolution, tithing and religious teaching were to early social welfare, and competition and information are to free markets. It is also just as important that it be fluid and organic, and not mechanically absolute, as those other attributes.

Today's world

A problem with much of today's prerecorded media art (such as sound recordings and movies) is the method of discovery. Introduction to new artists and their work is done through advertising, paid placement (narrow radio and TV play lists), and other mass marketing techniques. These are very expensive, and the difficulty of rising above the noise becomes yet more and more expensive. There is a self-fulfilling prophecy where only huge sellers bringing in large revenues are pursued. Small fan bases, even if solid and large enough to fully fund the artist themselves with a very acceptable life compared to other professions, do not fit in this model. A few big hits are viewed as more important than a myriad of small ones, each with a happy artist and happy fans. There seems to be a drive by the major companies in the media industry to create a few "superstars" instead of many full-time artists. This is bad economics if in catering to the big players we develop technologies and norms that hamper the "business models" of the smaller players.

Technology is making the cost of practicing many types of art less expensive. For example, recording and editing equipment of high quality that used to cost hundreds of thousands or millions of dollars is becoming something even a hobbyist can afford and use. Manufacturing and distribution of many media forms are becoming almost cost-free. Communications to a widely dispersed fan base has dropped to a minor cost as mailing and the need for advertising is replaced with email and web sites. (When I discussed this with someone in the computer industry, he basically asked: "Is the Britney Spears model the mainframe of the music business?")

There is a difference between few, centrally controlled sources of performance with huge audiences and many smaller sources of performance with smaller, often overlapping audiences. In trying to understand why the online market of eBay was worth so much more than OnSale, David Reed[17] formulated what has become known as "Reed's Law."[18] He showed mathematically that the value of "group forming networks" grows faster (exponentially) than centralized distribution (which grows linearly, according to Sarnoff's Law). Just like the myriad auctions on eBay for everything from Beanie Babies to Corvette sports cars have resulted in one of the dominant players in online commerce, the totality of all the artists and their fan bases, given the right ecosystem, can be more valuable to society than the few "superstars" of the recording industry

---

[17]David P. Reed, www.reed.com, is a friend that I met when we both worked on the Multics project in 1970. He is well known as a pioneer in the design and construction of the Internet protocols, distributed data storage, and PC software systems and applications. He is coinventor of the end-to-end argument, often called the fundamental architectural principle of the Internet.

[18]http://www.reed.com/gfn/docs/reedslaw.html

and Hollywood. Given the wrong ecosystem, this valuable and crucial source of art could die. While for certain forms of art centralized production and distribution are a valuable component, it must not be the only component.

Something that bothers me about the talk about Digital Rights Management (DRM), both technical and legislative, is the whole disregard for the ecosystem needed for widespread advancement of the arts. The free-form of a variety and a mixture of funding models, and the benefits of unintended free release, are part of what makes things work with art and society. Responding to opportunities that present themselves requires flexibility. The DRM systems we hear about today are rigid procrustean beds that could kill this ecology. They are wedded to narrow, simplistic business models dominated by large publishing businesses.

In computers, we've seen that fluid, general-purpose programs like word processors and spreadsheets have usually prevailed over the more structured systems. People do with them what they want, not what the creator envisioned. (I can tell you that firsthand with the spreadsheet . . .) DRM systems we hear about are based on a particular model of use, with an aim for absolute control being part of that model.

With art, which is usually used or experienced by others for their own purposes, there must be generality and lack of control to let others do what they want with it. An ecosystem with many ways for unintended free release is a requirement. Therefore, an ecosystem which looks to a mixture of the traditional amateur, performance, patronage, and commission forms of payment is a requirement. Depending upon rigid enforcement of performance payments will disrupt the balance.

Listening to representatives from the recording and movie industries, you would think that selling fixed artifacts is the only way that artists can get paid. That has never been the case, and should not be in the future, or else society and art itself will suffer.[19] Those publishing businesses may be based on that one form of payment, but the artists' livelihood need not.

---

[19]See also "Copy Protection Robs the Future" in Chapter 9. This brings up another problem with DRM, which affects the artists' desire to have a long-term impact through their work.

Reaction to the essay, April 21, 2003

Mark Bernstein's posting and my response:

Patronage and Peril

Dan Bricklin justly rebukes Big Music in his essay, "How Will Artists Get Paid?" He argues that

"...an ecosystem which looks to a mixture of the traditional amateur, performance, patronage, and commission forms of payment is a requirement. Depending upon rigid enforcement of performance payments will disrupt the balance."

As Bricklin observes, publishing is not the only business model for artists. However, it remains the best business model for artists, the business model that gives them the greatest independence and dignity. Patronage is better than starvation or giving up, but the zealots (not Bricklin!) who want to save art from commerce would return it to the Prince and the Priest, making artists subservient once more to the whims of government agencies and the desires of deep pockets.

It's nice to have a grant, but it's nicer to have lots of grants; it's good to have the support of your management, but it's even nicer to have the support of customers. If your funding, however lavish, depends on one or two powerful people, how free can your work be?

Bricklin's case study of Buskin and Batteau cuts both ways. He sees a healthy ecosystem that gave two talented folksingers a variety of job opportunities. I see two talented performers who spent the 90's writing jingles to sell Chevies and recruit kids to join the US Army.

Not long ago, I heard an interview with Pete Seeger in which he recalled a long car ride he took "with Martin" (Luther King) back in '57. The Reverend mentioned a song he'd heard Pete sing the previous night. "That song really sticks with you, doesn't it?" The song, of course, was "We Shall Overcome."

Mark Bernstein, April 15, 2003[20]

My response:

---

[20]http://www.markbernstein.org/Apr0301/PatronageandPeril.html

Mark Bernstein had some comments in reaction to this essay and the Buskin and Batteau example, especially with regard to commissioned work and patronage. He brings up the problems of ". . . making artists subservient once more to the whims of government agencies and the desires of deep pockets . . . [Dan] sees a healthy ecosystem that gave two talented folksingers a variety of job opportunities. [Mark sees] two talented performers who spent the 90's writing jingles to sell Chevies and recruit kids to join the US Army."

My response, defending some of the benefits of commissioned work, included the following:

I found a quote from Robin Batteau in an article on the Web written by Gary Eskow for *Mix* magazine:

> *"I like the immediacy of the advertising business," he says. "You can work for two years on an album, and when it doesn't turn into The Beatles' 'White Album' be very upset. But a jingle is written and cut very quickly, and it's on the air shortly thereafter, and that's satisfying. There's also something about getting your first idea down as the end result. Sometimes when you refine a song over and over again, you lose touch with your original impulse. There's none of that danger with jingles because of the pressure to complete your work quickly."*
>
> *Jingle writers, no matter how successful, have to make peace with the fact that advertising is considered a second-class art in certain circles. I asked Batteau for his take on the topic. "Who knows how the future will judge the art of this time?" he asks. "Andy Warhol was simply painting Campbell's soup cans, and now they're considered important pieces of art. Maybe the most creative advertising music will be thought of as art in the future. You don't know what throw-away art is going to become . . ."*
>
> Gary Eskow, Mix, May 1, 2000[21]

I find that doing creative work for a particular purpose is often a wonderful thing to do. It's like sticking to a particular poetry form, or that scene in the

---

[21]http://web.archive.org/web/20030628182650/http://mixonline.com/ar/audio_joey_levine_television/index.htm

movie *Apollo 13* where the engineers are given the parts available and told, "Make it work." Is commissioned work any worse than having to write stuff you don't like just because the audience likes it? Or playing that old hit song for the 40 thousandth time 20 years later to have them leave the concert happy?

I like your statement, "It's nice to have a grant, but it's nicer to have lots of grants," hence my invoking of Reed's Law. When I hear "depends on one or two powerful people," I don't hear rich patron but rather big record company, with whom personal relationships have little sway, and altruism for payment is unlikely.

As far as I can tell, Buskin and Batteau spent time helping other artists, too, in many ways (Shawn Colvin was Batteau's assistant at one point, according to one report), and doing lots of fund-raisers. I think it was Batteau who also wrote material for Clinton to help him get elected. Not the image of slaves to big business you sort of imply. If you know their comedy leanings and style, I think it sounds more like they felt they were exploiting big business. As I try to show, things are very fluid.

Great you bring up that story about Martin Luther King's reaction to hearing "We Shall Overcome." I hadn't heard it. It's even better if you look at this quote from Pete Seeger.[22] The one you heard is probably on this show on NPR.

The evolution of "We Shall Overcome" is a great example of how songs move along, with some changes, and can have great social effect. [It started, as far as we know, as a combination of religious hymns, was sung by striking employees with changes, and eventually passed along to Pete Seeger who published a copy and passed it on to others and eventually to Dr. King.] Being exposed to something and reacting to it, reusing it, is very important. As one who has had his work move on (and many ones that did not), I can tell you there are great psychic rewards for knowing that the pebble you dropped in the pond made great waves, even if the journey there meant you didn't get the full economic benefit that was theoretically possible.

http://www.bricklin.com/artistspaid.htm

[22]http://web.archive.org/web/20030504224613/http://www.learncentereded. org/Seeger/Civil+Rights.html
The link in the original essay to the NPR show recording no longer works. Also, NPR apparently had a setting on their web site that requested that Archive.org not preserve copies, so I couldn't find it there either.

Attribution: An Alternate Method of Payment

For many artists, and other people who create new things, having their work attributed to them is a major motivation. Sometimes it has only psychic rewards, but often it also has important economic rewards as it builds up the creator's reputation and the demand for their other work. This next essay discusses an ancient problem of attribution, or more specifically, the ancient problem of ensuring attribution. It ties together the Internet, the speed with which some forms of expression can now virally spread around the world without your control, and attribution.

February 22, 1999

ATTRIBUTING A JOKE

How do you let people know you were the author when the email gets forwarded around the world without attribution?

It's amazing how the problems we run into in the new world of the Internet are really just the same problems of old, often with similar solutions. Here is an example:

There is a custom among many Jews during the Rosh Hashanah holiday to symbolically get rid of their sins by throwing bits of bread into a body of water, such as a river. The practice is known as *Tashlich* (pronounced "TAHSH-lich"). My friend Robbie Fein had the idea that it would be fun to associate different types of breads with different types of sins. He mentioned this to a friend of his, Rabbi Dick Israel of Newton, Massachusetts. Dick liked the idea and wrote a humorous piece listing several different sin/bread combinations for a sermon. For example:

> For ordinary sins, use—White Bread
> For exotic sins—French Bread
> For particularly dark sins—Pumpernickel
> For complex sins—Multi-grain
> For twisted sins—Pretzels
> (You get the idea . . .)

Dick participates in an email mailing list for rabbis, and he sent a copy to the list. Like many professional mailing lists, this was supposed to be a closed list, with no sharing of the material outside of the list. Unfortunately, that's not what happened with his piece. Within hours of posting the *Tashlich* list, people all over the world were forwarding each other copies. Dick was soon getting back copies of his own joke. While he was flattered by the widespread delight at his humor, he was upset that the attribution to him was removed and didn't travel with it. (In the academic and spiritual world, of course, attribution is important.)

Dick described it this way:

> *"It was circulated not only with no attribution, but also with spurious attribution. If A sent it to B, B assumed that A wrote it and gave A credit. There were any number of A's who were given such credit. But the worst was when someone showed me a copy of the list which they thought was clever and I responded that I had written it. 'You did not!' He said, 'No one wrote it.' It had become folk-lore and it was apparently my lot to have my fifteen minutes of fame anonymously."*

One of the people who wrote him was his friend Richard Dale. Richard had received a copy of the *Tashlich* piece from a friend in England. Understanding Dick's problem, Richard proposed a rabbinical solution to keeping the attribution with the text. He suggested that Dick send out an updated list with additional entries. This time, Dick should encode his own name in the text using a method common to the poems of old: make the first letters of each entry spell out his name. Richard found it a little strange to propose a solution that came from his religious background rather than his technical background. It is well known to most Jews that some prayers, such as the *Lecha Dodi* sung every Friday evening, have the author's name encoded this way (in that case, Shlomo HaLevi, who lived in the 16th century).

Dick followed Richard's advice, and now the new version circulates with his name "Richard Israel" encoded inside as the first letters of the last 13 items.

The problem that Dick ran into is an important one in the Internet world. People with content, including images, programs, text, music, video, and more, face the problem of attributing ownership and authorship. Digital watermarks in pictures, encrypted file formats, and more are being developed. But the problem is not new. The content creators of hundreds of years ago left "watermarks" in their works that have survived copying for generations. Hopefully we can come up with simple and powerful enough methods so that our signatures will last as long.

Dick Israel is the author of *The Kosher Pig: And Other Curiosities of Modern Jewish Life* and *Jewish Identity Games: A How-To-Do-It Book.*[23]

This essay was written in early 1999. Tragically, Dick passed away in the summer of 2000. May his memory be a blessing!

http://www.bricklin.com/jokeattrib.htm

RICHARD ISRAEL'S CRUMB LIST

Dick sent me his latest version, with an introduction, for inclusion here:

My crumb list has yielded a great deal of fun, both from writing it and the suggestions I have gotten from others. It has also been quite aggravating. I had been working on the piece before Rosh Hashanah, off and on for the past several years, during those times I couldn't stand working on a *drashah*.[24] I had assumed that I would get it just right after a few more years and would publish it. That all changed when someone leaked it from private emailing, sent it to a friend, and the friend sent it to the world. It then began appearing on every known Jewish net list either without attribution or with inaccurate attribution. I was in danger of losing all connection with the piece, but trying to get it back was like trying to return feathers to a torn cushion in a high wind.

Following the practice of our ancestors who wrote their names into liturgical poems (which I now understand for the first time) I spelled my name into the list (the last 13 entries from "Rearing children . . ." on). Should have done it a long time ago. Now let people mail it out without attribution and claim it! It appeared in *Sh'ma* last Purim so at least at a formal level, I have rights to it.

The list was certainly not intended to be an exercise in earnestness, but it was also more than a joke. I hoped that it would be a light-spirited way to get people to think about *Tashlich*. (Yes, even sins can be funny.) I can't be sure that this was what made the difference, but after I read it at services more people turned up at our local pond than we have ever seen before. I think that is probably a good thing. I am less sure that it was good for the fish.

---

[23]*The Kosher Pig: And Other Curiosities of Modern Jewish Life*, 1994, Alef Design Group, ISBN: 1881283151

Jewish Identity Games: A How-To-Do-It Book, 1993, Torah Aura Productions, ISBN: 0933873786

[24]A *drashah* is a Hebrew word often translated as "sermon" but that has more of the specific connotation of exploring the meaning within a Biblical passage.

There was also the goose problem. Signs were posted saying firmly, "Do not feed the Canada geese, they will forget that they are supposed to migrate."

"But officer, we are not feeding the geese. They are just taking advantage of our sins." It doesn't sound very convincing. Luckily, we didn't get caught.

~~~~~~

Tashlich Supplement:
(c) 1997 Richard J Israel

Taking a few crumbs to Tashlich from whatever old bread is in the house lacks subtlety, nuance and religious sensitivity. I would suggest that we can do better. Instead:

> For ordinary sins, use—White Bread
> For exotic sins—French Bread
> For particularly dark sins—Pumpernickel
> For complex sins—Multi-grain
> For twisted sins—Pretzels
> For tasteless sins—Rice Cakes
> For sins of indecision—Waffles
> For sins committed in haste—Matzah
> For sins committed in less than eighteen minutes—Shmurah Matzah
> For sins of chutzpah—Fresh Bread
> For substance abuse/marijuana—Stoned Wheat
> For substance abuse/heavy drugs—Poppy Seed
> For arson—Toast
> For timidity—Milk Toast
> For high-handedness—Napoleons
> For being sulky—Sourdough
> For silliness—Nut Bread
> For not giving full value—Short bread
> For jingoism—Yankee Doodles
> For telling bad jokes—Corn Bread
> For being money-hungry—Enriched Bread or Raw Dough
> For telling small lies—Fudge
> For war-mongering—Kaiser Rolls
> For promiscuity—Hot Buns

For racism—Crackers

For sophisticated racism—Ritz Crackers

For being holier-than-thou—Bagels

For unfairly up-braiding others—Challah

For provocative dressing—Wonton Wrappers

For snobbery—Upper Crusts

For indecent photography—Cheese Cake

For trashing the environment—Dumplings

For the sin of laziness—Any Very Long Loaf

For being hyper-critical—Pan Cakes

For political skullduggery—Bismarcks

For over-eating—Stuffing Bread or Bulkie Rolls

For gambling—Fortune Cookies

For pride—Puff Pastry

For cheating—Bread made with Nutrasweet and Olestra

For being snappish—Ginger Bread

For dropping in without calling beforehand—Popovers

For trying to improve everyone within sight—Angel Food Cake

For being up-tight and irritable—High Fiber or Bran Muffins

For sycophancy—Brownies

For rearing children incompetently—Raisin Bread

For immodest behavior—Tarts

For causing injury or damage to others—Tortes

For hardening our hearts—Jelly doughnuts

For abrasiveness—Grits

For recurring slip ups—Banana Bread

For davening off tune—Flat Bread

For impetuosity—Quick Bread

For silliness—Nut Bread

For risking one's life unnecessarily—Hero Bread

For auto theft—Caraway

For excessive use of irony—Rye Bread

For larceny (especially of copyright material)—Stollen

etc., etc.

Remember, you don't have to show your crumbs to anyone.

February 22, 1999

For those who require a wide selection of crumbs, an attempt will be made to have pre-packaged Tashlich Mix available in three grades (Tashlich Lite, Medium and Industrial Strength) at your local Jewish bookstore.

~~~~~~

With thanks to Robbie Fein who suggested the original formula.
Richard J. Israel

http://www.bricklin.com/crumblist.htm

Self-Expression

The last part of this chapter expands on the idea of what people will pay money for. The iPod I refer to is an early, all-white one, before the mini, the nano, the Touch, etc.

January 29, 2004

PAYING FOR STYLE

People pay for expressing themselves personally through style.

Over the years, there has been continuing interest in my July 2000 essay "What will people pay for?" An edited version was reprinted in the *Harvard Business Review* back in September of 2001, and it still gets readers every day on my web site. It lists the following things regular people will pay for in addition to basic human needs like food, shelter, etc., and other "practical" things: (1) Interacting with people they care about (e.g., talking on a cell phone and email), and (2) experiencing "other forms of emotion" like listening to music or seeing something beautiful (including buying art, paying to watch a performance, etc.).

I continue to be interested in what people pay for. I presented some related thoughts in my "How will the artists get paid?" essay. There I add: (3) Practicing an "art" as an amateur, and (4) subsidizing an artist they especially like as a form of philanthropy.

As I sit here on a plane listening to music on my Apple iPod, and after seeing lots of people with many different backgrounds on the train ride to the airport, I thought about another time when many regular people spend money that "they don't have to." That is for (5): Personal expression through something with style. To many people, expressing themselves through designs, combinations of products, and attention to detail is worth paying money. They buy and wear products (and deliberate mixtures and juxtapositions of products) that "say something." What they are saying may be, "I identify with this brand—if you know what that brand means you'll know something about me." It may be, "I have strong feeling for a form of art, and I practice that art form in the choice of clothes, hair style, makeup, whatever." They may have nothing to say but rather are just driven to express themselves for themselves by a love of that "art form." Some artists are driven to paint in oils, others to choose certain fabric patterns. While there is sometimes a conformity drive behind what people wear, or a practicality trade-off between price and "doesn't look too bad," I believe that a significant portion of the population has an artistic drive and expresses that drive through their choices of clothes, accessories (worn, carried, used), ornaments (desk, room, cubicle, etc.), tools, and more. Like amateur artists, they pay extra to express themselves.

What's interesting about this is that it isn't about being rich. Style is in no way connected to wealth. I believe that the percentage of one's "disposable" wealth that is knowingly and purposefully spent on style is a factor of who you are and not on how much you have. In good times you'll spend larger amounts, but it is always viewed as a "necessity" by such "artists."

To profitably sell something that meets the needs for such people you must have a product in an area where an economic number of people are willing to put their "expression dollars." (When I say "economic," I mean considering your company's particular cost structure.) You have to be priced with a premium that is acceptable, given the perceived value of adding expression over the utilitarian value of the product itself. You have to have the styling itself "right" for the way that an economic segment of that population wants to do the expression. Getting the balance of all these conditions right to make money is all very tricky. A premium-priced product with desirable style in an inexpensive category may sell many more units than one in an expensive category or have lower per-unit marketing costs. Some people have a real understanding of this area for certain products and are repeatedly successful (such as Steve Jobs and his associates at Apple, as well as many well-known clothing and home-furnishing designers). Others just luck out. In any event, expressing one's self through style is responsible for a significant amount of spending that is important to the individuals involved.

It is interesting that the Apple iPod addresses multiple categories here. It is for listening to music (#2), it is from a company some people like to support (#4), and it exudes a variety of style attributes (#5) as it appeals through the stark color carried through even to the earpieces and wires, the smooth, compact, and sealed physical design, the minimalist simplicity and responsiveness of operation, and more.

http://www.bricklin.com/stylepay.htm

In this chapter we have covered a variety of forces that are not driven primarily by simple financial needs but rather by human feelings. We also touched on how technology has moved from just something utilitarian to something involving feelings and style. Taking these forces into account is important when constructing a model for how your business makes money.

Apple has continued to be a leader in this movement, from the streamlined case and color display of the original Apple II in a world of techie boxes with monochrome monitors, to the "organic-looking" display of the first Mac, to the iPod, and now to the iPhone. In the years since the last essay, the practice of juxtaposing brands as a part of expression has only grown.

We also looked at how providing the money to support artists in their work has many components, and how there are many different configurations of those components that can be beneficial.

The better-connected world enabled by the Internet has increased the reach of even simple creations. Reach means that an artist's reputation can be around the world instead of just among a few physically close friends. Even obscure creations can have a big following when it is an inch deep and 25,000 miles wide. The technological advances since these essays were written have only increased that reach.

In the next chapter we'll look at how technology is changing the music industry and how the industry has been reacting. Does the industry look to the ideas in this chapter or are they like the early telephone people, clinging to an old model?

3

The Recording Industry and Copying

This chapter provides a look at the recording industry as a case study in the issues brought up in Chapter 2 and relates them to a business situation being adversely affected by technology. These issues include the problem of a big business with one method for paying artists, free release, fan bases, and methods of discovering new artists. As I did in Chapter 2's "How will the artists get paid?" essay, I try to take a view from the level of society's needs in addition to those of the specific players themselves. Some of the material in this chapter is also an example of trying to do some deeper numerical analysis of an issue rather than just using gut feelings.

The issue of music recordings downloaded from the Internet was thrust into the center of the public stage with the rapid growth of Napster in 2000 and the lawsuits that eventually shut it down. To help argue for a position on what was going on, words like *sharing*, *stealing*, and *piracy* were used by people arguing for the different sides.

Given the high visibility of the music industry, despite its small size in relation to other businesses, politicians became involved in this issue. Laws were proposed that were thought by their authors to be limited to the entertainment industry and only to address the real issues causing problems. Technologists, though, realized that such legislation could have detrimental effects in other areas. This potential for overreacting spurred me to write several essays and many blog posts.

The popularity of the original Napster[1] and related file-sharing systems, I believe, helped drive the demand for home high-speed Internet connections. While most web sites of the day could be accessed in just a few seconds at

---

[1] Napster was a system created initially by Shawn Fanning that operated from 1999 through 2001. The name was later used on other, different systems. When I write about Napster in this book, I am referring to the original system.

dial-up speeds,[2] a typical 4 MB Top 40 song could easily take 15 minutes or more to download. With a cable modem, it would take something more like 15 seconds. The widespread adoption of fast, always-on, so-called "broadband" connections in the years after 2000 made all sorts of other advances possible, leading to popular applications such as YouTube and Skype.

Napster showed that the Internet could be used for more than just email and informational web sites. The personal computer became the communications and entertainment center for many people, especially college students, and some of these went on to invent new personal uses for computers like Facebook and YouTube.[3]

Napster was a system for finding and transferring copies of music files from one personal computer to another. It was started in June 1999, and a lawsuit eventually shut it down in July 2001.

Here is how Napster worked: You first downloaded a copy of the program from the Napster web site. This program ran on your personal computer. You would log on to the Napster company's computers using the program. You could then type in part of the name of a song. The Napster program on your computer would display a list of names of files that other people who were also logged in had on their computers (in a special sharing directory for this purpose) that matched what you typed.[4] You could select one or more of these files for download.

The Napster program would then establish a direct connection (called "peer-to-peer") between your computer and that other person's computer and it would automatically transfer a copy without the copy going through the Napster company's computers. When you got the copy, you could play it using MP3-playing software. Because the file was copied into your sharing directory, it was now also available for others to copy from you, increasing the likelihood that someone would be logged in who had any given song. The

---

[2] For example, the CNN.com home page on August 15, 2000, when retrieved from Archive.org, is only 17KB of text and 17KB for the main photo and an average of about 1–2KB for each of the few dozen other little images that make up the design. That would be readable in a few seconds and fully loaded in 15–20 seconds. The CNN.com home page in 2008, while still only about 20KB of text, has Flash video playing, over 300KB of JavaScript and CSS, etc., and is much more tuned to a higher-speed connection.

[3] http://www.usatoday.com/tech/news/2006-10-11-youtube-karim_x.htm

[4] Normally people would name an MP3 file with the name of the song it contained. Most programs that copied from CDs to computer MP3 files (a process called "ripping") named the files automatically with the help of a special online service called CDDB. (CDDB is described in Chapter 4.)

September 9, 2002

Napster program would continue running in the background while you did other things. The Napster system was an Internet system, not just the World Wide Web part of the Internet. It did not involve a browser.[5]

We start with this essay:

THE RECORDING INDUSTRY IS TRYING TO KILL THE GOOSE THAT LAYS THE GOLDEN EGG

> *Given the slight dip in CD sales despite so many reasons for there to be a much larger drop, it seems that the effect of downloading, burning, and sharing is one of the few bright lights helping the music industry with their most loyal customers.*

Josh Bernoff, who once worked with me at Software Arts, did an interesting survey for Forrester Research. He's quoted in a Forrester press release[6] titled "Downloads Did Not Cause The Music Slump, But They Can Cure It" as saying, "There is no denying that times are tough for the music business, but not because of downloading. Based on surveys of 1,000 online consumers, we see no evidence of decreased CD buying among frequent digital music consumers . . . Plenty of other causes are viable, including the economic recession and competition from surging video game and DVD sales . . ." Intrigued, I thought I'd look a little closer to see what might be causing the decrease in CD buying.

What is affecting CD buying according to the data?

To get some data to understand CD buying, I looked to both Forrester and the Recording Industry Association of America (RIAA). First, I looked to find more of what Josh Bernoff found. Some of that is presented on the Forrester web site on the "Downloads Save The Music Business" page.[7] I also looked at the RIAA "News Archive" page[8] to get some of their numbers and statements. Finally, I looked around me to see behavior on the streets, and among friends and relatives.

Josh breaks down the music download/burning and CD-buying public into various categories. The categories, from lowest use of downloading and burning

---

[5] I cover more of what we learned from Napster, and explain how using a browser is different, in Chapter 4.

[6] http://www.forrester.com/ER/Press/Release/0,1769,741,FF.html

[7] http://www.forrester.com/ER/Research/Report/Summary/0,1338,14854,FF.html

[8] http://web.archive.org/web/20021015124808/http://www.riaa.com/News_Archive.cfm

to highest, are: the "Offline" people; the "Nonusers" of digital music; then the "Dabblers" who have tried it but do it infrequently; the "Digital Music Learners" who do some (downloads, rips, or burns 3 to 8 times a month); and finally, the "Digital Music Lovers" (over 9 times a month). Based on the full report he kindly sent me when he learned of this analysis, I calculated: People who never download or burn their own ("Offline" and "Nonusers") make up about 54% of the population and only buy about 39% of the CDs. Using values explained below of about 881.9 million CDs and 239 million people over 9 years old, that yields a value of 2.7 CDs purchased per year per person. Those who sometimes download and burn their own (combining the other categories) make up 46% of the population yet buy 61% of the CDs (4.9 per year each). Of those, the "Lovers" and "Learners" make up only 22% of the surveyed population, yet buy 36% of all CDs (6.1 per year each). The "Lovers" alone make up about 5% of the population and buy about 15% of the CDs (9.7 per year each). So, it seems the more you buy, the more likely you are to download and burn your own, or, to put it another way, "the more you burn the more you buy."

Bernoff, in his Forrester report, discusses what he sees as the real reasons for a drop in CD sales: the economy (he says on his video presentation that in the pre-Internet early 1990s economic downturn there was a "significant drop in the growth of CD sales"), competition from other forms of entertainment (including the yearly $6 billion of video games and the rush to the new DVD video format), and finally the shorter playlists on radio (partially a result of Clear Channel's control of 60% of rock radio listening and their style) that lead to fewer new musicians becoming well known. I also hear that MTV is playing fewer music videos, and in general, there is a record industry strategy to push a narrower range of musicians. You can imagine that the death of Internet Radio will also cut down on the ways to find out about new music.

The RIAA also provides numbers. I looked at its web site and looked at the yearly reports that come out in January or so, giving the sales figures for the previous year. They include the number of "units" of music sold, and the dollar amount of revenue that those units represent at retail. They also break things down by different media types, such as CD albums, CD "singles" (another, no longer popular, format), cassette tapes, etc. I looked at the 2000 report and the 2001 report to get numbers from 1991 through 2001. I typed some of them into a spreadsheet and crunched the numbers a bit to figure out average retail price (sales dollars divided by units) and year-to-year change expressed as a percent. Here is what I came up with (there may be rounding effects, and I haven't rechecked all of my typing):

September 9, 2002

	1991	1992	1993	1994	1995	1996	1997	1998	1999	2000	2001
Units	801M	896	956	1123	1113	1137	1063	1124	1161	1079	969
Change		+12%	+7%	+17%	-1%	+2%	-6%	+6%	+3%	-7%	-10%
Revenue@list	$7.8B	9.0	10.0	12.1	12.3	12.5	12.2	13.7	14.6	14.3	13.7
Change		+15%	111%	+20%	+2%	+2%	-2%	+12%	+6%	-2%	-4%
$/unit	$9.78	10.08	10.51	10.75	11.07	11.02	11.51	12.20	12.57	13.27	14.19
Change		+3%	+4%	+2%	+3%	0%	+4%	+6%	+3%	+6%	+7%
$/CD (album)	$13.01	13.07	13.14	12.78	12.97	12.75	13.17	13.48	13.65	14.02	14.64
Change		0%	+1%	-3%	+1%	-2%	+3%	+2%	+1%	+3%	+4%
CD/unit	42%	46%	52%	59%	65%	68%	71%	75%	81%	87%	91%
Change		+9%	+14%	+14%	+10%	+5%	+3%	+6%	+7%	+8%	+4%
CD singles/unit	0.7%	0.8%	0.8%	0.8%	1.9%	3.8%	6.3%	5.0%	4.8%	3.2%	1.8%
CD singles/Rev	0.4%	0.5%	0.5%	0.5%	0.9%	1.5%	2.2%	1.6%	1.5%	1.0%	0.6%
Cassette/unit	45%	41%	36%	31%	24%	20%	16%	14%	11%	7%	5%
Cassette/Rev	39%	35%	29%	25%	19%	15%	12%	10%	7%	4%	3%
Cassette $/unit	$8.39	8.61	8.59	8.62	8.45	8.46	8.82	8.96	8.59	8.24	8.08

Unit sales have dropped, but revenue has not dropped as much because of an unprecedented 7% rise in prices. With a poor economy, basic economics says that a rise in price of a discretionary item already priced above the optimum point may result in a drop in total receipts. The history of results from large rises in CD album prices shows consistent negative changes in unit sales. As you can see with CD singles and cassettes, there is a life cycle with each format and CDs should be no different. Examples of other factors that affect sales that RIAA mentions[9] include the 1997 effect of tighter retail inventory controls and retail consolidation that they blame for the 1997 drop in revenues (no mention of the price rises). In early 1997, trying to explain a 2%-growth year after years of CD-driven, double-digit growth followed by a drop in unit sales after a CD price rise, RIAA president Hilary Rosen said that, "Two percent growth [in 1996] is positive news."[10] She neglected to say "prices were the same or lower."

Trying to make a case against digital music downloading and burning, RIAA also reported that its own survey of music buyers showed ". . . over 50 percent of those music fans that have downloaded music for free have made copies of it. Just two years ago, only 13 percent copied it onto a portable device or a CD

[9] http://web.archive.org/web/20020818103835/www.riaa.com/PR_Story.cfm?id=148

[10] http://web.archive.org/web/20020818104758/www.riaa.com/PR_Story.cfm?id=152

burner."[11] They also report that in 2001 40% of all "music consumers" owned a CD burner, compared to 14% in 1999. (This matches Forrester's 45% number from mid-2002.) They say that "23 percent of those music consumers surveyed said that they did not buy more music in 2001 because they downloaded or copied most of their music for free." It is unclear if those people didn't buy any music, or just didn't buy more than they did (but since they call them "consumers" and not "fans," they imply that those people do buy), nor whether the other 17% who have burners said they bought more. (Bernoff says this is the case: ". . . while 13% [of Digital Music Lovers] say downloading will decrease their music purchases, 39% say exposure to new music online increases their CD buys.") In any case, it is clear that those people who download and burn music generally still buy a lot of music when they could have gotten it "for free." In fact, they still buy most of all music.

If downloading invariably led to a cessation of buying, as RIAA implies, music sales would be off by a much, much larger amount. Further trying to bolster their argument for controlling digital music, RIAA claims that, "If just half of the blank discs sold in 2001 were used to copy music, that would mean that the number of burned music CDs worldwide is about the same as the number of CDs sold at retail." You'd have to assume, reading such material, that if it weren't for personally copied music, CD sales would be double, and with the copying they should have dropped by at least half, not 10%. (Like the RIAA, I'm ignoring here the effects of illegal, unlicensed commercial copying that has been around for years.) This doesn't match what we're seeing in the sales numbers, so something must be wrong with their logic despite its seeming "obviousness" to those of us who don't buy many or burn many music CDs. (I do burn a lot of data CDs, though, to share my photos and back up my data.)

To put the RIAA's claim that the "number of burned music CDs worldwide is about the same as the number of CDs sold at retail" in perspective, let's look at another way that music fans learn about and sample music: radio. If you assume there are 1,000 U.S. radio stations each reaching 50,000 people, playing 10 songs an hour for 10 hours a day, you get $1,000 \times 50,000 \times 10 \times 10 = 5$ billion songs heard each day. (Since Clear Channel has about 1,000 radio stations alone, and claims 110 million listeners every week, this is probably a reasonable estimation.) If you assume about 15 songs per CD, and that each CD is played by its owner 20 times, then radio would equal all the playing of the approximately 900 million CDs bought last year about every two months, or 6 times a year. (I'm

---

[11]http://web.archive.org/web/20020809140119/www.riaa.com/News_Story.cfm?id=491

September 9, 2002

assuming about 1 in 5 CDs you buy becomes a "favorite" that you play over and over for years, and most others just get played a few times.) If "free" listening is a problem, then radio is much more a factor to be feared.

Why the "obvious" answer may be incorrect

When trying to understand people's motivation and behavior, introspection is inappropriate if you aren't one who thinks like those you are trying to understand. You need to use something else, like surveys, research, and real numbers dealing with how those people actually behave. Unfortunately, Bernoff reports that, "The music label executives we spoke with are so sure piracy is destroying their business, that they seemed strangely uninterested in the truth." Politicians who listen to such people do society and musicians a disservice.

I remember when in the old days of telephone hacking In the early 1970s one very active phone-hacker at MIT was interviewed by Bell Telephone people for a magazine article. The Bell people were completely dumbfounded when he told them that his personal telephone bill was often over $100 a month (in 1970 dollars!). They assumed it would be near zero. It turned out that he liked communicating by telephone, and blue-boxes and other telephone hacking devices weren't for everything at all times. The "free" calls led to him spending more. (In this case, his "free" calls were "subsidized" by actual phone company equipment and phone company payment of international calling fees. In the case of music, the music industry does not subsidize the shared music with out-of-pocket costs, like they do with music videos or radio payola.)

I believe that there is a segment of the population that buys a disproportionate amount of the music (that old "80/20" rule). At least one such segment showed up in Josh Bernoff's numbers. According to the RIAA numbers, given the 239 million U.S. residents over the age of 9 reported by the Census Bureau, the average person must have bought about 4 units of music in 2001, 91% of them CDs. If you didn't buy a lot of CDs before Napster (let's say, more than 6 a year), your feelings don't count, since you probably haven't downloaded music, and probably buy most of your music on impulse at concerts or such, or as gifts. What we want to understand are those people who always did buy most of the music and are now downloading. We want to understand those people who have CDs playing constantly in their lives—in their homes and as they stroll, commute, or travel.

The buying cycle

What we haven't seen is a detailed model of how music buying comes about. The RIAA would have you believe that there is a simple fixed demand that is then diminished by any copies people make on their own of music obtained from others. That is clearly too simplistic a model for almost any emotionally charged buying behavior. How does the demand occur? Is there a difference in the buyer's mind between a "real" CD and downloaded copies? What is the relationship between the "fan" and the artist and what role does the physical CD play in that relationship? All of these are important questions, and there are many others.

For example, demand can occur when you learn of a musician you've never heard before through hearing one or more of their songs "for free." You find out about the "new" musician through friends, radio, and other means. (For example, some musicians are getting their big break by having one of their songs used as the music in a commercial.) After sampling the music enough times you may decide that you like it enough to buy an entire CD, or perhaps previous recordings from the musician. As you become a "fan," you may start collecting posters, CDs, and other tokens, and attend concerts. When new recordings are released, you are primed to "add the latest" to your collection. Sometimes, the first exposure may be at a concert (e.g., the new band is the warm-up band for another) and you buy the CD there. Sometimes you go to a musical in a theater and buy the CD on impulse as part of expressing your feelings about what you saw and heard. The model of exactly what role familiarity plays in purchasing is very important and is ignored in the simplistic "downloading is bad" theories. "Free music" has always been a factor in demand (remember the dual-deck cassette player/recorders?), you just have to figure out how it fits in to the entire picture.

Music that you download at the suggestion of others, or in response to hearing something else by that artist, counts as sampling just like listening on the radio (maybe more so, since you get immediate gratification and your tastes are taken into account by your friends). The importance of radio sampling, and the problems of the cost of "paying" for it, are of great interest to the music industry, as you can see in their writings about consolidation and payola.[12] Marketing music through means such as music videos and radio playing is a major cost to the music industry—"perhaps the most expensive part of the music business today" according to the RIAA.[13]

Some examples of how we could use such a model were suggested by a friend: What is the role of MP3 players, which hold more music than I normally

---

[12]http://web.archive.org/web/20021029051549/http://www.aftra.org/resources/pr/0502/stmt524.html

[13]http://web.archive.org/web/20020924131502/http://www.riaa.org/MD-US-7.cfm

carry? Does an old portable CD player only let me carry just my few "favorites" that I listen to over and over again, and the larger capacity of the MP3 player means I can sample ones I'm just learning about? Does the proliferation of automobile CD players have an effect? Do people load up the car CD holder with 20 of their "favorites" every 6–12 months and just listen to them instead of learning about new artists on the radio?

The role of cell phone usage

There is an effect that I noticed while walking around the streets of New York City, and then again in Toronto, on campuses, and elsewhere. Less and less do you find people walking along, in their own worlds, listening on headphones to personal music devices. More likely than a Walkman or Discman, I see people with cell phones clutched to their ears. Style of dress doesn't matter . . . rich or not, working or strolling, they are talking to someone else. Maybe it isn't just music or mass entertainment we want when we tune out the world around us, but rather something else to do of our own choosing. And that something else, if we had our druthers, would be to talk to someone we know and like. We don't just want "content" that many other people would enjoy, too. The young people who buy many CDs, as far as I can tell, are not just the asocial people who don't talk to others. "Popular" kids buy a lot of music. This move to more communicating when traveling, and less music listening, is something I understand and have experienced personally.

Maybe there is a drop in music sales that is the result of an increase in cell phone usage. Cell phone ownership (especially among those in the CD-buying ages—as reported by the Cahners In-Stat Group[14]) has been growing the last few years. In addition, the number of minutes used is going up. According to[15] the wireless association CTIA numbers (details on their web site[16]), total billable cellular minutes were up 76% from 2000 to 2001, with an average of 296 minutes per month per subscriber and with 17% more subscribers. In order to drive sales, there continues to be a war among cellular carriers to see who can provide the most "unlimited evening and weekend" minutes to talk to friends and family (and thereby get you used to talking on a cell phone when it costs money, too). People have only so many waking hours a day. Extra talking while you're walking will undoubtedly cut down on time when you

---

[14]http://web.archive.org/web/20021021110419/http://www.instat.com/pr/2000/wp0007md_pr.htm

[15]http://www.mobile.seitti.com/story.php?s=7&story_id=1700&nl=2002-05-24

[16]http://files.ctia.org/pdf/CTIA_Survey_Mid_Year_2008_Graphics.pdf

can listen to music. With 500–1,000 minutes a month to talk, that's enough to listen to 10 CDs. If we say that you listen to each CD you buy 20 times (1,480 minutes) that means that avid CD buyers would probably buy 1–6 fewer CDs per year once they start using a cell phone heavily. In addition, talking on the phone while walking or driving cuts down on time to listen to the radio and be exposed to new music. This could be having a huge effect on CD sales. This is in addition to the moving of limited discretionary spending from music to cell phone fees.

The entertainment industry is trying to turn peer-to-peer into a bad name. This is wrong. Fax machines are peer-to-peer. Telephones are peer-to-peer. Email is peer-to-peer. Cell phones are peer-to-peer. As we see here, maybe the peer-to-peer systems they should be complaining about are sold by AT&T Wireless, Verizon, and Voicestream.

Gifts

There is another thing that I've noticed. Not all giving others copies of music is to avoid payment. People make mixes of songs for other people as gifts. (PCs make this really easy compared to the cassette tape days.) Those songs are sometimes ones that remind them of times together because they are the main ones they listened to over and over again when working, riding in a car, at camp, etc. Those songs come from CDs, often purchased, that one or both parties own. The "gift" is the compilation—the mix—not the music, since they already have the music. (That's interesting, because a compilation can be an expressive thing, maybe even worthy of its own copyright protection.) Our use of music is evolving, and it isn't just to save money.

Opposite effects that increase CD sales

What effects are increasing CD sales? The one I keep hearing about from people I know who buy many CDs is learning about new musicians from friends and sampling their songs through downloads and other means of sharing. Once they find out they like the musicians, they then seek out their CDs for purchase (recent and past) as well as go to their concerts. This is of great importance to the health of the music industry. Another area is buying CDs as gifts. A "real" CD is even more special today, and that makes it an even more special gift. You show you care enough to get the pretty shrink-wrapped copy, not the hand-labeled, home-burned one.

Given the slight dip in CD sales despite so many reasons for there to be a much larger drop, it seems that the effect of downloading, burning, and sharing is one of the few bright lights helping the music industry with its most loyal customers. Perhaps the real reason for some of the drop in sales was the shutdown of Napster and other crackdowns by the music industry.

Record companies complain[17] about the consolidation of radio station ownership and the cost of paying off radio stations to play their music so we can listen for "free" and figure out what we'd like to buy. At the same time they are trying to kill a goose that is laying a golden egg by fighting Digital Music Use rather than, as Forrester's Bernoff suggests, understanding and joining it. Worse yet, they are trying to use legislation to hobble computing in general to get what they incorrectly think they need. This is wrong and shortsighted, and will result in many undesirable side effects (for example, see my "Copy Protection Robs The Future" essay[18]). It is bad for them and it is bad for society.[19]

http://www.bricklin.com/recordsales.htm

September 9, 2002

Example from Another Industry

I wrote this piece in 2000 when the original Napster was still operating and in the midst of lawsuits. At the time, portable MP3 players were in their infancy, with the Apple iPod still more than a year away.

THE SOFTWARE POLICE VS. THE CD LAWYERS

The recording industry needs to learn more from the software industry than just suing people involved in copying.

Reading the statements of the recording industry about Napster and seeing its legal maneuvering, I've felt somewhat conflicted. I feel something is wrong with

August 26, 2000

---

[17]http://web.archive.org/web/20021029051549/http://www.aftra.org/resources/pr/0502/stmt524.html

[18]Included in this book in Chapter 9. See also the "How will the artists get paid?" essay in Chapter 2.

[19]Some real research: See "The Effect of File Sharing on Record Sales: An Empirical Analysis" by Oberholzer and Strumpf, March 2004. Observed, carefully measured behavior shows that file sharing does not hurt record sales in the ways claimed by the recording industry and is probably good for society. http://www.unc.edu/~cigar/papers/FileSharing_March2004.pdf

how the music recording industry is going about it, being so heavy-handed and uncompromising. Yet, I'm reminded of my tenure on the board of the SPA (the Software Publishers Association, now known as the Software and Information Industry Association, SIIA[20]). We had a campaign, started a decade ago and still going, that got us and related organizations the nickname of the "Software Police." We'd go after "pirates" who made illegal copies of computer software. We'd participate in raids with law enforcement agents where illegal copies were confiscated and millions in "makeup" payments were made. It was effective. Piracy in U.S. corporations slowed substantially, and a vibrant software industry flourished with many people paying for our software.

Why isn't what the recording industry doing the same as the SPA, looking to emulate our success?

Here are some thoughts:

The software industry

There were two types of "pirates" that the SPA concentrated on for legal action: corporations that used more copies than they paid for and companies or individuals who made unauthorized, counterfeit copies and resold them (usually at low prices, or preloaded on systems to make their PCs more desirable).

The corporations were the actual end users (well, actually their employees were, but it was on the corporation's behalf that they used the software). They used the software exactly as they would have had they paid for it; they just saved the money or the hassle of keeping track of how many copies they bought. The threat of lawsuits and penalties by SPA offset the savings, and SPA provided easy-to-use auditing software to make the job of keeping track of what they had bought vs. what they were actually using more palatable.

The counterfeiters were just middlemen who were trying to make money. They served no purpose to the users of the software other than to, perhaps, lower the price. In some cases, especially outside the U.S., their versions were inferior because of poorly printed documentation, poor duplication, etc.

Other copiers of software were normal users who shared copies with their friends. SPA approached them with an educational campaign, such as a "Don't Copy That Floppy" rap video with a syllabus for use in schools and other videos for companies. These explained the economics of software (no money means no version 2), ethics (please pay the poor developer), etc. We tried to be careful about negative publicity. We rarely, if ever, sued kids.

---

[20]http://www.siia.net

The organization doing this campaign, the SPA, was actually made up of software developers. The people suing were the companies who, in most cases, actually wrote the software and documentation. Those software developers were directly hurt by lost sales. There were no alternatives for income. (As a software "star," I can tell you I rarely get paid for my personal appearances. The most I usually get is free admission to a conference, but I still pay airfare and hotel . . .).[21]

In the early days of PC software, we had copy-protection schemes.[22] Users hated this, especially when those schemes got in the way of their rightful use of a product. To "protect our rights," we made it harder for the users. We found out that when we made it easier to use our software (i.e., no copy protection) users were happier, and we still got paid. When we made it hard, they just didn't buy, or they used special programs to get around our schemes. The support costs of helping users deal with our "protection" were very high. The idea of getting them just used to paying was much better.

Users of software usually found the prices charged "reasonable" for how they used it. For example, the software used by a secretary would cost a very small fraction of what a company would pay in salary, benefits, etc., per year, yet make that person much more productive. There were "professional" versions as well as "home" and "personal" versions of products, priced to be "reasonable" in light of how they were used. Over time prices dropped, often at the same time there were more capabilities. It used to cost $495 for Lotus 1-2-3, and hundreds more for WordPerfect and perhaps a database. Then there were professional-level suites for a few hundred. Now the "Works" versions are powerful enough for most people and cost even less.

We listened in other ways besides copy protection and price. Users liked buying products bundled together, paying much less than individual products for features they probably wouldn't use but wanted available already on

---

[21]Update: Now that I do a lot of consulting and am involved in Open Source software for which there is no charge, I sometimes get a speaking fee, especially when I am there in a teaching capacity. When I appear on behalf of a company I am consulting for, though, the conference doesn't pay me, just as it didn't when I was representing my company and had a proprietary software product to promote. In any case, speaking fees don't pay enough to run a multiperson software development firm.

[22]Copy protection was accomplished through means such as requiring the original floppy disk to always be present or a special device connected to the computer. Sometimes a special code was stored on the hard disk which led to problems when the disk had errors or was reformatted.

their machine "just in case." They liked common software preloaded on their computers and other distribution methods. They liked "trial" versions.

In general, we tried to listen to our customers and give them the products they wanted in the forms they wanted so they could use them in the ways they wanted.

The recording industry

The recording industry is different. The product they are selling is basically the same it has been since the 33 ⅓ record came in many years ago (further back than I can remember). The distribution channels the end user sees are the same. And, at least for the last 35 years as far as I remember, the prices have stayed the same or gone up. The only real innovation to the user has been portable players (the Sony Walkman) and slightly improved quality.

The users of recorded music want to use it differently than it is delivered. For example, they like mixing and matching songs. Getting just the songs you want is one of the great features of Napster. Kids love making mixes for themselves or friends. One of the things driving David Winer of UserLand's work with Radio UserLand is sharing playlists. We listen to radios that don't play whole albums, just mixed songs, and hop from station to station. Yet, despite this way of use, the recording industry still sells albums of multiple songs that they decide to put together. Singles, which are rarely available, are quite expensive. To get the equivalent of a medium-sized Napster-acquired collection of music that you might listen to for a few months (one or two songs each from a hundred albums) would cost hundreds or thousands of dollars, not a "reasonable" amount in terms of the spending money of many of the users. The days of buying an album or two a month are over.

Look at who the recording industry is suing. Not the people who actually want the different use. Rather they are suing the companies that are trying to figure out how to get those users what they want. They think that by stopping the people providing what people want they will stop the need. This is not how the software industry fought piracy. The software industry tried to figure out how to give people what they wanted, even if it meant changing the distribution methods, bundling methods, or pricing. The software industry grew incredibly and is well respected. The recording industry needs to copy more from the software industry than just hiring lawyers.

http://www.bricklin.com/softwarepolice.htm

A Book Publisher Speaks

Tim O'Reilly, founder and CEO of O'Reilly Media, Inc., posted an essay titled "Piracy is Progressive Taxation, and Other Thoughts on the Evolution of Online Distribution" on December 11, 2002.[23] Here are some excerpts:

> The continuing controversy over online file sharing sparks me to offer a few thoughts as an author and publisher. To be sure, I write and publish neither movies nor music, but books. But I think that some of the lessons of my experience still apply.
>
> Lesson 1: Obscurity is a far greater threat to authors and creative artists than piracy.
>
> Lesson 2: Piracy is progressive taxation.
>
> Lesson 3: Customers want to do the right thing, if they can.
>
> Lesson 4: Shoplifting is a bigger threat than piracy.
>
> Lesson 5: File sharing networks don't threaten book, music, or film publishing. They threaten existing publishers.
>
> Lesson 6: "Free" is eventually replaced by a higher-quality paid service.
>
> Lesson 7: There's more than one way to do it.
>
> Interestingly, some of our most successful print/online hybrids have come about where we present the same material in different ways for the print and online contexts. For example, much of the content of our bestselling book Programming Perl (more than 600,000 copies in print) is available online as part of the standard Perl documentation. But the entire package—not to mention the convenience of a paper copy, and the aesthetic pleasure of the strongly branded packaging—is only available in print. Multiple ways to present the same information and the same product increase the overall size and richness of the market.[24]

---

[23]http://www.openp2p.com/pub/a/p2p/2002/12/11/piracy.html

[24]You can read my www.bricklin.com web site for free. Most of the material in this book is available there or elsewhere on the Web, but organized in a much more haphazard manner. It will be interesting to see whether people will pay for a book like this one.

And that's the ultimate lesson. "Give the wookie what he wants!" as
Han Solo said so memorably in the first Star Wars movie. Give it
to him in as many ways as you can find, at a fair price, and let him
choose which works best for him.

Tim O'Reilly

What Happened Since

For a long time after my essay "The Recording Industry is Trying to Kill the
Goose That Lays the Golden Egg" appeared in 2002, I wondered whether
things would get so bad for the industry that my ideas would be proven wrong.
CD album sales continued to drop. According to RIAA reports,[25] the units
of CD albums sold went from 882 million in 2001 to 511 million in 2007, a drop
of about 40%. (The average prices seemed to be only slightly lower, dropping
from $14.64 to $14.58, an insignificant 0.4% change over 6 years, compared to
past yearly swings of 3–4%.) Despite legal efforts that include suing individuals
and companies, nonauthorized transfer of music continues on the Internet,
seemingly unaffected by the shutdown of Napster and others.

In my essay "The Software Police vs. the CD Lawyers," I point to the issue of
music singles vs. albums. Listeners are often very interested in particular songs
and not just in complete albums. The industry did not address this interest
well. Given how they were mired in a world of physical distribution and fear
of online distribution, there was little cost savings possible to enable selling
a single song for significantly less than an album. (With a $14 album having
16 songs, you would expect the cost per song to be something like $1. They
charged over $4 for a CD single.) This mirrored the "old industry thinking" of
the telegraph veterans who ran the early telephone industry that I discussed
in the "Acceptance of Cell Phone Uses Similar to Landline's Acceptance" section in Chapter 2.

However, another industry did address the singles issue—the computer
industry. Specifically, Apple produced an enticing device, the iPod, which
could hold an entire music collection and still fit in the palm of your hand.
They married it to an Internet-based service, the iTunes Store, that made the
finding, sampling for free, and downloading for a fee of individual songs (in
addition to albums) quick and basically effortless. The record companies get
a substantial portion of the iTunes Store revenues for music.

---

[25]http://www.riaa.com/keystatistics.php

Having a collection of thousands of songs always with you gave you less reason to buy entire new albums. In the old days, you could carry only a few CDs with you at a time, so the "extra" songs that made up an entire CD were an important part of the total minutes of music you could carry with you. When you have many of your favorite songs on your MP3 player, most of which you haven't heard in a long time, there is always something good that you already own. However, being able to buy singles means that you can fill in your collection with missing songs from your favorite artists or genres at a reasonable cost.

If you assume that listeners, on the average, would want only two songs from an individual album (assuming they were spending the same amount of money, but spreading it over multiple albums), the drop in CD album unit sales from the 943-million peak in 2000 to 511-million in 2007 represents a missed demand in 2007 of 864 million songs.[26]

Surprisingly, according to the RIAA, the for-pay digital download singles in 2007 totaled 810 million units (plus 42 million downloaded for pay albums), not far from my estimated 864 million "lost" songs. It seems that given a convenient way to buy music, people are still buying a similar amount of music. Given that this method is dominated by one vendor, Apple, and that the method is still in its infancy, you'd expect the digital download market to be less than its potential. There was also a substantial (361-million-unit) mobile market that includes ringtones and other mobile downloads. This shows that the market for music did not drop off a cliff never to recover in the drastic way predicted by the recording industry.[27] The ease with which fans can buy artist-related merchandise, from T-shirts to posters, through the Internet is another way that artists make up for lost CD sales. These examples show that ingenuity can create new systems that get artists paid. There are surely additional systems that will be invented that will bring even more money to the artists.[28]

So, given the continued rise in cell phone use for talking, texting, and Internet access, the success of for-pay music downloads, the addition of other

---

[26]The calculation was performed as follows: 943 minus 511 equals 432 fewer albums, multiplied by 2 desired songs per album yields 864 million desired songs.

[27]The fact that the price paid for each song dropped to about $1 vs. the $7 ($14 divided by 2 songs) is balanced to some extent by the drop in production, distribution, and inventory costs. In 2000, CD singles were selling for a little over $4, so the "extra" songs on a 16-track, $14 album went for less than $0.50 each.

[28]http://www.rollingstone.com/news/story/20830491/rocks_new_economy_making_money_when_cds_dont_sell

forms of time-using entertainment such as Netflix,[29] YouTube, Hulu, etc., my 2002 essay seems to hold up. Whew!

Is it reasonable to think you can come up with new ways to make money? We can look at an example in another area of finding methods to make money that occurred around the same time period: Internet search. Google started out in the late 1990s by getting other Internet companies to pay them to do the search function, since Google was so much better than most other systems of the day, thanks to Google's innovative technology and constant investment. At that point, highly visual banner ads (first appearing on the HotWired web site in October 1994 and evolving to today's Flash video and more) were supposed to be where the money was.

It turned out that there was an additional, very effective way to make money on search pages without annoying the user with large, eye-catching, intrusive ads. Learning from and improving upon the method pioneered in 1998 by Goto.com of automatically auctioning simple text advertisements displayed in response to particular keywords in a search, in 2000 Google developed a way to bring in billions of dollars in revenue with AdWords. Instead of signing a few contracts with large advertisers for large ads like national-network television, it figured out how to harness hundreds of thousands of small contracts for tiny, but effective, ads. Most of these advertisers could manage their accounts themselves through online tools, keeping the overhead cost to Google low.

Google's sales have grown to over $16 billion (in 2007), a substantial portion coming from those tiny ads. (The RIAA reports that the total retail dollar value of recordings sold was about $14.7 billion in 1999, their peak year.) Finding new ways to get money when you have something people want is not an unusual occurrence.

Legal Issues with Copying

This next section includes comments relating to the legal aspects of copying in the United States.

The copyright law states:

> *Copyright protection subsists, in accordance with this title, in original works of authorship fixed in any tangible medium of expression,*

---

[29]Netflix started its popular monthly subscription movie-rental service in September 1999. By mid-2002 it had over 500,000 subscribers, and by late 2006, over 5.6 million.

*now known or later developed, from which they can be perceived,
reproduced, or otherwise communicated, either directly or with the
aid of a machine or device.*

U.S. Code Title 17 section 102

Copyright applies only to the "expression" of ideas, not to the ideas themselves. The "idea" of painting a picture of your mother is not covered by
copyright law. There is a particular expression of that idea in the painting
Arrangement in Grey and Black: The Artist's Mother by James Whistler (better
known as *Whistler's Mother*). That would be covered by copyright law (if it
were painted today).

Copyright law reserves for the owner of the copyright the exclusive right:

(1) to reproduce the copyrighted work in copies or phonorecords;

(2) to prepare derivative works based upon the copyrighted work;

*(3) to distribute copies or phonorecords of the copyrighted work to
the public by sale or other transfer of ownership, or by rental, lease,
or lending;*

*(4) in the case of literary, musical, dramatic, and choreographic
works, pantomimes, and motion pictures and other audiovisual
works, to perform the copyrighted work publicly;*

*(5) in the case of literary, musical, dramatic, and choreographic
works, pantomimes, and pictorial, graphic, or sculptural works,
including the individual images of a motion picture or other audiovisual work, to display the copyrighted work publicly; and*

*(6) in the case of sound recordings, to perform the copyrighted work
publicly by means of a digital audio transmission.*

U.S. Code Title 17 section 106[30]

An important concept is that of a derivative work:

*A "derivative work" is a work based upon one or more preexisting
works, such as a translation, musical arrangement, dramatiza-
tion, fictionalization, motion picture version, sound recording, art*

---

[30]http://www.copyright.gov/title17/92chap1.html

> *reproduction, abridgment, condensation, or any other form in which*
> *a work may be recast, transformed, or adapted. A work consisting*
> *of editorial revisions, annotations, elaborations, or other modifica-*
> *tions, which, as a whole, represent an original work of authorship, is*
> *a "derivative work".*

U.S. Code Title 17 section 101

When is something a derivative work, so the copyright owner controls use, and not just something completely new, where the new author has control? That is an area where you will find differing opinions with regard to many specific cases.

Another concept is that of "fair use." There are cases where the use of a copyrighted work is considered "fair" and may not be limited by the copyright owner. These include certain cases when the purpose is criticism, commentary, news reporting, teaching (including making multiple copies for classroom use), scholarship, or research. The particular cases where a use is a "fair use" are not always easy to determine from the law. It depends, according to the law, on a mixture of the specific purpose (including the degree to which the use is commercial), the particular work, the amount that is used, and "the effect of the use upon the potential market for or value of the copyrighted work."[31]

Since the reason given for copyright protection in the U.S. Constitution is "To promote the progress of science and useful arts," there is an ongoing discussion of what will best do that promotion. The following blog posts join in that discussion.

Thursday, October 10, 2002
THE RIGHT TO CREATE DERIVATIVE WORKS IS IMPORTANT

I've been reading a lot about yesterday's *Eldred v. Ashcroft*[32] hearing and listening to some commentary on the radio. People keep talking about the right to make copies. What they keep forgetting about is one of the most important

---

[31]U.S. Code Title 17 section 107

[32]The *Eldred v. Ashcroft* case was being argued before the Supreme Court of the United States. It concerned a law passed by Congress that extended the length of time that existing copyrights applied. One issue was that the law conveniently extended Disney's exclusivity to the old Mickey Mouse character, hence my reference to Snow White. Once a work stops being covered by the limited-time limitations of copyright and it enters the "public domain," anybody may make copies as well as derivative works.

things to our culture: the right to make derivative works. It isn't that I'm lazy or cheap and just want to take from you [by simply making copies] (the image that keeps on being portrayed, incorrectly, of those who value the public domain). It's that unless it's in the public domain, I can't build on what you did. Disney told Snow White in a different, and in some ways for some people, better way than the Brothers Grimm. My compilation for a textbook may present the history of the early part of the century better than the original material by itself. My performance may express things better than previous performers. The value of Open Source to many people stems from the modifications others make. Building on the work of others is, and has always been, important to progress for society. Fair use derivations (like satire) are not the only valuable uses to society.

http://www.satn.org/archive/2002_10_06_archive.html

Monday, July 7, 2003
FAIR USE RULING

I found this through Slashdot.org: The U.S. 9th Circuit Court of Appeals issued an opinion about Fair Use. The issue was whether a search engine that indexed images from the Web and presented them as thumbnails was fair use under copyright law. They decided that it was fair use and allowed under law.

I found a couple of things interesting here. The concept of Fair Use (the right to use copyrighted material without permission in certain cases) is very important to the workings of society and was part of the compromises made when drafting copyright law. Digital Rights Management (DRM) will make fair use harder to accomplish, even when it's legal. Reading this opinion[33] helps you learn about the concept of Fair Use and see why it can be so at odds with DRM.[34] "Transformative uses" weigh in the favor of allowing use, and that doctrine was key to this case. A transformative use adds ". . . a further purpose

---

[33] http://www.ca9.uscourts.gov/ca9/newopinions.nsf/8E22982657C96BE188256D5C00 518BF5/$file/0055521oop.pdf?openelement

[34] The ruling goes into helpful detail about how it determined Fair Use in this case. It also includes statements like this: "The Copyright Act was intended to promote creativity, thereby benefitting the artist and the public alike. To preserve the potential future use of artistic works for purposes of teaching, research, criticism, and news reporting, Congress created the fair use exception."

or different character . . ." rather than ". . . merely supersedes the object of the originals . . ." (searching vs. pretty pictures in this case). These are the types of uses so hard to take into account with DRM. How do you allow for unforeseen uses?

http://www.satn.org/archive/2003_07_06_archive.html

Monday, September 2, 2002
COPYRIGHT PROTECTION IS NOT "SUPER SIMPLE"

In response to some discussion about duration of copyright protection for software, blogging pioneer Dave Winer wrote: ". . . it's super simple. If I build a house I can live in it as long as I want. If I want to rent out rooms I can do that too, as long as I want."[35] Copyright law should only be so simple, but since it deals with the real world, there are lots of complexities. (Even with a house, can you really live in it as long as you want? What if you don't own the land, or don't pay your taxes, or if the town wants to build a road through it, or if you abandon it, etc? Each of these conditions can affect your rights.)

Drawing fine lines to determine what you control and what you don't is very hard. Suppose I paint a painting. If you take it from me without my permission, I no longer have it. That's often called stealing. What if you take a photograph of it? I still have the painting. Is that "stealing"? What if you sell copies of that photograph? What if you see my painting and, remembering what you saw, paint a similar one? What if you peered into the window of my house to see the supposedly hidden painting? What if it wasn't a painting, but was a sculpture? If you take a photograph of a sculpture, a different medium, is that "stealing"? What if it wasn't a sculpture, but rather a building? Does it change things if it's useful and not a "work of art"? Can you take a picture of my building? Can you reverse engineer my design from the photograph and make a building like it? What if my building is really big and stands out in the skyline? What if it doesn't? Can I control pictures of the skyline that happen to have my building in them? What if I paint my painting on the side of the building? All of these relate to various "intellectual property" issues. In all cases, the person whose work is being "taken" in some way worked really hard to create the work.

---

[35] http://www.scripting.com/2002/08/28.html#When:2:54:00PM

Does all work (effort) "deserve" to be rewarded (with some form of exclusive rights)? What type of "work" does and what type doesn't?

"Pirates" of old took physical property by force. The victim of piracy, if left alive, was left without something he or she physically had before. Dave talks of renting a room in a house. Once rented, he cannot rent it to others, nor use it himself for that period of time. "Pirated" software does not consist of software that was physically taken. It is a copy that does not diminish the original except in the predicted potential sale that may or may not have been lost. The author most likely does not even know of the copying, unlike the occupants of a ship that has been boarded by pirates.

These issues are very tough, and these differences matter. Saying "what I do should be protected" isn't enough. There are many links in a chain, and each seems to think his or her link is the last one needing protection (with whatever definition they think "protection" should have). Getting this clear enough so that laws based on this understanding will work with ever-changing technology (as David Reed pointed out last week here[36] on SATN.org) is hard. Discussing proposals, even those that may put "my work" on the "wrong side" of a line, is important. However, our Constitution, with its call for granting ". . . for limited times to authors and inventors the exclusive right to their respective writings and discoveries," makes the quest for appropriate laws something that must be done.

http://www.satn.org/archive/2002_09_01_archive.html

Monday, April 28, 2003
ONLINE PIRACY IS NOT LIKE SHOPLIFTING

I keep hearing the tag line, "Pirating works online is the same as shoplifting a videotape, book or computer program from a department store," or something to that effect. It seems to just be taken as a given, and then used as reason for all sorts of laws that distort the balance between authors, distributors, and the general public. But it's not true.

Each copy of a videotape, book, or computer program in a department store is separately bought and paid for by that store from a wholesaler before being

---

[36]http://www.satn.org/archive/2002_08_25_archive.html#85397587

put on the shelf. Each shoplifted copy is not just a missed sale, but it is also out-of-pocket money paid without a return. If the shoplifter never intended to buy the item, the store loses the same amount of money as it would if the shoplifter were a purchaser who decided to save money this time by breaking the law. To the distributor of the videotape, book, or computer program, or the author, the shoplifted copy is actually a boon—they get the wholesale payment for items that would not have been purchased in addition to the payments from all those that are or would have been. They have no direct loss in any case from shoplifting. Only the department store has a loss, and it is a very real loss, one-to-one with each shoplifted copy. The shoplifted copies, also, are not likely to have any benefit for the store. Unlike the artist, the enjoyment of that copy is not likely to benefit the store if it results in attendance at concerts or any other "new fan" benefits. In addition, the location and circumstances of the shoplifting are the same as purchasing: in the store with a physical object. With online piracy, the location and circumstances are different than purchasing a movie or book (at least until authorized online copies are as easy to get as unauthorized ones). Software is different. Buying software legally online is almost just as easy as pirating it today. Software has been susceptible to piracy for decades, yet, according to the BSA (an anti-piracy group) "the commercial software industry . . . [is] the fastest growing industry in the world." (I wrote about this back in August of 2000 in an essay titled "The Software Police vs. the CD Lawyers.")

Pirating material online is really more like kids watching a baseball game through a hole in the outfield wall, or listening to a concert just outside the gate. There is no out-of-pocket expense for that particular copy, just a possible loss of potential revenue. If your costs are low enough and you have some sales, you can tolerate lost sales that have no expense. You might still actually make a profit. (It's like some summer concerts where the patrons pay a lot to sit in seats up front while thousands of others sit on the field outside listening for free.) No matter what your costs, if you have to buy each copy in advance, and then lose copies to stealing, too much stealing will drive you out of business. (The actual costs of producing creative material are dropping through the benefits of technology, though the choice of certain distribution channels is making the cost of marketing that material go up. Choosing different distribution channels could lower that marketing cost, as well as distribution costs, substantially. Technology is always opening up new methods for distribution.)

So, if we are basing our laws on the belief that online sharing is the same as shoplifting, we are making a mistake. If we are trying to "make the punishment fit the crime," we must understand that the crimes are different. If we wonder why, "Students would never enter a Blockbuster store and with furtive glance stuff a DVD inside their jacket and walk out without paying,"[37] but do share digital copies, realize that the economics are different, and understood to be different by the ones making the copies. Let's argue the issue based on what copying is and not what it is not.

There are those who want to transform artistic works expressed in a medium that can easily be copied into discrete physical objects with all the restrictions that entails. This is not a good thing and will hurt society which is based upon building on the works of others without diminishing those original works. Let's not pretend that the transition has already occurred.

http://www.satn.org/archive/2003_04_27_archive.html

Wednesday, April 23, 2003
BOOK SHARING

Bob [Frankston] just asked me to post something about this, since he's too tied up with conferences and maintaining his tools, etc. (see below [in this blog, not this book]). His request: ". . . someone should put up a story about the new problem on colleges—the effort to crack down on the crime of book sharing by the Paper Industry. It's about time we stopped this willful violation of copyright!"

I guess Bob is concerned that if students are being sued for sharing their record collections within their dorms, why isn't it a problem that they share textbooks while studying? And, horror of horrors, the bookstores even help by letting them participate in a "Used Book" racket, depriving the publishers of yet more sales. In addition, when you read the textbook, if there is a passage you especially feel is important to you, you can write it down in your notes, preserving it for after you finish using the book and mixing it with other works. As I pointed out in my essay on paying artists, copyright holders are trying to put absolute legal and technical restrictions that don't have physical counterparts on media without showing how it all fits into a rich ecosystem that helps advance the arts and sciences. It is clear that they think it helps

---

[37]http://web.archive.org/web/20030602184630/http://www.mpaa.org/jack/2003/
2003_02_24.htm

advance the fiscal-quarter-to-fiscal-quarter pocketbooks of the current distribution middlemen of the works of some small subset of artists, but is that what
we as a society want?

There, Bob, I put up the story . . .

http://www.satn.org/archive/2003_04_20_archive.html

We see that the music industry and its issues with "piracy" are more complex than a simple view that easy copying using the Internet is a bad thing.
Society needs to look at the whole ecosystem of music generation and enjoyment. Continuing to do things as they have been done for previous decades is
not always a good answer in light of technological changes. Other industries
have survived making things easier for the public, and it looks like the music
industry will, too.

In Chapter 4 we'll look at the case of many individuals collectively doing
selfish things that end up being for the good of the group. Just as Google is able
to lower its costs for servicing it advertisers, Internet technology is enabling
valuable aggregation and dissemination of individual contributions for other
purposes.

4

Leveraging the Crowd

The previous two chapters are focused on the individual. In those chapters, I looked at communication between two individuals and between an artist and his or her audience and fans. I also looked at the needs of an artist. In this and the following few chapters, I look at using the enhanced connectivity made possible by the Internet to leverage larger groups of people. This includes the role of people who participate without being formally employed and paid for that purpose. I am very interested in the forces that seem to govern groups with a purpose.

This chapter mainly deals with one essay and the discussion on the Web and elsewhere of which it was a part. I present in print the flavor of what it was like to follow the discussion, reproducing some of the writings of others.

"The Cornucopia of the Commons" Essay

This has been one of the most cited essays that I've written and continues to get dozens of hits every day even though it is eight years old as I put this book together. In 2005, industry leader and pundit Tim O'Reilly wrote that it included ". . . one of the seminal insights that has shaped my thinking over the past couple of years."[1] (Tim, whom I quoted in Chapter 3, is the founder and CEO of O'Reilly Media, a book publisher as well as the host of various technology-related conferences.)

The essay was originally written in the days when Napster[2] was getting popular and you would find many references to the service in the technology press. Internet-based applications were something new to most people,

---

[1] http://radar.oreilly.com/2005/08/the-cornucopia-of-the-commons.html

[2] Napster is explained in the beginning of Chapter 3.

and Napster was different in many respects from the few well-known ones like email and web browsing. Like the story of the blind men examining an elephant, each saying it was like the part that he encountered, people pointed to different aspects as the key one.

Some people concentrated on the "peer-to-peer" (P2P) architecture of Napster. When you downloaded a song using the program, it came not through the traditional connection to special servers in one centralized data center but rather through a connection to another personal computer just like yours running Napster. All of these computers were basically treated as equals on the system; they were "peers." This was different from the timesharing systems, like AOL and Compuserve, that people were familiar with at the time, where every action required the complete involvement of computers owned and operated by some big company. It was also different from regular web sites, where browsers interacted directly with a centralized server, not with each other.

Timesharing, the Internet, and Peer-to-Peer

For those who didn't understand the previous paragraph, here is a little digression to help you understand the difference between those architectures.

In Figure 4-1 we have a representation of a timesharing system, like the original AOL and Compuserve.

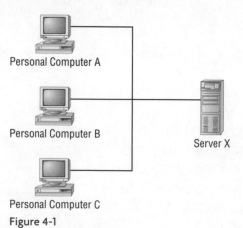

Figure 4-1

On the left you see computers that people use directly, with keyboards and screens. On the right is the computer system that provides service; for example, AOL's computers in their computer data centers. For you to access data, for example, to read a news report, you would use a program installed on your computer (in this case the AOL software that came on CDs that were given out everywhere) to connect your personal computer through a telephone connection directly to AOL's server. That server would then send the response back to your personal computer to be read.

You could connect to only one company's server computers at a time, each with a separate direct connection requiring either its own telephone line or a separate telephone call.

To send email or an instant message, you typed on your personal computer, and the text was sent to the AOL server. For someone else to read that text, they would need to have their computer connect to the AOL server to retrieve it.

In Figure 4-2 we have a representation of computers using the Internet.

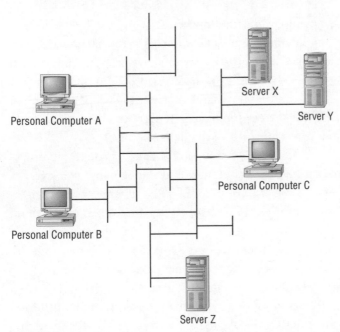

Figure 4-2

You can see both computers that people use directly, such as Personal Computer A, and computers that are located in computer rooms specifically to provide services to other computers, such as Server X. Each computer is connected through a network of communication links in such a way that it can communicate with any other computer "on the net." That is represented by the various lines between the computers. Only one connection is needed to each computer, and the computers can simultaneously communicate with any number of other computers at once. This heterogeneous amalgamation of different types of computers and connections is called "the Internet." It is not hierarchical like the timesharing configuration in Figure 4-1, but rather it uses a network topology. Each computer on the Internet can be connected to by using a unique address.

When you send an email, an email program on your computer connects to a server controlled by your email provider (such as Gmail.com). Your email program sends the text of the email along with the address of the server of the recipient's email provider (such as Hotmail.com). Your email provider's server then connects to the recipient's email provider's server and sends a copy of the text to it. Finally, the recipient connects to their email provider to retrieve a copy.

When you use a browser program (like Internet Explorer or Firefox) to look at pages on the Web, your personal computer connects to the particular server that holds each page and that has software specifically designed to connect to browser programs. As you click on links and "surf the Web" your browser program may first connect to one server and then another depending upon the address in the URL web address for each web page. In all cases, though, your computer goes to a server to retrieve the data.

With Napster, when you downloaded a song it came through a connection directly between your personal computer and the personal computer of the person "sharing" that song. Any number of such personal-computer-to-personal-computer connections could be happening simultaneously without any use of the Napster server computer.

You should notice that the architecture of the Internet (with any computer being able to quickly connect to any other computer on demand and consisting of both dedicated computers performing dedicated tasks and personally used computers used by individuals) lends itself to being used in many different ways and configurations. Email uses "PC to server to server to PC." Browsing the Web uses "PC to one server, then another, and another." Napster used "PC to server" to learn where a particular file resided, and then "PC to PC" to retrieve that file. The same style of use as Napster could be (and is) used for Instant Messaging and Internet voice communication. There are many other styles and many uses for each.

The Internet is very "fertile" for innovation. The basic building blocks can be arranged and used in different ways to create great, but previously unforeseen, applications. Technologies that lend themselves to repeated ongoing innovation like this are very important to society because they give us great leverage. Investment in that basic technology can be shared by all applications, multiplying its value to society. I like to drive that idea home by pointing out examples of where the Internet is used in ways that are different from the well-known Web way.

A Fixation on the Idea of Peer-to-Peer

Back in 2000 when the essay was written, there was a lot of talk about the Internet empowering individuals and of the movement of power from companies and centralized "broadcasters" to "the marketplace," from a view of "customers" to "participants." There were philosophical reasons to believe that Napster's success was from its use of P2P. Napster, to some, was a proof point of this philosophy.

For example, in his August 6, 2000, column in the *San Jose Mercury News*, Dan Gillmor wrote:

> *What matters more about Napster is its architecture, the way it works . . . Suddenly, you can be a Web site yourself—a publisher— creating content on your own computer . . . And venture capitalists are scurrying to finance entrepreneurs who are working on similar technology, which has taken on the "peer-to-peer" buzz phrase.*

> *San Jose Mercury News*

There were those who saw Napster in the light of community. They surmised that with all of those connected computers, each with its own unique screen name, perhaps it worked because people were purposely "giving" files to others. Maybe what was special was how it brought out altruism in some way, driving people to provide resources to "the community," again in a way unlike that with a company and its faceless customers.

On the other side, there were those who saw downsides to people being organized into a community that depended upon each other. They talked of "freeloading" and of how people made use of the system and weren't nice enough to "give back." There were thoughts that a large percentage of people had to participate, or else selfish behavior would cause the end of the service.[3]

You heard in the choice of words people used about Napster a hint of their philosophical views. Words like "generosity" and "freeloading" instead of "allowing access" and "use for downloading" exposed that point of view.

I read the commentary being written about Napster and tried to see if it rang true. I had been paying attention to how people I knew used Napster and noticed the cases when it was the best or only way to do something. I knew that many of these people didn't think of themselves as part of a "community" or of taking something from a system inappropriately. (The issue of music piracy is something else and will not be discussed along with this essay, because that is separate from the architecture of Napster. There were other ways to obtain music without paying that also existed. Architecture, even if illegal, can be something from which we can learn.) I also could see how many users of Napster did not add new songs to be "shared," yet the service kept growing despite all the "freeloading."

I thought about this question: What was really going on and how can we take something valuable away from it on how to build a successfully adopted service on the Internet?[4] My answer was this essay.

August 7, 2000

THE CORNUCOPIA OF THE COMMONS: HOW TO GET VOLUNTEER LABOR

> *Napster is an example of a manually filled database that has found a way to use volunteer labor such that normal use increases its value.*

There has been a lot of discussion lately about the success of Napster in becoming a popular application. I'd like to put in my two cents about what we can learn from it and other successful applications. The answer is not the common answer of "peer-to-peer communications."

---

[3] A classic article about freeloading on Internet P2P systems is "Free Riding on Gnutella" by Eytan Adar and Bernardo A. Huberman of the Xerox Palo Alto Research Center. It includes a section titled "The Tragedy of the Digital Commons." Published in October 2000, it is available at http://www.firstmonday.org/issues/issue5_10/adar/

[4] As I explain above, this is about the Internet, not the World Wide Web. Napster did not use an HTML-based browser, etc. It worked at a much lower level of communications protocol. People often confuse the Web, which is one use of the Internet, and the Internet, which is just what you get when many computers agree on a general-purpose method for transmitting data between them.

I think one of the main reasons Napster is successful is that you can find what you want (a particular song) and get it easily. This stems mainly from the fact that so many songs are available through Napster. If Napster let me only get a few popular songs, once I've downloaded those, I'd lose interest fast.[5]

It isn't that Napster uses peer-to-peer (P2P). That's plumbing, and most people don't care about plumbing. While the "look into other people's computers and copy directly" has some psychological benefit to some people who understand what's going on (see Tom Matrullo[6] on Doc Searls's weblog, also quoted in DaveNet), I think Napster would operate much better if, when you logged in by running Napster, it uploaded all new songs that weren't in Napster's database to Napster's servers, not just the names and who currently logged in has them. If they were copied to a master server, the same songs would be available for download provided by the same people, but at all times (not just when the "owner" happened to be connected to the Internet), and through (hopefully) more reliable and higher-speed connections to the Internet (Akamai, etc.?). Even the list of who had the songs could be maintained. Napster doesn't work this way partially because P2P may be more legal (they argue) and harder to litigate against. Other applications may not have this legal problem and would

---

[5] Other reasons for Napster's popularity:

The importance of access to a huge catalog of songs was something that was later pointed out in the discussions of the "Long Tail." (See Chapter 7 for a discussion of the Long Tail.) People I knew at the time had been "forced" to use Napster when they were searching for some obscure recordings that were unavailable no matter how many record stores they called.

Napster also let you obtain single songs. It did not package them as albums. With the advent of CD burners in personal computers, people liked making "mixes" of songs from multiple albums (a practice they also did with dual-deck boom boxes before). Napster made it easy to get just the right songs that you wanted to put together a mix. Often, of course, that mix was as a gift to someone else. But the gift you were giving was not the "free" music but rather the compilation of a specific series of songs to convey a message to the receiver or as something tailored to their needs. (This was in the days before portable MP3 players became popular. CD players were still dominant.)

At the time of this essay, turning a CD you had into a series of MP3 files was not something most people knew how to do. Even if you did know how, it could also be quite time-consuming. Napster made it much easier: Just type in the song you wanted, click on some buttons, and in a little while the songs were ready as MP3s for playing or CD burning.

[6] You can read a copy of Tom Matrullo's essay, "24 Notes on Napster: A Commonplace Book for Today," later in this chapter. Tom (interimtom.blogspot.com) has a background in comparative literature, print journalism, and editing.

therefore be able to benefit from more centralized servers. While I'm a strong proponent for P2P for some things, I don't think that is the main issue here.[7]

The issue is, can you get what you want from the application—"Is the data I want in the database?" So, I'd like to examine how a shared database gets filled with lots of what people want.

How shared databases are filled with data

There are three common ways to fill a shared database: "Organized Manual," "Organized Mechanical," and "Volunteer Manual." The original Yahoo! is the classic case of a database filled by organizing an army of people to put in data manually. Another example is the old legal databases, where armies of typists were paid to retype printed material into computers. The original AltaVista[8] is an example of an organized mechanically filled database—a program running on powerful computers followed links and domain names and "spidered" the Web, saving the information as it went. Newsgroups and SlashDot are examples of volunteer databases, where interested individuals provide the data because they feel passionate enough about doing so.

Many databases on the Web today are mechanically created by getting access to somebody else's data, sometimes for a fee. Examples are the street map and airline flight status databases. Some of those databases are by-products of automated processes.

Manually created databases

The more interesting databases (to us here) are the ones that involve manual creation. Some examples: Amazon.com's reviews (both house reviews and reader reviews) are a major asset. Yahoo!'s organized manual listings have helped get them to the lead for searching.

A more interesting one to me is the CDDB database. The CDDB database has information that allows your computer to identify a particular music CD in the CD drive and list its album title and track titles. Their service is used by RealJukebox, MusicMatch, WinAmp, and other software for playing music CDs on personal computers. The title information is not stored on most CDs. The only information in the CD data is the number of tracks (songs) and the length

---

[7] An observation in hindsight: For a while I wondered if I was right that a centralized store would be the right way. However, as it turns out, Apple's iTunes Store has done this and has proven extremely successful, being a dominant channel for music distribution, even though it charges for most music. It has a huge catalog and is easy to use.

[8] AltaVista was an early search engine.

of each. This is the information your CD player displays. What CDDB does is let the software on your PC take that track information, send a CD signature to CDDB through Internet protocols (if you're connected), and get back the titles. It works because songs are of relatively random length. The chances are good that almost all albums are unique and in practice this turns out to be true. (Figure there are about 10 songs on an album, and they each run from a minute and a half or so to three and a half minutes long, so the times vary by 100 seconds. There are 100x100x . . . x100 = 100^{10} = 10^{11} = 100 billion = an awful lot of possible combinations.) An album is identified by a signature that is a special arithmetic combination of the times of all the tracks.

You'd figure that CDDB just bought a standard database with all the times and titles. Well, there wasn't one. What they did was accept Internet-relayed postings with the track timing information and the titles typed in by a volunteer. Music-CD-playing software for personal computers was written that let people type in that information if CDDB didn't have it. Enough people using that software cared enough when they saw one of their albums not coming up with titles when they played them on their PCs to type in the information. Those people got the information for themselves, so they could more easily make their own playlists, and in the process also updated the shared database. Only one person with each (even obscure) album needed to do this to build the database. If you loved your CD collection, you'd want all the albums represented, or at least some people did. Not everybody needed to be the type who likes to be organized and label everything, just enough people to fill the database. Also, they only needed to rely on "volunteer" (user) labor until the database got big enough that it was valuable enough for other companies to pay for access.

CDDB's database is on dedicated servers, controlled by the company. Its web site says: "CDDB is now a totally secure and reliable service which is provided to users worldwide via a network of high availability, mirrored servers which each have multiple, high bandwidth connections to the Internet . . . boasting a database of nearly 620,000 album titles and over 7.5 million tracks."[9]

---

[9] CDDB is now known as Gracenote and was purchased by Sony. It continues to provide data used by many popular music-playing systems. Also, there has been an upgrade to the music CD format (CD-Text) so many new CDs have the track names included.

CDDB is another example of an Internet application, not a web application. It does not make use of a browser. It has a special computer-program-to-computer-program protocol that it uses for communicating between the music-playing program and the servers.

Napster

Napster is a manually created database created by volunteers. Somebody needs to actually buy (or borrow) a copy of a CD, convert it to MP3, and store it in his or her shared music directory. Or, somebody needs to create an MP3 out of a recording of one of their own performances that he or she wants to share. In both cases, creating the copy in the shared music directory can be a natural by-product of how a person normally works with the songs, for example, as part of downloading them to a portable music player or burning a personal-mix CD. Whenever that person is connected to the Internet and to the Napster server, those songs are then available to the world. Of course, that person may not be connected to the Napster server all the time, so the song is not fully available to all who want it (a problem with relying on P2P). However, whenever someone downloads a song using Napster and leaves the copy in his or her shared music directory, that person is increasing the number of Napster users who have that song and raises the chances you will find someone sharing it logged in to Napster when you want your copy. So, again, the value of the database increases through normal use.

What we see here is that increasing the value of the database by adding more information is a natural by-product of using the tool for your own benefit. No altruistic sharing motives need be present, especially since sharing is the default. It isn't even like the old song about "leaving a cup with water by the pump to let the next person have something to prime it with" where it just takes a little bit of effort, so why not be as nice to the next person as the last one was to you.

As Kevin Werbach wrote:

> What made Napster a threat to the record labels was its remarkable growth. That growth resulted from two things: Napster's user experience and its focus on music . . . What makes Napster different is that it's drop-dead simple to use. Its interface isn't pretty, but it achieves that magic resonance with user expectations that marks the most revolutionary software developments.

Kevin Werbach, Weblog 1.0, July 28, 2000[10]

---

[10]http://web.archive.org/web/20000816155817/http://release1.userland.com/
thoughts/napster

August 7, 2000

I would add that in using that simple, desirable user interface (UI), you also are adding to the value of the database without any extra work.

I believe that you can help predict the success of a particular UI used to build a shared database based on how much normal, selfish use adds to the database.

The Commons

There is the concept of "The Tragedy of the Commons"[11] popularized by Garrett Hardin in 1968:

> *Therein is the tragedy. Each man is locked into a system that compels him to increase his herd without limit—in a world that is limited. Ruin is the destination toward which all men rush, each pursuing his own best interest in a society that believes in the freedom of the commons. Freedom in a commons brings ruin to all.*

> Garrett Hardin, *Science*, Vol. 162. no. 3859[12]

In our case, we find the Cornucopia of the Commons: Use brings overflowing abundance.

[As I received various comments over time about this essay, I added some of them to the end on the same web page. Here they are, along with some context:]

Additional Thoughts

March 2, 2001

Evan Williams[13] wrote some comments that are relevant here. He points out that a good volunteer-created database should be designed with incentive for the entry of *accurate* information. One way is to use data that you rely on

---

[11]Dan Bricklin, April 23, 2001: It was pointed out to me that Prof. Hardin later said he should have named his essay "The Tragedy of the Unmanaged Commons." In 1994 he published a paper with that title.

[12]http://www.sciencemag.org/cgi/content/full/162/3859/1243

[13]Evan Williams, evhead.com, was cofounder of Pyra Labs, the company that developed the original Blogger system that helped popularize blogging. Blogger was one of the earliest systems that made it much easier for regular people to set up and maintain a blog with little technical knowledge. Since then, he has helped develop other products including the Twitter system.

yourself, such as with CDDB. You can read Evan's comments in his February 16, 2001 entry:[14]

Thoughts on The Cornucopia of the Commons

Yesterday, I caught Dan Bricklin's talk, The Cornucopia of the Commons. (He also wrote an essay, some version of which is also in O'Reilly's P2P anthology.[15]) Dan talks about user-created databases, which is really the key value to Napster. The unique approach to the plumbing in Napster gets all the attention and was necessary for legal and cost reasons, but the functionality that added the value was the shared database of all the user's music. Other examples Dan mentions are CDDB and AmIHotOrNot.[16] These are both great examples of user-generated, shared databases. But a distinction occurred to me, which I think is key to designing such systems: There should be a payoff to the user for entering accurate information. This exists for CDDB but not for (half) of AmIHotOrNot.

Many (most?) CD's get into CDDB because someone bought the CD and wants their computer to know what's on it, for their own use. That the information is useful to anyone else who has it is a nice side-effect, and I'm sure a major motivation to some people. But, essentially, if the user puts in good information, they are benefiting themselves (and everyone else), and if they put in bad, they are doing the opposite.

With AmIHotOrNot, there are two types of user-created data: the pictures and the votes. There is not much incentive to putting in non-real pictures. I mean, you can put in pictures that are not of you, but it doesn't really hurt the system anyway. However, there is no particular reason to put in "good" data on the other side—i.e., vote how you

---

[14] evhead.com/2001/02/thoughts-on-cornucopia-of-commons.asp

[15] *Peer-to-Peer: Harnessing the Power of Disruptive Technologies*, Andy Oram, 2001, O'Reilly Media, ISBN: 059600110X

[16] AmIHotOrNot was a web site where you could provide a photo of yourself. Visitors to the site were randomly shown photos and asked to rate the person on a numeric scale from "hot" to "not" and then given the cumulative score so far. You could track how your own photo was rated. It was enhanced with an ability to send an email to the person if you had joined as a paying customer. It used various simple manual techniques to keep the photos appropriate to a large audience. It is still running in 2008 as hotornot.com.

really feel. Most people probably do, but there is not as strong a motivation to. In fact, something Jim Gallagher wrote, in response to Dan's talk, "He didn't even mention that it is FUN to vote high for ugly chicks," implies that some people get more entertainment (which is the main value the site provides) by putting in "bad" data than good.

One could argue this doesn't really matter for something as arbitrary and non-serious as AmIHotOrNot, but obviously if the voting results were absolutely meaningless it would be less interesting for people. It obviously works well enough, and I'm not sure how it could be better, but in general I think this idea is an important point to keep in mind. CDDB was genius in that, by benefiting yourself, you're benefiting others without any extra effort.

Evan Williams, February 16, 2001

Talking to experienced Napster users, I've discovered another benefit from increasing the number of users: More users increases the likelihood that a song will be indexed in a way that helps you find it.

While songs have an "official" title, not everybody knows the song by that name. A normal, simple database would have just that text. With Napster, since people name the files in ways they feel will help them identify the songs themselves, many use more discoverable names than the "official" title, such as the chorus. Some people provide a mixture with one name in parenthesis. For example, Harvey Danger's song "Flagpole Sitta" is known by many people as "Paranoia," and a large percentage of the copies available through Napster are named that way, some with both. You'll find music files with both "Ode to Joy" and "9th Symphony" in the names. Note that you don't have to be the original provider of the song to add value this way—you could rename it after you got a copy to help yourself find it on your own system later.

So, here again, having more users increases the value, this time by adding human created variations.

This is another part of the bar that recording industry–provided systems will have to get over if they want to serve music lovers as well as Napster. It isn't just price.[17]

---

[17]This is a good introduction to the concept of "tagging." A tag is "metadata"—that is, information about data, but not the data itself. The song's name is still the name given by the artist. The filename is other data used to help locate and categorize the song. A song could have many tags or pieces of metadata, such as its genre (e.g., classic rock),

October 12, 2006

I wrote something somewhat related in January 2005 in a blog post titled "Systems without guilt where every contribution is appreciated" that bloggers sometimes refer to:

Systems without guilt where every contribution is appreciated

In reaction to, and support of, AKMA's[18] post about tagging, Dave Winer[19] writes that he stopped tagging the categories of blog posts. As soon as he missed one, he felt guilty, and then as the guilt grew, he tagged less. He started just assigning things to a couple of categories and then not tagging at all.

---

the singer's name, the songwriter's name, the track number, and the start of the chorus. These could be stored using means other than the filename.

Computers are very good at working with tags. Unlike physical shelves and an improvement over card catalogs, computers can use tags (or other metadata) to make access quick and easy to data through many filing schemes at once.

Having a community of users tagging things the way each of them wants to categorize those things, and not relying on a standard, "right" way, is one of the attributes of a "folksonomy." Approaching categorization this way has become much more popular in recent years.

Napster mainly had the track title (as written by the person who saved the file on their computer) as a way of aiding search. In today's world, there are many specialized web sites, for example, ones with the lyrics to particular classes of songs, that help you find the "official" name of a song for retrieval through iTunes or another means. On top of that, we have Google and other modern search engines to help us find those specialized pages.

Here we have one database, the search engine's, augmenting others, the specialized sites and the distributors of music.

[18]About AKMA (from his web site, akma.disseminary.org): A K M Adam (born September 10, 1957, Boston, Massachusetts) is a biblical scholar, theologian, author, priest, technologist, and blogger who has taught New Testament studies at several institutions, most recently at Duke Divinity School. He is a writer, speaker, and activist who simultaneously engages the worlds of theology and technology on topics including postmodern philosophy, hermeneutics, education, and collaborative discovery of truth and meaning.

[19]About Dave Winer (from his web site, www.scripting.com, in October 2008): Dave Winer, 53, pioneered the development of weblogs, syndication (RSS), podcasting, outlining, and web content management software; former contributing editor at *Wired* magazine, research fellow at Harvard Law School, entrepreneur, and investor in web media companies. A native New Yorker, he received a Master's in Computer Science from the University of Wisconsin, a Bachelor's in Mathematics from Tulane University, and currently lives in Berkeley, California.

Dave's writings and developments have had a major impact on me as well as many others in the field. You will see his name come up repeatedly in this book.

For context, here are the two posts, first AKMA's and then Dave's:

Poll Tags

When I read about Technorati tags, I was excited. In fact, I knew to be excited about it because Kevin messaged me, and first thing I read about them online was David Weinberger's encomium, and when Kevin and David are excited about something, I know enough to realize that it's good. And when it involves searching (Kevin's area) and epistemological taxonomy (David's area of concentration), somebody who respects those guys as much as I do simply must get excited. So I did.

But I should pause to say that I'm not a natural for "tags." I've hardly ever used deli.cio.us tags. I didn't begin tagging my pictures for flickr for ages; even now I'm liable to tag pretty cursorily (no, I don't mean "with a computer pointing device"). I don't use categories in my own Moveable Type posts, although the Seabury site that used to be (and may someday live again) integrated categories into its architectural rationale. And once I started thinking about tags, I felt chagrined; the folksonomized Web that David envisioned, that Kevin and Stewart and all had begun to implement, presents such a tremendous opportunity — but here I was, too lazy to tag. I had worked myself up to care about valid mark-up, and I emphasized this aspect of the Seabury site. But I just wasn't sure I had the determination to add Technorati tags to my posts. You're too polite to complain, but I get long-winded — how would I tag my monologues without repeating most of the words? I was going to be a stick between the spokes of the organic semantic Web, when my friends were building and turning the wheels.

So I didn't blog about tags at all. I thought they were a great idea, but I didn't have the energy to implement them here, and I didn't want to be a party pooper. Who knows? Maybe if the haphazard-HTML writer I once was can become a CSS ascetic, even lazy AKMA could become a tags-onomist.

But now Shelley [Powers] has spoken up and even illustrated her wise words, and I think I have to agree with her (I didn't implement "nofollow" either, so she's my official Webby Oracle this week). It's not so much the vulnerability to spam; it's not so much the imprecision; it's not so much the bother tagging; but the cumulative effect of a number of "it's-not-the"s tarnishes the luster of this really great idea.

Brilliance still peeks out from beneath the tarnish. The idea excited me at first, and it still does in a murky way. I expect that the fantastic organic semantic webbiness of the idea will come to expression in more spam-resistant, more precise, less cumbersome ways, and I expect that I'll get on board in a while (no doubt before it's really easy and an obvious thing to do); that far, I share David's ultimate confidence in a grassroots taxonomic web. For now, though, I remain unconvinced about this step toward the Web of tags.

A K M Adam, January 28, 2005[20]

Guilt about categories

AKMA writes about Technorati's tags.

I've seen the same thing. I have a very easy category routing system built-in to my blogging software. To route an item to a category, I just right-click and choose a category from a hierarchy of menus. I can't imagine that it could be easier. Yet I don't do it.

It's also very easy to add a new category, or to even reorganize my whole taxonomy. Never do those things either.

I have a theory that it's like desktop calendar software, which people were very excited about in 1985 or so (they called them Personal Information Managers or PIMs). Seemed like every new Mac software product had a calendar in it. John Sculley and Mitch Kapor were singing their praises. Users got all excited about them too, and set them up imagining how great it was going to be to finally have an orderly life. They happily entered appointments, until they spaced out or got lazy and didn't enter one. All it takes is one for the excitement to turn to guilt. You don't even want to look at the thing because you screwed up. Quickly you never use it. I've seen this happen both in my own work, and in others.

---

[20] akma.disseminary.org/archives/2005/01/poll_tags.html

The category stuff works the same way. At first I delighted in the ease of routing stuff to categories. Eventually I would only route to one or two categories, and then I stopped altogether. Not because it wasn't easy enough, but because the guilt had taken over.

Dave Winer, January 29, 2005[21]

What I wrote continues:

I think Dave has pointed out a key problem with tagging. It seems like a nice idea, but it requires us to always do it. The system wants 100% participation. If you don't do it even once, or don't do it well enough (by not choosing the "right" categories), then you are at fault for messing it up for others—the searches won't be complete or will return wrong results. Guilt. But because it's manual and requires judgment, you can't help but mess up sometimes, so guilt is guaranteed. Doing it makes you feel bad because you can't ever really do it right. So, you might as well not play at all and just not tag.

This is the opposite of what I was getting at in my old "Cornucopia of the Commons" essay about volunteer labor. In that case, in a good system, just doing what you normally would do to help yourself helps everybody. Even helping a bit once in a while (like typing in the track names of a CD nobody else had ever entered) benefited you *and* the system. **Instead of making you feel bad for "only" doing 99%, a well-designed system makes you feel good for doing 1%.** People complain about systems that have lots of "freeloaders." Systems that do well with lots of "freeloading" and make the best of periodic participation are good. Open Source software fits this criteria well, and its success speaks for itself.

So, here we have another design criteria for a type of successful system: guiltlessness. Not only should people just need to do what's best for them when they help others, they need to not need to always do it.

http://www.bricklin.com/cornucopia.htm

---

[21]www.scripting.com/2005/01/29.html#guiltAboutCategories

I put some additional discussion in a later blog post:

Wednesday, February 2, 2005
MORE ON WHO DOES TAGGING

Hmm, that last statement above, "Let our readers figure out how to use it,"[22] brings up a point to add to my post about guilt and tagging. Many people are pointing to Clay Shirky's observation[23] that there is good, cheap tagging going on, but that it's done by readers and not authors. Bingo! (Over the years I've found that Clay is so good at pointing out some things that sometimes it makes me smile in awe.) That's my point: Tagging by authors is what's hard, error prone, guilt ridden, etc. Google uses tagging (through linking and the words around it) to help do search.[24] That's "reader tags" (i.e., the tagging is performed by readers who then link to the material that they read and characterize it at the point of the link in their text). Authors "tag" well enough in many cases by putting in words that describe how they understand something and search engines like Google have gotten pretty good at finding those words and other clues. The "other" words to search for are often not ones the author would think of or else they'd say it. Sometimes the "tag" comes about after the item is written and has to do with how it is received (I remember a reporter who was asked about "that" article by a CEO and he knew exactly what was meant) or what it is in relation to something else. In my Cornucopia essay's "Additional Thoughts" (at the end of the essay) I point to the observation that Napster had the added benefit of letting listeners name songs by how they remembered them instead of the "official" name and thereby added that additional value to the search database.

---

[22]This blog post followed one that ended with this: Bloggers often get joy out of just letting you know a fact or observation. Things like: "I found a new device I really like," "Here's an interesting picture," "I figured out what the Senator meant." A lot of today's "professional" journalism is about showing conflict, people changing, horse races, etc. They are looking for some "you win/you lose" situation. Reporters are honing their skills at finding conflict at the expense of the skills of deep understanding. Many of us who blog are obsessed with understanding and feeling and communicating our experiences and what we find out. Let our readers figure out how to use it.

[23]Clay Shirky's essay is included later in this chapter.

[24]When Google's computers index web pages, they also look for links on pages on other web sites that point to the page being indexed. The words related to those links on the other web sites, and other material created by those other authors, help the indexing computers figure out which keywords best relate to the page being indexed.

Unfortunately, there is software development work in the tagging area that involves requiring tags in the original source of an item. That is the problem Clay and I are pointing out. I guess we're seeing that the original source is not a good place to require all tags. We learned that from Google and others. Clay shows that sometimes the tagging need only be done by those who like to tag. Not many people need to set the price of ketchup, even one would do.

Some of the metadata Clay talks about (people choosing a particular product over another being one vote for "this is better than that") is for sifting through and weighing (input into setting the price of ketchup). Google tells me which are the most "popular" items for a given tag. That works in the aggregate, but in search engine technology people worry about accuracy and reach. Some of the things we may want are only In one place (reach), so depending upon the accuracy improvement provided through aggregation of many other items may not be good enough when there's little to aggregate. That's where we want every author to tag every "thing" and to do it "correctly," but it's not to be, I guess.

http://danbricklin.com/log/2005_01_28.htm#moretagging

Here is a copy of Clay Shirky's[25] essay:

February 1, 2005

In What Do Tags Mean, Tim Bray says "There is no cheap metadata" (quoting himself from the earlier On Search.) He's right, of course, in both the mathematical sense (metadata, like all entropy-fighting moves, requires energy) and in the human sense — in On Search, he talks about the difficulties of getting users to enter metadata.

And yet I keep having this feeling that folksonomy, and particularly amateur tagging, is profound in a way that the 'no cheap metadata' dictum doesn't cover.

---

[25]Clay Shirky (www.shirky.com) consults, teaches, and writes on the social and economic effects of Internet technologies. His consulting practice is focused on the rise of decentralized technologies such as peer-to-peer, web services, and wireless networks that provide alternatives to the wired client/server infrastructure that characterizes the Web. He is an adjunct professor in NYU's graduate Interactive Telecommunications Program (ITP).

Imagine a world where there was really no cheap metadata. In that world, let's say you head on down to the local Winn-Dixie to do your weekly grocery accrual. In that world, once you pilot your cart abreast of the checkout clerk, the bargaining begins.

You tell her what you think a 28 oz of Heinz ketchup should cost. She tells you there's a premium for the squeezable bottle, and if you're penny-pinching, you should get the Del Monte. You counter by saying you could shop elsewhere. And so on, until you arrive at a price for the ketchup. Next out of your cart, the Mrs. Paul's fish sticks . . .

Meanwhile, back in the real world, you don't have to do anything of the kind. When you get to the store, you find that, mirabile dictu, the metadata you need is already there, attached to the shelves in advance of your arrival!

Consider what goes into pricing a bottle of Heinz: the profit margin of the tomato grower, the price of a barrel of oil, local commercial rents, average disposable incomes in your area, and the cost of providing soap in the employee bathrooms. Yet all those inputs have already been calculated, and the resulting price then listed on handy little stickers right there on the shelves. And you didn't have to do any work to produce that metadata.

Except, of course, you did. Everytime you pick between the Heinz and the Del Monte, it's like clicking a link, the simplest possible informative transaction. Your choice says "The Heinz, at $2.25 per 28 oz., is a better buy than the Del Monte at $1.89." This is so simple it doesn't seem like you're producing metadata at all — you're just getting ketchup for your fish sticks. But in aggregate, those choices tell Del Monte and Heinz how to capture the business of the price-sensitive and premium-tropic, respectively.

That looks like cheap metadata to me. And the secret is that that metadata is created through aggregate interaction. We know how much more Heinz ketchup should cost than Del Monte because Heinz Inc. has watched what customers do when they raise or lower their prices, and those millions of tiny, self-interested transactions have created the metadata that you take for granted. And when you buy ketchup, you add your little bit of preference data to the mix.

So this is my Get Out of Jail Free card to Tim's conundrum. Cheap metadata is metadata made by someone else, or rather by many someone elses. Or, put another way, the most important ingredient in folksonomy is people.

I think cheap metadata has (at least) these characteristics:

1. *It's made by someone else*
2. *Its creation requires very few learned rules*
3. *It's produced out of self-interest (Corrolary: it is guilt-free)*
4. *Its value grows with aggregation*
5. *It does not break when there is incomplete or degenerate data*

And this is what's special about tagging. Lots of people tag links on del.icio.us, so I gets lots of other people's metadata for free. There is no long list of rules for tagging things 'well,' so there are few deflecting effects from transaction cost. People tag things for themselves, so there are no motivation issues. The more tags the better, because with more tags, I can better see both communal judgment and the full range of opinion. And no one cares, for example, that when I tag things 'loc' I mean the Library of Congress—the system doesn't break with tags that are opaque to other users.

This is what's missing in the "Users don't tag their own blog posts!"[26] hand wringing—they're not supposed to. Tagging is done by other people. As Cory has pointed out, people are not good at producing metadata about their own stuff, for a variety of reasons.

But other people will tag your posts if they need to group them, find them later, or classify them for any other reason. And out of this welter of tiny transactions comes something useful for someone else. And because the added value from the aggregate tags is simply the product of self-interest + ease of use + processor time, the resulting metadata is cheap. It's not free, of course, but it is cheap.

Clay Shirky, February 1, 2005[27]

---

[26]The words in quotes are linked to my January 2005 "Systems without guilt where every contribution is appreciated" blog post included earlier in this chapter.

[27]http://many.corante.com/archives/2005/02/01/folksonomy_the_soylent_green_of_the_21st_century.php

Related Writings

Here are two writings related to the original "Cornucopia of the Commons" essay. The first is the essay by Tom Matrullo I referred to that brings up the concept of "looking into other people's computers."

Tom's essay, written in 2000, shows an emotional, poetic reaction at the time to Napster.

24 Notes on Napster: A Commonplace Book for Today

Tom Matrullo

Mozart once heard a piece of music so piercingly beautiful he was moved to write it down from memory after hearing it performed in a church. He had no choice. The church believed it "owned" the music, and forbade anyone to copy it. So, Mozart pulled a Napster. The piece has been in the public domain ever since, for all to enjoy.

Napster www.napster.com—a simple tool, crafted with no unnecessary arabesques of code—is organic software: Dionysus who knows no boundaries. Such a natural tool seems obvious in hindsight, like an evolutionary "Eureka!": the moment when life figured out the heart.

Why wasn't Napster obvious before it stared us in the face?

Open Napster and you're looking out over dizzying vistas of other people's music (OPM) on Other People's Hard Drives (OPHDs). It's like suddenly gaining several thousand generous, musically literate friends. You have highly compressed conversations sharing intimate knowledge of the music you love, without ums, uhs and other inessential articulations.

In a commercial culture, this tool was nearly unable to be thought. But here it is, offering me Sara Brightman in full-throated ease, thanks to some angel named SWAT18.

Napster has been called the third quantum jump in software, after VisiCalc and Mosaic.[28] Not because of any technical complexity. Its designer, Shawn Fanning, bought a book to figure out how to write

---

[28]Mosaic was an early web browser that pioneered functionality that helped make the Web popular.

the program. The coding wasn't hard to do. The concept was hard to think.

If the Cluetrain Manifesto[29] turns notions of markets upside down, Napster turns the trucking template inside out. Napster enables the nonce deployment of love via self-organizing labyrinths that defy central distribution models. Like the Manifesto's position that "Markets are conversations," Napster gives us a place for people's music to be held in common, not consumed.

Music has always had underground modes of dissemination. Remember how every working musician had his or her cheap, Xeroxed "fake books"? Napster was difficult to conceive because we forgot sharing. Central distribution of intellectual property (IntelProp) via channels, trucks, ships, presses, wires and microwaves ("trucking" for short) was all we could remember. In that system, music is not what gladdens our souls. It is mediated Product inserted into dead bodies, shipped and sold for good hard cash.

We used to need the corpses: CDs, vinyl, tape, etc. We, the sorry-assed multitudes who couldn't get to the Met, La Scala, or Ozzfest to bask in the unmediated presence of the Voice, the Artist. IntelProp vampires fed on our failure to arrive at the live act. Trucking is the wounding prosthetic that grows inside our disability to be present, as advertising infects us with discontent on which it dines.

And this spawned Content. Corporate distributors only see numbers, units, penetration, market share. To understand Content, you must ignore it. Pay attention only to containers.

If you imagine there is something called Content, you won't like Napster.

Courtney Love nailed it: "What the hell is content? Nobody buys content. Real people pay money for music because it means something to them."[30]

Being a "content provider" is prostitution work that devalues our art and doesn't satisfy our spirits. Artistic expression has to be

---

[29]http://www.cluetrain.com

[30]http://archive.salon.com/tech/feature/2000/06/14/love/

provocative. The problem with artists and the Internet: Once their art is reduced to content, they may never have the opportunity to retrieve their souls.

Napster doesn't distribute Content. Instead, it offers a voyeuristic look into OPM on OPHDs—a glimpse into the intimate specificity of other people's loves. More than a look, we have permission to "take" what we like, secure in the knowledge we are welcome to it. A regular Dionysian orgy of passions.

Other people's loves: Downloaded music is like the commonplace books of old, in which people would preserve snippets from books that held special meaning for them. Napster feels more personal than "personalized" sites. Without leering, it offers constellations of love affairs people have had with music—each one different, each reflecting a soul.

Napster is ingenuity powered by enthusiasm and generosity of spirit. It is the negative image of those porn sites that promise you'll be nuzzling 417,000 nubile young women within 30 seconds of handing over your credit card.

Interestingly, it is also the negative image of the piratical record company model described in detail by Courtney Love—how did porn sites and record companies get into the same slimy category? Hmmmm.

Sons of Napster will add features to its basic model: links to all kinds of info about music one is downloading, about the artists, where they're appearing, etc. And a means of stopping a download and restarting without having to start over. Or, a way of finding out if the only guy with the song you've needed for years is going to log off in the middle of your download. So what? Napster gives so much that any quibble is downright mean-spirited.

We can already hear the coming fuss, when bandwidth and grandsons of Napster permit us to exchange our passions for videos, films and other IntelProp.

Some good things will never be transferred this way. Like cuttings from flowering plants. Too bad, because I'm sure gardeners love to share their cuttings exactly as music lovers enjoy sharing their cuts.

The analogy isn't all that lousy, really. The gardener buys seeds, or borrows a cutting, and grows a plant; the plant makes possible its own replication, but only in real life, not virtually. The point is, the gardener who owns something he/she wants to share will always make a cutting. The cutting gives away part of the whole to create a new whole.

With Napster, we are made more whole: music sings without trucks, dances without dead limbs.

The act of downloading a song is labor, sort of. A broadband declension of the medieval passion of monks for manuscripts. When I play a song I've downloaded, I experience every note more intimately for having had a hand in its replication.

Napster brings closer a paradisiacal economy—a realm of abundance where trucking (and advertising) is hard to imagine. Where Mozart doesn't have to kidnap music. That is why it is embattled.[31]

When musicians work, they need to be compensated. They can either become one with the vampires, or look to salaries or tips—patrons or fans. That way requires faith, if songs are to be free.

Copyright © 2000 Tom Matrullo All Rights Reserved

Tom Matrullo (used with permission)[32]

This second related writing consists of the slides I added to a talk about the "Cornucopia of the Commons" essay that provides a more detached, mathematical view of applying my theory. This is the analytic MBA speaking. The last slide is a rough mathematical formula that helps explain why systems can be financially viable even if there is a lot of freeloading. It depends upon the cost of new users and the value of contributions. The declining cost of computing and communications have made more and more systems viable.

---

[31]http://www.salon.com/tech/log/2000/06/14/napster/index.html

[32]http://www.spark-online.com/august00/trends/matrullo.html

ADDITIONS TO CORNUCOPIA OF THE COMMONS PRESENTED AT THE O'REILLY P2P CONFERENCE, FEBRUARY 14, 2001

AmIHotOrNot.com
- People post their pictures and others rate them on a scale of 1 to 10: Are they Hot or Not?
- Large audience means lots of people to vote
- Lots of people wanting to be rated leads to ever-changing content

Won't it fall over by the "Tragedy of the Commons"?
- Worry over growth overwhelming benefit
- Xerox PARC study implies too much selfish use is bad

But we don't always see the curves you'd expect with growth

Increasing the value of the database by adding more information is a natural by-product of using the tool for your own benefit
- Passionate users make major additions
- Regular users add value or are of negligible cost

Per New User Financials
- Costs: Disk, Server, Bandwidth, Setup (one time)
- Revenues: Subscription or base fees, Per transaction fees, Advertising and other side-effect usage-based revenues, Philanthropy
- Revenue must be greater than Costs

Effect of a New User
- Breadth of data or choices
- Size of audience
- Interest of audience
- Access: speed, availability, reliability
- Cost
- Quality of data

Donations
- Different classes of donations to the database: breadth, depth, access, updates, testing
- Initial value of donation
- Decay of donation value over time

- Does donation benefit all users or just attract a single contingent of users?
- Result of passion or side-effect of normal use?
- Change in rate of donation over time

Adding a new user must be positive

Simplistic equation:

$$Dp \times \%P + Ds + deltaNU - deltaSys + \$Unew > 0$$

Where:

Dp = Value of passion donations to system
%P = Proportion of users who make passion donations
Ds = Value of selfish or side-effect use donations per user
deltaNU = Change in value of database from effect of a new user
deltaSys = Cost to keep system at normal performance[33]
$Unew = Revenue of new user

http://www.bricklin.com/speeches/c-of-c/

In this chapter we applied what drives individuals in their own quest for personal benefit or altruism to the task of helping the whole group. Through appropriate design, systems can be constructed such that the more people use them the more they increase in value. One hundred percent of users being active contributors, or even a majority contributing, is not always needed. Improved technology and acceptance of the Internet is letting us apply this type of design in a wider range of situations.

I showed in the previous chapters that "free release" is something that artists have been able to deal with, and even benefit from. Here we see that "freeloading" on a service that depends upon active participation by users can be tolerated, too. As before, it is the crafting of the right mixture, the details of the service, and its costs and benefits.

---

[33]Thanks to Moore's Law effects, the continually dropping costs to keep a system at normal performance mean more and more things may be done with just a few contributors, or you can have more resource-intensive services. Probably the most popular example of the second is YouTube.

In the next chapter I move from blog posts to transcripts of interviews with experts discussing interaction among people, especially in a community. These interviews are about "free" vs. "for pay," the importance of the "social world" and "social contracts," and other nonmonetary driving forces relating to working with others on a personal as well as a national and international level.

5 Cooperation

One of the ways that we get leverage from a group, making the whole greater than the sum of its parts, is through cooperation. Cooperation can take many forms. One way is through the simple act of sharing information, letting others find out what you are doing or what you know. Other ways include working together towards a common goal and sacrificing personal benefit for the good of the group.

I start this chapter with a blog post about an example of people observing the behavior of others and getting the idea to watch a particular event.

Friday, November 12, 2004
TIED INTO POP CULTURE ON JETBLUE

I had a strange experience just now. I'm flying JetBlue for the first time. They have personal flat-panel displays at each seat, with satellite feeds. Thirty-six channels (well, not all were working). When I flew a few weeks ago on United during an historic Red Sox game, we were lucky to hear updates every half inning from the pilot (I made it home in time to watch the end). I was putting the final touches on a keynote speech I'm giving next week at the Computer Reseller News Hall of Fame Awards. One of the points I make is about mobility, connectivity, and the move from point products to modular systems. Then I started listening to Adam Curry's November 11th podcast. This was the first one of his that I'd listened to (I tend more to the IT Conversations type of podcasts so far). Adam is more tilted to pop culture than Doc Searls and the Gillmor Gang, with his music and his background[1] and stuff. Then I got a real

---
[1] Adam Curry was an early MTV "video jockey" many years ago and an important person in the development of podcasting. IT Conversations produced some of the first major podcasting shows, with an emphasis on technical topics.

dose of pop culture: Up on the screen of the person next to me was Court TV. The Scott Peterson trial verdict was going to be announced in a few minutes. They were going to have a live audio feed. (I haven't followed this trial at all, so I wasn't too interested, but from the number of times I've heard reference to it in the news, I guess it's a big deal to lots of people.) Looking down the aisle, as the time grew closer, more and more screens were showing Court TV. Finally the verdict: Guilty. (Even I paused Adam, and moved my earphones from MP3 player to seat phone jack so I could take a picture at the correct moment.) A few minutes later, most people were back to watching the other stuff. Court TV was still talking about the trial—hours and hours on the same thing during this flight. I listened to some classical music on my MP3 player and blogged.

Watching TV

The Peterson verdict

http://danbricklin.com/log/2004_10_15.htm#jetblue

I find it interesting how individuals monitor others to make choices, including which information to use. Often, they use what I'll call an "editor" to do the sifting, instead of doing it themselves. I use the term "editor" to refer to any person who surveys a lot of information and then chooses a subset and whose choices are then relied upon by others. This may be the editor at a newspaper desk who decides which stories to put on the front page or an enthusiast friend who you rely upon to introduce you to the work of new musicians. Editors, in turn, are influenced by their readers and people who the editors have decided over time are worth listening to (i.e., other editors). Readers choose which editors consistently make the choices that most meet their needs. For a given situation, people choose which editor(s) they feel is appropriate for that case—they don't use one editor for everything. Sometimes they just look at the raw data themselves.

During my plane flight, we got to take advantage of the people around us who channel-surfed the different TV programs or who had looked around and saw a program on someone else's screen and liked it. (The latter is the common "viral" method of having information repeatedly move from the limited sphere around one person to the sphere around another and then another.) It was the unusual situation, at the time, of being able to see which media many others were consuming in real time (and simultaneously showing them what we chose). It was a very unusual crossing of personal boundaries, with so many strangers being stuffed into that confined space, much as if we were looking into apartment windows to see what people were watching in their living rooms while they looked into ours.

New services on the Internet are giving us other ways to see what other people find of interest. These include the popular "del.icio.us" shared bookmarking and tagging service and the Digg content sharing and ranking service. Millions of people have found them useful. Many blogs serve the useful purpose of being an editor, pointing you to material on the Internet that you wouldn't otherwise have known about.

Dan Ariely, March 2, 2008

In 2008, behavioral economics Professor Dan Ariely published a book titled *Predictably Irrational: The Hidden Forces That Shape Our Decisions.*[2] I interviewed Dan at a conference a few weeks after the book's release. I concentrated

---

[2] HarperCollins, ISBN: 006135323X

my questions on issues related to Open Source software (a cooperative development method popularized by the success of products such as the Linux operating system and the Firefox browser) and the differences between doing something for free vs. for pay.

This is the first of three transcribed interviews in this chapter. The interviews were done informally, either sitting in a corner off a hotel lobby at a conference or on the phone. They were then released as podcasts on my web site that people could, and did, download to listen to on their computers or MP3 players. They are like long blog posts to share my experiences with others.

I'm not a professional interviewer and these transcripts are pretty raw and true to the actual audio. Most people, especially me, do not speak in full, well-formed paragraphs or sometimes even sentences. Try to read these as conversations, not speeches. You may also want to listen to the original recordings by going to the web site (the appropriate URL is noted for each of the interviews). The timecodes in the transcripts should help you jump to a particular part.

Transcript of Interview with Dan Ariely[3]

Dan Bricklin as Announcer: [0:01] This interview with author Dan Ariely was recorded at the Diamond Management and Technology Consultants Diamond Exchange Meeting, March 2, 2008, by Dan Bricklin.

Dan Bricklin: [0:15] Hi, this is Dan, and I'm sitting here with Dan Ariely, so it may get confusing with two Dans. Dan is the author of a book called *Predictably Irrational: The Hidden Forces that Shape our Decisions*, and Dan's book just came out.

It's now on the *New York Times* best-seller list. He's been interviewed on NPR. But, I'm going to be asking questions that you probably wouldn't hear on NPR. But, we'll start with: Dan, tell me a little bit about yourself and about the book.

Dan Ariely: [0:47] So, I'm a behavioral economist, which means I'm interested in the behaviors we all make day in and day out: shopping, decisions about marriage, decisions about where to work, and so on, but without assuming that people are rational.

And the book is basically a description of many years of research on this topic, and I look at different facets of life. I look through all of the expectations, and I look at how we make decisions about buying, and I look at how

---

[3] http://danbricklin.com/podcast.html#danbcast-2008-03-06-20-15-14

we fall in love with things and how we decide about our passion for work and all kinds of those.

And I look empirically at those things and then I try to think about, if those empirical facts are correct and accurate and describe our behavior and they are not exactly rational, what does it mean for policy? What does it mean about how we should think about life in general?

Dan Bricklin: [1:35] OK. Now, you're a professor at MIT in two departments?

Dan Ariely: [1:39] Yes, so I'm the Alfred P. Sloan Professor of Behavioral Economics, and I'm at the Sloan School, it's the business school, and at the Media Lab.[4]

Dan Bricklin: [1:47] The media lab where they do all the cool electronic stuff and computer things?

Dan Ariely: [1:51] That's right. And I've been really privileged to be a part of that. It's a fantastic environment and a real treat.

Dan Bricklin: [2:00] Now, what I found really good about the book is that first of all, you're very experimental, experiment-centric, and what you do is you come up with these clever, really simple experiments to do things. (You might give an example of a simple one.) But then you apply the experiment results to diverse situations.

So, it's first finding something about people, why do they procrastinate, is there procrastination, you can give me all those things, and then the simple little experiment, some of it's audacious, you know, and then taking from that, how you then go from it. Is that . . .

Dan Ariely: [2:44] Yeah, so you know, I think about a scientist with a chemistry set and my chemistry set includes everything in the world. So, I do experiments on beer and on wine and on pencil, and chocolate. Everything in life is a perfectly reasonable topic to study.

Dan Bricklin: [3:02] Chocolate?

Dan Ariely: [3:03] Yes, actually, chocolate is a great thing. Let me describe to you one experiment on beer that will just give you an example. So, we go to a pub, and we give people two samples of beer—one is a regular beer and one is a beer with balsamic vinegar.

And some people, we don't tell them about it. We just say, "Here are two cups of beer. Try them both and see which one you like better and we'll give

---

[4] Dan is now a professor at Duke University as well as at the MIT Media Lab.

you a full glass of it." And as it turns out, balsamic vinegar improves beer, so more people want the beer with the balsamic vinegar.

But, it turns out that when you tell people upfront that one of the beers has balsamic vinegar, they hate it. And no matter how much they taste it, they still hate it. Now, if you think of it, it's an experiment about beer and vinegar, but the real point is: What happens when our expectations go a certain way and our tastes go a different way?

Which one of those overpowers each other? And the idea is that under certain circumstances, our expectation can actually overpower reality. What we expect to see and to taste, and so on, can actually be what becomes the reality.

Dan Bricklin: [4:03] Now, you did experiments that have to do with social norms and things like that?

Dan Ariely: [4:11] Yes. So, we have a set of studies that talk about motivation to exert labor, and we basically have the following argument: People live in two different worlds. We live in a social world, in which the rules seem to be different. This is something that we do for our friends and family and for our spouses and kids, and then we live in the work place, in which we work for money and the relationship is more clear between input and output.

And then between those things, there is the modern labor place, which is kind of an interesting mix because we don't exactly end the work day at any particular point, and the persons who employ us usually don't want us to think so. They want us to work at home and at night and be passionate and so on.

And I think open source is even more extreme on that continuum where it's even less work and more social. So, the thing to understand is these two extremes, the social world and the financial, the money norms, actually work very differently, and when they mix, sometimes counterintuitive things happen. So, for example, in our experiments, sometimes we ask people to do something for us for free, as a favor. And they work very hard when we ask them.

Dan Bricklin: [5:29] So, what type of simple, it was a simple thing?

Dan Ariely: [5:31] We ask people to help us move a sofa. We can ask people to drag some circles on the computer. We can ask them to do all kinds of things that are not particularly exciting.

So, they work hard if we pay them nothing. They also work hard if we pay them a substantial amount—$60.00 per hour and so on. But, what if we pay them a little bit? What if we pay them just a couple of dollars?

It turns out that when you pay them a couple of dollars, they don't say to themselves, "Gee, I get to help these experimenters plus I get some money." Instead, the money replaces the social motivation. They think of it as work, and now they don't work at all.

So, when we don't pay them, they think about it in a social domain as doing us a favor, and they're willing to work for free. When we offer them money, it's not free plus money. Now it's a little bit of money. They think about it very differently, and they don't like it at all. And they work very little.

Dan Bricklin: [6:23] Now you did experiments about—there was the one that has to do with being in the social domain vs. being in the economic, the financial domain.

Dan Ariely: [6.34] Yeah.

Dan Bricklin: [6:34] And another one about the difference between free and not free. That there is—even one penny . . .

Dan Ariely: [6:39] That's right. So, maybe the cutest experiment, but of course this is just one of those, was that kids who came to my house on Halloween one day, I gave them initially three Hershey's Kisses.

And then to half of them, I said, "Look. I have another deal for you. You can get either a small Snickers bar or a big Snickers bar. You can give me one Hershey's Kiss; I'll give you the small Snickers bar. Or you can give me two Hershey's Kisses; I'll give you the big one."

Now, this was a very good deal because the small Snickers bar was one ounce, the big one was two ounces. They would get a ninefold return on investment for the extra Hershey's Kiss. So, it was a really good deal, and all the kids basically took the big Snickers bar.

To other kids, I discounted both Snickers bars by the same amount. So, I said, "Look. I have two Snickers bars here—a small and a big one. You can get the small for free or the big one for one Hershey's Kiss." Now the difference between them is still one Hershey's Kiss, and it's still good to pay that extra Hershey's Kiss and get the big Snickers bar.

It's still a return of nine times investment, but now the free was so tempting that the kids went for the free. Now, by the way, it's not just kids, it's adults. And it's not just chocolate, it's also Amazon gift certificates and all kinds of things.

Whenever you have free, there's an emotional temptation from it. It actually puts us in a very different situation than when we pay. And in fact, you can think generally that payment is something very different than nonpayment.

We think about it very differently. We have a different emotional reaction. We apply different norms. We think about it very differently.

Let me say one more thing about labor. We did the following simple experiment. We got people to come to the lab and to build Bionicles. These are little Lego robots. And we paid people. We paid them $3.00 for the first one they built, $2.70 for the next, $2.40 for the next, and so on.

And people were supposed to stop when their supply of labor, when their desire to build these things was below what they were making. Right? So, what's the stopping rule? But here's the thing. When people were building this, some of them, every Lego they finished, every robot they finished, we put it in a box below the table, and we told them when they finished, we will disassemble all of them.

To the other half of the people, every time they started working on a new Bionicle, we start disassembling the old one in front of their face. So, as they were building it, we were disassembling it.

From a rational standard perspective, it does not matter. They were clearly just producing labor. They were building these things. We were paying them. They all knew that we will disassemble them at some point.

But, for those people who saw their work being demolished in front of their eyes, it was a very different experience. They stopped much earlier.

So, it is interesting. If you think about it, even when you do something that has really no particular meaning—they were not saving lives or being physicians or doing something exciting, they were building robots that they knew would be destroyed later—even the ability to suspend disbelief about the uselessness of your work for a little bit can create incredible motivational power for people to work.

Dan Bricklin: [9:57] Wow. So, let's look at this in terms of applying a lot of what you have been looking at to open source software and things of that sort and the social stuff we build, wikis or stuff like that.

So, I guess we should just go through each of the chapters and see if there is something applicable there. Chapter one, about things being relative, about that we don't really know the price of things but it is in relation to something else, even if it was arbitrary that we started with.

Dan Ariely: [10:31] That's right. And it is not just price. It is in fact a lot of things that we don't know how we value them. So, it is very easy to think about price in this way. It's not really clear how much we value, how much utility we get from two gallons of milk. But, it's very simple to think that it is double one gallon.

Dan Bricklin: [10:48] So, how would that apply? Since open source software is free, does that mean that people would undervalue because the price is lower and they think it wouldn't be as good? Is that one of the things against open source? We are not talking about the free stuff where we know that the other pull is that free is so strong that you said.

Dan Ariely: [11:12] Yeah. So, I think that if open source ever tried to start charging money, there would be a real issue because there will be this relative comparison.

Right now, I think open source and non–open source software are kind of considered in two separate bins. We don't actually compare them head-to-head with each other. Sure, you can take and say do I want Microsoft Word or do I want the open source version. But, we don't compare them head-to-head.

They are sufficiently different that they are kept in different buckets, and we compare them within the bucket. Now what will happen if open source all of a sudden became for pay? Under those conditions, we will compare the two of them, and then we might evaluate very, very differently.

Dan Bricklin: [11:59] So, that says that when you have open source that is free, you are viewing it differently. Now you have some experiments to show where we cross the line maybe.

But, then once we already assume, once we figure out that it is as good as, then you can start charging because you can go head-to-head.

Dan Ariely: [12:18] I'm not so sure. Let's think about email for free. When the Internet was kind of at the initial hype, there was all this idea of let's give people things for free and let's assume that they will realize the benefits of those things, and later we could charge them for it.

But, that assumes that when people experience something, they can actually rationalize their benefit in terms of money. So, they use email and they say, "Oh, this is really a good thing. I am willing to pay at least $19.75 for it."

It turns out that translation to money is very, very hard. In fact, we can say to ourselves, "Well, I have used it for free. It was perfectly fine. But, now that you are charging, I am starting to think about it very differently."

It is a different mindset. Free and nonfree are two different mindsets. Switching from free to nonfree changes a lot of things. It is not just the price.

Dan Bricklin: [13:10] So, free as in beer vs. not free is a dichotomy.[5] What about free as in freedom vs. not? Well, we'll get into that I guess when we get to options and stuff about how there are some values there. Why don't we talk about options, about the value of options and keeping so many options, and is that good or bad.

Because one of the things about open source software is that it gives you options that you don't have in proprietary software because you could, if you wanted to, make changes, etc.[6]

Dan Ariely: [13:45] Yeah. So, what we basically find is people have an over tendency to keep doors open, to keep options open. We love options. In fact, we love them too much because when we create situations in which keeping options open is costly, inefficient and financially costly, people still do that.

For example, in our experiments, I will give you an analogy. Imagine you're dating three women. Dating women is costly. You need to spend time and money with them. If one of those three women seems like she is the one that you should stay with for life, the question is, are you willing to abandon the other two?

Now, if you don't abandon the other two and you still spend some time and effort on them, your main significant other will not get enough attention and your relationship might not develop sufficiently well. It turns out that that is basically what we end up doing.

We end up spreading our efforts across too many options, even the dominated ones—the ones that are not as good. By doing so, we take away from our main relationship.

---

[5] In discussions about open source software there is also the concept of "Free Software." The distinctions and overlap between the two terms are not important for us here, but do matter to many of the people who create software for others to use. In general, Dan and I loosely used the term "open source" to refer to the whole area.

　　A major player in the Free Software world is the Free Software Foundation (www.fsf.org), the creators of the GNU General Public License (known as the GPL). The Linux operating system was released under the GPL, as are a large number of other free and open source software packages.

　　In describing what they mean by the word "free" in Free Software, the Free Software Foundation distinguishes between "free" as in free beer, and "free" as in free speech. They care most about the latter. Dan and I discussed both.

[6] With open source software, the source code, the computer code used to create the product, is made available by the author for reading and modification by the user. (While regular people might not be able to modify the code themselves, they could also pay others to do it for them.) You may give those modified copies to others if you wish. That is not normally the case with proprietary software, where the source code is not available for modification.

Dan Bricklin: [14:50] You have tested things like that with little computer games and things like that, right?

Dan Ariely: [14:54] That's right. We have tested this in a very abstract way when people make money and the doors are closing and they have to examine this and we have different conditions.

But, I think the question for open source is at what level do people keep too many options open. Is it the individual level or is it the society, or the level of all the people who are working on it? And what are the real costs of keeping those options open?

Dan Bricklin: [15:20] So, what I heard is that keeping options open is a driver. Even if it is bad for us and even if we know it is bad, we will do it. So, therefore the fact that open source gives you options is a pull in the direction of open source, especially since it isn't bad in many cases.

So, that is a positive thing with it. But, you are saying when you are designing certain products and stuff, if what you are doing will give options where people have the option of cutting down on options or not and it is bad for them not to cut down, you had better watch out because they will tend towards leaving options open.

Dan Ariely: [15:57] That's right. I think that what we see in terms of features and software is like that. There are more and more features. There are more and more things you can do.

It would be very hard for people to say, "I am willing to pay more money to have software with less options and less menus and so on." But at the same time, it might be actually more useful software.

So, how do you play that balance act? It is actually very difficult. But, I agree that more options are creating a pull, even if it is not good for people. So, the task is, do people who are on the verge of using open source, do they realize that this is one of the benefits or not?

Dan Bricklin: [16:35] As a developer, you should realize that your internal pull to leave options open is not optimal necessarily and you had better use some other things than your gut feel about options, unless you have been proven good at not doing that.

But, a normal person's gut feel on leaving options open is not optimal.

Dan Ariely: [16:57] That's right. We leave too many options open. Now, in a world with no cost, it's perfectly fine. But, this is not the world we live in.

Dan Bricklin: [17:06] For more detail, they should read the book.

So, the cost of zero-cost, is that applicable here? Did we talk about that?

Dan Ariely: [17:17] Yeah. That is the Halloween experiment. It's all about the cost of zero.

I think, actually I am interested in one of your thoughts on this. Some open source you get to buy, like Red Hat [Linux operating system].

Dan Bricklin: [17:34] Right.

Dan Ariely: [17:35] Right. How does that work and how do you think it changes the open source community?

Dan Bricklin: [17:40] Well, you're not really buying it. You're buying the service. It's more or less—let's say MySQL, where you could buy it with one license or another. You are afraid of one of the licenses (which we might get into about some of that), I think, for some security reasons, I mean feeling secure type of reasons, not software security reasons.[7]

But, it gives you something else. Like you want to know that it is supported in certain ways and things like that. You could actually, you had the option of being able to do it for free, but you would rather do it I guess the way that makes you feel comfortable because that is the way you have always done it.

That's a whole other thing you have about always doing it, right?

Dan Ariely: [18:26] Yeah. But, going back to the Red Hat question, do you think that the fact that they call it that you are "paying for the service" makes it easier for them to charge for it than if they call it that you're "paying for the software"?

Dan Bricklin: [18:36] But, you are paying for the service because you can't call otherwise. And for many of the people who are doing it, they want that service and they want to be able call, even though—well, that gets into one of the issues with social things that if you have an Open Source community that will support something for whatever altruistic or other reasons, statistically, it may give you better support than knowing that you have a contract with somebody.

---

[7] This relates to the aversion some companies' legal departments and management have to software available under the very common GPL Free Software license.

The MySQL database system, a software product, was released under two different licenses by the author. (The author of a copyrighted work has the right to give different people different deals for use of their work.) You could use the software as if it was licensed under the GPL. In that case, there was no charge for the product, but any modifications you made to it (and other software related to it in certain ways) had to also be licensed under the GPL and given away for no charge. Alternatively, you could buy the identical software from them, get technical support, and feel secure that none of the software you connected to the MySQL database also had to be released under the GPL.

And there's this thing about feeling that companies think that contracts are secure while social contracts and other things, they don't understand how strong they are. Now, your research says that social contracts can be very strong.

Dan Ariely: [19:23] That's right. The best example to think about is marriage; when you're married to somebody, of course we know that marriages don't always last, but for the time that they last, they're basically a promise that you will be there for the other person when bad things happen. This is very different than your contract with your gardener who's mowing your lawn and the moment something doesn't work for either of you, you go away.

And I think, that's the strength of social contracts, that they're not perfectly specified and it's not exactly clear what each of you are doing at each period of the game, but you know that when something goes really bad, the other person will not just abandon you.

They are fantastically useful for personal things and I think they can also be used for software things because what happens when something really bad happens? In software we have these things, it's not just that the software's crashing, it crashes your hard drive. There are all these catastrophical things happening. With regular contracts, it's out of the contract, it's not a part of the complete contract.

Dan Bricklin: [20:33] So, if my company suddenly needed something and I was part of the community for that product, the community may come together for me if it's a community, but it wouldn't come together if it was a contract. And we need help; we need a modification to it to support this new thing because we're in trouble or whatever.

Dan Ariely: [20:56] This is going back to the question of flexibility, that complete contracts are complete contracts. They spell out specifically what you deserve and don't deserve. And if you buy a piece of software and it crashes your computer and destroys your hard drive, tough. It's not in the contract that they will do anything about it. They might ship you a new box of software or send you a patch or something like that.

When you have an incomplete contract and the real feeling of community, there's a sense that the other side of it has some responsibility and flexibility to decide what the right thing to do is at the right moment. That's where the strength of it is coming from.

Dan Bricklin: [21:37] Now you found that, going from the social contract to a financial contract, all it takes is charging or something, and you have research to say when it switches from one to the other. And you also said it's very hard to move back once you're in there.

So, therefore, if you have an open source project, there are things you might do to the project that would mess it up and turn it from social to financial and then you lose this contract. It switches, and that you have to watch out for. Do you have some thoughts on that and research in that area?

Dan Ariely: [22:19] Yes. The research we've done is the following: We get people to work very hard for us when we pay them nothing, and we get them to work very little when we pay them a little bit of money, and we get them to work hard again if we pay them a lot of money. If we give them gifts, it doesn't matter what gift we give them, they always work hard. But, if we give them a gift and we tell them how much the gift cost us, they get upset again with a small gift.

Now, the analogy here is what happens if you're in an open source community and all of a sudden you start paying somebody to do something? You say, "Look, I really need help with these two things and nobody's able to do it right now, nobody seems to be doing it. I'll pay somebody to do that." How does it change the way you think, the way they think, and the way the community is thinking about it, where all of sudden there is payment involved?

And there's actually a very old project that was done with kids many years ago when they paid kids to play with Magic Markers. And it turns out if you pay kids to play with Magic Markers, they play with them a lot. But, when you stop paying them, they stop liking it.

They basically abandoned Magic Markers. It became a job. It wasn't fun. It wasn't something they took pride in any more. And they just stopped doing it. So, the financial motivation can actually chase away our internal motivation and pride.

I think that open source is about the pride we take in the work. Right? It's about the Lego condition, where it's not destroyed, it's continued and other people are building on it and we see actually a lot of pride in seeing other people taking what we have done and improving it.

It's kind of offsprings of our kids in many ways. It's incredibly rewarding. But, we find the same thing with ideation. When we create a system for people to generate ideas, and we reward them not by their ideas but by how much other people build on their ideas, people produce more ideas than if we pay them directly for their ideas.

Now, if you think about that, you want to say, "How do you create more social reinforcement and rewards in that community?" And I think it's about reputation. It's about how people create central ideas that other people then expand on it, and you want to go back and give people credit for being the first one to do it.

Dan Bricklin: [24:47] Do you have research on that?

Dan Ariely: [24:47] I don't have research on this, just on the ideation thing. But I think that the analogy is very clear, that you want people to have ownership and pride in it, and you want that when other people build on it, their pride, in some sense, is increasing in that.

Now, all of that can really backfire if we start paying people. And it even becomes worse when we just pay *some* people. You don't have even to pay everybody.

Imagine that you came to one of your friends to help them move some sofas, and you're happy to do it, but all of sudden, they also invite some movers that they pay money to. And you're working side by side with these movers. You can't be happy any more.

Dan Bricklin: [25:30] Oh. So, that gets to the structure. Now, I was thinking, there are people that are paid to work on open source, but I view that as if done right, it's like a gift from the company to let you spend all your time working on the project that you love, if it's viewed that way, I guess.

Or one of the things you can do is to say, "The company can give you the gift of allowing you to work after hours on other projects and not use their noncompete, we-own-all-your-inventions [employment agreement] clause," or type of thing like that. So, how does one make it feel like a gift vs. that it's being paid?

Dan Ariely: [26:07] Yeah, so I think if you take a salaried employee and you just say, "Look, you can do that," it's basically just making people like a research scientist and giving them some big honor and saying you can just work on whatever you want because we don't know what you're going to do.

So, there's something very "incomplete contract" about that to people, which is fine. I think that if you start creating more financial incentives, if you pay people by the hour, if you tie their yearly bonus to how much the open source community is going to be advanced, if you tie it to more financial things, then you're starting to have real problems.

Dan Bricklin: [26:44] So, you've done research about when things are considered money or not, and some of it has to do with morality in terms of: Will they do things ethically or not? Will they cheat or not?

But, you found out that there's a line between when it's money and when it's not money. And there are things you can do that are not money that let you think one way, and things that are money. So, there is the way of doing this.

So, for example, if I pay you specifically to work on this feature vs. what you just said was, "I'll let you work on anything you want on this open source project." There's a difference between that. And what about the money thing, too?

Dan Ariely: [27:25] So, money is really kind of a fabulous idea, you know. It's a very important invention, and it has all these other side effects. So, we talked about the fact that when free is substantially different than one penny, it creates a very different emotional feel, very different appeal.

We talked about the idea that when you pay people, you transfer them to a different type of norm. They use very different rules about what's appropriate and not appropriate. And it's also the case that people have different moral considerations when money's involved and when money's not involved. In particular, what we find is then when people have a chance to cheat for nonmoney, they cheat much more.

And I'll describe one experiment—we've done many of those—but, in one experiment, I distributed six packs of Cokes in the dorm refrigerators at MIT and I measured what is technically known as the half-life time of Coke, and it's a very short time.[8] People just take the cans all the time.

And when I leave money instead of Coke cans, nobody ever takes the money. It's because stealing money has a clear implication as theft, but taking Coke you can tell yourself all kinds of stories about that.

Now, with open source, I don't know exactly where the opportunity is to cheat, but the idea is that if there are the opportunities to cheat that are outside the domain of money, people would have an easier time doing that. For example, my guess is that if you have some kind of software that is about advertising, it would be easier to cheat than if you wrote something for a bank that actually does some conversions because it's a step removed from cash and it's easier to do.

Dan Bricklin: [29:14] You've done research that, when it comes to cheating, if people get their mindset in a moral [frame]—like if instead of reading a list of book titles, they have to remember titles of books, they have to remember the Ten Commandments—that just trying to remember alone puts them in the mind-set of being less likely to cheat?

Is it that if you know you're working on something that says, "I'm [licensed under the Free Software Foundation's] GPL [license]," at the beginning, it puts you in a more altruistic [frame of mind] because you're sharing with the community? Is there something about the placement of that and knowing the

---

[8] "Half-life" is a term from nuclear science but is used in other contexts. It refers to the time to decay to half of what you had originally.

type of license and the name of the license—does that put people in a different mindset?

Dan Ariely: [29:56] Yeah, I think, that would be the implication is that when there are no well-defined rules and we make our own rules and we follow our selfish interests a little too much, in our case, it was to cheat. But, when you have rules and when they're apparent and at the top of the mind, people would use those.

So, in our experiments with cheating, the moment that people recited the Ten Commandments they thought about morality and as a consequence, they behaved better even though there were no negative sides of behaving dishonestly.

And I think the same thing for the open source community, the question is: What are the rules that are in place, and are they on top of people's minds when they're doing it? And are you going to have different societies that have different rules and different regulations?

But, standards of conduct and adherence of them are actually very, very important because without them people might stray away.

Dan Bricklin: [30:55] Now, you've done research on the difference in decision making when you're aroused. And I'm wondering when it comes to software and stuff, some products just are so cool it's a high of some sort. And I'm wondering if there is some applicability to "techie" products or something, because I wonder if the high you get from certain products or from cool responsive things, does that make a difference like the difference you get when you're sitting next to a girlfriend?

Dan Ariely: [31:31] I'll tell you what I think, the reason writing software is so exciting is because we actually had a very hard time seeing the product of our creation in the marketplace. Most people have jobs that they do part of something and most of it is just lost.

We're really kind of in the Charlie Chaplin days [in the movie *Modern Times*], we're moving away from days when we created something to days when we're creating a *part* of something and often the part of what we created doesn't seem particularly useful, exciting, or doesn't even see the light of day.

And software is not like that because you get to actually do something, you get to do something complete, you get to see it working, which is very exciting. And I think that's part of the intoxicating aspect of it.

Dan Bricklin: [32:20] So, given that it's intoxicating, what does that mean?

Dan Ariely: [32:24] I think it means that it's very much a rewarding process. There's a lot of work that was done in the '60s on animal learning, and Skinner was the most known of course, and casinos are the ones who were using it most routinely in day-to-day life.

When we found out the schedule of reinforcement—that if a rat pecks a key or presses a lever 10 times and it gets the pellet, it's not as exciting. But, if it's a random number between 1 and 100, even when you take the food away, the rat just keeps on doing it for a long time.

And I think software's a little bit like that. When you write something you don't know who will use it and what reward you will get and if it will work or if it won't work. When it does, it's such a high and it actually keeps us going for a very, very long time.

Dan Bricklin: [33:15] It's like you hit bug after bug and then finally you get it, and the thing computes correctly.

Dan Ariely: [33:21] And that's really a part of understanding the meaning of labor, which is something that we just do really badly. All the theories we have about production of labor are like when labor is aversive and people do it because they just want to be paid and they hate doing it, it's kind of old philosophy.

But, really trying to understand where the motivation is and the passion and the enjoyment and the affiliation, I think, we just don't understand it as an academic discipline. And the open source community is the most interesting part of it because there you just have joy so it's clearly just that part.

Dan Bricklin: [34:02] Let's see, going through some of your other parts, procrastination and self-control, is there anything there applicable?

Dan Ariely: [34:10] Actually, procrastination and self-control is the idea that when we get emotional we behave differently, sometimes we behave in a very bad way. The best example, of course, is safe sex; most people think they won't have affairs or when they have sex, they'll have safe sex, but when the moment comes and people get aroused, they do things that they wish they hadn't.

Dan Bricklin: [34:37] You did research to find that out.

Dan Ariely: [34:39] [laughs] That's right. So, we found that people become so different that they don't realize themselves how different they would become. For example, people think that they will use condoms in different situations, but when they get aroused, they all of a sudden really change their mind in a way that they don't appreciate beforehand.

By the way, that's one of the reasons why there are so many STDs among kids who are in the "Just Say No" camp. Why? Because in a cold state, when they're unaroused, they say no; when they get hot, they say yes, and they don't have a condom. And, as a consequence, they even have more STDs than kids who are not in the "Just Say No" camp.

Dan Bricklin: [35:20] Because, you go through the research in the book, that really your decision making does change.

Dan Ariely: [35:26] And it does change in ways that we don't predict. When we get angry or hungry or any of those emotions, we become different people. You can think of it evolutionarily. So if you're an animal in a jungle and you see a tiger, you don't want to start thinking, "Is this good, is this bad, what should I do, what are my options?" You want a system that takes over and executes a command. You want it outside of your consideration.

And this is what emotions do; they make us into different people and execute on the emotions. So, when we're angry, we can say things that we would never say when we're not. By the way, the same thing with our spouses; when they get angry, they can also say things they wouldn't. It's just hard for us to understand that they are different people at that moment.

Dan Bricklin: [36:08] They really are. From what your measurements are, it isn't that they were latently that way, it's that things actually change.

Dan Ariely: [36:15] That's right. I think that, going back to our issue, the question is that when people get excited about those things, they do get into a very different mindset, and the same thing happens when they get annoyed.

Dan Bricklin: [36:40] So, working on something that you're annoyed about is different than working on something that makes you feel good about it.

Dan Ariely: [36:48] That's right. Now, let me give you one of my hopes for the open source community. If you understand some of those problems, if you understand that when you're in the hot state you're different than in a cold state, you might actually think: How do you solve some of the social problems we have? How do you solve impulse shopping? How do you solve lack of savings? How do you solve the problem that in the here and now nobody wants to go through aversive medical testing, but in the long term it's good for us? And think about what are the software solutions that actually augment the kind of things we're not good at.

So, think about—actually think generally about where do people fail, what are the things that we don't do well? So one of the things we don't do well is we don't think about the opportunity cost of money.

When you go to buy a cup of coffee at Starbucks you don't really think about what else could you do with this $2.50. In fact, even when people go to buy a Toyota, they don't think about what they're giving up in the future because of that.

Can you think about software that would help us understand what it is that we're giving up when we're doing that? Or with emotions, how do you create software that binds people's decisions for the future?

So, credit cards really work against us because we always have too much credit and we're always tempted. And it's in the here and now, and we don't feel any pain when we pay that because we always—it's a delayed payment. How would a gentler, kinder, humane credit card look like?

One of the things I'm proposing in the book is a self-controlled credit card where you as a—when you're unaroused and unexcited, and don't see anything, you would say, "How do I want to spend my money? I don't want to spend more than $20 a week on coffee, and I don't want to spend more that $40 a week on 'X,' and I don't want to spend more than $200 a month on clothes, and I want something to happen when I bypass this. I want an email sent to my wife; I want something that the community will know."

What kind of mechanisms can we use to get people to behave more in line with what's good for us?

Dan Bricklin: [39:02] Mm, hmm.

Dan Ariely: [39:02] Again the domains are saving and health care. [They] are the two big ones.

Dan Bricklin: [39:05] You're right with that. Another section you have has to do with the high price of ownership. How we overvalue what we have. Which is sort of like getting stuck once you're—this is being involved in a project and wanting to stay in a project. Is that . . .

Dan Ariely: [39:22] Yes, so I think, in the open source world this has both positive and negative. When we create something, we fall in love with it. We love it, we get attached to it. As a consequence, we're willing to spend a lot of effort to keep it going and to keep its influence on. And that's very good.

Dan Bricklin: [39:41] So that's one of the reasons why it works, is that you— once you're with something, you'll stay with it even if there may be something that is technically as good or maybe a little better. You'll still overvalue what you're in and you'll think your thing is good enough—is so much better you'll keep it going. Which is part of the reason that you don't have to worry about staying with an old product that may be obsolete. Kind of because there's people that keep it going anyway. Is that . . .

Dan Ariely: [40:06] That's right. So . . .

Dan Bricklin: [40:06] The psychology behind that.

Dan Ariely: [40:08] That's right. So, if people fall in love with what they create . . .

Dan Bricklin: [40:08] Yes.

Dan Ariely: [40:12] . . . it means that there will be longevity to that. You know I don't mean this in a funny way, but think about our kids. If I said, "How much would you sell your kid for?"

Dan Bricklin: [40:22] Yes.

Dan Ariely: [40:22] Right, people would give you a—I mean they would be outraged. But, outside of the outrage they would really value that kid incredibly. But, then if you asked them, "What if it wasn't your kid, they're just *somebody else's* kid and you saw this kid and you knew everything about them, how much would you pay for *that* kid?"

It's not that much. In some sense the value of the kid is not the attribute, it's the fact that it's yours. And when you create something that's a part of it.

By the way, I was amazed writing this book how much pride and ownership I feel about it. Much more than I expected to feel. Now . . .

Dan Bricklin: [40:57] Do you have the research like the one about the tickets to the ballgame at Duke, and how there's such a divergent difference between the same identical thing once when you have it vs. didn't have it? Even though you had to work just as hard in both cases.

Dan Ariely: [41:12] That's right. So, Duke has an interesting thing where people stand in line for a couple of days to get tickets for the Final Four;[9] and at the end of the day there are more students in line than there are tickets, so they do a lottery. So, usually when we have owners and non-owners, the owners chose to be owners, and the non-owners chose not to be owners. Here we had the situation that everybody wanted to participate.

Dan Bricklin: [41:33] And worked really hard to get there.

Dan Ariely: [41:35] And worked really hard to get there. And now we had people who became owner and not-owner, and the gaps between them are fantastic, are amazing. People who don't have the ticket are willing to spend $170 to get the ticket, and they think about it in very financial terms: What else they could do with the money?

People who have the ticket are not willing to get rid of it for $2,400, but—and they talk about it very differently. They talk about it as their crowning moment at Duke, and the experience of a lifetime. Something incredibly long-term.

---

[9] This experiment was conducted in 1994 when Duke played in the NCAA basketball championship game.

So, for the open source community there is a good and bad. The good is that when we create something, we love it, and we're willing to dedicate a lot to it.

The bad side is that we might love it too much, and even if it's not optimal, and as you said, it might not be the right technology, the optimal technology, we might still be too attached to it.

Dan Bricklin: [42:26] But from a viewpoint of somebody who is deciding to use an open source project that somebody else is supporting and all that, realizing that there are forces that mean that people may make it go longer than you would expect, which may make it more valuable, more reliable than you would have thought.

That a lot of these things—there are these forces in here that actually are—you have to take them into account because if you use your normal feeling of saying, "Oh, as soon as there is something better, it will be abandoned."

I was trying to understand why are all these projects that are out there? You know, why are they still supporting that old thing?

That this ownership, that shows that maybe it's worth taking a risk because, from a corporate viewpoint if you had corporations writing it, they're completely financial. And soon as it flips financially not worth it, the thing's dead, and there's no support.

Dan Ariely: [43:28] Yes, I think, that's a very nice perspective on this, is that the inefficiency from an individual perspective could be very efficient from somebody who is afraid of switching costs later on. And of course if corporations are really interested in it, the question is how do you create pride in something and actually prolong this period?

By the way I think, this same thing is about the "not invented here" phenomenon. As an MIT grad, I know you know this phenomenon. [laughs]

Dan Bricklin: [43:58] It's all over the place, yes. Whether a company feels that way or not. Yes.

Dan Ariely: [44:02] That's right. And I think, that's a part of this, is that the moment it's invented here it becomes the center of the universe, everything is valued relative to it. You know it's better, it's a part of your identity, and you're much more invested in it.

Dan Bricklin: [44:15] Or in the case of your community, once you're part of a community with that. And now there's a lot of social software, you know, and the Facebooks and stuff like that. . .

First of all, understanding the line between financial relationships and social relationships. You really have—it's a fine line, it's hard to understand, but it's not a linear—you go a little more a little less, is the . . .

You can mess things up if you get people the wrong way and—but these are very strong forces. And you have to understand that stuff, and that's why some things that seem like they shouldn't work do work. Is that . . .

Dan Ariely: [44:57] Yes. And I think, that's—just take Facebook as an example. What would happen if they start charging? Presumably, there are a lot of people now who experience a lot of value from those things.

You could imagine they could have started charging and just debate how much money they can make a month. I think the moment they started charging, it would switch the experience for many people. It would be a very different story, and maybe people would abandon them immediately.

It would be very hard to map the value of Facebook into $17.95 or $13.82 or something like that. The other thing is that Facebook has this fundamental social aspect to it, and I think the whole money-making endeavor could dramatically backfire. Because, depending on what they start charging, for some reason we're all willing to have these sidebars with advertising on Google and so on, and don't really look at them too badly. But, I think if they start doing other things, they might get into trouble.

Dan Bricklin: [45:58] As soon as we view people as money-grubbing "whatevers," it changes our relationship. We don't cut them slack and stuff like that.

Dan Ariely: [46:03] That's right. Now, it's a financial exchange, and we started viewing things very differently. So, imagine the Facebook crowd. How loyal are they to Facebook? How much are they willing to invest time in improving features and creating content, and doing stuff for the community. I think the moment the platform will become non-community-centered and financial, all of those things would go away.

Dan Bricklin: [46:31] Giving the right feeling of community and authenticity about that is so important, because as soon as you lose authenticity of whatever, you're in a different world and people act differently. And this affects all sorts of products we are talking about.

Dan Ariely: [46:45] That's right. Just for example, imagine that Microsoft all of a sudden created, gave a lot of infrastructure, to create some open source software in some domain, and they even promise that they will never, never sell it, right?

How likely would you [be] to develop something on the Microsoft platform, knowing it's Microsoft, right? I mean, this could be a completely separate initiative, and then they could be well-meaning. But, the moment they have this underlying structure, it will be very hard to forget that and use pure social norms for that.

Dan Bricklin: [47:22] Now, your whole thing, the way you work is that you are so experimental-centric, and it's like, "Let's do an experiment to figure things out." You're really into that, where all these things, like if you don't believe that social software works or open source works, because it feels wrong, we'll do an experiment to figure out and find a simple experiment. Is that right?

Dan Ariely: [47:46] Yeah, that's right, so I don't, I haven't done experiments on Open Source software. Of course, I would love to do it. We usually start by doing simple experiments.

Dan Bricklin: [48:01] So, how does a person come up with these simple— you seem to have this knack for coming up for, you're picking those but a lot of them are yours, that are really simple experiments to get to the essence of answering a question.

And the corporations, you're worried, either don't do any experiments or try to do too big an experiment rather than in a small area to answer some of these questions.

Dan Ariely: [48:21] That's right, I try to think about what is the psychological phenomenon that I want to isolate and what experiment would test that particular thing in the best way, in the simple way but it would, I would still feel, have some face validity about the real problem?

But, by the way, we don't stop there, so when we do an experiment about, people helping us move a sofa, we found something about willingness to help, and that's a great start, but now there's the second step of how will this play out in the world, so I can speculate about how this will play out in the world.

But, of course it will be great to do some real experiment, it's just that the world outside doesn't always give us these opportunities. And companies, it's a general thing, just don't experiment, almost never, and I just don't understand this, but they almost never do any experiments.

Dan Bricklin: [49:12] They don't believe, a lot of them, a company understanding that social things and lot of the other forces you've talked about, actually work and can be measured, to show that they work.

Just so, now we can, that you should take them into account, you shouldn't just say, we'll use financial measures because it's the only one. It's like that lamppost problem, why you've lost something over there, why are you searching here where the light's better.

It's that just because, you're used to those things, you should do experiments in the other area, even though you may feel it's wrong, it may be right about that or may be wrong.

Dan Ariely: [49:52] That's right, so I heard a great example today, about somebody who talked about the health care, for their employees. He basically said that they set up these financial incentives for people to do all kinds things and get money back for their health care, and people hated it.

In my world, in my world view, health care benefits is about social norms. It's about taking care of your employees, about showing your employees that you care about them. The moment you start translating into money and say, "I will give you this amount and you give me this amount," you take away all these social benefits of health care, which is the deepest way in which a company can tell its employees, "I am going to take care of you if something bad happens." And he said that the financial structure was perfectly fine and reasonable, but that's not how people operate.

Dan Bricklin: [50:41] So, one of the things about open source is that because it gets rid of the money, it gets rid of that issue, so suddenly we can be in the different space where it's more squishy and more, you can expect more of people, you get more.

You may not be able to depend as much or whatever, but it makes up for it, because not having money in it, that alone, ignoring any of the other altruistic reasons or stuff like that, just removing money from the equation, gives you some freedoms in crafting things.

Dan Ariely: [51:15] That's right. Actually, now that I think about it; I think that open source is a bit like Burning Man.[10] It's a society without money, that you and people just give each other stuff and it's really fantastic feeling. You know when I'll go to Burning Man and I give gifts to people, I feel good and they feel good, everybody is happy.

There are very different norms and the fact that these norms are allowed to emerge is because money is out of it.

Now the question for you is what do you think would happen if people didn't, I mean I think, paying is a bad thing, but we change the norms, what if people donated equipment or bandwidth or stuff like that? Would this be like gifts, that you're sharing?

Dan Bricklin: [51:59] So, being in the gift—so, that's the thing, because you found out that gifts are different than money. And so there're these different pieces we can start creating. I mean, open source was an experiment in a way. Where we got to find out that when you removed money, free (as in

---

[10]Burning Man (www.burningman.com) is an annual festival held in the Black Rock Desert in Nevada "... dedicated to community, art, self-expression, and self-reliance."

beer), you got rid of the money issues, then you could experiment in other ways, and that gives us freedom to find out that you can actually structure things differently.

Also, legally, it made it possible to do some of those things.

So, gifts are one area we can experiment with and 'cause there's the philosophical thing of "software wants to be free," and I should, you know, that's a valid thing for many people and that's one part, but as a business viewpoint looking at from the society, as we structure different ways of doing things. Maybe we should structure with other parts to it.

Dan Ariely: [52:55] Yeah, so you know I don't have the answer for this, but the implication of our research is that you could, you could give the community things in different ways, that wouldn't be money. It would bypass this ban on money.

Dan Bricklin: [53:09] So, a donation of bandwidth may be more important for a company doing that than just providing money. If you had to create a foundation or something, you give the foundation money, that's one thing. But if you just provide the free bandwidth or you provide the free service, which is much easier in many cases, that may actually work better.

Dan Ariely: [53:31] That's right, that's right and I wondered that, and on top of that of course is the question of, "Should the community create a hierarchy of social rewards?" Right? How do you build reputation in this thing?

Could we make a more a systematic way of reputation-building that would actually give people more social benefits from the work that they are doing?

Dan Bricklin: [53:58] And what your research has shown is that it's the difference in things, the relative difference that matters, not the absolute from many things, that people pricing things, their mindset based on some random number, like the last two digits of their security number, is enough to change their mindset of what is a reasonable amount of money to pay. And that everything after that becomes relative. Is that . . . ?[11]

Dan Ariely: [54:22] That's right, and what this basically says is that the force of this, of this social element, or the force of the society, or the emerging norms are amazing, because these norms of, what's an appropriate behavior,

---

[11]This refers to an experiment I had heard Dan talk about at one point in a presentation. As I recall, subjects were first asked to write down the last two digits of their Social Security number (an assumed random value) as a price for something. They then were asked to estimate prices for some variation. There was a correlation between the random starting number and the supposedly unrelated other numbers they then came up with. The starting number seemed to have a big influence on subsequent numbers.

and appropriate of contribution, and so on, have huge implications, because people would start judging themselves relative to those standards. Whatever standards you create are going to become the point of comparison.

Dan Bricklin: [54:48] Right, so the beginning really matters, where you first, what you normally reward people, how do you normally give attribution to people. How do you normally do this, you know, all of those initial things set the point, that then becomes the relative position, or the absolute position that everything is relative to after that.

Dan Ariely: [55:08] That's right, that's right.

Dan Bricklin: [55:10] Well, thank you very much! This was, God, we've been going on for, what is it, almost 50, 55 minutes. This is really amazing, thank you very much Dan.

For those of you listening to this: I've been talking to Dan Ariely, and the book is called *Predictably Irrational* and I love the book, but on the other hand I know Dan, so I had a relationship, a social relationship, but I thought it was really cool and I hope you found this thing interesting. Thank you very much, Dan.

Dan as Announcer: [55:42] This recording was produced by Dan Bricklin, as part of the Dan Bricklin's Log Podcast Series. To find out about other recordings I've done, go to Bricklin.com.

Learning About Cooperation from the Navy

The next set of interviews is with Vice Admiral (Ret.) John Morgan of the U.S. Navy. I became acquainted with John at a series of conferences hosted by Diamond Management and Technology Consultants. I am a "Diamond Fellow," which means I can go to these get-togethers with senior corporate executives along with other Diamond Fellows, such as computer pioneers Alan Kay and Gordon Bell, MIT Media Lab's Andy Lippman and Dan Ariely, and University of Chicago Graduate School of Business professor Marvin Zonis. In recent years, some senior people in the U.S. Navy have also been attending, joining the corporate executives.

As I did with Dan Ariely, earlier in the chapter, I recorded an interview with John Morgan during a break in one of the conferences. (I routinely travel to such things with podcast-recording equipment just in case I find an opportunity to share my hallway discussions with the readers of my blog.) A year and a half later, after he retired from the Navy in the summer of 2008, I recorded another interview with John over the phone to take a longer-term perspective.

It's nice to talk about theories of cooperation, but you do also have to look to real-world experiences. Instead of thinking how in the future we might communicate in the control room of the Starship Enterprise in science fiction, here I get to ask questions of someone who actually commanded the USS Enterprise in war. As Deputy Chief of Naval Operations, he was involved in life-and-death issues around the world and helped set the new strategy for the Navy.

To give some background, I start with this essay, written at a point in time between the two interviews:

December 27, 2007

TRUST AND COOPERATION CANNOT BE SURGED: FROM U.S. MARITIME STRATEGY TO THE LITTLE PRINCE AND THE FOX

Repeated simple encounters (in person or electronically) help develop trust and friendships.

Social software is a hot area in today's world. Facebook is valued at over $10 billion, Wikipedia and other wikis are major sources of information, and Twitter is captivating many industry pundits. Millions of people participate in special moments in other people's lives through YouTube. Short text messages connect a huge portion of the world's population and are a major carrier of social contact for a whole generation.

At first glance, a lot of what goes on in these communications channels seems mundane and worthless. As I've pointed out, though, in my "What will people pay for?" essay back in July 2000,[12] people like to interact with people they care about. The interactions are often simple and repetitive, but personally important. They are willing to pay money for this.

There is another aspect, though. These social systems, by allowing (and encouraging) repeated, simple, personal interactions, actually help build community and trust. Understanding how that happens is important.

I want to look at two references that might help. One is from the Chief Naval Officer, and the other is from Antoine de Saint-Exupéry's *The Little Prince*.

Let me start with a community of cooperating organizations and people that is "a matter of consequence" (to borrow a term from *The Little Prince*, but I mean it for real). When Admiral Mike Mullen was Chief of Naval Operations (the CNO—the head of the U.S. Navy) he advocated the "1,000-ship Navy."

---

[12]Found in this book in Chapter 2.

This is a pooling of the resources among nations, a community of trust that includes the sharing of information among navies of countries that may otherwise be untrusting of each other for political or economic reasons. A "free-form, self-organizing network of maritime partners." This is a somewhat informal relationship, more like the one that grew the Internet than the command-and-control style of more traditional military or corporate relationships.

Admiral Mullen himself talks about it in a series of podcasts that he did starting in June 2007. (These are a little hard to find on the Navy's web site, but I found the old RSS feed[13] on this page.[14]) One of his podcasts (here's the MP3 file[15]) included a description of his return to Vietnam, this time not in a war but rather to meet with his counterpart. In addition, I have a recorded interview that I did with Vice Admiral John Morgan (who worked with Admiral Mullen) in March 2007 where he explains this "community of trust." (For more about the 1,000-ship Navy and the podcast, see my blog post "Interview with Vice Admiral John Morgan: Building a community of trust in a Pier-to-Pier world."[16])

Admiral Mullen is now [(in late 2007)] the new Chairman of the Joint Chiefs of Staff. The new CNO, Admiral Gary Roughead, recently restarted the CNO Podcast series with his own podcast.[17] While listening to the first installment of Admiral Roughead's podcast series I was struck by his explanation of how to build up this community among the naval personnel in different countries. He elaborated on a phrase in the Maritime Strategy document presented in October 17, 2007, at the International Seapower Symposium, "A Cooperative Strategy for 21st Century Seapower."[18] The phrase, on page 11, is: "Trust and cooperation cannot be surged." He explains (at about 9:30 in the podcast) that when he sits down and has tea with the heads of other navies, it is often the first time that they've met. He hopes that by participating in activities together over the years, the younger officers of today will develop lifelong friendships with their counterparts. Then, when they sit down for that cup of tea, they are not sitting down for the first time, but are talking as friends. He believes that

---

[13]http://web.archive.org/web/20070920104436/http://www.navy.mil/podcast/cno/cno.xml

[14]http://www.navy.mil/podcast/podcast.asp

[15]http://www.navy.mil/media/audio/cno/CNO-PODCAST-062607.mp3

[16]http://danbricklin.com/log/2007_01_25.htm#navy

[17]http://www.navy.mil/navydata/cnopList.asp

[18]http://www.navy.mil/maritime/MaritimeStrategy.pdf

if we do that, the problems of the world, the issues that we face, will be much easier solved than they are today.

What I hear him saying is that it takes time and repeated interactions to develop trust. Those interactions may be as simple as having tea or doing training exercises together, but they build up trust over time. This trust is a key ingredient for cooperation-based organizations. Remember the rationale for the 1,000-ship Navy: We can't provide all those ships ourselves, we have to cooperate with others to build the big navy out of many smaller ones, and that cooperation-based organizations are a more efficient way of getting things done at a large scale.

The use of the word "surge" (instead of the more common "hurried," "rushed," etc.) stuck out when I heard it, given that it's a word with heavy political connotations today. Thinking about it a bit, I can see the concept used to support a wide range of different opinions about the war in Iraq, but I won't follow that further. However, I think the use was a signal that this is something important to think about for our country and the world, and it may have life-and-death consequences. (Or maybe it's just a common military expression . . .)

This brings us to *The Little Prince*. Starting back in December 2000, when I discuss online community building, I often make reference to Antoine de Saint-Exupéry's book, *The Little Prince*. In light of today's social software, even more so than the growing popularity of blogs in those days, it is worth reading all of chapter 21, the story of the Little Prince and the fox (it is so much better written than what I can paraphrase, and I want to respect the copyright—I'm sitting next to my copy as I write this).

The Little Prince encounters a fox and asks the fox to play with him. The fox replies that he can't play with the Little Prince because he isn't tamed. He explains that "taming" means to "establish ties." If they establish those ties, then they will need each other. They will each be unique to the other. And, this great quote: "One only understands the things that one tames." Taming takes time. It takes repeated simple encounters. It takes simple "rites" that make certain times special. The Little Prince "tames" the fox by visiting each day, first sitting at a distance, and then moving closer. The closing thought: "You become responsible, forever, for what you have tamed."

This idea, that repeated simple encounters (in person or, today, electronically) help develop trust and friendships, is an important concept to grasp. The Navy gets it (they've been building cooperating teams for hundreds of years). The CNO emphasizes the importance of the growth in understanding of others that occurs. We should look to this idea, too, in our evaluation of social software. People may make fun of blog or Twitter posts about what someone had for breakfast or how they like a certain video game, but it is all part of how humans build a cooperating society that works. It can't be rushed, and it can be nurtured, even with simple text messages.

http://www.bricklin.com/trustthrutime.htm

John Morgan, March 5, 2007[19]

Dan Bricklin: [00:00] Hi this is Dan. I'm at the Diamond Management and Technology Consultants Exchange Conference and with me is Vice Admiral John G. Morgan. He's Vice Admiral and Deputy Chief of Naval Operations. Hi.

John Morgan: [00:14] Hi Dan. How are you?

Dan: [00:15] Fine. So what is your position? What does it mean to be the Deputy Chief of Naval Operations?

John: [00:20] Well actually, my portfolio is current operations around the world, and also I act as the strategist for the Navy. So, I advise the head of the Navy, Admiral Mike Mullen, in his role as what we call the Chief of Naval Operations. So, I sort of look at both today and tomorrow.

Dan: [00:38] OK. So tell me, you're going around the country and you're talking to people about new thinking and stuff like that. What are you telling people? What's interesting is we are at a conference here where we're talking about competing in the networked economy.

John: [00:55] Right.

Dan: [00:57] And yet, we're talking about the Navy. We're talking about peer-to-peer, whereas I think Paul Carroll said that the Navy would spell peer-to-peer differently than those of us in the computer industry. And I actually heard Navy and wikis mentioned as related—not that they'd use them, but that their thinking is similar. How does all this fit?

John: [01:16] Right. Well, I think that there's a lot in common between the Navy's interest, corporate interests here in the United States, even academic interest. And here's what the common intersection is . . . The common intersection is, we are all dealing in an era of profound change. We're seeing rapid change in technology. I think we're seeing change in economic markets. I think

---

[19]http://danbricklin.com/podcast.html#danbcast-2007-03-07-22-24-06

we're seeing change in relationships around the world. I think we're seeing new players come on the scene. How do we fit into that? What contribution does the Naval Service make in that profoundly changing world?

Under Admiral Mullen's leadership, what we're doing, Dan, is we are rethinking the maritime strategy for the country. This country has always been organized around its maritime interests. The original 13 colonies had 13 sea ports—whether they were on the oceans or major rivers. It's really one of the key influences in our history as a country.

Dan: [02:16] So what changes are you making? What are we moving from? You always think of guns and boats. So how are you changing the Navy?

John: [02:26] Well, here's what we're doing—we recognized some key attributes to this planet. First of all, 70 percent of the planet is water. 80 percent of the world's population lives within 200 miles of a coast, and 90 percent of the world's commerce flows across the oceans. When you realize, in those terms, what vast interest we have in being a sea power nation, we now have to say, "In light of that profound change that's going on, how do we have to change as an institution?"

Dan: [03:06] So how does that relate to . . . well, there's this thought of a 1,000-ship Navy, when we don't have 1,000 ships.

John: [03:12] Right.

Dan: [03:15] There's the issue of like what we saw during Katrina, and the tsunami, and Lebanon, where the Navy did things that aren't normally what you think of as the Navy. How does that all fit?

John: [03:26] Here's how it fits—let me step back one step further. Right now, because of the background factors that I've just given you, we're actually embarked upon an effort that we call "Conversation with the Country." We're actually going around to major cities in the country, not just coastal cities but major cities in the country, to talk with Americans about: Historically, we understand how sea power has helped us get where we are, but where is sea power going to take us in the future?

And then there are some interesting concepts like the "1,000-ship Navy." We recognize that we're the most powerful Navy on the face of the earth, but we have our limitations. Because of the changing nature of the players involved, we're looking at efforts of how we can do cooperative security without having to be a member of a fancy organization or an alliance. It's actually playing pretty well. People are interested in how we can help each other, we can recognize our own sovereign rights, we can take care of our own economic interest, but we can approach things from a cooperative way in terms of maritime power. It's all pretty interesting.

Dan: [04:35] I heard it explained like: In New York City, after a baseball game the taxis show up but there's no organizing automatic thing—it's sort of self-organizing. You're talking about rather than an "us in control," telling everybody what to do, something more cooperative, which is where we're talking wiki-like. Give an example of that.

John: [04:55] Well, a couple of examples. One was certainly the tragic tsunami that hit Banda Aceh [in December 2004]. There was nobody from Washington or London or Bonn or Tokyo or Beijing that ordered all those ships there—they just sort of showed up. They showed up because people were in distress, they just simply wanted to help. So that's a great example.

The same thing happened in Katrina [in August 2005]. Naval vessels from all over the world started showing up off of New Orleans. U.S. Navy ships arrived, other navies sent their ships to help, carrying food and medical supplies, reconstruction supplies. Sometimes that's the only way you can get there

Dan: [05:35] How is the decision made? Did the ship captain say, "Hey everybody! Let's turn around! Quick, let's go there," or . . . ?

John: [05:41] No. In some cases in the U.S. Navy we certainly have the ability to do that to an extent—I mean we follow a certain form and structure, so we can't always make it up as we go. But when anybody's in distress, we have latitude to suddenly turn and go help. But so do other countries, and that's the nature of being a seaman.

Dan: [06:08] What is that nature? I hear this, that there's something interesting here. The Navy—obviously in the computer industry, because the Navy funded the original ARPA work and stuff like that led to a lot of computing we know, the ARPAnet, etc. There's a history there, but there's a history that goes back much further about what it means to be on the sea helping others. Is that right?

John: [06:30] Well, I think part of our culture in the Navy is that we probably have a well-deserved reputation of being pretty independent, and that independence comes because when you go to sea, you're often alone. The captain of a ship and his or her crew really have to fight those elements, and historically ships would sail off for months, if not years, with no orders whatsoever, and then come back. So, culturally it's ingrained in us to be able to think quickly on our feet, to react to a very dynamic environment called the ocean—storms come up and go down and bad weather blows through, very seldom do things go as scripted, so culturally we're sort of known for being able to adapt very quickly.

Dan: [07:23] How about, though, cooperating? Having the fact that you have to be able to cooperate with people who are ostensibly enemies, per se, or at least people that you're in heavy competition with.

John: [07:33] Right. Here's a unique bond that we all share if you go to sea: That is that we have one common enemy, and that's the ocean. The ocean is the most powerful force on the face of the earth, I think. We all have a hearty respect for the ocean because of its power. We want to be good stewards of the ocean. It's those characteristics that unite us regardless what of our political differences are, so when anybody's in distress on the seas, everybody tries to help.

Dan: [08:05] How are we seeing this? I know there are issues to deal with—there's piracy out there that affects commerce, etc. Are we seeing some benefits of this attitude, this cooperation, already?

John: [08:17] Absolutely! One of the best specific examples I can give you is in the Straits of Malacca around Singapore, where three countries, Singapore, Malaysia, and Indonesia, have all said, "Hey, let's cooperate together. Let's make sure that because these vital sea lanes are so important through the Straits of Malacca, that we want to patrol them together, we want to look for transnational crime, we want to look for illegal immigration, we want to stop piracy." And over the course of the last 3 or 4 years they've made remarkable progress—so much so that the piracy incidents in the Straits of Malacca are significantly down. Lloyd's of London has reduced their insurance rates going through the Straits of Malacca because of it. It's just a shining example of what cooperative security can be.

Dan: [09:01] So this idea of cooperating, you're being a model in some ways as the rest of us are trying to figure out about companies cooperating. This whole thing—open source movement obviously cares about this stuff. Sharing secrets and data with people who you used to keep things apart from—that's a military thing now? That's the way we do things?

John: [09:34] We are certainly exploring better ways to build that community, and it's a community of trust. There's a lot of unclassified information that heretofore we had not been sharing and we're going out of our way now to share that information. We think it's to everybody's benefit. You know, we may be a model in some respects, but we look to technologists like you and leading corporations who are pioneering new ways of doing business, and we're saying, "Will that work for us? Can we do it that way?" And so, it gets back to sort of that independent nature of ours that we're willing to say, "Oohh, that's a good idea, and how can we apply it?"

Dan: [10:18] And you're taking technology and giving it to others and stuff like that?

John: [10:22] Yes. One of the technological solutions we have right now is a system called the Automatic Identification System, AIS. It's like a little OnStar,[20] you know, on your ship. And, what we try to do is we just share locating information of where all the ships are in the oceans.

And, there are now international standards that say if you're greater than 300 metric tons, you're required to have one of these systems. Can we enforce that around the world? I mean, it's not ours, the U.S. Navy's, to do that, but slowly but surely, those standards are being established, they're being complied to, and we in the United States Navy are installing them on all of our ships.

Dan: [11:05] This is a cooperative effort and it's sort of ad hoc? It's sort of like you guys go off, a few of you admirals go off and talk to some of their admirals, and then you sort of make the decision, with OK from on top, I guess, but that's, is it, I mean it's not like there's an organization gets together that votes and then goes down to its members, or . . .

John: [11:27] Well, it's not necessarily a formal organization, but it's not a group of ad hoc admirals like myself just going around and calling up your friends. I mean, actually, the Chief of Naval Operations, Admiral Mike Mullen, who heads our Navy, he actually sponsors what's called an International Sea Power Symposium. And, in September of 2005, a year and a half ago, he held a conference. He held that symposium in Newport, Rhode Island. And, he gathered 50 heads of navies from around the world. And, he proposed this notion at that conference about the 1,000-ship Navy. How can we help each other? How can we build this community to cooperate along the lines of 1,000-ship Navy? And from there, it sort of took off.

You really need to credit him with his strong leadership. And now, there are regional symposiums around the world. There's a regional symposium in Europe. There's one in South America. There's even one in Africa now, certainly out in Asia, where navies of the world get together and say, "Well, what works in the Mediterranean may not work in the Straits of Gibraltar."

---

[20]OnStar is a product from General Motors for communications in automobiles. Among other things, it can let a remote OnStar emergency operator know where your vehicle is in the event of an airbag deployment.

But, now we're sharing best practices. The U.S. doesn't always lead. We're happy—there was just a Pakistani admiral in charge of coalition forces in the north Arabian Sea. And so, this is really gaining momentum.

Dan: [12:55] It's interesting because I know that in the tech world we're having a lot of these gatherings, conferences, or un-conferences, for people to sort of talk about what's interesting, and things come out of it . . .

John: [13:04] Right.

Dan: [13:05] . . . hack-o-thons or something . . .

John: [13:06] Sure.

Dan: [13:07] . . . so basically, it's you get together, somebody has some ideas. And so, it isn't like a governing body which has official heads, but it's the schmoozing in the hallways and stuff like that, so to speak?

John: [13:19] Yeah, and it goes, it probably goes beyond schmoozing, but doesn't arise to, you know, to the central committee of NATO, you know. So, there's something in between there.

Dan: [13:30] OK. But, it's more ad hoc and more relationship-oriented?

John: [13:34] I think it's more about it being a community. I really do. How do you build that chat room, those network friends, that community there? So, it's really about those types of relationships.

Dan: [13:49] Now, thinking about community, in the Navy, when you're on a ship, you have a community.

John: [13:53] We do.

Dan: [13:54] Right. And, when you have your Special Forces . . .

John: [13:56] Yes.

Dan: [13:58] . . . that's a real tight community.

John: [13:58] That's a very tight community.

Dan: [14:01] And, a lot of peer-to-peer type of work, too . . .

John: [14:03] Yes.

Dan: [14:03] . . . in terms of how they work. So, you've learned stuff. Are you applying ideas from that? Because I'm learning from the conference we're sitting at, we're hearing Navy people and corporate people talk about working with their competitors, working with other companies outside. We're all sort of feeling our way there.

John: [14:22] Sure.

Dan: [14:23] So, what have you learned? Is that from that area you've learned?

John: [14:26] Well, I think so. Certainly internally we learn in that way, and also externally. I mean, we watch how other navies operate. We welcome other navies to participate with us. We just had a major exercise last summer where we invited the Chinese to come to sea with us. So, we think it's very, very important to have military-to-military relationships, even with potential adversaries.

We would certainly love to see the day where we're all constructive rivals, not destructive rivals. But, even if there is some tension, if you have a military-to-military relationship already established, you can pick up a phone, you can say, "Wait a minute, I'm not sure I understand why tensions are rising here." And, you certainly want to avoid mistakes.

We recognize that we don't live in a perfect world. But one of the great contributions I think that the Navy makes is that one of our core strategic missions is, one, to prevent the next war if we can. And if conflict does break out, we want to limit and localize the conflict.

Dan: [15:36] One of the roles of the Navy is it isn't just to whomp the other guy. You can bring a ship into, near another country, for example, or a city . . .

John: [15:46] Right.

Dan: [15:47] . . . without invading . . .

John: [15:47] Right.

Dan: [15:48] . . . and you can leave without leaving a trace . . .

John: [15:50] Right.

Dan: [15:50] . . . just a wake behind you, but that you provide other services. So, is that part of your mission? If I was, you know, counseling somebody about should they go into the Navy or something like that, what other than, you know, that I'm defending my country militarily, what else am I doing?

John: [16:10] Well, in the Navy, and my hat's off to all the services. We all have our own cultures to some degree. We try to work very closely together. But, one of the things about the Navy that probably a lot of people don't understand is that we have both what I call "soft power" and "hard power." The phrase was coined by somebody else, but it's a good description. And, in some times it's our soft power that we can bring to bear that will help prevent that war or prevent that crisis, avoid it altogether.

And then, if the soft power doesn't work, then we can bring our hard power to bear. Perhaps not by employing our fire power, but by just arriving. And, maybe that's enough to deter an untoward action until diplomats can step in and say, "Let's go to our corners here." And so, we try to avoid this conflict.

Dan: [17:04] What are some of the soft power things you do? Examples.

John: [17:08] Well, after everybody rushed to help in Banda Aceh, about 7 months later we sent our hospital ship, Mercy, back. She spent about 5 months in Indonesia, saw close to 150,000 patients, issued I think it was 11,000 pairs of eyeglasses. This is the largest Muslim country in the world, and we were there to help. And so, long after the crisis had subsided, we came back. And, our hospital ships are great examples of our soft power.

But, we have Seabees[21] who can go in and help reconstruct areas after they're damaged. They build schools. They build roads. There are all kinds of things that we can bring to bear in terms of our soft power.

Dan: [17:54] OK. Anything else that, did you try to make sure that, you know, you want your audiences to know that may be a misconception, or just to, you know, about the Navy or about how people who, like a person who's chosen a career like you've chosen . . .

John: [18:11] Right.

Dan: [18:12] . . . to serve your country this way about that?

John: [18:15] Well, I think if there's any one central message that I'd like to make sure people are aware of, it is that sea power has played an enormous role in our country's history. I firmly believe it's going to play a big role in our future. And, to be candid, I worry sometimes that the sea power elements of our history are now taken for granted and are not well understood.

Any means we can to talk about and debate the merits of sea power, that's why we're going around and having this conversation with the country, not necessarily to convince people, and quite honestly, we actually listen more than we talk. And, we've been delighted at the response that we've gotten in the major cities we've gone into.

I appreciate the opportunity to sit down with you today to discuss this.

Dan: [19:03] Oh, I appreciate that. The image I get with this so much of commerce traveling over the sea . . .

John: [19:08] Right.

Dan: [19:09] . . . and, almost all of the international electronic commerce traveling under the sea . . .[22]

John: [19:13] Right.

Dan: [19:14] . . . that you're protecting . . .

John: [19:15] Right.

Dan: [19:15] . . . and fixing, or whatever. I mean that's, it's important.

---

[21]Seabees are the Construction Battalions (CBs) of the U.S. Navy.

[22]This is a reference to underwater communications cables used for Internet and other purposes.

John: [19:19] And, also to protect the environment. We think we are good stewards of the environment. And, we want to protect the environment. So, you have the environment, you've got the commerce that's flowing on top of the sea, the infrastructure that's now underneath the sea. We think, as I said, the definition of geography alone where 70 percent of the planet is water, we think it's important we need to take good care of it.

Dan: [19:46] Thank you very much.

John: [19:47] OK, great, Dan.

John Morgan, September 25, 2008[23]

Dan Bricklin: [0:00] Hi, this is Dan, and with me is retired Vice Admiral John Morgan of the U.S. Navy. Admiral Morgan has an economics degree from the University of Virginia. He entered the U.S. Navy in 1972 and for the next 36 years was steeped in the practical side of planning, execution and organizational leadership.

On September 11, 2001, John was commanding 10,000 men and women of the USS Enterprise Carrier Group, just then exiting the Strait of Hormuz. Upon getting word of the second plane hitting the World Trade Center, he immediately turned the group—on his own authority—to be the first in the theatre of operations against Al-Qaeda and the Taliban.

Morgan capped his Navy career as a key adviser to Mike Mullen, then Chief of Naval Operations and, starting in 2007, Chairman of the Joint Chiefs. In that capacity he directed the creation of "A Cooperative Strategy for 21st Century Seapower."

Two years in the making, the global strategy is now in effect and reflects the input of national and international leaders in business, military, civic organizations, and think tanks, and is aimed at protecting vital interests in an increasingly interconnected and changing world.

Welcome, John.

John Morgan: [1:13] It's great to be with you today, Dan.

Dan: [1:15] Thanks a lot for being willing to do another podcast with me. You've worked on both operations and on strategy, what's going on today, and what's going on tomorrow. You have a vast experience in a variety of diverse areas. And having retired after 36 years, I think I'd like to take advantage of that perspective, asking some questions.

---

[23]http://danbricklin.com/podcast.html#danbcast-2008-09-26-03-54-45

Here's where I'm coming from. I'm not a person with a military background, and I'm not looking at the current military situation in the Middle East or U.S. party politics in this discussion. I have interests as part of the high-tech ecosystem and the economy that creates new systems and provides new tools for the world.

And when I say tool, I mean it very generally—it's systems and products that leverage people. I have personal experience of how designing the right tool can leverage millions of others in their work to do a better job. And we're now building systems that provide the new fabric through which much of interpersonal communications takes place.

It's enabled by computing power, the Internet, and ubiquitous connectivity. It went from email to MySpace, Facebook, YouTube, blogs, Wikipedia, the original Napster, and Skype. And now with mobile we have SMS text messaging,[24] iPhone, Twitter, Qik with live video [streamed from cell phones], and they connect millions and millions of people. So, my questions will be driving at information that can be useful in that context.

First, anything about your background that people may not get from the short bio that might be helpful?

John: [2:54] Well, Dan, you and I have grown up in different worlds, but it's interesting that we've arrived at a common point of view. I admire the work that you have done across your adult life, and I think your efforts to try to find systems and products that leverage each other for the betterment of mankind is exactly where I am at the end of my 36-year naval career.

Dan: [3:24] My background as an MBA and as an engineer gives me a particular viewpoint. What would be the viewpoint of somebody with your background, having commanded large fleets and strategies for countries and having the weight of the world on your shoulders?

John: [3:41] Dan, you know it's funny, as you've described your interests and as I concluded that my interests were very much along the lines that you are pursuing. I'll tell you; here's the higher thought that's important to both of us. Despite our different upbringings and perspectives, we both would agree that there's a global system at work right now. And that global system is very important to maintain.

I tried to defend and protect that global system and in so doing I think you have, too. You tried to understand the inner connectivity of that global system and make it work more efficiently.

---

[24]SMS (Short Message Service) refers to the technology behind text messages on cell phones, also known as "texting."

Dan: [4:24] OK, so that's where your goals are. Let me ask some questions about what you've seen over these 36 years. We have to get this question out of the way: How has the role of computer technology changed in the Navy?

John: [4:43] It's been a huge change. For instance, just for us to be able to gather what we call situation awareness, high-speed computing has brought that kind of information to us all the time. And it's only gotten better and better and better over time.

My ability, when I was the commander of the Enterprise Carrier Group off of Afghanistan after 9/11, was I was never at want for information. I had plenty of information. In fact, the challenge for the military commander is managing a lot of complex information and deciphering what's important and what's not.

High-speed computing has been essential to military commanders for their ability to have an accurate sense of the situation around them.

Dan: [5:35] And have you seen changes? How is it different doing something now than it was, let's say, back 30 years ago?

John: [5:44] Let me give you a very specific military example. You are right, I brought the Enterprise Battle Group south through the Straits of Hormuz on the night of the 10th of September, and on the 11th of September we watched the events unfold in New York and in Washington and in Pennsylvania and the reaction around the world, and we pressed up off the coast of Pakistan.

But, when we launched the first strike into Afghanistan we did so by firing Tomahawk cruise missiles.

And here's the technology example: We directed all those Tomahawk cruise missiles by means of a chat room. It's staggering.

Dan: [6:24] Chat?

John: [6:25] Yeah, by chat.

Dan: [6:26] You, running the aircraft carrier Enterprise and all that were using chat rooms?

John: [6:33] We were using a chat room for the Tomahawk cruise missiles. I can't go into the specifics because that gets classified. But, the use of now Internet tools like chat, obviously secure chat, is going on every day. The means of us exchanging large volumes of information from overhead satellite photography is because of our high-speed computing capabilities.

And our computer protection in defense is going to be very important to us in the future because militaries follow the trend of technologies, and this is one good example of it.

Dan: [7:12] So, back 30 years ago you weren't doing it that way?

John: [7:15] We were not doing it, no; 30 years ago there were no chat rooms. I don't want to tell you that every detail was passed through a chat room, that's not the case. But, the advent of chat rooms, and you find them around the world today with military applications, some can be classified, some are unclassified. But, chat rooms didn't exist 10 years ago, much less 30 years ago in military applications.

Dan: [7:42] One of the things about that is, with a chat room, as opposed to walkie-talkies, or the equivalent . . .

John: [7:47] Or radios.

Dan: [7:48] . . . radios . . . is that you have multiple people sharing and some people lurking,[25] some people talking?

John: [7:55] Absolutely, and it did a couple of things that I found fascinating. As I first looked at it I said, "We can't be doing it this way because that's not the way I grew up, this will never work."

But, what I found was, Dan, these two things: One, it made our command centers much more quiet. There were not people talking, multiple conversations going on on radios. It was all being done on computer screens. So, it almost induced a sense of calm and order and discipline.

The second thing it contributed to was this collaborative nature. That somebody somewhere could say, "Wait a minute, I think that's wrong." And that kind of information was made accessible to me as well. It was a very interesting combination of how new technology was being applied in the military scenario.

Dan: [8:53] It's not just new technology, it's the use of groups working together. Are these huge groups, medium groups?

John: [9:01] We had multiple ships, and each command center, my command center was probably the largest, but each command center must have had 30 or 40 people in it. I couldn't give you a tally of the number of people, but I would say there had to be a couple of hundred people in chat rooms.

Dan: [9:23] In one chat room? Now, is this one or are you doing multiple at the same time?

John: [9:27] They're multiple chat rooms.

Dan: [9:29] OK, boy! So, are these people who know each other face-to-face?

John: [9:34] Sometimes they've never met.

Dan: [9:37] The mixture is, in general, people who have worked with each other before? Are they people who are together for the first time?

---

[25]Lurking refers to following an online conversation but not participating.

John: [9:47] Well in the case of the Enterprise Battle Group, we had worked together closely for over a year, half of that time being before the group deployed and then during the 6-month deployment, which actually ended up being about 8, 8½ months.

All these people are located on different ships. So, they're obviously separated by space and distance across water obviously. So, it really was this collaborative group of people that may not necessarily have seen each other's face.

Dan: [10:21] Now, do people know the rank of people? Do they know anything about them, background or anything like that?

John: [10:30] I wouldn't say they're anonymous. I mean there certainly is a relationship in different, what we call "watch stations," where the senior officer present will be the senior person there, or the coordinator for a given mission will be probably a mid-grade officer. So, their identities were never hidden, but they were never as apparent as if you were in a command center together and you could see which rank a person you're talking to.

Dan: [11:00] So that when somebody participates, they could be talking to someone way over their rank without having to go through each of the steps going up?

John: [11:09] Either that, or certainly somebody much more senior to them could be observing on their computer screen what's going on in the chat room.

Dan: [11:17] So, you as commander could sit there and have a feel for what's going on, lurking. It's sort of like watching Twitter[26] in today's world.

John: [11:24] Yeah, that's a very good example.

Dan: [11:26] Wow! So that puts Twitter in a different perspective. Now, what about nontext stuff? You have all those images and stuff. How does that tie in—live video feeds, things like that?

John: [11:43] In many respects what we use that for in that specific application, was we would certainly look at that type of imagery as we prepared to launch missions, so we could understand that an anti-aircraft site wasn't completely destroyed. Should we have to continue to worry about that? We

---

[26]Twitter is an Internet service accessible through web browsers as well as normal cell phone text messaging. When you post a message, always 140 characters or less to meet the restrictions of cell phone texting, that message is added to the top of each of the combined lists of messages viewable by the other subscribers who are "following" you. That way, each person can view their own list of just the messages from people they are following. It is like a chat room with only those people you want in your room, but something you type shows up at the same time in all the other rooms that other people have made you a part of.

When I wrote of repeated, simple encounters in the "Trust and cooperation" essay earlier in this chapter, I was referring to systems like Twitter.

could watch for logistics flow, lines of trucks moving, anything along those lines.

We would certainly do that before we left for a mission, and then after a mission we call it a "damage assessment." Did we destroy the target that we wanted to get to? So, rapid access from imagery to do that was most helpful to us.

Dan: [12:29] To sort of pivot a little bit from that, over these years, how has the community aspects of ships and the Special Forces changed, over the last 30-something years?

John: [12:39] Well, I think that the Special Forces, and I know many of them well, and I've worked with them for well over 30 years. I think the need for Special Forces is obviously increasing. They bring such a diverse set of talents. They're so skillful in so many ways. Many times our Special Forces spend more time helping avert a conflict than actually fighting in a conflict.

They're obviously very heavily engaged in both Iraq and Afghanistan today, but they are a very, very special group of men, and they're doing remarkable things. I think because of the changing nature of conflict, and I think there's almost a new generational level of conflict that's about us, I think Special Forces will be increasingly important in the future.

Dan: [13:32] They're like a really cohesive group, and has their sense of community changed? Are things different with the technology of communications? Are they more connected now? Are they less connected now? How do they work with each other?

John: [13:49] Well, I think that they're more connected now, but I don't think it's affected their bond. I mean they are such a special and such an elite group that they fundamentally depend upon each other, more so than depending upon technology. They understand and take advantage of technology, all that it can bring to them. Their core of camaraderie, of being part of a team, of being part of a very elite group of people, I don't think that's changed at all, and if anything it's just stronger.

Dan: [14:23] Oh, is there a connection from them to the outside more, to the other forces and stuff like that, or has that more or less been the same?

John: [14:32] No, they're certainly well connected not only to other forces, but to the general situational and global awareness. So, they certainly take advantage of being much better connected today than they ever been, but it has not altered their core camaraderie.

Dan: [14:50] OK, and then what about ships, the community aspects of ships? Now that you can be on daily connectivity with your spouse and your family, is there any change in the community aspect? Are people, because of these chats and stuff like that, are they closer with people in the ships, any changes over the years?

John: [15:10] Well, I think they're closer with their families while they're so far away in distant places, and that's been a huge improvement. The ability to stay in touch with your loved ones at home, friends and family, has been an enormous benefit for all of us. That difference is light years than what it used to be just 10–15 years ago.

Dan: [15:34] So, it's not a distraction, it's viewed as a positive thing from on top?

John: [15:38] I think it is a positive thing. I think your thoughts are certainly about the mission at hand, but we in the military are not made of wood. We have emotional relationships, and I think if you're balanced emotionally, you're better prepared for your mission.

Dan: [15:58] Now, you talk a lot about community, like communities of trust and things like that in discussions we've had and writings you have. How do you define community? What are the attributes of a community?

John: [16:10] Oh, I think the attributes are grouping of people with similar aspirations, and ambitions, and desires, similar interests obviously; that's what brings a community together. It goes back to my point earlier about, the larger point here is about a global system, and the global system is made up of a variety of local systems.

It's that system approach, and I don't mean it in a pure system engineering approach, Dan. It's the notion that there's something that's larger than self, that you benefit by a community benefiting. It's that notion that's central to where I think you're channeling your efforts, and where I'm now channeling my efforts.

Dan: [17:03] What have you learned about self-forming groups, or enhancing cohesion? Obviously, that's one of the things you have to do when you have new recruits and stuff like that on the ship. Self-forming groups are things that come about on their own or something, or like the experience you had putting together the 1,000-ship Navy.

John: [17:24] Indeed, Dan. I think self-forming groups are very important. I was watching a video on "TED Talks" by Clay Shirky.[27] Clay gave a presentation in Oxford, I think in 2005. He spoke about how institutions in the future

---

[27]http://www.ted.com/index.php/talks/clay_shirky_on_institutions_versus_collaboration.html

are going to be challenged by what he called "interactive infrastructures," and I think Clay was exactly right.

I think interactive infrastructures, communities in some cases, can be very, very powerful things. Clay's assertion is that they're going to become more powerful over time. It may take some time. It may take 30 or 40 or 50 years. He sees the emergence of interactive infrastructures as almost akin to the advent of the printing press.

Dan: [18:18] How's that applying to some of the stuff that you've been involved with?

John: [18:22] I think military men and women aren't any different from citizens in the United States, or around the world. I mean any tool that we have, and I am a fundamental believer that I like collaborative approaches . . . I'm a "wisdom of the crowd" kind of guy from Jim Surowiecki. It always made us stronger and in what we do, obviously there are life-and-death implications to what we do, you're constantly in search of the best idea, and I think communities and groups help you find that best idea.

Dan: [19:05] How has the nature of adversaries and other challenges changed?

John: [19:11] Well, I think we are in a transition now. I think perhaps there's a new generation of warfare emerging. Certainly in Iraq what we saw was a significant insurgency, and how you fight an insurgency is far different from how you fight state-on-state or nation war. And we're becoming, unfortunately, very experienced at that in the American military. But, there's probably no more experienced force in the world right now than the United States military as to dealing with that type of danger. And it is a real danger.

You may agree or disagree with what went on in Iraq, but there are going to be sources of conflict in the future. They may arise for different reasons in the future. It would not surprise me if someday conflict arises over a competition for resources. One of the most fundamental resources may be water. Some of the things that are going on in Darfur right now, some people are claiming it really has its genesis in the environmental change due to climate warming. And that nature of conflict is so dreadful and so different from state-on-state war that somebody is going to have to understand that.

Dan: [20:41] So, it's going from nations to different groups than nations. The individual is getting more powerful. Are we talking about them alone? In formal groups? In ad hoc groups?

John: [20:56] Well certainly I think the threat of state-on-state conflict is diminished somewhat, but it has not gone away. There are militaries around the world that are expanding, and in some areas of the world there is a rise in nationalism.

In other areas of the world there are these groups that are forming: Al-Qaeda, the Taliban, they're prime examples. There are other terrorist groups around the world and they are somewhat more ad hoc than, obviously, a nation-state. But, make no mistake, they're very dedicated to their beliefs, to their cause, and they will resort to violent means to achieve those. And that's one of the dangers we face in this world.

Dan: [21:47] So, is a lot of it from the group or is it individuals who are leading the group? Is that a difference?

John: [22:03] I think there's always a role, Dan, for leaders that emerge. Clearly there's a leadership cell in Al-Qaeda. Every tribe has a leader. Obviously every nation has a leader. So, leaders will still be important. But, how they motivate and inspire and compel the groups they belong to, to act in the manner in which they desire is important. Some are more rigidly formed, others are more loosely formed, I'm not so sure "one size fits all."

Dan: [22:12] Reports have been that they use the same chat rooms and stuff like that—the same technologies that everybody else does.

John: [22:48] Absolutely. Sure. Internet cafes are a very popular place for global terrorists.

Dan: [23:00] Now, what have you learned about being members of multiple groups that have sometimes conflicting goals and needs?

John: [23:09] That's constantly present and will never go away, and it's how do you, not necessarily arbitrate those conflicts, but how do you at least understand them? How do you find, when there are competing interests, one beneficial path where most of the groups get most of what they want? That's the delicacy of diplomacy. In some cases that's the need for enlightened leadership—is to be able to suggest to the varying groups with varying interests, that it's this common path that serves most of their interests. Once again, I think that's the notion that comes back to keeping the global system intact. That's a fundamental concern of mine.

Dan: [24:01] Of keeping it intact?

John: [24:03] Yeah. Not breaking it. It will never be in perfect harmony, but the bigger question, Dan, is, "Is there a global system running in the world today?" I think the answer is, yes. I spend a lot of my time now thinking, "What could break that global system?"

And then I spend a lot of my time figuring out ways to try to sense that there's a danger rising that could potentially break that global system. And then, what do we do to prevent that?

During the course of my military career I spent time thinking about, "How do I win a conflict?" I'm now spending time, maybe it's a function of my age, trying to avoid a conflict, realizing that the world is not perfect, it is not safe, and until it is safe I understand that we may, once again, have to resort to our hard power. But, the military has a number of elements of soft power that can try to prevent the breaking of that global system.

Dan: [25:12] So, we have this system that's working and we have some definition of what would be "bad," of what happens when it starts breaking in some bad way.

John: [25:24] Right.

Dan: [25:25] And you're looking for indicators that something is into a feedback loop or some loop that's about to break off.

John: [25:33] Right.

Dan: [25:33] OK. So, you're looking for something that can be squashed in the bud, so to speak.

John: [25:40] Right.

Dan: [25:41] Nipped in the bud, sorry. So, what type of examples of that . . . obviously we have some in the financial world right now, there were leading indicators and stuff like that,[28] but how did you know that it would spiral as opposed to dampen?

John: [26:00] Precisely. I think today's financial crisis is a great example, Dan. I've been with some leading business men and women who I've asked if their businesses have been affected by the financial crisis and some clearly it has. But, a handful of those business leaders said, "You know, we saw this coming about a year ago and we began to protect our positions and we began to strengthen other elements." So, there were people who were able to see this financial crisis coming and did something about it. Now, they did something about it at their local business level, but you wonder if that kind of foresight could be applied on a global scale.

Dan: [26:46] Right. At the system level, at the higher level.

John: [26:48] Yeah. And so I'm working with a couple of people who are trying to see if that's possible. You know, we're not going to be able to predict who's going to win the World Series this year, but we certainly think that

---

[28]This interview took place in late September 2008, when Congress was debating a financial bailout bill as investment institutions were failing, credit was tightening, etc. I was making reference to a presentation I heard a few weeks before, right after the collapse of Lehman, by a senior person at Goldman Sachs who discussed information systems Goldman had put in place over many years, and at great development cost, that helped detect high risk and were helping them get through the crisis.

with the use of high-speed computing and in some cases the use of some behavioral insight, can we anticipate that something is really beginning to go south here? And then, how do you gather the group of people with greater insights than your own who can say, "Jeez, maybe there is something going wrong here and maybe we can find it in the early stages so remedial action can be taken sooner"?

Dan: [27:32] I can think of one example that I know about with a friend of mine who works in public health. What they do is try to get daily reports on things from emergency rooms to see if there is a spike that you wouldn't expect, to be able to catch epidemics or attacks of various sorts quickly before they become an epidemic, which is an example of that. Can you give examples of other things you're thinking of?

John: [28:00] Well, I think that's one of the best examples, and there are a couple of others. But, just think about what the rapid spread of disease would do in this global system that we've talked about.

If you were to ask me, Dan, "John, what things could disrupt the global system?" One of the things that I would tell you is, one causation for breakage would be, a global pandemic. And in the global transportation system today something can spread from Africa to London in 12 hours.

Do we have a network on a global basis, not just a local emergency room, that can say that one strain could potentially spread to a global pandemic? Certainly that was the concern with Avian Flu. And there are means right now to be able to fence that global system.

Other things that I think could break this global system would be a major state-on-state war. God forbid if the United States and China ever went to war, it would probably set back the world economy by 50 years. You can understand why the elevation of the prevention of something is terribly important in my judgment.

Dan: [29:23] That's not what you are taught in military school, I take it, or didn't use to be?

John: [29:29] I'll credit Admiral Mullen, the current Chairman of the Joint Chiefs of Staff now. One of the tenets that we subscribe to in the new maritime strategy is that we've elevated the notion of the prevention of war to rival that of winning war.

Once again, we don't think the future's a panacea and no one should interpret that people in uniform have become pacifists. That's not the case; we understand there are harsh realities about life in the world. And our job is often to prepare for the worst and hope for the best.

We understand that there are elements of military soft power that can help prevent, and if prevention doesn't work, then you can rely upon us to prevail. But, it is a more nuanced, more sophisticated, I think, a very mature look. And I credit Admiral Mullen for really being the champion of this notion of preventing the next fight. And the corollary is to preventative medicine.

Dan: [30:35] When you are practicing something, what would you practice doing to be able to stop something before it gets too big, rather than being able to get in there and just wipe out the other side?

John: [30:51] One of the clear things that we're doing these days is that the U.S. military is promoting military-to-military relationships with China. We want the Chinese military to get to better know us, and we want to get to better know them.

We think, through the exchange, particularly educational opportunities, and I think the next generation of leaders, both in their military and our military, if we're closer, and if we get to a situation where we don't understand what the other side is doing, you would hope that somebody could pick up a telephone, enter a chat room, send an email to somebody that they've know for 10 or 15 or 20 years, and say, "I just don't understand what you're doing, can we talk about this? Is there something else we ought to consider?" That's the kind of dialog that we need to foster, I think.

Dan: [31:43] I get this image that instead of the hotline phone that you pick up that there's this chat room that major governmental people around the world are involved in.

John: [31:54] I think whatever means available, Dan. Sometimes there's no replacement for a face-to-face meeting. But, otherwise if you can quickly get on the phone and say, "Ahh, I didn't understand that's what you really meant to say." Those are the types of things that we need to be better off at doing to once again get back to the central notion of "how would we prevent state-on-state conflict?"

Dan: [32:20] So, misunderstanding, paranoia, those which you may think of as individual problems in individual relationships, we have that at a state level, and we have to prevent that.

John: [32:32] Indeed, and the other factor that I would throw in there is a cultural bias. What don't we understand about an adversary's culture? Why are they motivated to do what they do?

Dan: [32:46] So, this is the thing of when somebody says something, we misinterpret it as meaning something else.

John: [32:52] Indeed.

Dan: [32:53] And then we say, "Do you really mean that?" And they say, "of course," and that's a spiraling thing, a spiral to negative area, to the wrong place.

John: [33:01] It can be that. There was a great Greek philosopher Thucydides who once said, "People fight for fear, honor, and interest," and I think that's exactly right. In time of fear groups and nations can behave irrationally.

Dan: [33:22] And it's often unfounded fears that we're talking about.

John: [33:24] Indeed.

Dan: [33:25] The way of finding out if it's unfounded or not, some of it has to do with the trust of actually knowing the people and of having more than one meeting, but actually having a tested relationship with the other side.

John: [33:41] Precisely, and I think it takes years to build those relationships and it takes years to build that trust.

Dan: [33:49] How do you practice having people in situations where there's a perturbation so that they may swing out of control, and instead learn how to be able to put the brakes on and say, "Whoa, this is spiraling out of control; I'd better double check."

John: [34:05] I think, there are a couple of very encouraging signs in the U.S. government, quite honestly, in its approach that's called DIME, D-I-M-E. What DIME stands for is, "Diplomatic, Information, Military, and Economics." And what military leaders and generations behind me are now being schooled in and have become experienced in is that there is more than just a military solution to a problem.

There are diplomatic avenues, there are information avenues, clearly there are military avenues. But, that M in DIME for Military can either be a big M or a small m. The big M is probably our hard power; the small m is our soft power. And then there are economic conditions.

And across the government I think there's a growing realization that there's this more sophisticated approach to resolving conflicting interests and it is this DIME approach. But, that almost goes back to your question earlier, Dan, about how do you get groups with competing interests and desires to cooperate or not try to kill each other at least?

Dan: [35:19] Since you have had to work with people who had opposing interests, how did you do it? There's work with the Chinese, work with all sorts of people, putting together the 1,000-ship Navy, for example.

John: [35:38] The 1,000-ship Navy is a great example. The first thing that we did is that we wrote about it. We wrote about the need to cooperate in this global system. That it's in nobody's interest, it's not in the Chinese's interests, it's not in the Americans' interests, it's not in the Iranians' interests, it's not in the Iraqis' interest, it's not in the Russians' interests if we break the global system.

It's in everybody's interest if we can keep the global system running as smoothly as it can be running. Not running perfectly, but as smoothly as it can be running. And there are global indications of financial crisis right now, that's in nobody's interest.

Dan: [36:15] You have to teach people that it isn't zero-sum everywhere.[29]

John: [36:18] You got it. When people put aside their nationalistic interests, their selfish interests, they begin to understand that and they're far more inclined to cooperate in a larger whole, because it's to their benefit. That's why we named the maritime strategy a "Cooperative Strategy for 21st Century Seapower." The word American is not even on the cover of the document.

Dan: [36:48] The first paragraph, "Security, prosperity and vital interest of the United States are increasingly coupled to those of other nations. Our nation's interests are best served by fostering a peaceful global system comprised of interdependent networks of trade, finance, information, law, people and governance."

"Preventing wars is as important as winning wars," and one of the things in it is that "trust and cooperation cannot be surged." That you can't decide at the last minute, "OK, we've changed to a different way."

John: [37:21] Exactly.

Dan: [37:22] You basically have to agree that cooperation and working as a group is important, or as cooperating multiple groups with divergent needs.

John: [37:35] That's the answer to your question, Dan. I mean, so I have to credit the leadership of not only Admiral Mullen, but the head of the Navy, Admiral Gary Roughead, and the head of the Marine Corps, General Jim Conway, and the head of the Coast Guard, Admiral Thad Allen.

I mean those leaders were bold enough to put this philosophical belief in writing. They signed it for the first time in history of the United States Military, they've testified before Congress for it. So, our belief system is there for the public to scrutinize.

Dan: [38:10] So, it's so non-isolationist.

John: [38:12] Right.

---

[29]Zero-sum is a term from game theory that refers to situations where one side's gain or loss corresponds, respectively, to the losses or gains of the other sides. That is, it's an "I win, you lose" situation. In non-zero-sum situations, there are often ways where both sides can be benefited.

Dan: [38:13] Because that's the world we depend upon isn't, can't be that way.

John: [38:16] Indeed, and I mean that's what technologists like yourself have done for us. I mean the Internet alone just opened up an enormous world for people that they never saw before.

Dan: [38:29] How so? Example?

John: [38:31] I mean just the whole connectivity of knowledge. Now it can be used for bad purposes, I understand that, but on whole the sharing of information, how it's changed people lives, that you can pay your bills in your living room if you want to, that you can access information in the Library of Congress, that you can try to understand cultural differences better all from just your laptop or now your cell phone.

Dan: [38:58] So, now for those of us who are designing things, how should we design them so they are more likely to be used for good and less likely ill? Everything's a "double-edged sword" as they say, so what properties enhance things being used for good?

So, like something that's decentralized is usually more robust and less brittle.

John: [39:23] Right.

Dan: [39:24] On the other hand, you have less control over it in certain situations.

John: [39:26] Right.

Dan: [39:28] So, any ideas about if I was designing a system? If I'm building the next Facebook or the next MySpace, which are probably used by some pretty bad people just as much as by some really good people?

John: [39:42] Right. Dan, I'm not an expert in the business, and so I don't have a good pat answer for you. I do believe, though, that on balance, the openness of the system and the flexibility of the system probably outweighs the detriment.

As you inject safety measures, and there have to be some logical safety measures—from sexual misconduct, to stealing money, to fostering hatred, those types of things. I think there have to be some safeguards, but on balance I think the goodness of the system will tend to beat down the bad—maybe I'm too naive there.

Dan: [40:28] Well, you've seen some pretty bad stuff though over the years.

John: [40:31] I've seen some pretty bad stuff.

Dan: [40:33] How do you not overreact in terms of clamping down? I mean there are crazy ideas that really end up being key important things, the whole concept of "innocent until proven guilty." You don't want to have a system that ends up looking for anything that's deviant and squashing it, like may have happened way back when in history when governments and religious institutions were trying to have a very strong orthodoxy.

John: [41:01] Yeah, I think there's a balance point to be found between freedom and responsibility. I mean that's one of the things we're seeing in the financial crisis today. If markets run too unregulated, the greed and avarice really seep in and a handful of people make a bunch of money, while a large group of people lose a lot of money.

So, where the balance point is between regulation and freedom, it's been a constant debate across the history of our country. I think more often than not, Americans have fallen on the side of more freedoms, but complete freedom introduces other difficulties as well.

Dan: [41:49] When you start throwing in the concept of personal security coming in, people worry about "Well, they're going to wipe us out," etc., then maybe you can overreact in terms of, "Will this help?" What you're saying is sometimes that too much holding back just in case, to have overkill of protection, may be "throwing out the baby with the bathwater."

John: [42:17] It could be, and once again, I'm not an Internet expert, and I've not studied the intricacies of the law; nor the philosophy behind it all. Certainly an example that I'm aware of is how Wikipedia balances out correct information from bad information, and how self-organizing groups can begin to say, "Wait a second, that's not right!" and whether it's factually incorrect or, "Wait a minute, that's not a proper practice." I don't think you're ever going to be able to completely rely on self-organizing groups, but my sense is, in the aggregate, more freedom is probably better than restricted freedom.

Dan: [43:02] That's great to hear, because you worry about that, "Oh, my God!" whenever you hear that some bad guy is using the things that you championed or that you helped develop, "Oh, my God! I helped Al-Qaeda." I mean, God forbid.

John: [43:18] Right.

Dan: [43:21] You want to also realize the other way around. Well, the worry I would have is that people in your position probably go, "Oh, you horrible technologist! You've opened up Pandora's box for us, and we have to put it back together." That doesn't sound like what I'm hearing from you?

John: [43:39] No, it's not, Dan. I agree that some very evil people have used tools that they didn't have 10 or 15 years ago to their great benefit and to our detriment, and we just have to understand that those tools are fair game. Then what we need to do is understand how we can better use those tools to attack their vulnerabilities as they use those same tools, and then if the abundance of evidence is that something is really amiss here, then we can take some action.

Dan: [44:15] That's interesting. So, the thing is that rather than say, "Oh, my God! Bad guys will use something," this goes to everything from copy protection, of people who have rights and all, too, others.

John: [44:24] Right.

Dan: [44:30] It's, well, there's a technology, learn to use it and to take advantage of learning to use it, and think how to use it for good, rather than worrying about how it might be used for bad.

John: [44:40] Precisely.

Dan: [44:41] Because the good might, like cooperating with bad people, cooperating with our enemies, which is what you're doing in the military right now in order to stop piracy and things like that. It's more important for us all than . . .

John: [45:01] Right.

Dan: [45:02] . . . making sure that the guys we don't like don't get any benefit. "A rising tide raises all ships," or whatever.

John: [45:07] Right.

Dan: [45:08] So, what happened in the straits around Indonesia where there was cooperation against pirates? That's worked very well.

John: [45:18] It has worked very well.

Dan: [45:20] Is it still working that well?

John: [45:22] It really is. You have to applaud what Singapore, Malaysia, and Indonesia are doing. Once again, those are three countries that were not necessarily the closest of friends, but they had a common interest, and that was the maritime straits that flow by all three of their countries.

About 5 years ago, Dan, if you were the owner of a private ship that was transiting through the Straits of Malacca, you were paying Lloyd's of London wartime shipping rates for insurance, and it was all because of piracy.

About 5 years ago, Indonesia, Singapore, and Malaysia got together and said, "How could we cooperate to better see what's going on in the straits, and patrol the straits?" They did exactly that, and today if you were that private ship owner, you'd be paying peacetime shipping rates to the Lloyd's of London, just out of cooperation.

Dan: [46:19] And that's still holding?

John: [46:20] It's still holding, and they're doing a great job, and I commend them for it.

Dan: [46:23] What type of cooperation are they doing to do that?

John: [46:26] They have a specific program called "Eyes in the Sky." What they do is they use aircraft to patrol the straits, and there are always members of all three of those countries present. It's just been a great story of cooperation, of information sharing, and how they've really turned a situation around. Now, I can't say the same is the case with piracy off of Somalia. Unfortunately, piracy there is really beginning to have a very negative impact on humanitarian aid getting into drought-stricken Somalia, and it's a shame.

Dan: [47:06] Is there a difference in the parties cooperating or anything? Or is it just the pirates are worse, or what?

John: [47:12] Well, the problem in Somalia is that you don't have a recognized government in Somalia, and so there is no basis for cooperation. There's a degree of lawlessness that prevails, and there are limits the United States needs to recognize, even if they don't recognize the government of Somalia.

So, we abide by international law, so we can't go inside. There's a line drawn at 12 miles off of a coast. The pirates know that the line is drawn 12 miles off the coast. The United States won't go inside that 12 miles.

Dan: [47:49] There's no cooperation from inside to help you?

John: [47:51] There's no cooperation from inside to help us.

Dan: [47:53] So, that's the example which is, while it's not working, it helps prove the thesis.

John: [48:02] Right. What's not working about it is what's missing.

Dan: [48:07] What about where we have transponders on ships, and we're sharing that information with the whole world?

John: [48:16] Right.

Dan: [48:16] So that information is given to people who are economic and perhaps military adversaries?

John: [48:23] Right.

Dan: [48:23] How's that been working? That's more in, like what, Mediterranean, Black Sea, and things like that?

John: [48:30] Yeah. It really started in earnest in the Mediterranean. A good friend of mine, Admiral Harry Ulrich, was really a champion of that system. For your listeners, I'll draw a relationship that you probably can better understand.

Whenever you get on an airplane to travel either domestically, or even internationally, there are transponders on that airplane that share information with anybody in the world.

In fact, you can log on to your computer right now, and you can see air traffic patterns around the United States, around the world. All that information is unclassified. There's no military application to it, none of that, and it's all shared in the global system.

Unfortunately, the same is not true for what's sailing on the surface of the oceans of the world. When you realize that 70 percent of the earth is water, there's a lot of commercial traffic going across the oceans of the world. The amazing realization is that 90 percent of the global GDP flows across the oceans of the world. Yet we don't have a similar type of system that's in the air space around the globe.

It's not a technology limitation, Dan. We have the technology to share this information; people have just not wanted to share the information.

Dan: [49:43] Have we started doing that?

John: [49:44] We have started doing that. There's a major program that's going on, certainly in the United States government, called Maritime Domain Awareness, where there's a Department of Defense, Department of Homeland Security, the Navy, and the Coast Guard that spreads to the Department of Transportation, Department of Commerce, Department of Energy.

We all have a vested interest in understanding where commercial goods are flowing across the oceans of the world, and lots of other places, as well.

You know, you go back to Singapore. Singapore, now, is requiring you, even if you have a 50-foot Chris-Craft boat that you want to just spend on the water on the weekends, you're now required to have these kind of transponders. They know everything that's moving in and around the Straits of Malacca.

Dan: [50:36] Are you worried with something like the transponders on the airplanes? That means that people know where airplanes are at and can shoot them down and stuff like that. But, I guess we worry about the bad side, but we haven't seen that.

John: [50:50] But in fact, it's just the opposite that's happening. Because it is transparent, because it is cooperative, because the information is shared we think less bad things happen, not more bad things happen.

Dan: [51:05] Huh. Well, that's interesting to hear. And some things are pointing that out. So, what do you see for coming about in the future? Where do you see some of the stuff going?

John: [51:20] Well, Dan, I think the global system is in transition today. I think a number of local systems are in transition. There's a phrase used in Europe that I like and the phrase is, "Radical novelties about what the system looks like." Honestly, I also think that the nature of power is changing.

So, I think it's a remarkable time right now and I think those are the three major forces at work, based upon the vantage point that I've had over the four years as the chief strategist of the Navy. I think we probably need everybody's help to try to tackle this challenge.

Dan: [52:03] What do you mean the nature of power is changing?

John: [52:06] Well, I think the nature of power is changing this way: I think we're moving toward a more power-sharing arrangement in the global system. I think, from the period of time where from the end of the Cold War up to the recent present, I think that people would not argue that America was the dominant power.

But, I think the challenge for America is how do we begin to share some of that power in the global system without sacrificing our American way of life or our American interest? I think that will be important.

I think you can see in the financial markets today that power is changing. I mean, just the shift a couple of days ago. Goldman Sachs is now a banking holding company [instead of] a pure investment firm. Then the nature of their financial power just changed rapidly. I think the demise of some companies, because of the financial crisis, I think you can see the nature of power is changing in Fannie Mae and Freddie Mac.

I think the nature of power is changing almost on an individual basis in ways that technologists like you have enabled—this growing power, the individual, through access to greater and greater information. That's a power change as well.

And I think it's going to take some time. I think what Clay Shirky talked about, the notion of the power of the institution vs. the power of an interactive infrastructure—I think that's another example of how the nature of power is changing.

Dan: [53:41] Does this have any historical precedent?

John: [53:47] I certainly think that the global system has been in transition before. I mean, the Roman Empire was probably the first major change in the global system. I think the Westphalian state, where states were recognized as the big power brokers in the world, was another indicator of when the global system was in transition. But, I think the global system is back in transition now, and I think it will take a lot of cooperative help to make sure it transitions in the best way.

Dan: [54:15] So, it's moving from absolute "I win, you lose," to, what, to we each win in our own way?

John: [54:27] I hope it's moving in that direction, Dan. I think we may be at a juncture. I mean, I don't want that to sound as if it's an ultimatum, but I think the world collectively can make a bad choice.

I think we can go back to a point of a binary solution to our challenges of win or lose. Or I think we can find a more secure, more prosperous way where we keep larger systems intact and we understand and reap the benefits of why they stay intact.

Dan: [55:06] We end up with systems that have to be maintained in equilibrium, that there are normal things that might cause it to spiral out.

John: [55:16] Yeah. I'm a big fan of balance and equilibrium, Dan.

You know, winner-takes-all, the consolidation of power, I think, is probably behind us. If we were to return to that, it would probably mean that the system was broken in order for somebody to consolidate that power.

Dan: [55:33] OK. Well, thanks very much. Do you have anything else you want to say to these listeners; anybody who got this far?

John: [55:39] No, Dan. I really appreciate it. I'm always stimulated by the chance to chat with you, Dan, once again. I have admired your body of work over the last many years, and it's striking that we're sort of looking at the world in the same lens.

Dan: [55:55] Well, thanks very much.

My web site has more than just blog posts and essays with my opinion. I like to share some of my experiences through other means. I started using sound recordings in November 1999. The first was a few seconds of the sound of me running through a pile of crunchy leaves in the New England fall. In those days, recordings took up too much bandwidth for frequent use on web sites like mine that were often accessed through dial-up connections. I kept my use of sound short and infrequent. Over time, though, the common technology changed, and today it is not unusual to provide much longer recordings such as these. I periodically use this podcast format to let the people who come to my blog get a fuller flavor of my discussions with people than they could with just my one-sided write-up from memory.

In the case of the interviews in this chapter, we got to look at some of the nuances of interpersonal relationships, cooperation, and motivation as seen by people outside of the technical field. Understanding these nuances can be helpful in understanding what goes on when people cooperate with the help of technology. It also takes some of the mystery out of cooperative development efforts, such as open source software.

Next we'll look in detail at the evolution of one pervasive use of Internet technology for communicating between individuals and large groups: blogging and, to a lesser extent, podcasting. Some of the areas we'll cover are these: What is blogging like? How was it first viewed? What are some examples of it in relation to society and the more traditional means of communication? Where is it special or different from what came before?

6

Blogging and Podcasting: Observations through Their Development

The Internet has given us enhanced connectivity for communicating with others. It has lowered the cost of sending messages or publishing thoughts to virtually zero. Many different means for exploiting this technology for communication have been developed, and new ones are emerging all the time.

One very visible and important development has been that of blogs and blogging. A blog is basically a simple personal web site where a named (either real or pseudonymous) author (the blogger) posts written items listed in reverse chronological order, with the most recent on top. Each post may be referred to through its own web address—a permanent link, or "perma-link." Some blogs have facilities for readers to directly post comments that become associated online with the original post without needing to email them to the blogger, but not all do. (My blog does not support direct comments.) The term *blogging* is what we commonly use today. In the early days, we also used the terms *personal web site*, *log*, *web log*, *online diary*, and others. The term *blog* is simply a contraction of the phrase *web log*.

Creating and publishing the HTML computer code to display text through a browser is somewhat technical and tedious. HTML, which stands for Hypertext Markup Language, is a programming language used to specify the contents of a web page. It is the language that browsers translate into what you see. Web pages are usually stored on web servers as files written in HTML. Software tools were developed to aid in creating HTML. These let you type in text to what seemed like a simple word processor, but when you pressed Save, all of the needed HTML files were automatically created for you and stored on a web server. One of the most popular early such tools (and still very popular in its latest incarnation) is the Blogger system. That also, I guess, helped popularize the term blogging, as many people started their first blog using Blogger.

I started blogging in 1999 and have continued to this day with a frequency that varies from once a day to once a month. Throughout that time,

I have included observations about blogging, both introspective about what I was finding and through observations of others. Here are some of those observations.

The Importance of Permanent Links

Understanding the concept of a permanent link is important to understanding the role of individual blog posts and the structure of most blogs.

In most blogs, there is a front page that lists the most recent posts to that blog, one right after the other in reverse chronological order. Only the most recent posts are displayed. As new posts are added, older posts at the bottom of the page are usually removed. Alternatively, some blogs batch up the most recent day or month's worth of posts on the front page.

The old blog posts are usually moved to an archive page, which is different from the home page. Archives can be made up of many pages, often organized by date, or with one page per blog post. Each page is given a unique name and web address (URL). This sequence is different from that of a traditional web site, where old material is usually just removed, or where material always starts out on the one web page where it will stay.

When the posts are on the front page, they may be accessed on the web using the web address of that page, such as `www.blogname.com`, or `www.companyname.com/blog`. This makes it easy to find the latest material on a blog: It is always on the front page. If the author of a blog on another web site needed a web address (URL) to make a link to refer to a post, initially that front page address could be used. However, after a time, as the front page changed with the addition of new blog posts, the post the other blog was trying to refer to would no longer be at that front page web address.

A perma-link is the web address of the archived version of a blog post. When a new post is added to a blog, most blogging software systems make two copies: One copy is added to the front page, and one copy is added to an archive page (creating that archive page if need be). For example, a new blog post may be added to both `www.blogname.com` as well as `www.blogname.com/archive/2008/12/24/post109.html`. On the front page, as part of the blog post's identifying information such as the date and title, a link to that "permanent" web address is also inserted. Other bloggers have learned to use those web addresses when referring to a blog post, not just the front page name.

The automatic creation of perma-links became common in blogging software around 2000 or so. The title, date, or time text of a blog post on the front page, or a little icon of some sort near the title or end, is often linked to the permanent web address.

With the growing use of perma-links early in the history of blogging, it became much easier to have "conversations" that spanned more than one blog. Blogger A could make a comment about a particular post by Blogger B, and then Blogger B could refer back to that post, and so on, secure in knowing that the links to each post would still point to "the right thing" even after the posts were superceded on the front pages.

Perma-links also increased the value of blogs in other ways. Because every post had its own, permanent web address, search engines could find and index each post separately. Otherwise, the result of a search would always end up with the front page of a blog and show the new text and not the post from long ago with the information you wanted.

Notice how simple conventions like perma-links can make a huge difference in the use and value of a system on the Internet.

PAMPHLETEERS AND WEB SITES

There is a similarity between the pamphlets of the American Revolution and today's personal web sites.

April 23, 2001

A few years ago, while thinking about personal web sites and personal publishing, my friend Chris Daly pointed out the similarity to pamphlets during the American Revolution. (Chris spent years as a reporter, including being a New England correspondent for the *Washington Post*. He's now a professor of journalism at Boston University. He was a major contributor to the start of my www.GoodDocuments.com web site.) He lent me his well-worn copy of Bernard Bailyn's *The Ideological Origins of the American Revolution*.[1] I've quoted from it a few times in speeches. This is an essay that ties it to personal web sites. (All quotes are from Bailyn's book, Chapter I, "The Literature of Revolution," unless otherwise noted.)

To help learn about what was going on in people's minds back in the 1700s for his book, *The Ideological Origins of the American Revolution* (published in 1967, and still available), Bernard Bailyn turned to hundreds of pamphlets from the time. While written public discussions about issues appeared in all

---

[1] Belknap Press, 1967, ISBN: 0674443020. Copyright 1967, 1992 by the President and Fellows of Harvard College. All rights reserved. Excerpts used with permission.

mediums, including newspapers, broadsides (single sheets of paper with any amount of writing, often posted or shared), and almanacs, he writes:

> Above all, there were pamphlets: booklets consisting of a few print-
> er's sheets, folded in various ways so as to make various sizes and
> numbers of pages, and sold—the pages stitched together loosely,
> unbound and uncovered—usually for a shilling or two.
>
> *The Ideological Origins of the American Revolution*, page 2

To me, the pamphlet is analogous to the personal web site. Like a personal web site, a pamphlet can vary in size and is controlled by the author. (It is interesting to note that the authors could charge, albeit a small amount, for their work. Perhaps this is akin to today the reader paying for ISP access. Maybe it bodes well for future business models.)

I think reading some of what Bailyn had to say back in 1967 about the 1700s can help us better understand the role and peculiarities of today's writers who use web sites (web logs or essays).

Bailyn goes on to say:

> It was in this form—as pamphlets—that much of the most important
> and characteristic writing of the American Revolution appeared. For
> the Revolutionary generation, as for its predecessors back to the early
> sixteenth century, the pamphlet had peculiar virtues as a medium of
> communication. Then, as now, it was seen that the pamphlet allowed
> one to do things that were not possible in any other form.
>
> *The Ideological Origins of the American Revolution*, page 2

He quotes from George Orwell, ("Introduction," in George Orwell and Reginald Reynolds, eds., *British Pamphleteers*):

> The pamphlet [George Orwell, a modern pamphleteer, has writ-
> ten] is a one-man show. One has complete freedom of expression,
> including, if one chooses, the freedom to be scurrilous, abusive, and
> seditious; or, on the other hand, to be more detailed, serious and
> "high-brow" than is ever possible in a newspaper or in most kinds of
> periodicals . . .
>
> *The Ideological Origins of the American Revolution*, page 2

In his book's Foreword, Bailyn writes:

> *The pamphlets [he looked at to write the book] include all sorts of writings—treatises on political theory, essays on history, political arguments, sermons, correspondence, poems—and they display all sorts of literary devices. But for all their variety they have in common one distinctive characteristic: they are, to an unusual degree, explanatory. They reveal not merely positions taken but the reasons why positions were taken . . .*
>
> The Ideological Origins of the American Revolution, pages ix-x

Back in his Chapter I, he groups the pamphlets into three categories:

> *The largest number were direct responses to the great events of the time . . .*
>
> *They resulted also, and to a considerable extent, from what might be called chain-reacting personal polemics: strings of individual exchanges—arguments, replies, rebuttals, and counter-rebuttals—in which may be found heated personifications of the larger conflict. A bold statement on a sensitive issue was often sufficient to start such a series, which characteristically proceeded with increasing shrillness until it ended in bitter personal vituperation. Thus East Apthorp's tract of 1763 on the Church of England's Society for the Propagation of the Gospel, inflaming as it did New Englanders' fears of an American bishopric, was answered at once by Jonathan Mayhew in a 176-page blast, and then, in the course of the next two years, by no less than nine other pamphleteers writing in a melee of thrusts and counterthrusts . . .*
>
> *A third type . . . was distinguished by the ritualistic character of its themes and language. In the course of the Revolutionary controversy, the regular, usually annual, publication in pamphlet form of commemorative orations came to constitute a significant addition to the body of Revolutionary literature.*
>
> The Ideological Origins of the American Revolution, pages 4-5

I found this mention of "inflaming" writing, predating the Internet "flame-wars," intriguing, given that he was writing this well before the term was used online.

It's also interesting to look at the style of writing that emerged:

> *One of the surprising aspects of the American writings is the extent*
> *to which they include the stylistic modes associated with the great*
> *age of English pamphleteering. Of satire . . . irony . . . parody . . .*
> *sarcasm . . .*
>
> *The most commonly attempted was the satire associated with pseud-*
> *onymous authorship.*
>
> The Ideological Origins of the American Revolution, pages 9, 11

SlashDot, *Wired*, etc.: the style is timeless.

The purpose of the pamphlet writing at that time was not literary, it was political. It was to struggle with ideas that led to the Revolution. (The rest of Bailyn's book sets forth those ideas and their development.) He writes:

> *And yet, for all this . . . the pamphlets of the American Revolution*
> *that seek artistic effects are not great documents . . .*
>
> *First and foremost, the American pamphleteers, though participants*
> *in a great tradition, were amateurs next to such polemicists as Swift*
> *and Defoe. Nowhere [were there writers who were] . . . capable, that*
> *is, of earning their living by their pens . . . [The closest were some of*
> *the printers, but other than Franklin they weren't principals in what*
> *was going on.]*
>
> *The American pamphleteers were almost to a man lawyers, min-*
> *isters, merchants, or planters heavily engaged in their regular*
> *occupations.*
>
> *. . . it is this amateurism, this lack of practiced technique, that*
> *explains much of the crudeness of the Revolutionary pamphlets con-*
> *sidered simply as literature . . .*
>
> *But there is more than amateurism behind the relative crude-*
> *ness of the artistic efforts in the American pamphlets. For if*
> *writers like Adams and Jefferson were amateur pamphleteers,*
> *their writings in other ways display formidable literary talents*
> *. . . The more deliberately artful writings were in a significant*
> *way—for reasons that reach into the heart of the Revolutionary*

April 23, 2001

movement—peripheral to the main lines of intellectual force developing through the period . . .

The American writers were profoundly reasonable people. Their pamphlets convey scorn, anger, and indignation; but rarely blind hate, rarely panic fear. They sought to convince their opponents, not, like the English pamphleteers of the eighteenth century, to annihilate them.

The Ideological Origins of the American Revolution, pages 12–19

Reading something like this, as a person whose main job is to create software and help run a business while expressing himself on a public web site, gives me a wonderful sense of fitting into the flow of history. Hopefully, our give and take on topics like liberty, empowerment, the role of government and big business, and the joys and dangers of technology, will lead to as meaningful result as theirs.

Here are some of the comments I received soon after writing this essay:

From Boston University Associate Professor Chris Daly:

One other feature of 18th C. pamphleteering deserves mention, one that may have a lot of relevance in other countries today where the Web is used for purposes of political insurrection. That is, the pamphlet was preferred by the rebels because it did not provide any target for retaliation by the Crown. It was a guerilla form of publishing in which an individual or small revolutionary group could make a point, then disappear. This was in contrast to the more established printers. Typically, the printer owned his shop, his press, his tools and all his stock. If he antagonized the Crown, they knew just where to find him, and the king's agents could easily shut him down. The hit-and-run, anonymous pamphleteer, on the other hand, was almost impossible to find and, thus, to stop.

From my coworker Ed Blachman:

I know you've made this point elsewhere, but it's acutely important in this context: we have a much better chance of being able to read some of those pamphlets 200 years from now than we have of being able to read any of today's personal websites at that point:

Pamphlets had large printings (compare even 1,000 paper copies of a pamphlet to a personal website that exists on only one server)

Paper is a durable, autonomous material (compared to a website that depends on the existence of an organization to support its server, to say nothing of the possibility of datawipe (accidental or intentional))

Paper and ink are and were a stable, autonomous technology (compared to a website that is inaccessible to roughly everyone in the absence of a particular technological base)

http://www.bricklin.com/pamphleteers.htm

In 2005, Professor Daly posted an essay about blogging in response to a lawsuit that Apple brought against a web site for publishing alleged secrets. Apple apparently was arguing, among other things, that online journalists do not deserve the same rights as "traditional" journalists. Here is my blog post about it:

Thursday, April 7, 2005
ARE BLOGGERS JOURNALISTS? LOOKING TO HISTORY

There has been a lot written about Apple going after bloggers and the question about whether or not bloggers have the same protections that journalists do. I just saw a slightly different answer.

My next door neighbor Chris Daly is an Associate Professor who teaches journalism at Boston University. Previously, he has been the New England correspondent for the *Washington Post*, a features writer, and an AP editor. On the Web he is best known as the main idea person behind the old GoodDocuments.com web site that I created back in 1999 that was quite popular at Netscape and around the Web.

Besides teaching, Chris is working on a book about the history of journalism in the United States.[2]

He just weighed in with an essay titled "Are Bloggers Journalists? Let's Ask Thomas Jefferson."[3] I found his perspectives helpful.

---

[2] See Chris's blog at www.journalismprofessor.com.

[3] http://www.bu.edu/cdaly/whoisajournalist.html

April 7, 2005

As I read what Chris wrote, these sentences stood out (though the whole thing is worth reading):

> Common Sense *and other pamphlets like it were precisely the kind of political journalism that Jefferson had in mind when he insisted on a constitutional amendment in 1790 to protect press freedom— anonymous, highly opinionated writing from diverse, independent sources. In historical terms, today's bloggers are much closer in spirit to the Revolutionary-era pamphleteers than today's giant, conglomerate mainstream media.*
>
> Chris Daly

So, it's the BigPubs ("traditional" big media like big newspapers and TV) that need to show that they are covered by the First Amendment—blogs are the easier case, not a harder case that needs to be proven. Newspapers as we know them now are a 19th- and 20th-century invention; the Constitution is from the 18th century.

The other thing Chris points out is the difference between reporting and other forms of journalism. This is an important distinction, and the history matters for legal questions. Saying "journalism" or "journalists" as if they are all doing the same thing is as bad as saying "blogging" is all the same. (There are other terms I think we need to be careful about, such as the different types of "editors"—some editors pick and choose and may change what you mean while others help you say what you want to say clearer and without grammatical mistakes.) Chris also talks about the difference between "prior restraint" (before publication) and liability after the fact.

As blogging is bringing up issues about journalism, having a detailed historical perspective can be quite helpful. After all, journalism has been evolving ever since the printing press was invented around 1438, with many additions over the last century or two.

Yet again, we have a personal web site where a person who knows an awful lot about an issue (in this case, a practitioner, teacher, and historian) shares what they know directly with all who might be interested, without a reporter (and their editor) as an intermediary. I'm looking forward to Chris's book (he tells me that some of the chapters may go up on the Web sometime soon for comment).

http://danbricklin.com/log/2005_02_12.htm

About Blogging

In early 2002, blogging was being widely discussed. For example, there was an article on February 25, 2002, in the *New York Times*.[4] It seemed to care more about whether blogging companies could become big, profitable businesses and cared less about the effects blogging might have on politics, customers' relationships with corporations, or any of the myriad other areas that have been affected by blogs in the years since.

The writings by the "professional" press about blogging resulted in reactions from bloggers on their blogs. Here are some examples:

> *Meg Hourihan, www.megnut.com*
>
> *monday, february 25[5]*
>
> *In the past few weeks, as I've been rather quiet on this site, there's been an explosion in weblog coverage by various news sources, including: Wired's Blah, Blah, Blah and Blog; Canada's National Post 'Bloggers' emerge from internet underground; Henry Jenkins (director of the Program in Comparative Media Studies at MIT), Blog This; three Guardian articles (1, 2, 3); Andrew Sullivan's, A Blogger Manifesto; and today's New York Times article, Is Weblog Technology Here to Stay or Just Another Fad?.*
>
> *Goodness, but that's a lot of coverage in a short amount of time. Unfortunately most of it fails, once again, to penetrate or probe in any sort of meaningful way. Of especial disappointment to me is the Times' piece asking whether blogging is just another fad, not because I'm afraid of the answer but because I think the question is so meaningless. Fad, especially as it relates to anything Internet, is a terribly loaded, and potentially dismissive, word. And its use in this instance precludes a more interesting examination of where the hype is coming from. Bob Tedeschi, the article's author, asks, "[I]s it simply that in this, the Internet's fallow period, anything even remotely buzzworthy is given more of a spotlight than it deserves. Is the Weblog, in other words, a fad that is destined to fade?"*

---

[4] http://query.nytimes.com/gst/fullpage.html?res= 9400E1D61E3EF936A15751C0A9649C8B63

[5] http://meg.hourihan.com/2002/02/the-big-blogging-fad

Previous Internet fads, which had all the longevity of a firecracker (the expectant hush, a boom and burst of light, and then nothing), included Portals, Vortals, Push, B2B, B2C, and the whole "dot-com" thing. But those fads emerged in a top-down fashion—they were created by marketers and analysts making big pronouncements because they had something to offer or gain by doing so. The weblog hype, for the most part, has come from the bottom up, from the people actually doing the weblogging. Sure the tool makers/bloggers (Dave Winer and LiveJournal come to mind) have spent a great deal of time proselytizing, but the majority of the weblog buzz has come from the individuals themselves. As the amount of bloggers has grown, so has the collective noise.

The term fad describes something that's popular for a short period of time. Whether blogging will be sustained, and more importantly, continue to evolve, remains to be seen, but I believe it has a greater chance of success than previous Internet fads because of its grass-roots beginning. The increase in professional media coverage simply demonstrates an increased awareness of the weblog phenomenon. And whether that's due to the dearth of more deserving fads, I cannot say.

[Snarky aside: The best part of this article was the analyst from Forrester who, "predicts the technology will be adopted by the big portal sites for reselling to their users." Portals + Weblogs = Two Great Fads that Taste Great Together! [Additional aside: Big portal sites? Who's left besides Yahoo!?]]

And speaking of professional media coverage, the "blogs-are-not-journalism" camp is quick to point out that capital J journalism is focused on researching and presenting facts. Journalism is concerned with credibility and to that end employs editors and fact-checkers to ensure that the public receives a valid and informed piece of writing. And yet with a quick glance at the articles above, I see errors—errors that have been continued from one weblog article to the next, the same "facts" repeated over and over. Of course Journalists are informed by previous pieces that have been published on the topic they're writing about, but does that relieve them of their fact-checking obligations?

Take for example this quote from Andrew Sullivan's "A Blogger Manifesto," which ran yesterday in the Sunday Times of London, "Blogger—pioneered and still run by one man, Evan Williams—makes that completely easy". People familiar with Blogger may recall that there were three of us at Pyra when that product was launched. And there were many more folks that poured lots of time and energy into Blogger, at various points in its lifecycle, to create the product that's seen today. It's even mentioned on the Blogger/About the Company page yet I've lost count of the number of articles that have given Evan credit for creating and building Blogger all by himself. I'm not trying to be a brat here, and in fact I've avoided pointing out most of these mistakes as they've occurred because whenever I do I get an inbox full of email saying, basically, "Sit down and shut up, you left Blogger so stop your whining." And perhaps because of that, because some other webloggers and I have not spoken up and pointed out mistakes, these mistruths prevail.

My point is we shouldn't be so quick to say that Journalists get it right and webloggers don't. I think the weblog articles are a good example of the often shallow approach taken by mainstream media towards "quirky" topics and demonstrate that fact-checking may consist of copying "facts" from previous articles on the same topic. Of course, it's easy for me to spot mistakes in these stories because I participated in the events being described. This isn't black or white, fact or opinion, journalism or weblog. We're well into shades of grey, into a fuzzy realm where the distinction between amateur and professional is blurred. Where and how articles are published should not overshadow the examination of the quality and credibility of what's being written.

[Note: the author does not wish any of the above to be construed as Journalism.]

Over at Jason's an interesting and related discussion is taking place.

Meg Hourihan, February 25, 2002[6]

---

[6] Meg Hourihan was the cofounder of Pyra Labs, the company that developed the original Blogger system that helped popularize blogging. She also coauthored the book *We Blog: Publishing Online with Weblogs*, 2002, Wiley, ISBN: 0764549626.

Dave Winer, www.scripting.com

Monday, February 25, 2002[7]

One more note before signing off for the night. One of the advantages the pros are supposed to have over amateurs is the time and skills they have to carefully research a topic. According to the legend, weblog people shoot from the hip, there's no time to research. This is an incorrect idea. In fact the best webloggers are domain experts. They spend their whole professional lives gathering knowledge and experience in their fields. A fantastic example of this is Glenn Fleishman, who pours his intelligence out to the Web in vast quantities. He doesn't take any shortcuts. The quality of his writing, and his integrity is in your face. Another example, with all possible humility, I've spent 25 years becoming an expert in several areas of software development. When I write about software, really, there's nothing shallow about it. I've got the scars to prove it. I wonder when some reporter is going to connect XML-RPC, SOAP, RSS and Radio to my weblog.[8] *Could any of these things have happened without the ability to communicate directly to users and developers? Don't they see the economic revolution. We've cut out a middleman who was subtracting value. It must be hard for them to see because the reporters are the middlemen. How can you explain a new idea when the reporters won't believe or even express the ideas behind the software. Therefore no new ideas get out. Until the Web. No more exclusive access to people's minds. A route-around. Lots more to say about this. Lightbulbs going on everywhere.*

BTW, there was a time when reporters got on top of a technology story, and some still do. My career in software was launched by a NY Times reporter almost 20 years ago. I'll never forget it.

Dave Winer, *Scripting News*, February 25, 2002

---

[7] http://archive.scripting.com/2002/02/25#1c118cefac2045b31322832cc3129cb04

[8] Radio is a blogging tool, and XML-RPC, SOAP, and RSS are important, well-established technologies for communicating between computers on the Internet. Dave was instrumental in developing all of these.

February 26, 2002

This next essay was my contribution in 2002:

OBSERVATIONS FROM A WEBLOGGER

When I write, I think that I'm writing to peers and to friends who are regular readers, as well as to people who are looking to learn something from a link they've followed provided by someone else whom they trust.

In the last few weeks there has been a lot written, both online and in print, about blogs, journalism, etc. Here are some of my thoughts.

I've learned that there is more to understand about the world of blogging than is obvious to those watching from the outside. This shouldn't be surprising, since many human endeavors may appear less than they are from the outside: Why would you want to risk life and limb sliding down a hill in the cold on snow? (Ask any avid skier.) Running hurts . . . what's this about a "runner's high"? This list goes on and on.

To help those of you who haven't participated, let me tell you what it feels like in my position, since I don't think it's that unusual, even if my background as an inventor is unusual.

About me: At this point, I've been maintaining a weblog for about 2 ¼ years, and just helped some friends start another one that appears to already be pretty popular. Prior to that, I had been putting up thoughts about various topics on somewhat less chronologically oriented web sites for another year and a half, though many of those posts were listed chronologically and had repeat readers. In addition, I've been reading many weblogs for years, as well as corresponding with some of the authors. I've also spoken with many web site creators as part of my work with Trellix. Finally, I have kept careful watch of the server logs[9]

---

[9] Many server computers on the Internet, when they respond to a request for a web page, log a record of that request in a special file called a server log file. Traditionally, for each web page or image request, the server adds one line of text to the server log file. That line includes the date and time of the request, the specific web page or image requested, and the numeric Internet address of the requesting computer. In addition, certain information provided by most browsers as part of the request for the web page is also included on the line: information about the browser (such as its name and operating system) and the web page address of the page which held the link that was clicked on to generate the request. That last piece of information is called the "referrer page."

By looking through the contents of a server log, usually with the aid of a special program for this purpose to handle the large amount of data, a web site owner can get an idea of information such as when pages are requested, which pages are most popular, and which other pages on the Internet link to each page and generate "traffic" to the site.

for all of my web sites over the years, and have a good idea of how readership works, who links to my work and what it says on the linking page, etc.

First, let's talk about web sites in general and their readership.

When I write something and post it on the web on a new web site, I immediately go and tell people I know about the web site. They give me feedback. Let's say it's a web site with pictures of a wedding. I usually let the parents of the bride and groom know first. (The couple is probably away for a while, so I hear from them later . . .) They tell me how wonderful it is and thank me very much, which encourages me to do it again at another wedding (with usually a different family). In addition, they email many of their friends and relatives, people who were both present and absent from the event. Readership of the web site blossoms, peaking over the first week or so. Within a few weeks only an occasional person reads it. Total of about 50–100 readers.

If the web site has more general interest, such as the www.GoodDocuments.com one I wrote years ago about business writing for the Web, or even a web site about an event that is more public, some of those readers add a link to my web site on their web site. Sometimes, one of those Web sites is a very popular one. That drives more readers, and a certain ongoing proportion of the new readers of those web sites. An example is a link on Jakob Nielsen's Useit.com web site to GoodDocuments that brought in hundreds of readers when first created and which still brings in 5–10 readers a day, even though that link is itself a few years old.

The next source of readers comes from the search engines and directories. If others link to my web site, or if I tell the search engines about it, there is a good chance it will eventually show up as a search result. If my pages are deemed "relevant" enough, I might even get a high ranking in searches or placed in a popular category in a directory. Here again, such listings bring in a constant flow of additional readers, who might then link to the web site, etc.

Finally, when I speak with people in person, a topic sometimes comes up where the answer is "I have a picture of him on Joe's wedding's web site" or "I wrote about that last year . . ." In that case, giving out the web page address (a URL, such as "www.mysite.com/joe-and-jane") is part of a physical conversation or speech.

So, readership comes from personal relationships, personal referrals, or active searching. The person reading has some external reason why they want to read my stuff, but no prior relationship to my writing. Readership of my static web sites ranges from 5–10 visitors for a web site with pictures from a very private event, to a few hundred readers a day years after the last change to the web site for GoodDocuments.

A weblog is different. It starts out the same. I create a web site, write a few things, and then tell some friends. They send me feedback. Some link to it. Perhaps a search engine finds it. Nothing much different.

Then I do a second posting, and then a third. Unlike with my more static web sites, some of the readers come back. Since I know some of my friends might be interested in a new posting (it may be about them), I tell them and find out which are reading it and which didn't know about it. I get more feedback. Suddenly, I get feedback from someone I didn't expect. From out of the blue I get a thoughtful comment from a stranger. An email conversation then follows, and now this stranger is an online acquaintance. I read another weblog and see comments about what I wrote. I write comments back on mine.

I analyze my server logs to see which URLs have referring links to my web log. I go to those web pages and read the comments. These are the most revealing, almost like eavesdropping at a party. Some people like what I've written: "Bricklin gets it right when he says. . ." Some are more critical: "If you can get past the poor writing, you'll find another opinion from Bricklin . . ." Sometimes it's even weirder: "Here's a guy who looks like Osama and posts pictures of himself brushing his teeth . . . Get a life!" (Somehow he found my purposely boring "Day in the life of a weblogger" web site[10] but knew nothing else about me except that I had a beard that needed trimming.)

Each time I post something, there's a chance I'll hear from some of my readers. I learn what they like and what they don't. They correct my errors and give suggestions for additional material. When writing, you now have that feeling that you are really talking to real people who will hold you responsible for what you write. If they don't email you, they may stop you in a store and say, "I saw what you wrote and told the guys in my firm who actually worked on those patents and . . ." There's nothing like posting something late one night and then minutes later getting an email with a spelling correction from a reader in France. Ask a question, and you often get responses. (See the series of postings I made about "Big Planes" on March 23 and April 10 of last year.)[11] My mother, brother, and other relatives read my weblog regularly so I use it to communicate more personal material than I might otherwise to an "arm's length" audience.

---

[10]Well over 160 people who write weblogs took pictures during a 24-hour period of their choice between 12:01 a.m. Sunday, September 17, 2000, and 11:59 p.m. Monday, September 18, 2000. Then, a few days later, each posted a photo album showing what they took. I posted mine at `http://www.bricklin.com/albums/btc2000/`.

[11]The "Big Planes" postings are reproduced later in this chapter in the "I Asked a Question and the World Answered" section.

February 26, 2002

When I write, I think that I'm writing to peers and to friends who are regular readers, as well as to people who are looking to learn something from a link they've followed provided by someone else whom they trust. When I write about people and events, I know that those people will possibly read it and comment back to me (I often tell them about it to make sure). My writing is part of relationships of all sorts that continue. Some of what I write may only make sense in light of past writings or knowledge of past parts of my relationship with my readers. To take one of my postings out of context sometimes seems as silly as hearing just the punch line of an in-joke at a party. (In reality, this is a more general statement about weblogs. For mine, I try to provide a little background, though for something I think will attract a large number of new, one-time readers, I write a more thorough, stand-alone essay like this.)

When I read the weblogs of others, I slowly get a sense for that person. It's like hearing a commentator on the radio day after day, or seeing sitcom "friends" week after week. Even though I may never have met that person, I feel the background of a relationship. Some of the responses they write in reaction to something is the same response I was thinking of but didn't write. I start to remember events or themes that recur in their writings. In some cases, I actually have met the person, and the weblog just fills things in, like phone calls between yearly visits to a relative. This feeling of "knowing" the person shows through in the tone of much of the email you get.

Weblogs like mine aren't traditional "journalism" in the sense used to describe an Associated Press news feed. They are individuals, sometimes individuals with particular knowledge or background, describing something or commenting upon things as they see them. They are closer to the source material used by press and historians. (See my "Pamphleteers and Web Sites" essay.) Letters from soldiers aren't the same as reports from correspondents, but they are valuable nonetheless for understanding what's going on. (Think of the value of something like Anne Frank's diary, even if she wasn't such a good writer.) The Internet lets others read these in almost real time and form their own opinion of things. Other weblogs serve as editors for those first-person reports as well as more traditional reports on news sites, helping make sense for their readers. The informal nature of many weblogs, the fact that the writer views it similarly to talking to friends over dinner, lends itself to open, somewhat unedited, and far-ranging material. Who knows what any given reader will find most interesting, especially when that reader months later may be the author themself?

Finally, since some of my readers have their own weblogs, our reactions can be part of what really is some sort "conversation" . . . that is, people making statements and others with whom they have an ongoing relationship reacting.

What about those "silly" web sites of kids writing, "I called Jane for a date again and . . ."? Think of their readership as a community that cares. As one who has found it fulfilling even when one of my web sites has a readership of just a few people (a few family members), I can tell you, with the ease of posting with tools like Blogger and Radio being similar to that of email, it's worthwhile even for something that others might make use of an email going to one or two people. It gives you a log of material you can read yourself and a better control of layout than individual emails. (In an email when you say "like last week's fiasco with Joe" can you depend upon your readers to have a copy to read to remember what you're talking about?) In fact, if I could justify the time, I find my weblog valuable to myself as a personal diary of work-related stuff. Most diaries are not read by much more than the author, yet they are considered "normal" to do for just this reason of augmenting the author's memory.

Journalists who evaluate weblogs on the basis of other motivations for writing can be misled. Not everybody is writing for a wide audience. Not everybody is writing "objectively." The "Hey! What's Up? . . . Oh, GTG, bye!" of Instant Messaging is akin to the "Hi! How's things? Fine!" of two people passing in the hallway. Some weblogs are more like the cell phone calls people make on the way home. Others are like the calls from a person at the scene of an event. In most cases, though, there is a feel for a relationship with the readership. In psychotherapy, I understand, there are various styles. Some therapists have a "blank wall" style where they try to completely keep their own feelings and reactions from the relationship with the patient. Others, to the horror of the first style, tell their patients of their own experiences and express opinions. Both styles have their place. Some journalists send their reports from the field, never even knowing if it's printed or in what form. Others hear from their readers immediately and may even write about the interactions. I believe that blogging gives a journalist a chance to have additional valuable conversations with an audience that would be otherwise unavailable. It's not the only way to communicate, but it sure is a valuable one for both readers and writers. Just ask my mother or my readers around the world or any weblogger. (Don't minimize the value of making your loved ones happy—after all, "Honor thy father and thy mother" is one of the Ten Commandments, and there's no "Be a reporter.") The main reason to stop, from my viewpoint, is that writing takes time. As with weekly telephone calls with our close friends, colleagues, and loved ones, we don't always have time for everything. Stopping doesn't mean it's not valuable.

http://www.bricklin.com/webloggerobservations.htm

Some General Comments about Creating Personal Material to Share on the Web

The next essay was written in 2000, when creating web pages was uncommon for most people. I was working for a company that created web site creation software, and because of that I was posting some material to help show the many ways you could use our tools. *Web site* is used here to refer to a group of related pages, such as photos from a wedding, a blog, or information about a vacation home for rent. A person may have a master web site that would consist of many such smaller sections.

In the years since this essay was written, many software systems have been developed to facilitate the creation of many specific types of web sites. They have made it even easier in those cases. However, the ideas in this essay about the different levels of work needed for different styles of results still hold.

January 18, 2000

HOW LONG DOES IT TAKE TO MAKE A WEB SITE?

One of the questions people considering a web site have is, "How long does it take to make a web site?" As with, "How long does it take to make a dinner?" the answer is, "It depends." I'd like to try to tackle the answer for a variety of personal web sites.

Some background:

The first thing it depends upon is what type of web site you want to create. There are many types of web sites for personal use. There is the web journal, like the one I keep. There is the event commemoration site, like one showing pictures from a wedding or birthday party. There is the nonprofit home page for small clubs and organizations, such as a chorus. There is the product information web site that you might use to describe an item you wish to sell by auction or a vacation home you wish to rent. The list goes on and on. I list the time it takes to create a variety of web site types below.

The second thing it depends upon is the tool you will be using to create the web site. Some tools require you to have some understanding of the HTML web page–programming language or create one page at a time and figure out the linking strategy yourself. For the purposes of this analysis, I'm assuming that you use Trellix Web.[12] It lets you concentrate just on the content of your site and takes care of almost all the linking and the "look" of your web site. When using Trellix Web, HTML knowledge is of little use in creating sites like the ones I mentioned. If you need to create your own design or use a tool that doesn't let you edit your whole site as easily as PowerPoint lets you go from slide to slide, add more time to the estimates below.

I'm also assuming that you have a server on which to place your web site. If you don't, Trellix Web has a variety of wizards to set you up with free advertising-supported services like Tripod and FortuneCity.com or with paid hosting companies.

Here are some things I've seen for myself and others using Trellix Web:

Common overhead

Design: Canned: 1–15 minutes. Custom design: 2 hours+++

If you use a canned design, you spend a minute choosing the design. (More if you're fussier or don't know the set from which you are choosing.) If you are not using a canned design "as is," you can spend from half an hour to several hours crafting the "look" of your web site. For example, my own www.bricklin. com web site used a custom design that took me a few hours to hone, including getting color suggestions from a professional. Many of my wedding and Bar/Bat-Mitzvah web sites use a standard design that comes with Trellix Web and only took the 30 seconds to scroll through some thumbnails and make a choice. If you need to make/get/buy custom artwork, the time can move to days or weeks, and the cost can go up quite high.

Preparing pictures: 5 minutes for every 10 pictures shot plus scanning or loading time

It takes time to choose the pictures, determine the order, and perhaps make minor adjustments with a photo editor (such as brightness, contrast, gamma, red eye, etc.). If you use a digital camera, you have to load the pictures onto your PC from the camera (1 to 10 minutes per 8MB of pictures—120 low

---

[12]Trellix Web was a product from the company I founded in 1996 and worked at that ran on your PC and published entire web sites, or parts of web sites, to the Web. It could publish to a web site you paid for as well as "free" ad-supported sites on providers of the time like Tripod and FortuneCity.com. Up through at least the writing of this book, I used Trellix Web for most of my personal web site and for my blog. (For business material, such as on SoftwareGarden.com, I write hand-crafted HTML. For a technical web site I share with two friends, www.satn.org, I've used Blogger.)

resolution, 20 higher resolution).[13] If you work from paper prints, you have to scan the pictures (a minute or so each?). While some pictures go quickly, you can waste a lot of time deciding between two almost identical ones, or getting the contrast and brightness just right.

Checking names and facts, linking to relevant information: 1 minute to 1 hour per page

There are different levels of checking the facts and spelling of names, linking to related web sites, etc. Here are some guidelines:

> **Off the top of your head:** Like a conversation at a cocktail party, you just type what comes to your mind, no checking. This takes up no more time than a quick email. Hopefully you proofread through once and spell check but usually don't.
>
> **Basic checking and linking:** Like a paper for distribution at a meeting, you check spelling, especially of people's names, their titles, give URLs for their web sites, etc. This can easily double the time it takes to write something. I find that even for family sites, like pictures of a wedding, I need help identifying people whose names I've "forgotten;" otherwise I'll just say "here are some pictures." You don't want to identify Aunt Jean (Jeane?) and neglect to name her husband (Joe? Joel? Jim?) smiling next to her.
>
> **"Reasonable" due diligence:** Like a paper for distribution to strangers, you follow the URLs to check that your assertions are correct, do extra research to make sure, look for related links perhaps, maybe get permission for using someone's picture or linking to their site as a courtesy. This can more than double or triple the time to create the page. When I did my report December 2nd about Howard Anderson's talk, I used a tape recorder to check quotes, etc. A lot different than just quickly typing what I remember.
>
> **Full checking:** Like a major publication, you not only do all the checking and more research, you have another person review it, call/email others to talk about it, etc. This is a full-time job.

---

[13]These are the times and sizes in 2000 when 1 or 2 megapixels was considered a high-resolution photo in consumer-level cameras.

Types of web sites

Here is a list of various types of personal web sites with estimates. This is not an exhaustive list.

A Quick Note Web Site: 10 to 30 minutes

This web site is probably just one page in length with a few pictures and a little bit of text. There is almost no fact-checking. Examples: "The tulips bloomed," "No more metal-mouth: I got my braces off," "A few pictures and results from the big race," "Directions to the party (with a picture) and where to park." This doesn't take much longer than an email with attachments.

Single Event Report: 1 to 4 hours

This is a 1- to 10-page web site with several pictures on each page, plus captions and/or descriptive paragraphs. It is organized into logical groupings, such as sub-events, different groups of people, etc. Examples are pictures from a birthday or other party, wedding, bar/bat-mitzvah, reunion, etc. If you are using a digital camera, you probably take 50 to 100 pictures or so.

A major determination of the amount of time is the number of photographs you use and the depth to which you produce a narrative. Saying, "Here are some dancing pictures," and inserting 5 pictures is a lot different than showing 10 couples, each with their names spelled right and a link to their email address, and a paragraph about what's new in their life since the last reunion. A page of the former takes 10 minutes to create, and the latter could take the good part of an afternoon or evening, or more. While the extra time may seem prohibitive, it can actually be quite enjoyable. Calling cousin Jim for an email address can result in a wonderful half-hour conversation; thinking about how to describe your feelings at seeing your daughter walk down the aisle is not wasted time. The feeling of tedium when writing in high school about Homer is quite different than as an adult describing a camping trip to your friends. Choosing among 100 different pictures of kids playing at a party you planned is not unpleasant.

Multiday event: Just pictures and simple captions: 4 hours; With detailed commentary and name/link checking: First page in 2–4 hours, finished in 20+ hours

This is a 5- to 30-page web site with several pictures on each page, plus descriptive paragraphs and/or a full narrative. It is organized by time and/or by event. Examples are my reports on www.bricklin.com about PC Forum, LCS 35th, the

Digital Storytelling Festival, Comdex '99, etc. If you are using a digital camera, unloading the pictures at least once a day, you may end up with 1,000 pictures. Other examples are vacations, wedding weekends, etc.

With this type of web site it is important to understand the time costs. I have seen people start such a site but not finish it well. Writing the narrative, choosing the pictures, checking names and affiliations, getting links to corporate web sites, etc., all over a dial-up hotel phone line with a modem, can add substantially to the time. I find that I can create the first page or two of an event site during the event in the late evening. As time goes on, though, the nights get longer, and you end up needing hours of extra work to finish the site on the plane and when you get home. Budget for this, or don't set the expectations too high at the beginning.

Ongoing web log or journal: 2 minutes per entry for simple note or link to 1–3+ hours for entries like in this log

Journals or logs are web sites to which you constantly add new entries. One common type, sometimes called a "blog" (short for weblog) has entries that are just short paragraphs describing links to other interesting things found on the Web. To do that, you just fire up your editing tool, type "Interesting article about blue frogs and politics on scienceworld2K.com," paste in the link, and publish. Finding the original article is the hard part.

Another type of journal, like the one I started in October 1999, has much longer entries with more original text, sometimes original pictures, researched names, etc. This could also be a "What's happened in my life" or "Another day in our vacation" journal. This type of journal takes 1 to 3 or more hours per entry. Essays like this (sometimes you have more to say than a normal entry) take even longer. It is very hard to keep up on a daily basis for a long period unless it is part of your job or a major hobby. For personal use, updating it just once a week, once a month, or once every three months may be more appropriate. Family members love this type of journal, so doing one you can keep up for the appropriate duration is important. I think the once-a-month one will become very popular and be a major supplement to infrequent phone calls to friends and relatives and improve upon the yearly Christmas letter.

Organization information site: 2 to 6 hours

This is a web site for an organization like a chorus, church group, budding nonprofit, amateur sports team, or group of friends. It gives you a place to send potential members/benefactors to learn more about you or to post pictures from an event. It initially runs 3 to 10 pages, with pages such as "About Us," "How to contact us," "Pictures of our members," "Our upcoming fundraiser," etc. The main time factor is deciding what to say and getting the correct words to say it. The design overhead factor can come into play here if you insist on having the look convey special, custom information. If you use a canned design and already have the pictures, this type of site can go up in an evening.

Other types of web sites

There are many other types of personal web sites, including fan/booster sites, very small business sites, family sites, etc. Hopefully the list here will give you some idea of the time to budget for whatever you create.

http://danbricklin.com/log/howlong.htm

I Asked a Question and the World Answered

In this series of blog posts, you get to see how the readers of my blog helped me answer a mundane, simple, but obscure, question.

Monday, March 19, 2001
TRAVELING WITH HANDHELD WIRELESS AND TRAINS

I've been doing a bit of traveling the last few weeks. Here are some notes:

I was at the Fort Lauderdale airport in Florida and noticed a huge plane just sitting there. Nobody knew what it was, but at least it had a big name on the tail:

Big plane and close-up of tail

Luckily I live in the new wireless Internet world! I pulled out my RIM 950,[14] and typed in the URL for the Google search engine:

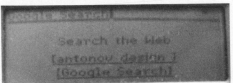

What is that plane? Call up Google on my RIM

It seems Google is tuned for such wireless use. The display was very simple and to the point. I found some references to the plane:

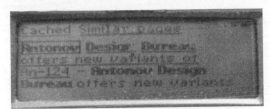

Search results list

Finally, I read that this was a Russian transport:

Details about the Antonov AN-124

Cool! Was finding this out worth $40 or so a month for a normal person? Probably not. Was it fast enough to answer questions in real life? Not if I wasn't

---

[14]The RIM 950 is an early version of the RIM BlackBerry (the service it used was called BlackBerry). It was not a cell phone, but rather a sophisticated pager with simple, and slow, web access.

just waiting around. Luckily, my plane was late, so I had time for playing around like this. Not good enough for a TV ad selling wireless . . .

I have an old write-up[15] of the RIM 950 where I timed typing on it. I tried "typing" on my cell phone to see, once I practiced, how long that same phrase would take. Cell phone: 8 words per minute (WPM), Palm Graffiti: 15 WPM, RIM: 25 WPM, and Stowaway keyboard: 65 WPM. (This is with practice—your results may vary. I usually go much slower in real life.)

The train

I'm typing this several days later while riding the train from Connecticut to Boston. (The train actually competes pretty well now with the plane from New York.) Here things are good: The ride is somewhat smooth (that "train" feel), but the business seats have a 120-volt outlet. The power goes off every once in a while when pulling out of a station, but just for a few seconds—no problem for a laptop. Even better, there's lots of room, even when the person in front of me puts his seat back.

Taking the train, with lots of room and power

[15]http://www.danbricklin.com/log/rimkeyboard.htm

If only they had 802.11b wireless Internet access, then things would be perfect . . .

http://www.danbricklin.com/log/2001_03_01.htm

Friday, March 23, 2001
AN EMAIL CLEARS UP THE PLANE MYSTERY

On Monday I posted my experience using a wireless device to do a web search to find out some information about a huge airplane I saw while waiting for a flight in Ft. Lauderdale. I wondered how valuable such a search capability was.

The huge transport plane I saw (lots of wheels!)

I received an email from Jørn Eriksen,[16] one of my readers:

> We Norwegians know a lot and I can tell you WHY that big Antonov
> was at the airport in Ft. Lauderdale, FL—It was used to trans-
> port two sailing boats from New Zealand to Florida. The boats
> (ehh—actually just one of them) is to compete in the Volvo Around
> the World Race that starts later this year. And yes—the team is
> Norwegian :-)

He sent me a link to a web site about the racing team with a March 8th press release about the plane trip. Thanks, Jørn!

So, two things: Now my mystery is completely cleared up, and I again see the value of person-to-person interaction through personal web sites and the Internet. Having a web site that is read by people around the world who care

---

[16]www.jorneriksen.com

is a wonderful thing, whether those people are friends and relatives or people you haven't met. The sense of community is very real. At the airport I asked some strangers standing next to me if they knew what the plane was. They were slightly annoyed and said "no." On the Web, I found someone who knew the answer and cared to tell me. In our society so many forces isolate us from community. It's nice to be part of one force that is drawing people together. Wireless services are "interesting" at this point, but Internet-aided personal communication is definitely worth paying for and using now.

http://www.danbricklin.com/log/2001_03_23.htm

Tuesday, April 10, 2001
MORE BIG PLANES

I received an email last night from another reader reacting to my story about the big plane in Florida:

> *If you think the plane you saw was big, what will you think of this wonderful plane:*
>
> http://perso.libertysurf.fr/jp.neymond/a3st.html[17]
>
> *This is an Airbus Beluga (to move pieces of planes from one city to another). I live in Nantes, France, one of the cities where there's an EADS (European Aeronautic Defence and Space Company) plant. They use the Beluga to move plane parts built in Nantes to Toulouse or other cities where the parts are assembled to make Airbus planes.*
>
> *Don't ask me how they move a Beluga !! ;-)*
>
> *The best place to learn about it:*
>
> http://www.airbustransport.com/
>
> —*Jean-Yves Stervinou*
>   http://www.stervinou.com/

---

[17]The linked-to page is no longer available.

So, while the Antonov was big, in Europe they often see an even bigger plane. Now I've taken my curiosity about a big plane I happened to see about as far as it can go, I guess. Ah, the joys of having friendly readers around the world looking out for you . . .

I was back going through the Ft. Lauderdale airport last week. The big plane was gone. I asked the driver who picked me up about it. He said there were two Russian planes at some point, but they moved. I asked him if he knew why they were there. He didn't, even though he picks up people at the airport every day. I asked him how he found out it was a Russian plane. He said he asked someone. I told him about the Norwegian boat . . .

The same driver knew my plane was late by using "the Internet" on his cell phone (Nextel, I think). He demonstrated. Later I asked what the weather was going to be. He whipped out his phone and punched a few keys and read off the forecast. "What about Akron, where I'll be going next to see my sister?" I asked. I wasn't sure of the zip code—so he first found the weather for Kentucky—but eventually got it right. (Cell phones are good for numbers and choosing from a small list, not words, I guess.) "Want to know the weather somewhere else?" he asked. His tone and enthusiasm reminded me of the early TV ads for automated teller machines. "Ooh! Let me stop and check my balance! Wow! Want to see me check it again?" Early adopters are fun to watch, but their enthusiasm is not always a leading indicator.

http://www.danbricklin.com/log/2001_03_23.htm

How Blogging Helped Blogger

As you can see, I like blogging and have felt for a long time that it is an important form of communication.

There was a time when the Blogger service was having financial difficulties. The last remaining employee, Evan Williams, wrote about their situation on his blog in a post titled "And Then There Was One."[18] He started out like this:

> *It's probably become obvious to the careful observer that all is not well in the Land of Pyra. Rather than wait for the public speculation*

---

[18]http://web.archive.org/web/20010410030419/www.evhead.com/longer/2200706_essays.asp

and debate, I'm going to say what exactly is going on (from my per-
spective—not speaking for anyone else on the team or as an official
Pyra/Blogger representative). I'm sure the public speculation and
debate will happen anyway, but I don't plan to take much part in it. I
have other things to do.

First of all, the company (Pyra) is not dead, and the service (Blog-
ger) is not going away. However: We are out of money, and I have
lost my team.

Evan Williams, January 31, 2001

Dave Winer linked to it in his blog, which brought it to my attention. Here is the account I later posted about what then transpired.

April 16, 2001

HOW THE BLOGGER DEAL HAPPENED

On April 16, 2001, Trellix and Pyra announced a relationship.
(You can read the press release at danbricklin.com/log/
bloggerrelease.htm.) *Here's my story behind it.*

Some background: Back in 1985, the company I founded that created VisiCalc, Software Arts, was in very bad shape. We had won an awful lawsuit filed against us by our old publisher and had released some new products, but we owed lots of money and needed a partner fast. We had talked to many companies, but they either didn't understand our urgency or wanted deals that tied me up personally with employment contracts I didn't like.

In the midst of this, I traveled to an industry trade show, SoftCon, hoping to find a good partner. Waiting to check in for the plane, I ran into Mitch Kapor, founder of Lotus. Mitch was a friend from back in the early days of Software Arts, but Lotus was now a major competitor. Despite our bad situation, I hadn't contacted him. Mitch asked me how I was doing. I said, "Lousy." He said, "No." I said, "Yes! Want to talk about it?" We spent time talking on the plane and it turned out there were some important synergies between what they needed and what we had. Within 5 days, we had a deal—one that Mitch helped structure in a way that gave me the freedom to do what I wanted. His approach to the deal made it happen and beat out our other suitors. (I ended up doing some consulting for Lotus for a few months and then went off and founded Software Garden to create the successful Dan Bricklin's Demo Program.)

April 16, 2001

Fast-forward. I've been a relatively long-term reader of Dave Winer's Davenet essays and Scripting News blog. In 1998, I created a public web site of my own that I updated frequently for a few months, GoodDocuments.com, to discuss issues related to our work at Trellix at the time. In early 1999, I started my own public personal web site, Bricklin.com, to, among other things, provide a platform for my writings.

Through Dave and others, I read about a new product called Blogger that a company called Pyra released in late August 1999. Internet people I respected started using it. In October 1999, I started my own log as a part of my web site, using Trellix's product of the time, Trellix Web (a desktop application).

I kept hearing about neat features in Blogger through Dave's writings. In February 2000, Trellix announced Trellix Web Express (TWE), a server-based web site creation system we were developing. In March 2000, Dave ran a panel at Esther Dyson's PC Forum on "Web-based Applications." It included Pyra founder Evan Williams as well as myself. I met Evan at the opening reception and we had a nice talk. You can read my report of that conference in my PC Forum 2000 Album.[19] Here are some pictures:

Clockwise from top left: The reception, Dave Winer,
Dave running the panel, Evan Williams

[19]http://www.bricklin.com/albums/pcforum2000/

We released TWE in May for Lycos/Tripod, and in September started rolling out other private-label versions for additional partners like ZDNet, CNet, About, and others.

February 1st, 2001, I returned from a PR tour. It was my mother's birthday and that night I was busy trying to find a way to tape "Jeopardy!" after she called saying she saw my name mentioned on it.[20] Later, reading Dave Winer's site before bed, I saw a posting about problems at Evan's company, Pyra. I read Evan's heartfelt story "And Then There Was One." I was really moved. This was the type of stuff I couldn't write about during our tough days at Software Arts.

As a believer in web logging, and an admirer of the product, I didn't like the idea of Blogger being lost in the dotCom crash. Personal web sites were growing and important. Losing the most well-known system used by many of the most visible people would be a blow to the industry. Also, our product, TWE, was tuned for creating normal multipage web sites, with lots of pictures, fancy layouts, etc.—great for photo, small business, informational, hobby, and personal expression web sites. It was not tuned for chronological, content-managed web logs. (Our old desktop product that I use for this log is a nice compromise, but desktop products don't have the widespread appeal of a server-based product like TWE.) Our server-based offering includes not only TWE, but also FTP, Frontpage extensions, and an HTML editor to serve as wide an audience as possible. I had always planned upon adding features to TWE to beef it up for blogging. Maybe, I thought, we could acquire some technology from Evan and help him and his users at the same time. (And, of course, there could be some good PR opportunities . . .)

I quickly sent off an email late that night to Evan asking if there was anything we at Trellix could do. The next day I talked to my CEO at Trellix, Don Bulens, and told him what I had read and asked him if it was OK to try to do something with them. He said yes.

A few days later Evan responded. Seeing that I was scheduled to speak at O'Reilly's P2P conference several days later [about my "Cornucopia of the Commons" essay], he said he'd like to chat if I had a chance when I was in California.

I arrived in California Wednesday, February 13th. All afternoon I accompanied Trellix people on sales calls. Finally, I arrived in the evening at the Westin St. Francis in downtown San Francisco where the conference was being held. I called Evan and we arranged to meet near the hotel registration. We did meet,

---

[20]http://danbricklin.com/log/2001_02_05.htm#jeopardy

and then walked through the lobby to go out to dinner (registration is straight through the opening in the middle left):

April 16, 2001

The St. Francis hotel lobby—really something!

We walked around a few blocks until we found a place that appealed to both of our eating requirements: Niko Niko Sushi. Here's what I recall of the conversation:

I asked Evan what his situation was and what we could do to help. I checked to see what he wanted, remembering my experience on the other side from Lotus and the other suitors way back when (I told him about that). He wanted to stay independent. He didn't want to move to Massachusetts [unhappy face icon in original]. He had talked to others, but they weren't proposing things he liked or weren't coming through. (Sounded familiar . . .) He was willing to license code and trademark. He could give us lots of time to help us get things working. He understood the benefit of our partners to his distribution. I asked about the code (some in ASP—bad for us—some in Java—good—and XML for data—good). I took notes. We went over monetary needs.

I told him I understood his situation and would try to be as responsive as possible. I would talk this all over with Don in the morning when the East Coast woke up and Don would be back to him by phone to work out a proposal that day if he wanted. I knew that the best way to do something like this (from Evan's viewpoint) was to move fast to an agreement so money can change hands and he could plan his future. Taking weeks to come to a decision could really hurt his future.

I forgot to bring a camera to record the meeting. All I have is a picture of the receipt I filed with my expense report. The notes were made that night.

Receipt from dinner ($41.10 plus $8.50 tip . . .)

I was happy since I thought we had the outline of a deal that would work for us both and there was a good possibility that it would happen. I was worried that Evan may not like it in the light of morning or not get along with Don when they went over details of what we'd need.

The next morning was the start of the conference. I took a seat where I could take pictures. They had 802.11b wireless, so I was hooked up to the Internet. I posted during the morning session. Evan posted something a bit later, showing he read my stuff and telling people that we had dinner together. I ran into Evan a couple of times, but we didn't talk about the deal. I kept calling Don to see if he connected with Evan. It took a while, given cell phones and Evan's schedule.

By Friday afternoon, Don had talked with Evan and emailed him a proposed outline of an agreement. (Not bad—Evan and I met Wednesday night.) Monday we heard back from Evan. He liked what he saw, but needed to think a bit and run it past some others. It took a little while to get that all together and fine-tune the term sheet. With lawyers and advisors involved, it took a little while to finish, but the basic deal worked out in the first 48 hours was finally signed on March 2nd (and money changed hands).

Over the following weeks, Evan had other work to do and both companies worked on a full contract which was eventually signed. I also noticed that Evan was quoting my writings more often [smiley face icon in original]. On April 9th Evan and one of his people, Matt, came to Trellix to install a copy of Blogger on an internal system here, teach us about it (inside and out), and plan for the future. We also worked on the press release.

Wednesday night they went home. Friday, Evan and I started briefing some of the press for official publication Monday. I spent the afternoon writing this. I posted it around the time our press release was scheduled to go up on the Trellix web site.

Me and Evan Williams, taken by Don Bulens in his office

Evan posted his account of the events on his blog in a post titled "How the Trellix Deal Happened—and What It Means."[21]

http://danbricklin.com/log/blogger.htm

From a product viewpoint, this deal ended up being only somewhat beneficial to Trellix. While we learned a lot from Evan and Matt, we ended up not using the Blogger code and used our own code for the simple blogging functionality that we added to our web site building system. The public relations benefit certainly justified the expense of the deal.[22]

---

[21]http://web.archive.org/web/20010418093357/http://www.evhead.com/longer/ trellix_essays.asp

[22]For example, there was a nice article in the *New York Times*: http://www.nytimes. com/2001/04/16/technology/16LOG.htm.

For the world, helping Blogger turned out to be very important. In his account, Evan wrote that by the time we met in San Francisco his finances had gotten to the point where he was considering cutting off all free service and starting to charge. In those early days of blogging, turning off the service used by a large percentage of the participants would have soured a lot of people on the concept and stunted its growth.

Eventually Blogger was sold to Google, where it is still available to this day. After a while Evan left Google to work on other projects, including Twitter.

Bloggers at the 2004 DNC in Boston

In late July 2004, the Democratic National Convention was held in Boston, Massachusetts. I live in Newton, Massachusetts, just a few miles away. In the blogging world this convention was a special moment and a big deal. A set of bloggers were issued official credentials to cover the event. They were given space to sit in the convention hall and given special briefings. The traditional press was very curious about this new player, and the interplay between press and bloggers was interesting to watch.

I didn't apply for credentials, but I did talk to some who were going and followed what they wrote carefully. I blogged about it, giving a view from outside: a view of the city and the bloggers writing about the convention rather than being inside the convention itself.

As I write this four years later, things have changed quite a bit. Not only are bloggers major players in the world of politics, it is even the case that major politicians now go to the blogger's conventions in addition to vice versa. Major professional journalists now also (or only) blog, such as professor, *New York Times*–columnist, economist, and Nobel Prize–winner Paul Krugman who writes for a blog hosted by the *New York Times* itself.

This series of blog posts and essays is an interesting snapshot at a critical time during the development of a means of Internet-enabled distributed communication of which that controversial *New York Times* piece asked in 2002, "Is the Weblog, in other words, a fad that is destined to fade?"

Wednesday, July 21, 2004
THE CONVENTION IS COMING, THE CONVENTION IS COMING . . .

I'm not one of the bloggers going to the Democratic National Convention. I didn't apply for various reasons, and am feeling mixed about that. It would be a real special experience, like a roller coaster or 3 Comdexes[23] at once, I assume. But I couldn't commit to all that time, nor did I really want that pressure (as I'd put on myself), and frankly I never thought about how special it might be until it was too late. (I also might not have been chosen—I'm a techie blogger with a specialized audience, not a political one.) The closest I got was being a catalyst in David Weinberger's pre-Convention camera purchase.

I feel very grateful to those who are blogging at the Convention. To me, they are the way we other bloggers (and blog readers) will get to vicariously feel what it's like to be there as a blogger. That's what I expect from reading the blogs—to get feelings of being there through the eyes of someone I get to follow through time. A "traditional journalist" gets us the facts—who, what, where, when, why. They try in many ways to be interchangeable, except that some may be closer to an "ideal" than others. Bloggers are different to me. They have a name and a history. I've seen how some of them have reacted to all sorts of things and know some of their perspectives. The Convention will fit in there in that stream from them over time, and the human element that they have already given us (or that we can read in old posts and in posts in the future) is something on which their reports will be carried. People see the world differently. I remember a child who when asked if they remembered visiting Cape Kennedy Space Center years before, said, "Is that the place where I saw the cat with her kittens?" with no mention of any huge rocket carcasses nearby. I want to hear the wonder at seeing things that are not supposed to be the "story" but that matter to someone. We know who is going to be nominated. What else do we learn instead from having so many people together for such a purpose with such emotion behind their reasons for being involved?

While I'm not in there, I guess I'll still write some of what I feel as a person nearby. The Convention has a force field that goes far beyond Causeway Street. That's a view I want to remember, too, and this log is where I often put things I want to remember.

Here are some observations:

Notice that I call it "the Convention," with a capital "C." In the Boston area this is a Big Thing. (I live a few miles from downtown in a close-by suburb,

---

[23]Comdex was a huge computer industry tradeshow.

but for this event we're all in "Boston.") You can feel the excitement in the air. We didn't expect to get it here, and have no idea what it will be like. We don't have something like it to look back at for comparison. The city is quite different than it was—the Fleet Center (where the Convention will be held) is relatively new, replacing the old Boston Garden where the Celtics and Bruins (sports teams) used to play. The Big Dig has changed the landscape, but isn't completely done. We have a new bridge next to the Fleet Center—one of the most beautiful in the world (at least in the eyes of many of us here). Since 9/11 happened, security takes on a whole new meaning. While not all the hijackers started in this area, some did, and I pass by two of the motels where they last slept very frequently—a strange reminder. Kerry is our senator, so it's all local and national at the same time. We've met him.

The new bridge, the old Customs tower, and the Fleet Center

The city is very nervous. We are on display. Our big chance. We've lost some of the big games on the national stage (with the Red Sox) and won some others (with the Patriots) in the near past (but always a great show!). How will this go? Is there some security thing that could have been done that will be "obvious" in tragic hindsight? Are we doing it wrong? People all over are affected. Basically, downtown will be closed to lots of normal traffic for the duration of the Convention, meaning people can't get to or from work as they used to and maybe not at all. Things keep changing, so we don't know what new roadblocks will be thrown up (literally and figuratively). Some people are being more selfish, taking advantage of the situation. There are pickets threatened, which embarrasses me. They are using the delegates' support of unions against them and the city that invited them. It's like playing out a family feud at the wedding you invited all your friends to. Many others are sacrificing for the good of the city with a smile on their faces.

Sign on the highway last week: I-93 North Closed 4 PM - 1 AM July 26 To July 29. One of many such signs. I-93 is the major road through downtown (taken with my cell phone camera as we zoomed by).

It's getting closer. As I returned from a trip last night, the airport had banners up welcoming people to the Convention. I received a copy of a book in the mail relating all sorts of great stories about the city (Scott Kirsner is one of the contributors, and he kindly mentions me and Bob in his essay about innovation). The top newspaper headlines show the uncertainty and struggle with the details: "Fast city-police accord ordered," "Protest zone draws ire," "By sea or land, private transport fills a gap," "Neighbors fume over can removal: Security measure yields untidy result" (public trash cans were removed from the streets so bombs can't be hidden in them, and then people put their trash in the empty metal can-holder frames).

Five more days. Lots of emotion, but the bottom line is I'm proud to be here in Boston and proud that we're the center of something big for the country.

Sunday, July 25, 2004
DNC BLOGGER DINNER

On my way back from a vacation up in Maine this weekend, I got a call from Bob Frankston on my cell phone. Was I going to the DNC blogger (and others) dinner that Dave Winer mentioned on his blog? Bob and I aren't "official" DNC bloggers, but it was an open invitation—so why not? A minor detour on the way home and I was there for Chinese dinner. I listened to stories about the facilities inside the Fleet Center, CNN being behind the bloggers, and more (Bob and I also talked to Dave about RSS and old times). You can see Dave's pictures from earlier up on his ConventionBloggers.com site. Here is a picture I took tonight at dinner:

A DNC Blogger pass with a *New York Times* strap

Bob drove Dave back to his hotel and then me home, and we passed by the Fleet Center, where there was surprisingly little traffic:

The Fleet Center on the right as we go over the Zakim Bridge (notice how close I-93 is to the building)

Driving down from Maine earlier, there were more signs about the Convention. Lots of "I-93 Closed Monday-Thursday 4 PM–1 AM" signs. People on overpasses with Kerry-Edwards signs waving (no Bush ones visible). Yesterday, the Red Sox won a very exciting, emotion-filled (including a big brawl) game against the Yankees. It was a great, come-from-behind win. Just what the city needed. The strikes are settled so the pickets should be off, but not early enough for a least one canceled state-delegate party. People are streaming in. In a surprise change, Kerry was one of them today and flew in to see the Red Sox-Yankees game tonight, throwing out a ceremonial "first pitch" on his way to a scheduled event in Florida tomorrow. I heard people mention it on the streets of Cambridge, which is just across the Charles River from the Convention site.

http://danbricklin.com/log/2004_06_29.htm

An Essay in the Midst of the Blog Posts

I wrote a longer-form piece, an essay, after a few days to put together more of my thoughts. You can see from the introduction that it is intended for a wider audience than my normal blog posts.

WHAT WE LEARN FROM THE CONVENTION BLOGGING

Thoughts from a long-term blogger after two days of the DNC

I write this Wednesday, after two days of the Democratic National Convention in Boston. Prior to the event, I posted a couple of entries in to my weblog. Now that it's been going on, there is more to say. Here are some personal thoughts from the narrow place where I sit in my home a few miles away.

First, in the blogging tradition, let me give some personal background so you'll understand some of my perspective. I've been using various forms of weblogs to "cover" events for several years. I've done family life-cycle events, like weddings, and public "industry" events, like the Digital Storytelling Festival and Comdex, since 1999. These were all "posted within 12 hours or 24 at most" affairs, not delayed items like my inspiration—"Travels With Samantha" from Philip Greenspun.[24] Some examples of my work can be found on the Albums

---

[24]http://philip.greenspun.com/samantha/

page of this web site,[25] including: the 1999 Digital Storytelling Festival, Fall Comdex 1999, the Foreign Policy Association's World Leadership Forum 2000, and PC Forum 2003.

I've learned a lot from doing those and watching my progression over time. Reacting to the Convention Blogging is bringing it into even better focus.

Event blogging is different from normal, daily blogging. In normal blogging, you watch the world go by and pick and choose things you want to comment upon. There is material online to point to and react to. There are ideas that well up and you take the time to write about, but few people may be waiting for them. There are many, many bloggers. Some read other blogs and choose the posts they think others should read. Through popular gateway blogs like some of the well known political blogs, and tools like Blogdex, Daypop, and more, things bubble to the top.

Events are another thing entirely. The time is very condensed and the amount of information is concentrated. If you are "covering" the event, you have to look at it all and provide perspective to a reader who doesn't see all of the context that you do. The event marches on and won't stop for you to take time for thinking and writing. Picking and choosing is harder—if you stop to blog, you might miss the keystone piece of what's going on.

I started out being the only person "covering" the events I attended on the Web. I tried to tell a story, to let you feel like you were there and experience it as fully as possible. I used pictures (with which I am more skilled than with writing—I've been doing that since I was a child, including high school yearbook work) to help me communicate.

Short events, like a wedding, are great. You take the pictures, go home and spend an hour or two with the right tools (I was CTO of a company I founded that made such tools), and *voila!*, you're done. It's hard, but worth it as a "gift" for the people putting on the event. Today, I usually just give them a CD with all my pictures and let them do with those pictures as they please. I rarely have the time to tell the whole story myself.

Long, multiday events are a killer. The "getting there" part is easy. Your first posts have detail. The first real day you end up staying up late, very late, and do an OK job. By the second or third day, you just can't keep up. The event itself takes up so much time that doing all the writing and editing and thinking interferes with you being there. The big "think piece" gets written on the plane back or perhaps the next day, but then you've got to get on with your life. Unless it's your job, it's really tough to "cover" an event.

---

[25]http://www.bricklin.com/albumlist.htm

July 28, 2004

I've adjusted by just publishing pictures, and not even taking the time to research names and spellings. (Compare my 1999 and 2000 albums linked above to my more recent ones.) People like them anyway, and it serves my purposes. That's how I cope.

There's another element coming into play: I'm now not the only person covering events on the Web. I don't have to tell you what people said. Heath Row does miraculous real-time transcription. David Weinberger is insightful and funny. AKMA shows the philosophical side. Winer links to items I'd never have seen, helping people find the pieces. The pressure is off me to cover the whole thing, and I get a niche. I'm known for taking good pictures indoors—something I've worked at my whole life. Weinberger is insightful for a living and used to write comedy, AKMA teaches at a seminary, etc.

The Convention brings in a new element. There are 15,000 paid professionals covering the event. There are live and edited TV feeds produced by thousands more. These full-time people had time to prepare. They are used to covering such events—that's what they do for a living year after year. What should the role of the blogger be? Their readers may or may not have seen any of those other reports. How do you integrate that in?

Bloggers who are used to commenting on a day-by-day world, thrust into covering a huge event, need to adjust. Unlike a normal conference or family event, with a single speaker, a single party, and a single hall to schmooze in, a convention has high-power meetings everywhere, media extravaganza presentations with waving signs, and thousands of interesting participants including some you only see on tabloid covers or the evening news and many, many others whose personal stories are gems. And it's something new for almost all of the bloggers.

The Convention Bloggers seem to be going through logical stages in handling all this. The preparation they probably did was arrange for accommodations and equipment. A few worked on the technical aspects of cameras and microphones, but couldn't even prepare for the all-important connectivity to the Internet until the day it started.

The first posts were like any new blog: "This is my first post." "Hello world!" Then the introspective, circular "Wow, I'm blogging in this situation" and then moving out to "That blogger I know is here and blogging, too" and "A news organization I know is here and sitting over there."

Like other event blogs, the "pre-" postings were "How I got here," "What the transportation here is like," and "Here's them setting up and here's someone I ran into."

Then we saw something new. The bloggers were news. They were special. The Blogger Breakfast was a curveball. The lights were shined on them. They were under the microscope, not looking through it. They reported what it's like to look back up the microscope and be the specimen. More circular, "what it feels like to be a blogger" stuff. For us other bloggers, this was a treat. We could relate to the writers and appreciate the "report from the front." Others probably saw that as blogger naiveté. Bloggers need to learn to be watched as well as do the watching. The traditional press has learned this (probably overly so). In the future, with more and more bloggers, so no one knows who is blogging nor which may turn out to be significant to the person trying to influence them, the problem may go away.

Coming through, though, with the "Gee, they care about us and treat us special" posts, were blogger observations. Some bloggers, in reporting the breakfast event,[26] reported the questions they themselves asked and the answers they received, getting back into the groove with their own biases and perspectives.

---

[26]There was a blogger breakfast hosted by the DNC which was also covered by traditional press. They were addressed by Howard Dean, Barack Obama, then running for the Senate and the convention keynoter, and others. Obama was relatively unknown at the time but the bloggers took him very seriously. It is eye-opening to read today some of what was written back then.

USA Today ran a piece about the breakfast (http://www.usatoday.com/news/politic-selections/nation/2004-07-26-convention-bloggers_x.htm). It included this line:

Keynote speaker Barack Obama, the party's candidate for U.S. Senate in Illinois, told the bloggers: "Although I can't match faces to blog sites, you guys have just been doing a fantastic job . . . One of the most exciting things is how you're energizing young people."

One of the bloggers quoted in the USA Today article was David Weinberger. You can read some of what David wrote at http://www.hyperorg.com/blogger/2004/07/. For example, after Obama's keynote he wrote (http://www.hyperorg.com/blogger/2004/07/28/tuesday-night-scorecard/):

Barack Obama: The good news for Hillary is that she might get State Department when Obama is President in 2012.

The next day he wrote (http://www.hyperorg.com/blogger/2004/07/29/more-convention-weirdness/):

Last night, in a self-reflective capstone to the list of weird media moments at the Convention, Melissa Fitzgerald—CJ's assistant, Carol, on The West Wing—came by to talk with the bloggers. She was there to promote Environment 2004's ecological agenda. Why come to the bloggers? Because we're the future of the media, etc. etc.

Being a celebrity, um, camp follower—and having utterly failed to satisfy my children's requirement that I come back with photos of The Daily Show correspondents—I interviewed her. What's her political background? Her parents know Gov. Ed Rendell and she's been around politics all her life, and she's happy to be on a show that has social relevance. Ok. Then she told me what issues she's here to support. As one of her Environment 2004 handlers had said, she was articulate: She rattled off the mercury in the fish and the Clear Skies Act oxymoron stuff. After she'd made her way pretty far down the list, I asked her

There was "Wow, they thought it was worth spending Obama's time with us! But, hmm, is he the real deal? What have I heard from others?"[27]

The rest of Monday seemed to be reporting what they saw, followed by Tuesday morning burnout from covering an event (at least in the several blogs I read). "What should I write about?" seemed to be a question that needed to be answered. "I'm overwhelmed with what's going on, with long stretches of boredom and quick surprises." In the midst of it all, there were more things to go to outside, learning the ropes of covering such an event. There was learning when to use time for blogging activities, when to sleep. What to watch.

Some of the bloggers just fell back into their normal modes. Wonkette.com had infrequent posts on topics that you'd expect. Dave Winer looked for things to point to and did experiments with audio[28] and stuff. They all were getting distracted by being interviewed while they were trying to do their thing.

By Wednesday morning I could see some things coming together. The Barack Obama story is a great one to follow. He seemed to impress the bloggers at the breakfast, but there were questions about whether he was special because he was the keynote or the keynote because he really was special. We heard[29] from some bloggers about how they (and the press) get preview copies of the speeches. We heard how different news anchors watched (or didn't watch) the stage since they may have already read what was going to be said. Then Mathew Gross (experienced at covering political stuff in blogs, I assume), put

---

if she thought anyone in the stadium disagreed with her. No, she said, but some people may not know the facts.

So, here was a multi-level disconnect. She's a good actor, but she failed to read my face that was practically screaming "Stop the list! You're telling me stuff I know." But, so what, it's not like my time is so valuable that I can't afford to spend an extra 45 seconds listening to an actor on one of my favorite shows. But, what does she expect me to write about in my blog, other than the meta crap I'm writing right now? Melissa Fitzgerald came by to tell us that Bush sucks on the environment, a point of view I'd ignored until it came from Carol on The West Wing?

[27] Steve Garfield, an early video blogger, posted a video of Howard Dean's visit to the blogger breakfast including comments from Dave Winer. His blog post about it is `http://stevegarfield.blogs.com/videoblog/2004/07/heres_my_third_.html`, and you can also watch it on YouTube: `http://www.youtube.com/watch?v=Gv6Bwx-UXio`.

[28] `http://archive.scripting.com/2004/07/25#When:9:36:41PM`
  This podcast recording, early in the development of the genre, really impressed me and showed me some of its potential. I've mentioned it many times since.

[29] `http://web.archive.org/web/20040802233651/http://www.centristcoalition.com/blog/archives/000894.html`

it all together:[30] Having read the speech, he then reviews how it's delivered and why it went over so well. That was contrasted[31] by blogger Jesse Taylor to Dan Rather's "journal" entry[32] written before the talk, where Rather says how dull things were and discusses the upcoming Obama speech in terms of being from an African American, not what he would say and how he'd say it. Winer[33] and others spoke of boredom on Monday, but only as a shared observation from a

---

[30]Mathew Gross launched the first presidential campaign weblog for Howard Dean in March of 2003 and became the Director of Internet Communications for the Dean campaign. He's done lots since and blogs at www.mathewgross.com. Here is what he wrote:

(http://web.archive.org/web/20040807112526/http://mathewgross.com/blog/archives/000498.html)

Reviewing Obama

You read the speech in advance and you think it's all there: a great biography, soaring rhetoric, and great stories of the beleagured middle class, who have suffered great losses as a result of George Bush's economic malfeasance.

And then he takes the stage, and you think it's all there: stunning good looks, a commanding presence, and a sea of blue Obama signs waving across the convention floor.

But at first there seems to be something missing in the delivery. It meanders a bit. When he hits the right notes, the crowd goes wild. But in-between there are these deep troughs, and you begin to wonder if he's not unlike an undisciplined songwriter—with flashes of brilliance, yes, but with the too-frequent flat tune.

But then he starts to hit more and more of the right notes. By the end, he's building; he's in command of the entire arena. The crowd hangs on every word. They want to cheer him. He smiles, holds up a hand to stave off the cheering crowd.

And then his voice goes down, quietly. The hall is hushed. Soon he's building again, calling out the names of states. He doesn't quite reach the crescendo that was incipient moments ago. But when he says thank you, the crowd is on its feet, roaring. Everyone here knows they have seen something special.

And even I, who had expected to be disappointed—for how could any man live up to the hype?—am captured by the energy in the room. He'll make a great Senator, yes. But thoughts are beyond this cycle; they are on future elections, and future conventions in other cities. He'll be back, we know it; we haven't seen the last of him. Magic is within his grasp.

Mathew Gross at 10:10 PM on July 27, 2004

[31]Jesse Taylor at http://web.archive.org/web/20040803121222/http://www.pandagon.net/mtarchives/002972.html:

Do any of these people even realize that they didn't carry the single most important moment of the convention (Obama's speech) thus far live? One of the truly great political moments of the past few years . . .

[32]http://www.cbsnews.com/stories/2004/07/27/politics/main632346.shtml

[33]http://archive.scripting.com/2004/07/26#When:5:01:42PM

person new to the event (who hadn't learned that it provided time to get other things done—they were in "take it all in" mode).

For me, a stunning moment was this morning when I opened the newspapers (a neighborhood one, the *Boston Globe*, the *New York Times*, and the *Wall Street Journal*). The blogs and TV (if it carried it) had emotion. Obama's speech seemed to get to the CNN pundits the night before. The bloggers had lots to say. Even though the speeches happened well before an away baseball game would have ended, there was little of the emotion from the speech, nor even about Teresa Heinz Kerry's talk, in the papers. It was as if they had just read the speeches and decided to mention it along with others in a scripted coverage they had decided upon in advance. Here was news (the keynote really was a keynote) and they turned it (as I saw it with a quick glance) into a dry report. At least the neighborhood paper (more personal, like a blog) ran pictures and stories about local people, including the kid who movingly played the violin the other day.

It seems that the traditional media has turned into distinguishing itself with exclusive stories and reports that are pasteurized with the emotion taken out. Politics is about hope. Hope for a better world through government and its members or despite government or despite big business, or whatever. In any case, it's about conveying (or selling) hope for the future. Hope is emotional, and as author Dr. Jerome Groopman writes, a very important part of being human. The press has moved to reporting facts about what happened around the event, on what it "means" (to whom?), and a "delta" difference from expectations (whose?). For many events, you really want to know how it feels. Political conventions today are about transmitting a feeling and the press tries to filter that out, leaving something strange and unnatural. You wonder how the traditional press would cover the Grand Canyon. You know what it's like before you get there, it hasn't changed much, but, oh my, is it emotional when you look out at it. They'd say "the temperature is running 2 degrees lower than normal this year": factual, unbiased, unhelpful in many cases, helpful in others. They serve a purpose here with the convention, of course, though I find C-SPAN with its simple gavel-to-gavel coverage just as "unbiased" and helpful as the more-sophisticated productions. There's no way bloggers could cover this all. But something is missing without them. Bloggers are allowed (and encouraged) to give you the feelings, too, so they add an important element.

I'm finding that a traditional role of blogging is falling down for me here. Bloggers read each other, and we depend upon them to point and act as a gateway. Here, many of them are too busy working on their own stuff, many of us are only reading them and not blogging about it (there's only so much time in the day), and things are moving too fast.

RSS[34] and automated tools are being harnessed to help deal with the huge flow of material, for example with Winer's ConventionBloggers.com (a great service through which I've been doing most of my reading). But that's missing something. Normally, in addition to my "favorites" list and Google, I use an RSS reader to automatically get me news. But, in advance, I manually chose which feeds to monitor. I know that some of those web sites manually select things I'll find of interest—the writers of those blogs act as the gatekeepers (and they read other gatekeepers, etc.), and I automatically aggregate posts from them and scan them for nuggets with my eyes. The timescale of DayPop and Google are too slow for following an event. (I don't have enough experience with Technorati in such situations to comment.) We need to figure out how to get the right mix of manual and automatic when dealing with huge unfolding events. Conventions are easy in a way, since we know about them in advance. Unexpected huge events (like 9/11 or an earthquake) are going to be even harder.[35]

These are just some of my thoughts at this midpoint. With so much coming in, even if just from the Convention Bloggers, I only see a biased small sample. Blogging includes thoughts before we know the final results, and these are some of mine. As usual on the Web, put them together with those of others. I wrote it because I feel that it's important for us to look at this event and learn from it for the future of our media and our society.

http://www.bricklin.com/conventionblogging.htm

---

[34]RSS stands for "Really Simple Syndication." It is a way to easily distribute a list of headlines, update notices, and sometimes content such as new blog posts to a wide number of people. It is used by computer programs that organize those headlines and notices for easy reading and has become an important part of Internet functionality. The widespread use of RSS has cut down on the need to repeatedly check multiple web sites to see if there are any new entries. See my July 2004 page "What is RSS?" at http://rss.softwaregarden.com/aboutrss.html. Dave Winer played a major part in developing and popularizing RSS.

[35]I discuss some advances since then in the concluding section of this book.

More Blog Posts about the Convention

Here are additional posts from my blog:

Wednesday, July 28, 2004
WHAT WE LEARN FROM THE CONVENTION BLOGGING

A few other observations that don't fit in the "What we learn from the Convention blogging" essay:

- At least one "real" journalist who was exposed to what is going on with the Convention blogging, Larry Magid, was pushed over the edge enough to start his own blog. See "LarrysWorld Blog."[36] This is quite fitting, since Larry has filed a few CBS Radio reports about Convention blogging, as reported[37] by David Weinberger (and reproduced by Larry on his main page).
- More local flavor to share: As a Boston-area resident, when Barack Obama said he is of Kenyan ancestry, that had a very special meaning to me. To many, that may mean poor and third world. To Boston, it means champion. The Kenyans have dominated[38] the Boston Marathon for well over a decade with 10 different men winning, and the Boston Marathon is very dear to our hearts, as I've written[39] before. If only he had also mentioned the fact that he's a Harvard Law graduate, too . . .
- I've been talking to various friends who are getting into the Convention or spending time near their homes nearby. It's the talk of the town and very exciting. So many stories. I've read, and heard, about friendly security people. I've heard that others involved with the Convention went through very specific "friendliness" training, and it sounds like it may have paid off. We should learn from this for all of our Homeland Security needs.

Thursday, July 29, 2004
BLOGGING IS WORKING WELL AT THE CONVENTION

I woke up this morning and saw that Dave Winer pointed to Anick Jesdanun's story as the "AP Internet Writer" titled "Convention Bloggers Are Feeling Their

[36]He's now blogging at pcanswer.com.

[37]http://www.hyperorg.com/blogger/mtarchive/002886.html

[38]http://www.bostonmarathon.org/BostonMarathon/PastChampions.asp

[39]http://danbricklin.com/log/marathon.htm

Way."[40] I notice how I, and lots of bloggers, tend to identify writers by name not just as "AP says." We know reporters as people and treat their work as that of an individual, much as we do ourselves, and weigh it based on our knowledge of that person and their writing. (Well, Dave didn't do that this morning, but he does quick posts . . .) Googling Anick, I find lots of good, detailed Internet-related articles, some I'd be proud to have written myself. (I had to call AP to find out that he is male, so that I can get my pronouns right in this post. Anick is not a name I'm familiar with, like Jack or Pradeep. In Google I found Anick Violette, who is a female Canadian photographer and windsurfer.)

The headline and much of the content mirrored some of what I wrote yesterday—that it takes time to figure out how best to blog a convention and that you go through a process which we are watching. It's nice to know that a pro who spends his time following the Internet and speaking to people like Vint Cerf saw the same thing I thought I did. I loved how he pointed out some of the valuable things he found from the bloggers. He's doing his homework as he did in other articles.

What bothered me, though, was his tone about that process, that it meant blogging had some failing for needing to go through that process (even as he explained he himself went through just such a process in the past). The ending, "But as a member of the traditional media, I don't believe I need to look for a new job yet," seemed aimed at readers who are journalists like himself, not regular people who may wonder whether blogging may be something that might be important to them. He's being self-referential just as he faults the bloggers.

For someone who is so close to technology, it was strange that he didn't present this in a way that acknowledges the process we always go through in adopting and adapting new technologies. Rather than start with a lead declaring the arrival as hype and then temper that with "still trying to figure out their role," he could have used it more as a lesson in this common progression.

What I find amazing is how fast the bloggers at the Convention got in the groove (surely by last night). They feel the pressure and despite the distractions worthy of Super Bowl participants (in a relative sense . . .) are providing great value even in this first "experiment." They're fighting sleep and falling prey to illness as you'd expect, but pushing on. As I pointed out in my essay yesterday, blogging at an event is quite different than normal, daily blogging. That they are adapting so well is a testament to the robustness of the genre.

---

[40]http://web.archive.org/web/20040803061343/http://www.goupstate.com/apps/
pbcs.dll/article?AID=/20040729/APF/407290723

When it comes to the traditional press writing about blogging, I'm reminded of programmers reacting to developments like the spreadsheet when VisiCalc came out. Sure the "programs" people wrote with it, and the "databases" they kept as lists, were not up to the standards of "real" programmers. But "every-person programming and databasing" has proved a boon to society and has not really threatened the profession of "programmer." It has, though, changed the role of programmer by allowing many of the detailed, area-of-expertise-centric applications to be done quickly, effectively, and inexpensively. Likewise, personal online publishing, such as blogging, is providing a means for communicating feelings, facts, experience, and opinions that we're even seeing the benefit of in this first try on a national stage. Bravo!

Friday, July 30, 2004
MORE LOCAL COVERAGE

In response to my post earlier today, I found out about two related sites that provided feeds from local bloggers in the Boston area that might be of interest for looking at blog coverage of an event. From Adam Gaffin: the manually updated Boston Online/Politics,[41] and the automatic/manually fed Boston Online/Convention pages.

Thoughts right after the Convention

To members of the media and other non bloggers reading this: Much of my writing is aimed at the computer world, and I frequently have specific commentary that is meant as discussion among techies, or among bloggers, or among amateur photographers. Mixing roles together is part of the "reality" brought by blogging. Introspecting about blogging is part of my role as I see it. There are enough bloggers writing to other audiences. This is not circular, this is natural. When I write as an MBA and business person for *Harvard Business Review* targeting business people (which I have done), is that too circular? The DNC Bloggers were a small advance force scouting out a field for the hundreds of thousands or millions of others who blog. Their blogs were their main means to communicate back.

The Convention is over, and we can start looking back to learn from it in relation to bloggers. We will see the delayed effects from being at the Convention through posts coming in after the DNC Bloggers get home. We already can start to put together what worked and what didn't (from many viewpoints)

---

[41]http://www.boston-online.com/common/cat_politics.html

during the real-time part of the event. Hopefully, there is a snapshot for study somewhere online of all the full posts of all the DNC Bloggers and those that pointed to them or commented about them. Hopefully, we'll see how various stories or themes were carried throughout the blogosphere in future analysis by others out there better able to look through haystacks for needles.

We will use all this looking to figure out tools and techniques for doing event-blogging better. As I pointed out in my essay, the event blogging here lacked some of the scale aspects that have helped blogging, such as having gatekeepers and involving many participating bloggers (a few dozen is not that many in a genre that is used to hundreds of thousands). Unlike traditional media, which tries to use a few people to get the big picture, blogging as an Internet phenomenon uses a large distributed population. Blogging is aided by invented tools and techniques, some very simple such as the original Blogger and perma-links and others more complex such as blog-post popularity engines like Blogdex, specific search engines such as Feedster and Technorati, and the whole world of RSS. Event blogging will bring about others.

Most of the DNC Bloggers seemed to spend most of their preparation with logistics and not practicing for the sprint. That was good, in that they went with an open mind, trying things for us to learn from. It was an experiment. An innovative programmer among them, Dave Winer, did a quick experiment with his ConventionBloggers aggregator, as did Technorati and some others. The traditional press did lots of preparation, and tried to execute a plan. Don't judge blogging at this event that way. This wasn't, as Charles Cooper wrote today,[42] "put up or shut up" time. This was "start to learn time."

I've been repeatedly pointing to the local angle these last few days. I found another one that might be of interest to those trying to understand the local impact of such events and the role of a blogger. My colleague from Trellix days, Dave Owczarek, who has a strong command of operational and process issues in the Internet world and a very nice camera which he knows how to use, kept a blog from the viewpoint of a resident in a town that was supposed to get the brunt of the traffic effects of the Convention. Start at the bottom and read his coverage[43] of the traffic in Medford, Mass.

http://danbricklin.com/log/2004_06_29.htm

---

[42]http://news.cnet.com/2010-1028-5289475.html?tag=nefd.acpro

[43]http://www.davesphotoblog.com/2004.07.25_arch.html

I was contacted by CNet's Charles Cooper and asked to write a "rebuttal piece" to his column on News.com that I disagreed with in that last blog post. What I wrote was published on August 2nd on CNet's web site:

August 2, 2004

PERSPECTIVE: BLOGGING BREAKTHROUGH IN BOSTON?

In his column "Cybertourists in Boston," News.com's Charles Cooper expresses his disappointment with the bloggers credentialed for the Democratic National Convention. I think he missed the point about what was taking place in Boston.

This was not a contest between the best of 15,000 traditional journalists and the total output of a few dozen Web loggers. We were watching the start of an important learning process.

As a columnist who has advocated for and understood the genre, such as in his post-9/11 "When blogging came of age," Cooper's comments are ones to examine.

As a traditional professional journalist, after years of hearing bloggers deriding those in his profession, Cooper saw the convention as a chance to "show off blogging's potential" and, more angrily, to "put up or shut up."

My main issue with his assertion that "blogging blew its big chance" is with his apparent premise that this was a head-to-head evaluation of similar products with a similar feature checklist. This was not a prize fight, and they weren't even going after the same prize.

Many have written about the special nature of blogging with its intimate, first-person style aimed at ongoing readers. I think that the DNC bloggers did a wonderful job, and I personally found their work quite valuable.

Even Rick Heller's "Clinton looks really small"[44] quote was part of a longer observation that, together with the work of other bloggers, helped many of us better understand how traditional media works. Despite all this, how good they were is not what I want to talk about. I want to look at this as an advancement of a technology.

---

[44]http://www.centristcoalition.com/blog/archives/000888.html

I was reacting to Charles Cooper's put down:

"I had to content myself with gems such as, 'Bill Clinton looks really small from the upper tiers of the Fleet Center.' Really? If that knocks your socks off, my advice would be to take in the view from the bleachers at Fenway Park sometime."

From my years of experience as a blogger, I have learned that blogging at an event is quite different from normal, daily blogging. Long, multiday events are the hardest. You have to learn how to do it.

While many bloggers are used to "covering" simple events like a technology conference, they are not used to covering an event that is also being covered by live television and thousands of paid journalists.

The DNC was a chance to start learning how blogging can fit into such a situation. It was an experiment that would be expected to have normal ups and downs. The "Hello, World!"–like first posts were reminiscent of any "Testing 1-2-3." The "I'm trying A, I'm trying B" mirrors test pilots.

The DNC situation lacked some of the scale aspects that have helped blogging, such as having gatekeepers and many participants (a few dozen is not that many in a genre that is used to hundreds of thousands).

Unlike traditional media, which tries to use a few people to get the big picture, blogging as an Internet phenomenon uses a large distributed population for that purpose. Blogging is aided by invented tools and techniques developed over many years. Some are simple, such as the original Blogger, while others are more complex, such as blog-popularity engines like Blogdex and RSS readers. The blogging world will use the DNC experiment to invent tools and techniques for doing event blogging better.

Unlike most of the media, most of the bloggers did little preplanning of such tools and techniques. The few tools that were developed, like Dave Winer's ConventionBloggers.com, helped and will be improved. Most bloggers were too busy with logistics, dealing with how they'd handle pictures or find a hotel. Many wanted to just go and see what happens, which in the long run is probably good for experimentation.

Blogging is a different form of communication—not one to replace others, just as instant messaging is different from e-mail which is different from a phone call. We need to know how best to use blogging when an unscheduled natural or man-made disaster hits. We need to experiment in order to learn.

There aren't that many events on such a large scale with which to experiment. Let us salute the DNC for letting it happen here. Let's measure this as an experiment and not compare it to existing techniques that have had years to experiment. Certainly in that regard, the DNC blogging was very successful.

http://news.cnet.com/Blogging-test-pilots-in-Boston/2010-1025_3-5293461.html

Here's how I blogged about that essay:

Monday, August 2, 2004
NEWS.COM PUBLISHES MY REACTION TO COOP'S COLUMN

At Charles Cooper's suggestion, I wrote a "600–750 word rebuttal" which was just posted on News.com. The text borrows heavily from what I've been writing here. Thank you to CNet and Coop for this opportunity!

Read "Blogging test pilots in Boston."[45]

Not to take away anything from what CNet did, here is something I found of interest:

As I was told in advance, they did only minor copy edits to my submitted text, such as adding paragraph breaks. Surprisingly they did remove the phrase ". . . and perma-links" after "the original Blogger" as an example of "simple" blogging tools and techniques, which changed the meaning slightly to my mind—removing a "technique." That was the only real change and is pretty minor.

The fact that the copy editor may not have understood its value as an example of a very simple technique with big implications (I would have dropped the "Blogger" example before perma-links) shows how little people really understand of what makes blogging work. (Blogger is actually more on the complex side than the simple side, and was created partially to help manage perma-links.) It may have been "too technical" for the News.com audience. That's a shame. Perma-links are an important piece of what holds the "blogosphere" together, making direct interblog and intrablog references work in a genre that puts many ideas on one page and then scrolls them off. They are not the same as plain old URLs. They usually point into a different place than the original web page (i.e., to an archive), and have special visible locations on the page for locating them in the flow of text. RSS takes advantage of perma-links. They are a simple idea that had major implications. I thought mentioning them would get an "aha!" from people, but I guessed wrong. Sigh.

(On this weblog, which uses an authoring tool without built-in perma-link support, I have to do lots of cut and pasting, and hope you notice the text at the bottom of the home page that tells you where to find the archives that have perma-link markers in them.)

http://danbricklin.com/log/2004_06_29.htm

---

[45]This was linked to the CNet URL.

In the years since the 2004 Convention in Boston, blogs and other personal forms of Internet publishing have become major components of the political and news worlds. How they fit in is evolving. Newspapers have been covering political conventions since before the Civil War, radio since 1924, and television since 1948. They, too, are evolving, and personal publishing will do the same. However, 2004 should be remembered as a landmark time when blogging started to be taken seriously.

Podcasting

Another form of personal publishing grew out of blogging called podcasting. With podcasting, a digital audio file of an interview (like the ones in the previous chapter), speech, commentary, variety show, traditional radio or TV program, or whatever is posted on a web site. In addition, a computer-readable notice of that posting is made available through RSS, and a human-readable posting is usually made to a blog. Listeners can retrieve the recording manually, or they can use special automatic "podcatching" software to await new recordings from producers of their choice and then automatically download them for listening. Most podcatching software is set to automatically load new recordings onto an MP3 player.

The net effect is that you can "subscribe" to "channels" of your choice, pull an MP3 player out of its charging stand each morning, and have the latest recordings that were downloaded overnight ready to listen to during a commute or exercise session.

Creating a podcast is relatively easy. You can start with a $10 microphone, or the one built into most laptops, some free or inexpensive software, and a web site that costs just a few dollars a month. You can use anything up to full professional-level equipment to improve the sound or the range of situations you can record.

Once the basic ideas and software tools of podcasting were developed (with the involvement of people like Dave Winer, Adam Curry, and many others) many people experimented with the medium, or used it as a means to distribute recordings they were trying to distribute through other means. For many of us technical people, the high-quality IT Conversations series, such as the then weekly "The Gillmor Gang" show, which included several regulars and periodic guests in a conference call, were must-listen-tos, and served as models to emulate. (I had the thrill of being a "guest" on "The Gillmor Gang.")

The rising popularity of the Apple iPod, and the mid-2005 addition of podcatching ability to its companion iTunes software, further helped the medium.

I have been making simple recordings and posting them since early in my blogging days. I have been producing a variety of podcast series and individual-event recordings since late 2004. I have a pretty high-level setup at this point and have produced recordings from a wide range of locations. I was helped by kind advice from IT Conversations' founder Doug Kaye.

This blog post, written right after the 2004 election, related to both blogging and podcasting:

Thursday, November 4, 2004
WEINBERGER AT BERKMAN AND BLOGGING COMPARED TO CASSETTE TAPES

I went to Dave Weinberger's open discussion last night at the Berkman Center For Internet & Society at Harvard University. The topic was called "The Net and Democracy." Coming off the election, discussion moved to what to do next, especially among those that felt that the Net hadn't contributed enough to make Democracy work out the way they would have liked. For me, more importantly, it was a time to see some friends who attended and meet some new people as well as think some big thoughts.

I wanted to talk at a high level (after all, we were on the grounds of Harvard Law School, just down the block from Harvard Divinity School), such as about rethinking how a society's decision making is structured for its benefit when you have the Net, or how the election exit poll results relate to the role of spiritual aspects of life (not just the specific issues, but that they came from the spiritual side of people) as opposed to their pocketbook or physical security side. (I've written about the importance of people's emotional side many times, including the popular "What will people pay for?" essay.) But many wanted to talk about tweaks to blogging tools and such. The energy from the election made some of us very action-oriented.

I pointed out that in the last day or so, the word "blog" was sometimes as common as "newspaper" or "telephone" (and more than "mailed literature") when we listened to major participants in the election on TV. Who would have thought that such a young technology would rise so fast to such prominence? It took 20 years for the computer mouse to become well-known enough to be part of a joke in a movie (*Star Trek IV*),[46] and over 10 years more to be on most desks. I also reminded people that technology can be used by everyone. Don't assume that it selects for one party or another.

This morning while jogging and listening to the podcast "The Future of Online Content"[47] that I picked up on IT Conversations,[48] I had another thought. We had mentioned podcasting as a potential technology to be used politically. Just as blogging has an analog in the old activity of pamphleteering (as I pointed out in "Pamphleteers and Web Sites"),[49] listening to recorded talks by noted individuals and passing them around has been used for years with audio cassette tapes and is still used. I remembered how we keep hearing of discoveries of cassette tapes of speeches when terrorist hideaways are raided. Look at this discussion of the styles of presenting material on cassettes I found: "Islamist Cassettes & Tradition in Yemen."[50] It tells of messages on the covers of cassettes such as "In the summons to God's righteous path, the Islamic cassette is a superb means," or "May God grant blessings on whomever helps disseminate this cassette." Podcasting is not as related to music and the RIAA as it is to religious and other leaders and books on tape. The value podcasting brings is in the ease of reproduction (just bits), distribution (server or email or CD or flash disk), and recommendation (a link or term to Google). The emotional love of music is getting people to buy MP3 players, and there's lots of extra room on them for podcasts. Many people's lives have time slots in them that lend themselves to listening, even if only in 10 or 20 minute chunks (unlike radio, podcasts can be paused or repeated). Just wait and see what happens when sending 60 minutes of audio (about 20MB or so) is considered as low-resource as forwarding a joke or photo is today. Like most technology, it can be used by all parties, for good or bad. Like pamphleteering in Revolutionary times, or cassette tapes in the last decade, you ignore this technology at your peril.[51]

http://danbricklin.com/log/2004_10_15.htm

---

[46]http://www.startrek.com/startrek/galleryview?id=1091&count=9

[47]http://itc.conversationsnetwork.org/shows/detail223.html

[48]http://www.itconversations.com/

[49]That essay is included at the beginning of this chapter.

[50]http://web.archive.org/web/20041209203605/http://nmit.georgetown.edu/papers/fmiller.htm

[51]In hindsight, the last few sentences are interesting. In today's world, downloading a 2-, 10-, or 30-minute video is quite normal. YouTube and related Internet video (most importantly, with audio) have proven to be a key element in political discourse and have had a major impact on elections.

Here are some other blog posts about podcasting:

Wednesday, January 19, 2005

AUDIO RECORDINGS AND TRANSPARENCY

Dan Gillmor has an important post about "The End of Objectivity"[52] and how the goal of "being objective" as a journalist should be replaced by ". . . four other notions that may add up to the same thing. They are pillars of good journalism: thoroughness, accuracy, fairness and transparency." For transparency he suggests providing links to source material. In a later post,[53] he points to David Berlind's latest efforts[54] where David (of ZDNet) includes a link to the full MP3 of an interview with an executive quoted in the article, including the time codes for each quote so you can see if he represented the executive correctly. This is really good stuff.

I've noticed something that happened with the reports about Eric Kriss's announcement last week about Open Formats and Microsoft.[55] (Actually, while Eric made the announcement, I've seen that there were others in government and at Microsoft who worked real hard on this and should also get credit. As a very senior official, though, he should get credit for championing this, too.) The early reports were from news postings by reporters trying to tell a quick story (I know how quick—I went home to post, and some of their stories beat me by quite a bit, and they probably went through editors). They didn't have all the background that I did to work with and had to put things in the context of other presentations at the meeting that weren't meant to be juxtaposed but that were. Those early reports got picked up by an article on SourceLicense.com that was then picked up by Slashdot.[56] Reading the responses on Slashdot you can see people were trying to figure things out based on feelings and reactions to reports of the short reports. Most people didn't seem to understand what was

---

[52]http://dangillmor.typepad.com/dan_gillmor_on_grassroots/2005/01/the_end_of_obje.html

[53]http://dangillmor.typepad.com/dan_gillmor_on_grassroots/2005/01/pointing_to_the.html

[54]http://news.zdnet.com/2100-9588_22-140767.html

[55]Eric Kriss was Secretary of Administration and Finance of the Commonwealth of Massachusetts. The announcement being discussed was of great interest to the computer software community, including those who use the online discussion forum Slashdot.org. People were trying to figure out exactly what effect the state government might be having on use and sales of Microsoft Office and competing products.

[56]http://slashdot.org/article.pl?sid=05/01/15/1420205

really going on. It seems that Eric Kriss himself posted there on Slashdot[57] to ask for a correction of where the article said that Open Formats were replacing Open Standards, not extending them (a correction was made).

I had made a recording of the talk (with my little iRiver iFP-890 flash MP3 player) while sitting on stage (I introduced Eric). I transcribed part of the recording and posted[58] that transcript along with some of my own comments here on my blog. I emailed Pamela Jones over at Groklaw.net and gave her permission to quote me liberally. (Since this was an "informal" announcement, after the talk I asked Secretary Kriss if this was OK, and he said yes.) PJ posted[59] my material with lots of links to background material. This resulted in lots of what I think was better understanding in the comments than on Slashdot (though someone on Slashdot did point to PJ's post), but many people still didn't get what was going on nor Eric's sincerity towards openness.

PJ emailed me and Eric Kriss and asked permission to post my entire recording on Groklaw. We both agreed. She then transcribed the rest of it to make a complete transcript and posted[60] that transcript along with the MP3 and a more open-standard Ogg Vorbis sound format copy that she made. Her own comments, having now heard him speak, had greater feeling than her earlier post. Comments posted by others had a lot more heartfelt thanks to Eric than before, even though the written content wasn't that much different. The discussion, I feel, got down to the real issues being discussed and not just a reaction to what it was all generally about and how it related to their personal soapboxes. People responded in the more personal, helpful tone of a friendly give-and-take, not just the discussions of people in the third person often seen with such announcements. Wow, a real "conversation" with a very senior public official. Hearing the voice and "being there" with the recording seemed to open the relationship in a way similar to "knowing" a blogger through reading their blog over time. Things are more human this way. Maybe people will do fewer personal attacks when they feel they know the subject through experiencing the interaction that led to the story being written about (as in David Berlind's piece). Maybe podcasting will make things more personal (I'm getting to "know" the (Steve) Gillmor Gang people better by listening to them so frequently on their podcasts). Knowledgeable, civil discourse is good for our society.

---

[57]http://slashdot.org/comments.pl?sid=136172&cid=11374645

[58]http://danbricklin.com/log/2004_12_20.htm#openformats

[59]http://www.groklaw.net/article.php?story=2005011418070774

[60]http://www.groklaw.net/article.php?story=2005011807275883

Friday, January 21, 2005
MORE OF WHY PODCASTING IS GOOD

Following up on my last post about audio recording and transparency, I had some thoughts while listening to a Gillmor Gang podcast on the flight back from California. (Travel this week has given me time to listen to a few hours of podcasts while exercising, waiting, flying, etc.) The edition I was listening to was from January 14[61] with guest Adam Bosworth of Google, who is a database expert. I really like this series of "shows" ("The Gillmor Gang"). During this one it hit me why: It's done as a deep, serious show aimed at a professional in the area covered (in this case the IT world); it's not dumbed down, it's actually "smarted up."

The Eric Kriss announcement saga (as I chronicled it in my post [above]) showed that the news reports, and reports on them, were filtered, transformed, shortened, and simplified, losing a lot and evoking a different response in listeners than if they were exposed to the source. The reporting was by people who weren't practitioners steeped in the fine points and history of the field. They were reporters trained to ask questions and distill out a "story" and put it "in context" outside of the source as an "observer." That's their "product." On Groklaw, Pamela Jones and many of her readers strive to amass all the source documents and further ferret out and sift through as many related facts as possible. It is up to readers to figure out how to use it (who then often feed back that usage, proposing many "stories").

What I like about the IT Conversations type of podcasts is the depth, the aiming at a narrow audience who cares about the subject and wants to learn directly from people who know a lot about it. The Gillmor Gang is special in that the "regular" participants are all very knowledgeable in various parts of the field, and in what is going on in it at various companies. They ask probing questions and give opinions and anecdotes that draw out the conversation with the guest(s). Those guests are carefully chosen people who are involved at a high level in topics. They aren't just spokespeople but often the thinkers who know the subject very deeply from experience and who appreciate the opportunity to speak seriously and at a professional level. I feel that I'm learning, and the long format, with rambling into topics through the probing, and the informal nature of it being a "conversation" among topic insiders unafraid to use jargon and others unafraid to ask for clarification, is very engaging.

I feel that if I were a devotee of almost any other topic, just about all of which have depth (from knitting machines to nuclear safety), this format (as podcasting) would work. Regular broadcast "radio" wouldn't work for many reasons

---

[61]http://itc.conversationsnetwork.org/shows/detail405.html

on many of these topics. The fact that I can back up my MP3 player and listen to a passage again, or stop for a few minutes or days and then start up again a minute or two before where I stopped to help remember context, lends itself to this sometimes information-dense material. The material is often very technical and you need to hear some things said more than once. The material is also thought-provoking, so my mind wanders. I listen in places that sometimes have distractions. Finally, the shows are long, and I sometimes need to break up my listening into chunks. Another thing: With podcasts, you know that almost everybody listens from the start, with no dropping in (unless someone else sent them directly to a section knowing it stood on its own). No need to always have something when they tune the dial to catch them, no fear that you'd lose an audience to another channel, since they can fast-forward if a subtopic is boring. These conditions are killers to a traditional radio program, which just streams by without stop, and which by nature of the scarcity of available "airtime" can only go after topics with deep understanding to a wide audience, like sports or politics, or be presented in a way understandable to a more general population. Physical media, like CDs or tapes, are not timely enough and the distribution is too expensive for the wide range of topics and "shows" you'd need to get to that depth. Broadband and downloading don't have those problems.

Listening to Halley Suitt interviewing[62] Dan Gillmor and thinking about this topic, I also see how this long, informal format lends itself to getting to know a person. Since airtime isn't scarce, you can do a 30- or 60-minute interview with long answers, not the 10 or 20 minutes (including commercials) common in a TV interview. No need to edit out the personal "fluff" to just present the sensational "news." Isn't that one of the reasons Terry Gross's NPR "Fresh Air" radio show is so popular, with one person interviewed for 30 to 50 minutes with no breaks? "The Fresh Air" "about"[63] page explains how it's special by saying: "The show gives interviews as much time as needed . . ." The "getting to know someone" aspect of podcasting fits in with blogging, and relates to the "objectivity" question. Once you know someone, you don't need to have a "McReporter," each supposedly just as "objective" as the next. You understand more of their biases and tendencies and can put what they say or write in a context.

So, another rant about how special and different podcasting is.

http://danbricklin.com/log/2004_12_20.htm

---

[62]http://itc.conversationsnetwork.org/shows/detail404.html

[63]http://www.npr.org/templates/story/story.php?storyId=13

Just a few years ago, we had no more than a few newspapers in each city, and a handful of television stations, with consolidation cutting into those numbers. We waited expectantly for cable TV systems with the promised unbelievable number of 500 channels. To learn what was happening elsewhere in the world, you had to go to a news kiosk or use a shortwave radio. The idea that we would return to the world of our nation's founders with a modern form of pamphleteers, interacting with each other in a massive "conversation" in public, was not what the world of media foresaw.

Today it is not uncommon for someone being interviewed on television to be described with a phrase that consists of only "an expert who blogs at . . . " Dave Winer's Scripting News blog, www.scripting.com, the longest continually updated blog which he started on April 1, 1997, went from one of a handful to one of millions and millions worldwide. Most news programs, from NPR to "Meet the Press," are available as podcasts, joining thousands of popular alternatives in a wide variety of fields. "Amateur" video, scripted and documentary, is a staple of breaking news, politics, and entertainment. Most of the "amateurs" do it for reasons other than direct revenue or as small businesses. The question for the *New York Times* is not how blogging will make money but how newspapers will get paid.

When people figure out uses of technology, it often does not follow the "common wisdom" of the current dominant players. The old guard's skepticism doesn't always hold things back.

At this point, we've spent about half of this book focusing mainly on human behavior in relation to technology. In the following chapters, I'm going to focus more on the design of the interface between technology and people and how those uses of technology evolve.

7

Tools: My Philosophy about What We Should Be Developing

So far in this book, I have been looking at how people make use of new technology. Now let's look at the nature of tools themselves and of their relationship with people.

In this chapter, I start with some essays that contrast the popular idea of the computer acting as an assistant, interacting in a conversational manner, and following in the image of a robot butler, to that of a tool, more like a screwdriver or piano. Also included is another of my essays that continues to be cited by others and a new essay that I hadn't published yet when I put this book together.

THE "COMPUTER AS ASSISTANT" FALLACY

Learning to use things that are difficult to learn is part of being human.

The strange goal of computers as "natural assistants"

There has been a lot of talk lately about how computers are too hard to learn to use. There is a longing for devices you can just pick up and use without training. Microsoft's Kai-Fu Lee was quoted in the *New York Times* as saying when discussing the more "natural and intelligent" user interfaces he hopes to create, "My dream is that the computer of the future is going to be an assistant to the user."[1]

This type of thinking strikes me as strange. We don't ask for our automobiles to be more natural and intelligent, nor do we call for the next generation of cars to be like chauffeurs. With cars, we talk about responsiveness, comfort,

---

[1] *New York Times*, March 25, 2001, "Bill Gates's Brain Cells, Dressed Down for Action; Pressed to Innovate, Microsoft Relies Again on an Inner Circle"

power, cargo size, and safety. Tools are effective and appropriate to the task. Learning to use them is part of being human.

While a goal of simplicity may be worthwhile for many infrequently used devices that happen to use computing power, I have a real problem with this view of the computer in general, and especially the personal computer. I believe that the computer has a very important role to play in our society, and that that role will require us to continue to deal with its quirks and special needs.

Difficult things are part of life

This is not an unusual situation. The computer is no different from many other parts of people's lives. We trade the difficulties with things that matter against the desire for flexibility and effectiveness to the task.

This essay explores the space of human endeavors with aspects that, like personal computers, are difficult to learn. First, I want to define the type of computing I am referring to and those quirks and needs. Then, I'll talk about other human activities that have similar problems, yet are well integrated into most people's lives.

Things that we can just use without training or that act as "assistants" are usually things that are infrequently used, unimportant, or are peripheral to our main tasks. Things that are central to our lives are often things that require learning and practice.

The personal computer

The personal computer is a very special tool. It is a very general-purpose device. It has no real specific purpose other than to provide a means for supporting whatever type of computing-aided operation that can be accomplished with whatever can be plugged into it. The dominant form today is something used by an individual while sitting at a table or desk, using a screen that takes up a large amount of that individual's viewing area and some personal input devices, such as a keyboard and mouse. The software that drives the devices is changeable, as are the devices to which the PC is connected. The user is free to mix and match for whatever purpose he or she would like.

I talk about the evolving nature of the personal computer in an essay I wrote in late 1999 entitled "The Evolving Personal Computer."[2]

I think this general-purpose, mix-and-match, constantly changing nature of the personal computer is what makes it so special. It is a "platform" on

---

[2] See Chapter 10.

which we can use computing power and digital equipment to do many things. It is customizable, and able to do things unforeseen when it was designed and built. An example of the power and importance of this nature is the fact that with the simple addition of a little software (Netscape or AOL) and perhaps an inexpensive piece of hardware (a modem or sound card), most personal computers bought in the 1990s were able to be used for browsing the Web, Instant Messaging, or streaming media. Netscape and RealNetworks, fledgling companies at first, didn't have to get people to buy much extra hardware (though they sometimes needed to buy a little), or learn much more than their own service's special needs. Later on, Napster changed our view of navigating the world of music without planning on the part of PC manufacturers. Adding a CD burner made things even better.

Personal computing is filled with personal customization. Different people use it to do what they need, as well as what "everybody else" needs. Everybody has their own "special" needs and adds software and/or hardware for it. New uses come up, and people adopt them or not as they see fit. We can experiment without waiting for anybody else.

There are problems due to this general-purpose nature. The components are not always engineered to work well together. There is always something new to learn. The details of getting something to work may take careful reading and trial and error. You have to become "PC literate" and keep up-to-date. In fact, this being able to get things to work is what it means to be "PC literate"; it is not just knowing a particular existing tool.

The house

A comparable item in terms of its general-purpose nature in everyday life is the house. A house is basically a shell into which we install devices like heating systems and plumbing, kitchens and living rooms. By changing the "software" (furniture, pictures, rugs, wallpaper), and "hardware" (electronic equipment, plumbing, appliances, walls), we can completely change the nature of a house. Most houses are basically "the same," but they're also each different in meaningful ways. We don't want to each live in a Holiday Inn with identical rooms. Today's houses, even those that were built decades ago, are different from those of yesterday. For example, the role of the kitchen and the area around it changes from time to time.

The house, though, doesn't have the learning problems—or does it? New homeowners will tell you of all they had to learn to become "house literate."

Things like maintenance, turning off certain pipes in very cold weather, insects, where to get services, and "home improvement" work. These "problems" are a barrier to many people, and they opt for "managed" living arrangements, but many, many people put up with the problems. Some suddenly widowed men or women will tell you the amount of new things they have to learn in order to keep their house running.

In order to maintain or "improve" my house, I've learned to use a variety of tools. Some of these are hard to use and required training or much practice to learn to use safely and effectively (thank you, Dad!). There are often much better "professional" tools, but I don't have them, nor do I have the training to use them. I'll use a hammer or Vise-Grip wrench when it's not really the "right" tool to use, but it's the closest one I know how to use. My father's deformed nail on one finger was always there to remind me what can happen when you make a mistake with the more temperamental tools that are still used today because they are the best way to do something.

Other "unnatural" parts of our lives

The personal computer and the house are not the only general-purpose, "'unnatural' with lots of learning" parts of most people's lives. Here are a few others:

- **Automobiles.** Driving a car is a very unnatural endeavor. Having taught several people to drive, I can tell you, it takes hours of training to just "get around." It takes years of experience to become a "good" driver. But there is so much more that you have to learn to live in a "car" world. Luckily, some of it you pick up over the years if you watch your parents. For example: How to deal with problems (or how to even identify that there is a problem)? What is a flat tire? How do you get it fixed? How do you drive on ice and snow? How do you navigate from one location to another? What way to go is "best"? How do you deal with traffic jams? What do you do if you get stuck in an area? What is a motel? How do you "get a room"? What is a "reasonable price" for things? These are not "natural." "Simplifying" cars by making the transmission "automatic" isn't all it takes. In fact, many people like the feel of manual transmission driving, so it isn't always a benefit to automate things.

  Being hard to learn, very dangerous (prone to crashes if we don't pay careful attention, and even then not totally safe), and in constant need of maintenance (like getting fuel and oil), etc., has not held our society back from becoming dependent upon the automobile. It's just one of the things we need to learn and keep up with. My grandparents never learned to drive and were dependent upon their children and others to be taken around. Did they like to be dependent on their "assistants"? Were they better off? I doubt it, but they were afraid to take a chance and or didn't have the time to learn so much. They were not ignorant individuals—they were educated and very capable people who were successful in their fields.

Today, to lose one's license and always depend upon assistants to drive you is something most people dread (other than those who live in very crowded cities). We don't want to feel the same way about computing. Are those who speak of having digital assistants that will take care of us, like the now-paternal children of elderly drivers trying to get them off the road because driving is too hard and dangerous, trying to protect us from ever-more-powerful computers that we can't handle? I get the image of rich people with time on their hands calling to their servants to cater to their needs. Of course, we never talk about how long it took to teach that servant how to do things exactly the way we like . . .

- **Preparing Food.** Cooking and baking are things that are shared by all societies. A very large portion of the population learns to prepare food. Many individuals do not become proficient at it, other than for narrow areas, but most families have at least one individual who does. It's amazing how much you need to learn to be "food prep literate." You have to learn how to choose ingredients, how to prepare them, how to estimate needs, proportions, methods of using heat, serving, cleaning, storing, and more. There are whole courses in school just for basic, home-level food preparation. Recipes need to be obtained. A normal home's library of "how to" computer manuals is probably dwarfed by its library of cookbooks. Whenever you need to cook something that you haven't made before (or even recently), it's off to the cookbook or a call to an expert (like your mother).

I learned to cook the foods I liked for simple lunches when I was a child. When I went off to college, I learned how to cook the other meals I liked from frequent calls home and from friends and books and much trial and error. I've become relatively "cooking literate" and maybe even "cooking proficient" (though, sadly, you probably wouldn't pay any special premium to eat my food). I can improvise, and "cook with the

Force" in certain areas. For special occasions I've tried my hand at baking, but I'm basically "baking knowledgeable." I can't improvise much. Years of learning and practice.

Societies have advanced quite well with food preparation being unnatural and requiring training and practice.

- **Reading.** Literacy takes training, years of it. Enough said. Dumbing down language isn't enough.

- **Sports, Dancing, and Other Recreation.** Learning to ski or throw a ball takes time. They aren't natural. Nor are many dance moves. So many things, shared and loved by people the world over, are not things you "just pick up and do."

- **Etc., etc.** The list of such parts of people's lives goes on and on. In fact, there are theories that our intelligence as a species developed because there are so many special cases to know to survive that it couldn't all be wired in. The beauty of all of this is that training works, and practice brings a mastery of the variations we encounter in the real world.

Things that matter

For many day-to-day things that we encounter infrequently or that don't matter to us much or in which we can be inefficient, ease of learning or using an "assistant" is the way to go. But, to say that there won't be a major computing-centric platform that we treat as something we are willing to take the time to learn to use is to have little confidence in its importance. I believe general-purpose personal computing has proven its value.

Many people think that the barrier to some applications is how hard they are to learn to use and that they will only catch on when it's "brain dead simple" to learn. I think in many cases the real problem is that the application is just not that valuable to the people; they have ways to do the same thing that are OK or they just don't care. The challenge is in creating the right tools that are appropriate to the task as seen by the individual, and having the use be worthwhile. Making it "simple" often is translated into making it less flexible but it is often the flexibility we look for in our tools as humans.

For example, people look to products like Quicken and say how easy they are. Quicken wasn't easy to learn if you didn't know about checks, checking accounts, bills, paying them, keeping track for taxes, etc., as well as booting a PC, starting a program, keeping a printer working, etc. An awful large part of your brain has to work to get that far. What it did was remove the unnecessary (to most people for bill paying) requirement to understand professional accounting's debits and credits used in other computer systems, and removed the tedium of retyping the same thing every month, filing, etc., compared to doing it manually. It also was customizable. You could name things as you wished. You could have more than the accounts a "normal" person has. You could make mistakes and fix them, just like when you did it by hand. It was flexible. Finally, you needed to do what it does, and it did it better than alternatives when it came out. People cared enough to take the time to learn a lot in addition to all they already had learned.

The forms of general-purpose computing

I believe that, for the foreseeable future, general-purpose computing platforms will be an important part of more and more people's lives. There will probably be at least three such platforms: big, medium, and small. The big platform will be fixed in location, and have specialized things connected to it. These "servers" will be the least common of these devices, mainly controlled by people whose job it is to work with them. The medium devices are those used on the table or equivalent—the Personal Computer as we know it today. It will probably go through some mechanical transformations, mainly related to ergonomics like being carriable ("laptop") and to make adding new devices and capabilities easier. It will be used by most people as part of their work and hobbies if appropriate and for personal communication, information gathering, and some entertainment. You'll spend minutes to hours at a time using it. The small platform will be "holdable" (e.g., fit in a pocket) and be used for work, hobbies, communication, etc., but for applications that are much shorter in duration, such as seconds to minutes. Smaller devices will be more special purpose.[3]

http://www.bricklin.com/assistantfallacy.htm

I continued with these thoughts, describing what type of applications I think we should build, in another essay, "Metaphors, Not Conversations":

---

[3] I guess I predicted this correctly. Eight years later, we see that laptops are replacing desktops, and handheld devices like iPods and smart phones are major computer platforms.

METAPHORS, NOT CONVERSATIONS

Rather than make interacting with the computer act like a conversation with an assistant, make it like a tool you use yourself.

My essay "The 'Computer as Assistant' Fallacy" has proven popular. Among other places, it was linked to from Jakob Nielsen's Useit.com and Lawrence Lee's Tomalak's Realm.[4] Lawrence also linked to a July 2000 John Markoff article[5] in the *New York Times* about Microsoft research. (Jakob is also quoted in that *New York Times* article.) Reading that old article inspired me to be more explicit in describing the types of software interfaces I prefer and led to this essay.

Introduction

In John Markoff's July 2000 article, "Microsoft Sees Software 'Agent' as Way to Avoid Distractions," there is a description of a general human interface design: "Using statistical probability and decision-theory techniques that draw inferences from a user's behavior, the team is developing software meant to shield people from information overload [in email] while they are working." The software "decides" whether a message is something you should see and when to show it based upon sophisticated statistical analysis of various inputs. This is the same group that did the work behind the Microsoft Office "Paper Clip" and the email filter that blocked Blue Mountain Arts email greeting cards for a while. (John writes that the filtering ". . . was an important lesson . . . in the risk of artificial intelligence making poor judgments.")

Reading about this style of an "agent" program that "decides" what to do for me in the background bothered me. What, I thought as I walked the dog that night, is wrong? The "what's wrong" is what makes up the difference between an "agent" or "assistant" and a "tool." It isn't the end result (e.g., only reading what I want to at the time I want to) that's the problem but *how* the tool interfaces with me. That missing difference, I realized, is "transparency."

Programs that are "transparent"

The word "transparency" came to mind because of the reading I've done in the area of globalization.[6] The term is used to describe (countries') financial and political systems and measure how open they are with information that

---

[4] http://www.tomalak.org/todayslinks/2001/04/01.html

[5] http://www.nytimes.com/library/tech/00/07/biztech/articles/17lab.html

[6] Such as Thomas Friedman's book *The Lexus and the Olive Tree*, 2000, Anchor, ISBN: 0385499345.

allows outsiders to understand what's really going on. Countries with transparent systems have detailed, up-to-date statistics telling you the state of loans, money flows, agriculture, etc. Nontransparent countries have ministries that say "everything's fine—trust us." Investors like transparency. Countries whose systems are not transparent enough don't get much investment. If you don't know the details and can't find them out, it's hard to develop trust.

To me, a transparent user interface is one in which the user is presented with all the information he or she wants in a form that makes sense in light of their mental model of what's going on. The operations of the program should be consistent within the constraints of that model. One that isn't transparent just provides data with little context or model of where it came from or how it was derived or how to make adjustments.

Metaphors

The key to making a transparent interface work is in the presentation of the model of the world in which the program is operating. In the "old days" of the early 1980s, we used to talk of the "metaphor" represented by the program. A good metaphor aids in developing trust between the program and the user. Its strengths and weaknesses are apparent. It is a tool that the user can work "with." It provides a "space" of some sort that can be explored and manipulated for the user's purpose.

The metaphor proposed for many of the agents and assistants that I find so bothersome is of a "magic" program that says, "I know, trust me, I'll tell you." That's an easy metaphor to invent, but one with very little transparency. The idea of sophisticated software analyzing diverse inputs on my behalf is fine, but ending with a "this is the answer, trust me" interface is missing an important part of the product design.

What you want in a metaphor is a presentation of the data in a way that emphasizes what the user needs to see, exposing whatever they need when they need it in a visual or some other visceral manner that supports the meaning and manipulation of the data.

Too caught up in Artificial Intelligence

The problem with many of these Artificial Intelligence–style metaphors is that they seem to be designed to pass a Turing Test in which a human types a free-format question and the computer types back in prose, or the "Holy Grail" of conversing in voice.[7] They miss the part of the problem with the total interface to the user.

Just after I wrote the first draft of this essay, News.com posted an interview[8] with Microsoft Research's assistant director in which he's quoted as saying, "We'd like to be able to interact with a computer just like you interact with another human being." Again, there's that desire for the computer to be a person. Now, in the movies, people work with assistants all the time, but when they really need to get something done right, they decide to be "hands-on" and do it themselves. Shouldn't we have the computer help us do it ourselves for more control? Shouldn't the goal be to create tools that magnify what we can do, like tools in other areas? We want leverage like a Star Trek Tricorder, not the movie *2001*'s HAL.

(You might think that Microsoft, with those very rich employees, must be run by people who are used to servants at their beck and call. But from what I've seen, given their great wealth, Microsoft's leaders like Gates and Ballmer are amazingly unpretentious and hands-on in many aspects of their lives. It must not come from that. Maybe too much of the wrong science fiction?)

Examples of useful metaphors

There are many examples of useful metaphors. A classic one, of course, is the spreadsheet. [smiley face in original] The calculations, the formatting, and the presentation are all visible and under the user's control. The user-determined, two-dimensional nature of the data layout, along with optional text in the same layout, supports the understanding of the meaning of the data. There are "automatic" operations, such as copying cells, that make certain assumptions, but most of that is presented in an obvious way. The more clever automatic operations are often the most error-prone for the user, since they may not fit into an obvious mental model. We don't "ask" the computer to forecast costs, we "refine" our model.

Another popular metaphor is the word processor. The formatting of the text is right there for the user to see, and the automatic operations, such as word wrap, pagination, spell check, line numbering, etc., fit well in the metaphor and are obvious to the user. (Microsoft has done some useful innovation here.)

CAD/CAM products are a popular way to display and manipulate design data. Video editing tools let you manipulate snippets of recorded material.

---

[7] http://www-rci.rutgers.edu/~cfs/472_html/Intro/NYT_Intro/History/
MachineIntelligence1.html

[8] http://news.cnet.com/2008-1082-255170.html

April 4, 2001

Sound editing tools like Cool Edit and Sound Forge let you work in a space unapproachable without such tools. Image editing and music creation tools give indescribable control to the artist. (I use the term "indescribable" purposely.) These are all tools people value highly (even though some are quite inexpensive).

These applications have proven very popular. They are examples of WYSIWYG ("what you see is what you get") metaphors. That term refers to the output when printed, though in many cases now the results are rarely printed. More importantly they are direct manipulation metaphors and the user feels as if they are operating on a world that responds appropriately. That world is constructed in a way to promote leverage in the space covered by the application.

Rather than a robot-want-to-be Paper Clip winking at me as it condescendingly tries to show how much better it knows a program than I do, I would expect a help program to display a more inviting set of instructions than today's Help. Add to the "Contents," "Index," and "Find" tabs other useful tools, perhaps using (in a "transparent," understandable way) the information collected from my recent operations that would have driven the Paper Clip.

It's interesting that AOL, which had an awful problem with spam email, came up with the very easy to understand, "transparent" idea of a Buddy List. That simple solution worked for millions of users. Not much Artificial Intelligence (AI).

Wizards are not a complete answer

Since good, easy-to-understand metaphors are hard to create, many developers just present all of the data and expect the user to figure out how to make sense of it. To get things started, they create "Wizards" that extract initial information from the user step-by-step in an interrogation process. This is good in that the application gets populated with data relevant to the user. This is bad if the metaphor they end up in is not understandable. Wizards don't make up for poor interfaces if you ever need to go further. It becomes like a taxi driver that drops you off at a restaurant in an unfamiliar city after taking all the short cuts. Without a map, if the restaurant is closed, you have no idea how to get anywhere else.

Allow user control to do the unanticipated

In addition to the presentation of data, it is helpful to have tools that leave the user with enough control to do things not anticipated by the tool designers.

When I worked on VisiCalc, there was no way (despite my lauded MBA) that I could foresee all of its uses. Often, each individual has their own special needs or special insights into what needs to be done. Tools that allow for such user control seem to win out over more circumscribed ones. There were many "forecast my business" systems, based on the latest AI and business school teachings, but they didn't catch on once the more user-programmable spreadsheet was available. There is a tendency in product design to think you understand things more than the user. In the long run, when it comes to their particular needs, you often can't. Product designers should leave the users with the control. Bob Frankston addressed some of this in his "Prerogatives of Innovation"[9] essay on ZDNet.

This is not to say that tools cannot do things beyond the understanding of the users. Having "magic" under the covers is fine as long as it is presented in an understandable way to the user. For example, sound editing programs do mathematical transforms on the data whose theory would never be understood by most users, but the effects have useful names and can be tried to see what they do. Artists may not understand the chemistry of their paints, but they can still use them and do things unimagined by the paints' creators.

Conclusion

Finding appropriate metaphors is a challenge. Neglecting to do so, though, will leave many needed applications unadopted.

http://www.bricklin.com/metaphors.htm

Next is a further discussion of the interface between the computer-based tool and the user.

Widespread acceptance of a customizable computing system by regular people is often a required attribute of new products. Unfortunately, many systems that the programmer-developer found "easy" and obvious to use turned out to not be widely adopted by nonprogrammers. Therefore, analyzing different systems to see why they are, or are not, accepted is popular among product developers. This essay, which proposes a taxonomy for use in evaluating different designs, has proven popular over the years, with new references to it popping up periodically.

---

[9] http://www.frankston.com/public/?name=prerogatives

WHY JOHNNY CAN'T PROGRAM

How the author constructs instructions to a computer, and how the author can correctly anticipate the results, can affect acceptance of a system.

As a result of the Trellix blogging announcement,[10] I have been involved in a flurry of discussions with people about blogging, about various tools and features, and about differentiating the various blogging systems. One thing that came up in a discussion with Amy Wohl,[11] as a follow up to her article[12] about the Trellix offering, was this question: "How do you explain that function accessible through programming and function designed for consumers is not exactly the same thing?" Here are some of my thoughts (thank you, Amy, for inspiring me to address this!):

What is "programming"?

What is it about traditional "programming" that keeps regular people from routinely doing it? And, when they do control a computer, why do some programming systems find wide usage among the "nonprogrammers" (like spread sheets) and others don't (like C++)? I have some ideas why.

What is "programming"? A "program" could be defined as "a set of statements or instructions to be used directly or indirectly in a computer in order to bring about a certain result" (the "official" copyright law[13] definition). "Programming" is creating those statements or instructions. The key to our question here, I believe, is how the author constructs those statements or instructions, and how the author can correctly anticipate the results.

First, let's look at what makes up the "statements" or "instructions" in the program.

- In a "traditional" program, the instructions are entered by the author into the computer in the form of "statements" such as lines of a BASIC

---

[10]The company I founded and worked for at the time, Trellix Corporation, had just announced the addition of a blogging capability to its web site authoring system.

[11]Amy Wohl consults on new and emerging technologies, and on its commercialization. She was extremely well-known in the days when word processing and office software were first becoming popular and continued to be an influential voice as the computer industry advanced. Her clients have included extremely large corporations.

[12]http://www.wohl.com/wa0252.htm

[13]http://www.copyright.gov/title17/92chap1.html#101

program or cell contents in a spreadsheet. The computer "executes" the statements in some logical order to bring about the result.

- In less traditional "declarative" programming systems, the instructions are there, but the way the execution occurs is a little more mysterious, since the instructions are often more of constraints to be followed and relationships to use. A simplistic variant of this are systems where the constraints and relationships are specified using forms and pick-lists such as dialog boxes and menus.

- Further from our traditional view of a "program," but now a very common way of bringing about a certain result in a computer, is to use a "WYSIWYG"[14] environment, where there is what appears to be "direct manipulation" of the result. That manipulation is really changing instructions to bring about the result. It just looks like you are manipulating the result itself because the changes are made and the results recomputed so quickly. For example, dragging a column handle in a WYSIWYG HTML editor actually changes the "width=" attribute of the "<td>" tag. The HTML is a traditional programming language (remember the "L" in HTML is "language"). In WYSIWYG systems, there isn't always a human-readable form for the instructions—sometimes they are just stored in a computer-friendly form, with the results being enough for humans.

So, we have a variety of forms including: typed statements following a particular syntax, constraints and other declarations (sometimes each chosen from lists), and direct manipulation of results.

There are some hybrid forms. A very common one is based on a menu and dialog-box driven "fill-in-the-forms and drop downs" system but tied to a display of the results to give an almost WYSIWYG direct manipulation feel. These are declarative systems in that you usually just specify data, set relationships, etc., using the dialogs, and then the execution is done when you click "OK." They are tied to a graphical representation of the results so that when you click on appropriate places on the results the corresponding dialog box appears. They are "one-click-away direct manipulation"—not quite direct, but almost. (Trellix's TWE web site authoring system is built this way.)

---

[14]What You See Is What You Get (WYSIWYG)

What makes one system easier or harder than another?

In Don Norman's wonderful book, *The Psychology of Everyday Things* (now called *The Design of Everyday Things* in paperback[15]), he provides these "principles of good design" (at the end of Chapter 2):

> **Visibility.** *By looking, the user can tell the state of the device and the alternatives for action.*
>
> **A good conceptual model.** *The designer provides a good conceptual model for the user, with consistency in the presentation of operations and results and a coherent, consistent system image.*
>
> **Good mappings.** *It is possible to determine the relationships between actions and results, between controls and their effects, and between the system state and what is visible.*
>
> **Feedback.** *The user receives full and continuous feedback about the results of actions.*
>
> The Psychology of Everyday Things, pages 52-53

A traditional, "typed-statement" programming environment (traditional "procedural" or "declarative") falls down on all of these. It is often very difficult to determine the relationships between operations and results. The feedback is not continuous—because of syntax constraints there are many times that a program being modified is not in a state where you can see the results.

Menu and dialog-box driven "fill-in-the-forms and drop downs" systems for controlling a computer are better. The alternatives are easier to choose, and when well designed the conceptual model is part of the presentation of the input. Usually seeing the result is only a click away, leading to a fast feedback loop.

Direct manipulation systems are best, and if well designed help on all of these areas.

Immersing yourself in details

Programming is a very error-prone business, especially with "typed-statement" systems. Most of them are very intolerant of errors (even simple typos). You must really have a good conceptual model of how each individual statement (and its subcomponents) affects the result in conjunction with each other

---

[15]Basic Books, 2002, ISBN: 0465067107

statement. You have to know how to check for proper operation (testing) and how to find out what to fix if it isn't (debugging). Unless you are totally immersed in that particular programming system (understanding the varieties and subtleties of its statements and functions) it is very hard for most people to do this. Most people will not get immersed in such systems that way.

My coworker Ed Blachman points out that this is not to say that many people can't get immersed in systems that require such understanding. They do in many parts of their lives. For example, lawyers and tax accountants routinely work with such complexity in their contracts and planning. Doctors work with an untold number of variables. Someone planning a big party has to work out the food, matching paper goods, favors, invitation list, entertainment, etc. Yet, all of these people rarely program computers in addition. It's just that people who aren't professional or hobbyist programmers usually don't want to get so immersed in something that is infrequently done and not part of the rest of their lives. The question really isn't "why Johnny can't program," but rather "why Johnny *won't* or *doesn't choose* to program."

"Fill-in-the-forms and drop downs" and direct manipulation systems require less learning, testing of results, and debugging. There are fewer chances for error because of the constrained input choices. Rapid viewing of the results makes it easier to make simple changes and see what happens.

Testing and debugging

The problems of debugging cannot be underestimated. Figuring out what is happening so you can "make it right" can be very frustrating. Programmers are a special type of people because they can tolerate this, and have the patience to pore through manuals and stare at apparently incorrect lines of code to figure out how to fix problems. They have to author in a way to minimize the likelihood of errors. They need to figure out test cases to make the bugs show up earlier. This is not the way to get something done easily.

One of the problems with "typed-statement" systems is that even though each statement has an effect, you only see the final result. It is often unclear which statement (or interaction of statements) caused a particular problem. With a "Forms" or direct manipulation system, the granularity is often such that each input change has a corresponding result change.

In today's world, it is common for regular users encountering a "typed-statement" system (like HTML, JavaScript, and Perl, for example) to just copy sample statements provided by others and incorporate them into their system. Sometimes this works perfectly, especially with error-tolerant systems like

August 15, 2002

HTML. In most cases, though, this is very error-prone. A single typo, a slightly inappropriate placement of the copied code, an incorrectly set constant, or a lack of required libraries or other resources, can cause a result that just says "Error." Unless the author is well-versed in the system, doing debugging at this point, with the code consisting mainly of statements created by another, is very difficult and frustrating. It is common for the copier to be unaware of subtle errors in what they've done, since they don't know all of the test cases to try.

Intermediate results

David Reed commented to me that one of the good properties of a spreadsheet (leading to its wide acceptance) is that you usually set things up so that you can see the intermediate results of calculations. Rather than have one long formula in a cell, you use several cells, each with simpler formulas referring to some other cells. This makes testing and debugging much easier. Most traditional "typed-statement" systems make it very hard to show intermediate results, and require you to add "temporary" statements and output, or learn additional debugging systems. (That's why "Integrated Development Environments" have become so popular.) In addition to letting you see intermediate results, the recalculation ability of a spreadsheet, giving instant feedback, helped lead to Don Norman's conclusion that with a spreadsheet ". . . it felt as if you were working directly on the problem, not on a computer."[16]

Conclusions

From all of this, you can see that the way a system requires an author to enter instructions into the computer affects the likelihood of acceptance by regular people. The more constrained the instructions the better. The more the instructions are clearly tied to various results the better. The more obvious and quickly the results may be examined the better:

- Programming languages like Assembler, FORTRAN, C, C++, and Java are least likely to be well accepted by the masses. Their syntaxes are very unforgiving.
- Statement languages like HTML which are very forgiving of errors and with quick and obvious results are more likely to be accepted.
- Integrated development environments, like Visual Basic and the old Turbo Pascal, with quick syntax checking, integrated debugging, and

---

[16]*The Psychology of Everyday Things*, page 181

rapid movement to execution, are better than the old way for such languages.

- Something like a spreadsheet, with very tight syntax checking, usually obvious connection between results and the statements that caused them, and easy display of intermediate results, are even better.

- Use of dialog boxes for instructing a computer is generally more likely to be accepted than a "language." By additionally integrating a quick one-click-away display of the results with a connection back to the dialogs, this type of system has proven to be well accepted by regular nonprogrammers.

- Direct manipulation, if the results being displayed are related well enough to the results for which you are programming, is even more likely to lead to acceptance.

Responses

A comment from Ed Blachman after seeing a final draft:

> *Your discussion focuses on complexity and difficulty, without looking at the other side of the coin: power/freedom. It's generally (though far from universally) true that each step toward programming difficulty is also a step in the direction of power and freedom . . . at any given time.*
>
> *The two are not independent, as is illustrated by Trellix blogging. Formally speaking, Trellix blogging is an ease-of-use advance, because it does nothing that one could not have previously done manually in TWE. But the net effect to end users is a power advance: adding blogging to TWE doesn't affect TWE's overall ease-of-use, but does automate something that required a fairly complex set of manual activities.*

Ed Blachman, personal communication

A comment from Amy Wohl:

> *While it is often thought that "real" programmers like real programming environments (my husband, for instance, is perfectly happy in MF Assembler, which is pretty grim), most programmers seem to become pretty happy moving up to graphical user interfaces*

August 15, 2002

and visual environments where they choose from a list of "correct" choices. I don't think it is only users that can be more productive when they are better supported.

I believe there is a direct relationship between the ease of use of a product or environment and the number of users it attracts. I also think that how deeply the users take advantage of the environment's capabilities is also a function of how they are offered. Users don't like to play hide and seek.

Amy Wohl, personal communication

http://www.bricklin.com/wontprogram.htm

Some Specific Tools

Advances in computer technology have been increasing the range of media that can be easily created and manipulated by everyday personal computers. The explosion in the ability and desire to share "user-created content" is giving more people reasons to use these tools. This is an essay I started in the spring of 2008, but haven't published as of this writing, about the specific computer tools that should be commonly learned.

April 3, 2008

THE NEW COMPUTER LITERACY

I feel very strongly that being able to do video (and of course photo) editing is now part of what it means to be computer literate, just as knowing how to use word processing, spreadsheet, and presentation graphics have been for the last decade (and are now part of K-12 curricula).

What does it mean to be computer literate? How has that changed over the years?

First, let's look at what it means to be literate.

Normally, being "literate" means being able to read and to some extent write. But it is more than that. Being able to read one poem or book, or fill out one type of form, does not make you literate. Being literate means that you are able to read (and write) a wide range of material, most importantly material that you have not encountered before. The whole point of literacy is that you have a general skill that lets you work with an unlimited variety of new situations.

Being literate is more than just the skills to translate between marks on a page and sounds or concepts. Being literate also includes the peripheral and social aspects related to the skill. For example, understanding the nuances connoted by typography, the functions of book covers, tables of contents, and indexes.

One can be literate in more than just words on paper. One can be "telephone literate." Using a telephone involves skills including how to structure a conversation when you can't see the other person, how to initiate and receive calls, deciding what uses a call is appropriate for and what uses it is not, and more. Many people over 50 have lived through an evolution of learning new skills required to communicate "by phone." First we had to go from dial telephones to push buttons, a relatively easy move. Then we had to learn the role of the answering machine. At first this was considered an impersonal device, and in the greeting message the answering machine owner would apologize for having it and need to explain what to do. Later, not having an answering machine became viewed as less friendly. Cell phones brought in new things to learn. You didn't just type in a number and wait—you now needed to push the "Send" button. Many people remember how they had to be taught this. As cell phones moved from installed "car phones" to pocket phones, the situations in which you used a phone call expanded. This was not obvious to many first-time users. Being able to say, "I'll call you when I get there and we'll figure out how to find each other," was not always obvious to people with landline phone literacy. Being sensitive to "is this an OK time to talk?" became much more important.

Computer literacy has gone through an even greater evolution. Initially, being computer literate meant being able to program in a computer language like FORTRAN or BASIC. Computer classes in school were "Programming 101." These really didn't make most people very literate. Very few could actually do much that was useful with that training. It was more like "French 101," where you could sound out some of the words and knew some of the basic concepts, but you couldn't understand anything practical if you visited France or Quebec.

The first wave of tools: productivity applications

What I call real computer literacy came about after personal computers became generally available and when people started learning a variety of application packages, such as word processors and spreadsheets. They learned how to approach learning a new package, about concepts like saving their work, file systems, and about cursors and the ability to "insert above" something. They learned what people meant by "you can't break it by typing something wrong." They learned about instruction manuals, help systems, and what was OK to ask others. They learned about WYSIWYG and filling in forms.

If you were computer literate in those days, you knew how to use word processing concepts like insert/overwrite, copy/paste, word wrapping, pagination, and formatting. Hopefully you even knew spreadsheet and database concepts.

In any group of people (for example, a club, PTA activists, or extended family and friends) you could find someone who could "word process" the minutes of a meeting, keep track of receipts, etc., and produce printed output. As time went on, more and more of these concepts and skills were taught in the schools, to where today it is hard to graduate high school without "keyboarding" skills and reasonable proficiency with word processing and presentation graphics, and maybe even very simple spreadsheeting.

The availability and popularity of Graphical User Interface–based systems ("GUI" systems with icons, menus, and windows) added a new wrinkle to computer literacy. There was now a common set of operating principles for controlling applications and for discovering some of the functionality. Once you conquered using a mouse, internalized the meanings for various icons and widgets, and understood the operation of menus, you had a reasonable chance of being able to successfully operate a wide range of new applications with little training other than perhaps a quick demonstration of the concepts unique to that application.

So, computer literacy consisted of general operating principles (clicking, menus, plugging devices together and powering them up appropriately, not touching the diskette surface, etc.) and some specific data presentation and manipulation metaphors. Those metaphors included: the word processing metaphor for paragraphs of text; the multipage, two-dimensional drawing object metaphor of presentation graphics; the heterogeneous grid and recalculation of the spreadsheet; and the homogeneous records accessed through forms and reports of simple database programs.

The second wave: connectivity and browsing

What has been fascinating for me to watch has been the general user's progression in embracing new data presentation forms and manipulation metaphors.

This has been driven by the continuing advancements in processor speed, storage capacities, connectivity, and display and other input/output capabilities of digital devices at "affordable" prices.

After word processing and other office-centric uses moved to the home, we saw uses that involved accessing prepackaged text and images. We had encyclopedias and other information-centric uses on CD-ROMs, and we had games. Connectivity, first through proprietary services and dial-up modems and later through the open Internet and always-on "broadband," brought us email and then web browsing.

Knowing how to "do email" is part of being computer literate. So is browsing, using a search engine, and using e-commerce.

Added to literacy are now much more "self protection" skills, such as avoiding viruses, dealing with spam and phishing.

Media Creation

One special area with many implications is advancement in what type of "content creation," or editing, that regular people are expected to be able to do.

One of the first after the old office-suite-centric data is photographic images. For many, this started out as scanning paper or film photographs, with simple controls like cropping. This has moved to photo editing, referred popularly, using the name of the most prominent professional tool, as "using Photoshop." The overwhelming popularity of digital cameras (which happened for many good reasons) has led to a huge percentage of photographs being easily available for potential digital editing. Understanding the tools available in a photographic editing product, from red-eye removal to cropping to contrast and color adjustments, pixel-level "healing" and stitching, filter effects, and more, is a new type of literacy that helps regular people who are not professional graphic artists express themselves. In most any group of several people at least one probably knows how to do this.

What has happened in the last couple of years is the addition of another type of data and editing metaphor. The data is video and audio. The editing metaphor is the so-called nonlinear editing system popularized professionally by Avid many years ago, and then first made "standard" on home systems with Apple's iMovie. This metaphor consists of a bin of "clips" that can be assembled in a simple horizontal display of the data representing the successive captured data points, much like a linear "tape" laid out on a timeline. A cursor can be positioned on this timeline and then the data points may be "played" as video and/or audio, with output in a video window or through speakers. The linear display of the data points can be segmented, with parts copied, cut, and pasted to rearrange things. A selected series of data points can be modified to change properties such as color (for video) or amplitude (for sound). Two or more of these timelines may be presented simultaneously, one above the other, and the data points merged appropriately to add titles, mix two images, etc.

The types of manipulation that you can do with such a system are quite different in many ways than other editing metaphors because the operations are tuned to the type of data and what you often want to do with it. For example, positioning a cursor is not as simple as with a word processor. The granularity you want is down to the frame in video data (one static screen full displayed for about ⅓₀th of a second), with perhaps thousands of frames to be edited. You want to have control to move through those frames quickly but precisely. It is not as easy as just clicking on a letter in a word processing document . . . there's too much information to be displayed on the screen all at once. Various tools use sliders and "scrubbers," sometimes modeled on the controls of effective old, physical linear editing systems that actually moved linear magnetic tape. (The computer systems that let you jump around instantly from one scene to another are called "nonlinear" editors, in contrast to those old linear systems.) Like the myriad of cursor-moving controls of a keyboard-centric text editor (e.g., forward one character, move to end of word or sentence, move to matching bracket, etc.), good video editing systems give controls for quickly selecting and manipulating what you want. The "feel" of a product can affect the ease with which you can do needed operations, and the data processing capabilities can affect what types of changes you can make to the data, affecting the range of expression the tool gives you. Learning all of these operations at first can be very time-consuming because they are so different than other operations you have already internalized.

With any of the data manipulation metaphors, there's a question of what should be the core operations that all products have? What is the minimum set of features that separates a "useful" product from one that is too basic for normal use? We have seen this with word processing. I remember when spell checking was not an available feature and when the only tables were created with tabs. This is not acceptable today. Coming with our experience and expectations from desktop applications, we are now getting to watch the move to online, browser-based word processing as it gets more and more capable, and eventually crosses that line to "powerful enough for most or all of my work."

Some of what we want to do with our tools is influenced by what others commonly do in that medium. Professional printing has learned to use typographic effects to help better express or present concepts. Being used to that "language of expression," we expect to be able to express ourselves in a similar manner. A challenge in the design of software tools for regular people is making it not only possible but even straightforward to do such expression.

With home video editing, at first it was enough to just put a few clips together, add a title, and do some basic transitions. Professional systems have always dealt with very precise frame-level control, and have evolved a wide range of special effects to help better express things. Today, we are exposed to a huge quantity of professionally produced video. We know the language of expression, and something too simple looks as bland as a monospace, type-written report with no illustrations. While, in the right hands, even a simple presentation can be beautiful and expressive, it can be as tough for a normal person in a hurry as being restricted to writing to a 3rd-grade level or to only use words of five or fewer letters (an interesting exercise). Conversely, too much capability can lead to inappropriate choice of expression, much like the early "ransom letters" you frequently get from people who first encounter a word processor with font-choosing capability.

It will be interesting to see where we end up with video editing.

More about video editing

I first watched video editing when we produced a video to go along with a product announcement at Slate Corporation in the early 1990s. It was done on a linear editing system, run by professionals. I first did video editing myself on a professional Avid nonlinear editing system provided by a friend's company when I was producing a video for a school in the mid-1990s. The next time I really got into doing video editing was in 2005. I was producing my "A Developer's Introduction to Copyright and Open Source" training video.[17] I decided to spend the money to purchase equipment and do the production myself. I worked with a professional videographer who told me what to buy, helped me set up my "studio," etc. He recommended Final Cut Express to run on my Mac PowerBook, and a particular book to use to help learn it. I spent days going through all the exercises in the book and then many more days editing my material. By the end, I had a basic proficiency in using the product and produced a product that I'm pretty happy with (and that companies have paid money to show their employees). Today I use a variety of video editing systems, including Adobe's Premier Elements on my Windows laptop.

---

[17] http://www.softwaregarden.com/products/video/

April 3, 2008

I would recommend that everyone who needs to express themselves to others using computer-generated media learn to do video editing. I would make sure that you have a tool with a wide-enough range, but tuned to be usable by regular people. You can use the video recording capabilities of today's digital cameras for material, as well as tape-based or hard-disk-based cameras for longer or more demanding subjects. Sharing online on YouTube, Google Video, or similar services, or on DVDs for more private (and often better quality) distribution to family and friends, is easy and inexpensive enough to get you an appreciative audience with feedback to help make it worthwhile. In addition, when you really need to know how to do it, you will be ready. It's the latest part of computer literacy we need to have.

Not published online as of December 2008

The Value of Being General Purpose

In describing the value of a particular type of tool, flexibility and the ability to handle new situations is often mentioned. The following essay looks at that in a deeper and more explicit way.

February 19, 2006

WHEN THE LONG TAIL WAGS THE DOG

> *There are "must have" application areas and data files that will drive adoption of products. Many of them are far down the long tail of popularity. Serving a narrow, most popular set is a losing proposition.*

One of the hot concepts mentioned frequently when discussing Internet businesses and applications for the last year or two has been that of the "Long Tail." It was most recently popularized by Chris Anderson's October 2004 article in *Wired*[18] called "The Long Tail." I've written about some of the value of the long tail, as have many others: See "Small Players Matter"[19] from June 2002 and Jakob Nielsen's email there and his essays[20] with data back to 1997.

---

[18]http://www.wired.com/wired/archive/12.10/tail.html

[19]http://www.bricklin.com/smallplayers.htm

[20]http://www.useit.com/alertbox/9704b.html

From what I've seen, most of the writings derived from Anderson's article have to do with the additional value you get by serving the long tail of less-than-very-popular items made more financially viable by the Internet. In this essay I show why it is even more important to serve the long tail in some areas, and how systems that limit the ability to use inexpensively created custom content will have a hard time in the marketplace. I also relate the idea of the long tail to general-purpose authoring tools. The essay goes through the background that brought me to these conclusions.

What do we mean today by the long tail?

The standard discussion of the long tail includes a graph like this:

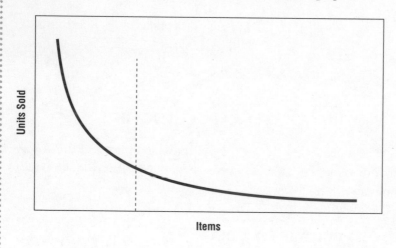

Items

Along the horizontal axis it has the full inventory of items or services available for purchase. The vertical axis shows the number of units of each sold. There is a classic curve with just a few of the products selling in any significant numbers compared to the others. In a traditional store or company only a subset of the products that could be sold is actually made available for sale . . . those to the left of the vertical dotted line. There are many reasons for this, such as cost of inventory, lack of shelf space, old-fashioned telecommunications architecture, need to focus sales and support in a narrow area, etc.

The long tail (the products to the right of the line) comes into play when the cost of making a much wider selection available drops. This may be because of new technology such as the Internet, business models that involve user-generated reviews and support, etc. In any case, in areas such as books and music there is a very long tail of additional products, each of value to its

February 19, 2006

purchasers few that they may be. If you look at the total sales you find that the large volume of niche products more than makes up for the few copies sold of each, with those products making up a significant portion of revenue and often profit. You get graphs like this:

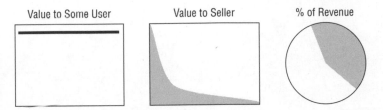

Hyperdifferentiation

Last year I heard a speech by University of Pennsylvania Professor Eric Clemons at a Diamond Management and Technology Consultants Exchange event. Prof. Clemons talked about "hyperdifferentiation." (See the paper he coauthored titled "Information, Hyperdifferentiation, and Delight: The Value of Being Different."[21]) Hyperdifferentiation is described as "the art of reducing the importance of price as the principal determinant of customers' selection among alternative goods and services . . . [It's] not about being better in any absolute sense nor [needing to be] more expensive to produce; rather it is about being better for each customer, and thus more profitable to sell."

He gives examples of products such as beer with a high content of hops. Most people don't like the taste, but for those who do like it that beer is something they will pay much more for than a more common brew. He also talks about certain hotels that just do things just the way he likes, and therefore make him feel the extra cost is "worth it."

The issue is shown graphically on the next page. The horizontal axis shows the range of items available, sorted by attributes that matter to the purchaser. The vertical dotted line is the point where the product's attributes are "ideal" for a particular purchaser. The vertical axis is the value to that particular purchaser.

Notice how the value peaks at "exactly what they want" and drops off as it meets the ideal less and less. Clemons and his coauthors write: "Assumption: With many choices available, a customer's willingness to pay for products and services falls off quickly when the fit between these offerings and his or her ideal product location decreases."

---

[21]http://opim.wharton.upenn.edu/~clemons/files/delight_info_paper_v2_1.pdf

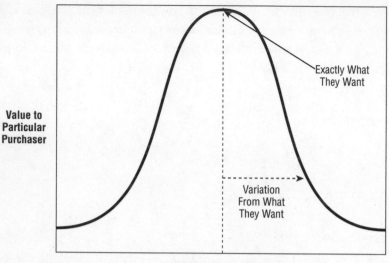

**Value to
Particular
Purchaser**

Exactly What
They Want

Variation
From What
They Want

Range of Items Available

Uncertainty

What struck me is the following graph, derived from what I remember of his talk and explained in the paper:

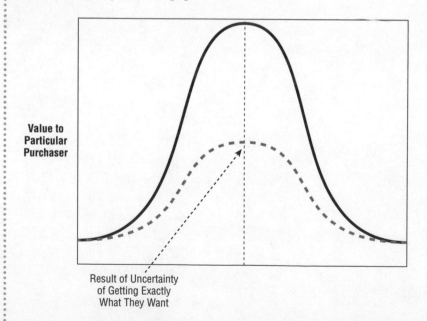

**Value to
Particular
Purchaser**

Result of Uncertainty
of Getting Exactly
What They Want

When you have uncertainty involved, not being sure that the product will be of consistent attributes or not being sure of your understanding of the likelihood of meeting your ideal, the value goes down. A hotel which is sometimes great and sometimes lousy is not one you will pay as much for as one that is always great. A hotel that you can't check out in advance through pictures or trusted recommendations will make you feel less comfortable about committing in advance to paying a high room rate. Some products (big fast food and hotel chains) often depend upon the value of certainty: Their attributes may not be the greatest, but they give you a very high certainty that you will get exactly what you expect and rarely get surprised on the downside, so they minimize the uncertainty effect.

Hearing this, I realized something. If I have a particular need that can be fulfilled by a tool, the tool I will choose is the one that I know will more likely fulfill that need. If I have to limit my "toolkit" in advance to just a few tools, I try to include those tools that will meet as wide a range of needs as possible from the range of needs that I think I will have in the future. Tools that can be used for a wide range of purposes therefore become very popular: hammers, screw drivers, pliers, word processors, personal automobiles, etc.

General-purpose tools

A digression about general-purpose computer-based tools:

I've learned from my work developing spreadsheet and word processing systems over the last 30 years that one of the reasons they are so popular (and have repeatedly beat out competing genres of products aiming for a subset of their uses) is that these tools are so general purpose and well understood.

People's needs with text and mixed text and data documents are quite diverse. When you get down to the details, most uses are custom. While an "income statement" may sound like a standard thing, so many of them are very specific to the company they report upon and the needs of the particular executives and others who use them. A production planning report is even more varied. A "letter" or "resume" may sound standard, but people like to craft each to be exactly their way and to fit the content.

The beauty of a computer tool like a spreadsheet or a word processor is that it provides an understandable framework with which the user can figure out by themselves how to create exactly what they want. (We sometimes call this framework a "metaphor.") The spreadsheet provides a framework by having a row and column system. That system imposes a slight order and restricts things a bit, but it opens up areas like summation on ranges and other operations.

The free-form positioning and arbitrary cell references keep the framework from getting in the way of making things exactly as you want them to be. The spreadsheet as a tool takes care of the tedious parts of producing a wide variety of output without defining the problem being solved. It has calculating (and recalculating) abilities, both text and numbers and straight lines, and numeric formatting—all tedious things otherwise.

General-purpose tools such as these are appropriate when you have very diverse situations. They handle unanticipated needs well. They are "tools," not automatons or agents. They allow for customizing (dealing with the unanticipated) as opposed to just choosing (dealing only with anticipated, predetermined needs).

An important aspect of the framework of a good general-purpose tool is that once you learn it, the range of areas it can be successfully applied to should be something you internalize. You know which things are easy to get done exactly as you want with a word processor or with a spreadsheet. You may never have used them for that particular application, but you know the "space" it covers well enough to know if the application is in that space. Tools whose applicable "problem-solving space" is broad become popular, from word processors to duct tape. A general-purpose tool that most people can't use easily or understand how to apply in new situations will be less popular.

General-purpose addresses hyperdifferentiation

Back to hyperdifferentiation: If you know that a product can be used for a range of needs, you will have less uncertainty about getting to your ideal. You may not be sure that public transportation will get you to a new friend's house, but you know an automobile can.

Here is another graph (see opposite page).

David Reed points out that this is related to option theory. You would be willing to pay very little for an option to have something that is unlikely to occur compared to the maximum potential value you would get if you exercised the option. On the other hand, an option to get something that is very likely to happen would be worth much closer to the value of buying it with certainty. The question with valuing an option is how do you know the likelihood of what will happen. When you have a tool with which you understand the range of problems to which it may be appropriately applied, and that range of problems covers your desired area completely, you can have greater certainty of success than a tool with which you feel there is a smaller range of problems to which it may be appropriately applied and that is unlikely to work for many of the problems that you may need solved.

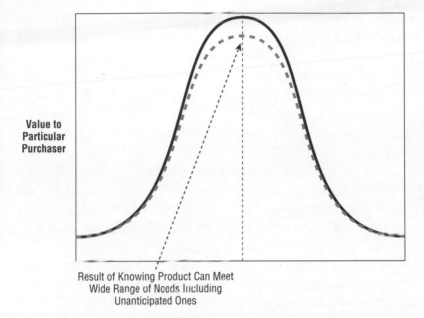

Value to
Particular
Purchaser

Result of Knowing Product Can Meet
Wide Range of Needs Including
Unanticipated Ones

David points out that the key is having a tool whose design is such that you feel confident in knowing what it can be applied to and a range of problems to be solved with which you understand the capabilities that are needed in order to solve them by using such a tool.

So, general purpose tools that people understand are more likely to serve a longer part of the "tail" of potential future needs and also be valued higher because of such likelihood.

Must haves

While interviewing ex–Palm Computing CEO Donna Dubinsky last year, I asked her about the applications people came up with for use on the original Palm handheld and their effect on the success of the product. What she said surprised me. In addition to using one or more of the few "popular" built-in applications (calendar, address/phone book, etc.), ". . . rather than adding 3–5 applications [to those existing built-in ones] on a device, customers would find one that was compelling for them, and that to them was a make it or break it thing. It might have been the stars and where the stars are, it might have been world traveler applications, or it might have been querying a detailed database at work, but there was always some additional compelling application for the Palm owner."

That statement struck me as very special. There are "must have" applications. Good versions of the popular, everybody-needs-them applications were a minimal requirement (and highly valued). But people bought the Palm instead of some cheaper limited device that could only do those popular applications because they had at least one other niche application that made the increment in cost worth it. More importantly, the Palm (joined later by similarly customizable Pocket PC competitors) became dominant beating out the cheaper, non-customizable devices. The "must have" applications were often quite limited in their appeal and often labors of love, but they made the Palm a successful product.

So, it isn't just the number of potential items that's of value, it's the kind of items. Some are of great value and their availability completely drives the purchase. For example, in the late 1990s, many people in their 40s and 50s didn't use personal computers or email. But when their children went away to college and email became a major form of communication available to stay in touch with those children, they got the computers, signed up for email, and started using it. That one application got them started. Once they were email users they would use it to communicate with people other than their children, but it was that one particular application (communicating with a particular loved one) that drove the purchase and adoption.

Applying this to the long tail

So, now we have another graph:

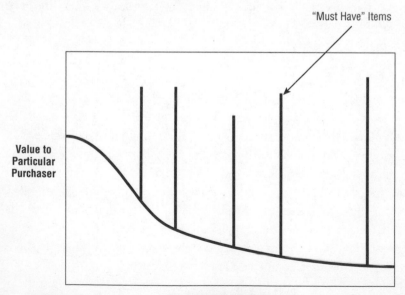

"Must Have" Items

Value to Particular Purchaser

Range of Items Available

The horizontal axis is the range of things you'll want to do sorted by popularity. The vertical axis is the value to a particular purchaser. For the sake of argument, I'll assume that in general the value of each item is reflected in its popularity. For example, with PDAs, everybody wants a calendar application and an address/phone book. What I've added is the occasional item that is a "must have." These are of great value to the purchaser.

Think of telephones (wired or wireless). Lots of people need to call airline reservations at some point. Fewer, but still many, need to call L.L. Bean. Many in a city will need to call for concert ticket reservations. Only those who live in the neighborhood will call a particular pizza restaurant. Finally, only a very few will need to call a particular automobile service station and even fewer a particular individual. However, there are some individuals (my friends, relatives, etc.) that I really, really want to talk to. When my car is making some funny sound and I'm about to start a long trip or when it breaks down I really want to talk to my car mechanic. That's why I pay for the phone service. I don't pay for it to just make calls to L.L. Bean or receive calls from a Verizon representative. Much of my use is only of interest to me. See my "What will people pay for?" essay from July 2000.[22]

Now, let's add the "must haves" that I don't know about yet but can easily anticipate and want to be prepared for. With the phone it includes friends I haven't met, future customers, and perhaps a doctor for a disease I haven't come down with yet. Here's the new graph:

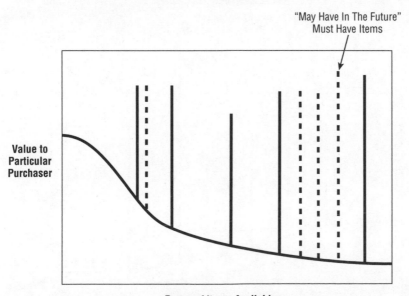

_{"May Have In The Future"} Must Have Items

Value to Particular Purchaser

Range of Items Available

---

[22]Presented here in Chapter 2.

If I'm buying a system to meet this general area of need, how do different system architectures fit? Here are two types: One is a restricted, special purpose system that meets the popular needs quite well. It is of high value for those needs, but not for the others. The other is a general-purpose system that I know will meet many, many more of my current and potential needs. It is of high value for a wider range. As David Reed says, general purpose gives you more options and in the right cases more higher-valued options because they are for the right kinds of high-value potential uses. Here's the graph:

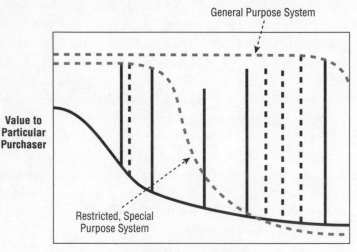

Another way to look at it:

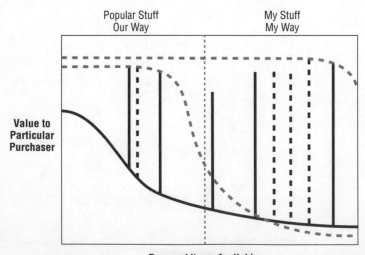

February 19, 2006

I believe that for many areas, only products that serve both the left and right side of the graph—providing popular applications/content as well as specific, niche ones—will be successful in the long run. The niches can be personal (my family photos, for example), commercial (internal-use-only corporate stuff), or by other means (buyers of Pez dispensers).

I also believe that even when the general-purpose system produces somewhat lesser value for those popular applications, the fact that it covers the "must have tail" more than makes up for that drop in value. I'll put up with the lower quality of the sound on a telephone over an FM radio to listen to my friends rather than just professional radio personalities. Many more people carry a cell phone with them than an FM radio, and they willingly pay much more for the phone.

Here is an example that has been in my thinking. You have a cell phone that can receive video and display video. Should it be tuned for the top 100 video feeds and make it hard or impossible to see the birthday videos of your grandkids or grandparents? Or should it let anybody inexpensively share content composed using any of the popular tools available? I maintain that given a choice, the latter products will win. There will be some content you need (for example, created by a loved one or on the topic of a hobby you are most passionate about) that would only be available on the general-purpose system, and you know it (or will find out quickly when you find out it's available). It may be that the niche content is the reason you buy the product in the first place.[23]

The conclusion

So, here is my theory which I call "When the Long Tail Wags the Dog":

In areas where results are often customized to people or situations and that can't be addressed directly in advance, such as when there is a high value to most users of at least some user-generated material, "open" general-purpose systems that address all these niches will dominate.

---

[23]The success of YouTube in comparison to specialized video systems is a case in point. YouTube's success wasn't clear when this article was written in early 2006, just a few months after its official start. Two months later, in March of 2006, it had 13 million unique visitors, and a year after this was written, now as part of Google through a $1.65 billion deal, it had over 79 million users. New cell phones, like the iPhone and the T-Mobile/Google G1, come with built-in support for YouTube.

This essay is partially a reaction to the limited video systems, tuned to "popular" material, being championed when this was written, which included the FLO system (http://www.qualcomm.com/news/releases/2006/060104_lg_electronics_mobilecomm.html).

I believe this helps explain the emergence of Internet email, cell phones, automobiles, and many other systems we take for granted today and is useful for evaluating systems and business models for the future.

Companies that develop closed systems that ignore generally created content and applications and that don't take advantage of widespread "open format" content/application creating tools (that is, those that produce output that is easily consumed by a wide range of different content-accessing or application-running tools) will be eventually wiped out by those that do.

http://www.bricklin.com/tailwagsdog.htm

In this chapter we saw how a tool is more than just functionality for producing or displaying output. How we control that functionality matters. Also, the range of applicable applications for the tool matters, too.

Next, let's look at a more specific aspect of interaction—the part of the computer we touch to control it.

8

Hands On: Tablet and Gestural Computing

Mobile and hand-operated computer-technology-based tools are an area that has been the subject of research and development for many years. It is now flourishing, most visibly with its use in products like the Apple iPhone. This way of having a person control computing power is much more intimate than the older deskbound and keyboard-controlled computers of the 1980s and 1990s.

I begin with an essay I wrote when the first of a new crop of what Microsoft called "Tablet PCs" were released in late 2002. Such machines are basically laptop computers with screens that are sensitive to being touched with a special pen. In some cases, these are called "convertibles," and the screens can be rotated or folded to alternate between covering and exposing a normal keyboard. In other cases, the keyboard is an optional-separate plug-in component, and the computer is just a slab with a screen on one side.

At the end of this chapter, I'll also look at the area of usability through a case study of a well-known non-computer-screen stylus system.

TABLET PC: FIRST IMPRESSIONS

Back in the early 1990s, I was heavily involved in the pen computing world. I cofounded Slate Corporation which developed application software for GO's Penpoint operating system, as well as Microsoft's Windows for Pen Computing and for the Apple Newton. I was exposed to software and hardware development, both at the operating system and application level, and had experience using a wide variety of machines. With the release of the new Tablet PCs based upon Microsoft's new software, I felt it was appropriate for me to comment upon that, given my perspective. You will find here my comments based on my general feelings as well as actual experiences using various equipment.

November 14, 2002

How I decided what to buy

At various points in time, starting with Bill Gates's Comdex 2000 talk,[1] I have been seeing public prototypes of Microsoft's Tablet PC software and the accompanying hardware. Most recently, I got to play with an Acer unit for a few minutes while waiting to get into Jeff Raikes's talk at TechXNY[2] (PC Expo). My ThinkPad was well over 3 years old, and I knew it was time for a new laptop. I decided to wait until the Tablet PCs became available, and probably get one of them. I had used a GRiD Convertible (a machine from late 1992) for years after it came out, and knew that a convertible could be a fine laptop, even if you didn't take advantage of the pen much, and I needed a lightweight laptop.

Now that the Tablet PCs have started shipping, I decided it was time for me to buy. Since I was spending my own money and knew this would have to last me for a while, I looked carefully. Given my needs, I narrowed it down to the Acer, Compaq, and Toshiba. The Acer has a maximum of 256M of RAM, so I decided that wouldn't work for me in case I wanted to do any development work, or run some of the photo manipulation apps I'd probably end up using for my photography work. I was really torn between the Compaq and the Toshiba. From the specs, both looked like they'd meet my needs. The Compaq is supposed to have much better battery life, has a stalk as the keyboard resident pointing device, has more buttons, and is lighter when the keyboard is detached. Its pen, though, is not pressure sensitive. The Toshiba has a bigger and supposedly brighter screen (better for showing pictures and presentations, which I do a lot), faster processor, a touchpad (which I don't like as much as the stalk), and is in a more traditional form factor. Configured as I wanted them, with warranties, etc., they were close enough in price. I've had two Toshiba Portégés over the years, so I was more familiar with them, but I worked with Compaq on a similar, earlier machine, so I had some loyalty (and they ended up with Slate's assets when we closed it down).

In the end, I couldn't find a Compaq to look at, but I found a Toshiba 3505 that was available at a CompUSA store in my area. After looking at it, I decided I might as well get the Toshiba. (I've presented the whole story of how I made my decision here not as an endorsement, but as an example of the type of thinking you might want to go through. I expect to spend time with some of the other units over the next few months, and will comment about them when I can.)

---

[1] http://www.bricklin.com/albums/comdex2000/sundaynight.htm

[2] http://danbricklin.com/log/2002_06_26.htm#techxny

My philosophical feelings about tablet computers

The most important thing to know about the Tablet PC, as far as I'm concerned so far, is that Microsoft did a great job—of naming it. Much as the press wants to call it a "pen" computer, it is a Tablet computer. You must understand that. The basis of the machine is that it is (or can be turned into) a tablet. The pen is secondary, and not always important. I think they did the right thing in concentrating on the tablet aspect.

Being a tablet means that it is much more mobile than laptops or desktops. You can do the things you do with a PC (read, web surf, email, etc.) in more situations (sitting without a desk, standing, etc.). The big change since earlier tablet computers like the GRiD Convertible is that so many more people read so much more on a computer. PCs used to be mainly for composing, doing "what if?", etc. Now we use it for those applications, but even more we spend time reading (Web, email, emailed documents) and quick communicating of simple stuff (IM). Another big change is that the main thing connected to a PC is not a printer, but rather all of computerdom, through LANs and the Internet. With 802.11 (WIFi), that connection can now be considered ubiquitous in more parts of our lives—we are no longer tied to a particular wall connector. These factors increase the value of a tablet, and define its use more. When you read, you mainly select things on the screen (which email message to read, which links to follow, or which "favorites" to revisit), or scroll. When you compose, you are much more concerned with text.

The pen is an obvious choice for an input device on a tablet. Since a tablet is often used in a horizontal position, and you can't be sure of a firm place to rest something like a mouse, a pen is appropriate for a pointing device. In a vertical orientation, like on a laptop, the pen isn't as appropriate for a pointing device as a mouse. In those cases we either connect an external mouse, or put up with even more limited pointing devices like touchpads or stalks. (I find the pen a much better pointing device than either a touchpad or stalk.) In both vertical and horizontal orientations, for any large amount of input of plain text, a keyboard (or in some cases dictation) is a very good solution. A mouse is a lousy text input device, and a touchpad even worse. A pen, though, is better than a mouse for text input, using either a touch keyboard on-screen or handwriting recognition. Handwriting recognition, though, is not the point of a pen, just like it isn't for a mouse. The pen is also much better than the mouse (or keyboard, touchpad, or stalk) for inputting graphical information, and has been well received in the graphic arts world for years. We've put up with all sorts of cumbersome, kludgy

UI workarounds to "draw" with a mouse, and consequently rarely use drawings in informal electronic communications as much as we would in a room with a whiteboard. The pen opens up new areas for applications using drawing, of which "digital ink" is one. Of course, every new input/output device added standard to a PC opens up vast new areas, from laser printers to CD-ROMs to sound cards to modems. The pen will be no different.

So, they are "pen" computers only in that being a tablet to some extent implies a pen. Like the touchpad and stalk in a traditional laptop, they are a reasonable compromise for doing the type of input you want to do with a PC. If you really wanted a "pen" computer, you'd probably want a desktop with a large dedicated writing surface like you find with the excellent pen tablets used by graphic artists. It's much easier to build a good pen system when it doesn't have to run through an electromagnetically noisy color display, and it's much better to make a screen without protection layers for a pen.

Impressions after using it

I'm not going to do my normal job of showing pictures, etc., of the computer in operation, since you can find pretty good Flash and video presentations on the web sites of Microsoft and the manufacturers. I'll just comment on what I've encountered. I assume most readers here have read lots of reviews and other material about the machines and software.

As I write this, I've had the Tablet PC for about a day or so. After I spend more time, I'll publish updated impressions.

It's a geek magnet

Like most any new device, but maybe more so, other people are *very* interested in seeing it. On the way home from buying it, I stopped to go to a Massachusetts Software and Internet Council committee meeting. When I explained that I was a bit late because I had just bought a Tablet PC, I was immediately kicked out of the meeting until I would go back to the car, get it out of the trunk, and return to show it to everybody. The machine was still in the sealed carton, so I had to open it up and show how the screen turned around and how light/heavy it was. (I didn't take the time from the meeting to turn it on and configure it, though.) Later that night, my friend Bob Frankston strongly encouraged me to come over and show it to him and let him play a bit (he's probably going to get one of the Tablets—he was also at Slate for part of the time). Anybody I tell about it says the same thing, "Can you bring it over for me to see? Please?" Just a warning.

You have to spend time learning how to set it up best for you

It took some fooling around (and there's still more to be done) to learn how to set up my Tablet PC to work the way that fits me best. For example, the Toshiba had "hibernate" as the default for closing the case, and "power off" for the power switch when it's in battery-powered mode. I had to change them both to "standby," so that I can wake up the Tablet in a few (about 5) seconds. I didn't want it to go into portrait mode when I switch to tablet, only on command, so I changed that setting.

The digitizer[3]

For input, I find that handwriting recognition works OK, so I sometimes use it for input in Tablet mode, and sometimes use the on-screen keyboard (the keyboard is better for passwords). The combination of cursive recognition and printing recognition is a nice step up from the machines I used in the old days. When I write in a way that my ink is readable (slowly and big), the recognition is surprisingly good, but not wonderful. Still, it sure beats writing with a mouse. For large amounts of text, I'll use the keyboard—that's why I wanted a convertible. I was buying a new laptop, not replacing a keyboard.

For note-taking, I set the Journal application to use the pressure sensitive feature of the pen. It makes the ink of my handwriting (even printing) look much more like real ink. In fact, while I was trying out the new settings (before fixing the digitizer), my cell phone rang, and I had to quickly jot down a number to call, and then take notes during the resulting call. It worked great. I just had to write somewhat bigger than I normally did, but with pressure sensitivity making it do different thicknesses as I pressed down it was very readable for me, and using a pen was a lot easier than holding a cell phone to my ear with one hand and typing with the other—and I got to doodle to boot! With a glass screen and some display delays, the Tablet PC may not feel better than paper for taking notes (ignoring the storage and searching features I haven't tried yet), but it sure makes the PC a more useful device. Some note taking is much better than none. Also, I'm happy I have the Toshiba with its pressure sensitive pen. When printed, the output looks like a felt-tip or fountain pen with varying thicknesses—certainly much more than adequate for producing

---

[3] This refers to the hardware that senses the pen and turns your pen movements into digital information used by the software.

In the essay published on the web site, this section started out with a discussion of some idiosyncrasies of my particular computer which were later fixed. I've left that discussion out in this book.

a printed binder of your notes for backup or sharing with others. They'll think you got a great scan of your paper notes.

Buttons help reading and probably other things

An important part of a tablet is being able to read, and an important part of reading on a computer screen is scrolling. The Tablet PCs have buttons you can push. The Compaq has a rocker switch, too. The Toshiba has basically 3 buttons, by default set to Up-Arrow, Down-Arrow, and Enter. This means when you're reading, you barely even need the pen. Very nice. I think buttons are real important, just like on PDAs. Remember, it's a Tablet PC, not a Pen PC.

An interesting thing about reading: I've noticed how pervasive the RIM Blackberry has become with financial people like venture capitalists and analysts. They sit there in meetings, and every once in a while hold their RIMs in their laps and check their email. A Tablet PC with 802.11 (WiFi) or connection to cellular wireless with Bluetooth or its own cell phone PCMCIA card gives you an even better way to read real email and share what you've found with others in a meeting. Having a personal communications or data storage device you can read with on your lap with the right form factor is already successful (the RIM, PDAs). Here is a device with wider applicability and real Internet connectivity and lots of storage, with ink as a socially acceptable reply method/ medium. The ability to turn the Tablet PC on or off in about 5 seconds with the push of a button is very helpful. (I think it takes a few more seconds to reconnect to 802.11, though.)

Portrait mode is a win

One of the properties of a tablet is being able to run in portrait as well as landscape mode. For reading on-screen this can be very helpful. Much of what you read fits better on a machine the size of a pad of paper when it's in portrait mode, especially when you only have 1024×768 resolution (or is it 768×1024?). I received some email that I read over breakfast that included images of several fax pages. Reading it on my Toshiba in portrait mode was really great. I never needed to scroll, I just tapped the Next Page button every once in a while. Of course, for many regular computer applications and web pages, landscape mode works better. Being able to switch is important. On my big desktop machine, with an 18″ 1280×1024 LCD display, I don't mind wasting the screen space when I read a portrait format page. With something I carry around, though, I don't want to have something any bigger than it has to be.

General-purpose machine

If reading on screen is so important, why not just build an electronic book for reading? The answer is simple. You need to have a portable general-purpose machine like a laptop anyway for composing, calculating, and running specialized applications. By the time you build a good enough "book" machine that can also connect to the Internet with whatever technique you have available (dial-up, 100baseT, 802.11) and connect to the devices you'd like (USB), and be upgradable, etc., you're already spending enough for most of a laptop. It's silly to pay twice, so the more general laptop has always won out. It's only in the case of a completely different form factor, and a price down in the range of a software package or PC peripheral (which is what a Palm cost and was positioned as) that you'd buy both. By making the Tablet PC a full-fledged Windows machine, with access to all the normal peripherals and applications, you don't have that tension of needing to pay twice as much.

How far have we come?

Using the Toshiba (and remembering the little time on the Acer, and seeing the demos at conferences and on the Web), Bob and I were both struck with how little advance there had been since the last try for pen computers in some respects. The pen/tablet software and hardware aspects appear just a bit better, especially given the huge increase in speed and capacity of today's computers vs. the ones of the early to mid-1990s (using the GRiD Convertible as an example). Of course, making it work with color displays, and integrating things into full Windows XP, did take work, I assume. The advance in features, though, seems more like a "next release" or two of things rather than 10 years passing.

This is not bad, though. Things were pretty good in the old days. The GRiD got hammered for its black-and-white screen just as color became standard (B&W being necessary for some of the digitizers of the day), and there wasn't as much advantage to a tablet back then. As I pointed out above, the big change is the environment in which the PC works. There are finally lots of real reasons for tablet computers. Also, the hardware has improved enough where the cost in weight and price is little different than the amount we've repeatedly spent for other new additions to laptops during that timeframe: CD drives, bigger screens, wireless, etc. Moore's Law eventually brought those costs down to where they became standard. Tablet-ability is the latest in that long line of new capabilities.

What's exciting to me, though, is that the way Microsoft is doing this will hopefully encourage tablet-centric innovation to start again throughout the hardware and software industry, so we'll continue these advances, and the rate of improvement will return to what it was in the early 1990s. The wide variations in Tablet PC form factors show the start of that innovation. There will be trial and error to learn all sorts of important issues, from number and placement of buttons, to inking techniques, to new ways to take advantage of the pen and sound.

Bottom line so far

So, one day in, my verdict: I can't see ever buying a portable laptop that isn't a convertible—the benefits are too great for me. It's a Tablet PC, not a Pen PC, and not a Clamshell PC, and that's a win. While these are clearly still basically a version 1 or 2, they are still very useful. If you read a lot on a PC, and move your laptop around a lot, and have benefited from 802.11, and don't mind using early software that works but is basic (like the original VisiCalc was), and are in the market for a new laptop, take the next step and move up to a tablet. Corporate evaluators must start learning about these systems, because as they improve and the price difference disappears, you'll have to figure out how to configure them, what type of software to insist upon, etc. If you always wanted to do your composing with a pen, and expect handwriting to be as reliable as a keyboard, stick with the keyboard, and wait for "handwriting computing" to happen, if it ever does. It's not that important. Tablet computing is. It will make reading on a computer even more pervasive. I think Microsoft and the hardware manufacturers who were willing to take a chance trying to advance the state of mainstream personal computing are to be commended for what they've done.

Further observations, January 22, 2003:

I have learned that the pen is quite nice to use instead of other nonmouse pointing devices on a laptop in normal laptop orientation. (Actually, that's the same experience I had with the old GRiD Convertible.) When reading Web-based email, with lots of spam to check off to delete, it sure beats a touchpad or stalk, and worked fine on the airplane in very cramped seats.

Finally, one of the congratulations I received about our acquisition[4] came from a user of a Tablet PC. It was handwritten in email. I hate to say it as a computer/email enthusiast from way back, but there was something very personal and special about getting a simple, handwritten, signed note as email. I printed it out and saved it.

http://danbricklin.com/log/tabletpc.htm

---

[4] The company I was working for, Trellix, was sold to Interland in Winter of 2002–2003. I continued working for Interland for a little over a year.

In response to reactions to the essay, I wrote another one looking at the reasoning behind some of my assertions. I explored a bit of the history of tablet hardware, as well as the state of application software for that hardware in the early 1990s. I even linked to a few patents to get detailed descriptions.

ABOUT TABLET COMPUTING OLD AND NEW

A discussion of PC tablet hardware and software from the 1990s, and why Microsoft's pushing of the new Tablet PCs will bring renewed innovation.

In my "Tablet PC: First Impressions" essay, I made some assertions about the amount of progress in tablet computing represented by the new Tablet PCs. Some sample quotes:

- Bob and I were both struck with how little advance there had been since the last try for pen computers in some respects.
- The advance in features, though, seems more like a "next release" or two of things rather than 10 years passing.
- Things were pretty good in the old days.
- The way Microsoft is doing this will hopefully encourage tablet-centric innovation to start again throughout the hardware and software industry, so we'll continue these advances, and the rate of improvement will return to what it was in the early 1990s.
- [The new machines are] still basically a version 1 or 2.
- I think Microsoft and the hardware manufacturers who were willing to take a chance trying to advance the state of mainstream personal computing are to be commended for what they've done.

It's hard for people who worked very hard bringing these new systems to market to hear me say it only looks like a "next release," and at the same time it's hard for others to understand why I believe things will advance so much further because of Microsoft and the manufacturers' recent actions. The purpose of this essay is to provide some of the reason for those statements.

The old hardware and OS software

To understand why it doesn't seem like such an advance, you have to be familiar with the hardware and software of the early 1990s.

The use of pens and tablets, and "light-pens" that you could point at the screen, goes very far back in the history of computers. For example, the SAGE[5] air defense system from the 1950s used a "light gun" to interact with the screen. CAD/CAM systems of the 1960s (like the pioneering *SketchPad*[6]) and 1970s used light pens or pens on opaque tablets to manipulate items on the screen.

A pen-based desktop system that was part of the personal computer world came from Wang in 1988. Called Wang Freestyle, it let you annotate screen captures, faxes, and scanned images, with "ink" from an electronic pen using an opaque tablet connected to a PC running normal applications, and manipulate thumbnails of those images by dragging them around using the pen. It let you synchronize recorded sound (using an attached telephone) to a recording of the pen motions. It let you then print, email, or fax the results. Freestyle was a big sensation at Comdex when shown. Even today, looking at a video of it in action demonstrated by the project lead Stephen Levine, it is impressive.

The first in the line of the "modern" tablet computers was the GRiDPad in 1989. Developed under R&D head Jeff Hawkins (who later founded Palm and Handspring), it was about $9'' \times 12'' \times 1.4''$ with a 10MHz 8086 running MS-DOS. It had a pen that was at the end of a wire, and worked by making contact with a coating on the screen. It could recognize hand-printed characters, and was used for data collection, like filling in forms.

The next really influential tablet system was from GO Corporation. The prototype "Lombard" was 80286 based, and ran a new, GUI operating system called PenPoint. GO was started in 1987. After announcing their product in January 1991, GO upgraded the base system to require an 80386 for the first real customer release (which was in April 1992). Later, after Penpoint development was taken over by a company named EO, the processor for PenPoint was changed again, this time to the AT&T Hobbit chip. Each time, software developers had to upgrade their software.

After GO started on PenPoint, Microsoft reacted with enhancements to Windows 3.1 to create Windows for Pen Computing, better known as PenWindows. (The head of that project was Jeff Raikes, who now heads Microsoft's Productivity and Business Services Group which includes the Tablet PC.[7]) Some machines produced at the time (such as the 3 lb. NCR 3125 pure tablet) could boot to either PenPoint or PenWindows. A variety of manufacturers

---

[5] http://www.eskimo.com/%7Ewow-ray/sage28.html

[6] http://en.wikipedia.org/wiki/Sketchpad

[7] In 2008, Jeff left Microsoft and is now CEO of the Bill & Melinda Gates Foundation.

November 22, 2002

made machines for PenWindows, including Samsung and later Compaq. The most interesting PenWindows computer, for me, was the GRiD Convertible, released in mid-1992. (I still have a working one which I used for years—most of the other pen-enabled computers in my collection are stowed away in a warehouse.) The GRiD Convertible was a normal Windows laptop, but when you closed the screen, it folded down in such a way that the screen faced out—like a tablet. It was started under Jeff Hawkins before he left to found Palm Computing. (Notice how these two Jeffs' names keep coming up.) NEC also made a variation on its laptop with a screen you could turn around, like some of today's tablets. Many other manufacturers tried their hands at tablet computers, including Wang and IBM. These computers all used either a Wacom digitizer and battery-less but electronically active pen (the same used in many of today's Tablet PCs, and very popular as a desktop accessory for graphic artists) or a battery-powered (or tethered on a wire) active pen from some other manufacturer. The reason for a special pen is to let the computer track the pen's location when it is held near, but not touching, the screen, much like a mouse is moved before clicking. Windows depends upon the ability to show different cursors, have "hovering" effects, etc. Unfortunately, some of the digitizing technology of the day did not work well with color screens which were just coming into a reasonable price range, so digitizers were left off of most later machines.

Another computer of the day was the Momenta, but it had pretty much its own variant of Windows, and a pen like the original GRiDPad—no hover.

One of the last of that crop of pen-enabled computers was the Apple Newton, first shipped in 1993. While Apple had experimented with other tablet computers, this was the one released to the most fanfare. The Newton's pen, as I recall, did not have hover—it was more like the later Palm computers which just sensed pressure on the screen from any object.

In all cases, the use of a pen as an input device was integrated into the operating system to varying degrees. The pen could be used for most mouse actions, such as clicking or dragging. Within almost any application, instead of typing on a keyboard, you could write on the screen or tap on a virtual keyboard. There were various "gestures" (special pen movements) that invoked certain functions, for example, Undo, or, like today's Tablet PCs, bring up a writing pad or virtual keyboard. All systems had handwriting recognition of some sort.

Looking at the machines of those days, and given the advances in hardware since, today's Tablet PCs are not very surprising. They are somewhat lighter and with much faster microprocessors and greater memory, but the pen additions and form factors are similar. The important thing, as I point out in my

November 22, 2002

"First Impressions" essay, is that today's machines come into an environment where you read more on a computer screen, and wireless connectivity to all of computerdom is commonplace. Now these machines have a much more important reason to exist.

The old applications

The first applications for the GRiDPad were very basic, in line with the simple forms capabilities of a basic browser. With the advent of PenPoint, though, developers started producing much more sophisticated products, pouring millions and millions of dollars into development. PenPoint itself had a very sophisticated, pen-centric user interface (UI). Coming before the convertibles, and trying to completely eliminate the keyboard, there were all sorts of user interface advances. Some of those ended up influencing Windows 95. It had OLE-like embedding well before it was viable on Windows; it required just a "tap" to launch apps which avoided the need for double-clicking, and more.

In early 1990, I cofounded a company called Slate Corporation (along with other PC veterans like Vern Raburn, Dottie Hall, and Tom Byers). Our mission was to create application software for the upcoming PenPoint and other tablet/pen operating systems. There were other companies that were creating application software specifically for these machines, but ours was the best funded, produced the most products, and is the one I know best, so I'll talk about it first.

We demonstrated the first of our software when GO announced PenPoint (286 version) in January 1991, and shipped our products in shrink-wrapped boxes in 1992 for both PenPoint and PenWindows. The products we developed were:

- PenApps, an application development system somewhat similar to Visual Basic (which was being developed around the same time). It had an object-oriented programming language (PenBasic) with support for ink as a data type, a drag-and-drop interface builder, and more. You could write on a form created with it, and when filling out forms it was smart about targeting the ink you wrote to the correct field (so you didn't have to carefully "write inside of the lines"). It had "deferred translation" where the ink was kept around so you didn't have to wait for each field to translate as you filled out a form, and you could check translated data against the original ink at any time. It had a built-in database. It was a major product.

- PenBook, an electronic book creation system. This was similar to Adobe's PDF system (being developed around the same time), but tuned for reading on a tablet computer. It could convert PostScript files output from most any program into its format, and then you could read the "books" with a special reader. The reader supported pen gestures for turning pages, annotating and highlighting, bookmarks that looked like paperclips, and more. It had searching and stored the "book" in a compressed format.

- At-Hand spreadsheet for PenPoint only. This was a full-fledged spreadsheet (mainly created by Bill Lynch who went on to work with Microsoft's Excel group for years) complete with a BASIC-like programming language with special spreadsheet data types and operators to react to tapped buttons and other events (developed by Bob Frankston before VBA came out from Microsoft in 1994) and a full graphing package (developed by Buzz Kelley, now with me at Trellix). It could read and write Excel and 1-2-3 files (thanks to Peter Levin, now with me at Trellix[8]). In addition to all this, it was completely operable with a pen, with lots of innovative features. You could write on the spreadsheet cell grid, and it would target your writing to the appropriate cell. If what you wrote was text, you got a label cell; if it was a number, you got a numeric value, appropriately formatted. If it couldn't recognize what you wrote well, you got ink reduced to fit in the cell (ready for correction or to be left alone). For entering formulas, there was a special input dialog tuned to the pen. A couple taps of the pen selected a range of cells, and writing a "+" put the "sum" function where you wrote it. There was a markup layer to annotate things with ink. The graphing system handled most of the popular graph types (including 3D and contour) yet scaled appropriately to work well when embedded on the sheet or elsewhere. A year or so later we created an Excel plug-in called PenPower that added many of those pen-centric capabilities to Excel running under PenWindows.

- Day-Timer Pen Scheduler for PenPoint or PenWindows. This was an electronic ink-based version of Day-Timer, Inc.'s organizer, with calendar-based day/week/month/year views, note-taking pages, to-do lists, and a name/address book (which used text and ink). With easy zooming, you could use "tiny text" to fit lots of data in any space ("Your pages are

---

[8] Buzz Kelley and Peter Levin have since moved to work at Adobe in the Boston area.

uncluttered, yet full of valuable information"). You could circle something of interest, and then file that snippet away in an index by topic, linked back to the original, all with a quick gesture.

- LooseLeaf Notetaker for PenWindows. This was an ink-based note-taking application for the GRiD Convertible with a variety of pens and markers.

In addition to Slate's products, there were deep, innovative products from other companies. For example, Pensoft produced a personal information manager that used recognized text and a database. A later company (founded in 1991) was Aha!, which created an ink-based note-taking product with extensive ink editing features. Among other things, it could "word wrap" text still in ink, and do background translation for later conversion or searching. Aha! was bought by Microsoft in 1996, and you can see how the Windows Journal program comes from it (without some of the cool word-wrapping features).

One of the issues we were working on at Slate in the mid-1990s was evangelizing the use of digital ink created with a digitizing pen as a normal data type among applications. We also had to deal with making the ink look true enough to your quick scribbles, so that even when you used a $6'' \times 8''$ screen to mark up an $8\frac{1}{2}'' \times 11''$ fax shrunk to fit, it would look "normal" printed out or re-faxed at full size. We did lots of work with growing and shrinking ink, and related issues. (When you shrink, you don't want the lines to get below a certain thickness or else it sometimes looks weird.) We also worked on some early pocket-sized prototypes, as well as software for Apple's Newton when it first shipped.

Learn from old patents

To learn more about the level of thinking that went into these old products, you can read some of the patents that came out of those efforts. Since patents are supposed to teach you what is novel and important, reading them should be like reading a techie-to-techie white paper about what's special and why. (Unlike when looking for infringement, just read the main body of these patents, not the claims. I list them here not to say whether or not they apply today, but rather as a source of learning about what was thought about in the past.)

- U.S. Patent 5,613,019: System and methods for spacing, storing and recognizing electronic representations of handwriting, printing and drawings. [Based on filings to the Patent Office done in May 1993.] This has the text of Aha!'s description. I found the middle section (it's a long patent) where it discusses how to determine what's a "word" (getting the dot over the letter "i" to be part of the right word, even if written much later) interesting. The patent mentions that the digitizers of those days sampled the pen's position about 200 times a second—faster than most Tablet PCs today.

- U.S. Patent 5,455,901: Input device with deferred translation. [Based on filings from November 1991.] This describes keeping the ink around to translate later, as well as for verification or instead of translation. It's the Slate PenApps patent. This and the other Slate patents are now owned by Compaq/HP. (Compaq bought Slate Corporation when we ran out of money when people refrained from buying the computers that ran our software.)

- U.S. Patents 5,717,939 and 5,848,187: Method and apparatus for entering and manipulating spreadsheet cell data. [These are based on filings from November 1991.] These are the Slate At-Hand spreadsheet patents (the two have similar text, but different claims). They describe targeting ink to cells, special spreadsheet gestures, improved recognition for a spreadsheet, and more.

- U.S. Patent 5,867,150: Graphic indexing system. [Based on filings from February 1992.] One of the Slate Pen Scheduler patents. This relates to selecting something on the screen by circling it and then quickly adding it to a graphical index or gallery. Sometimes it's easier to just put the image of a piece of a page into an index for quick scanning with your eyes than to type a description. This patent relates to such a feature.

- U.S. Patent 5,231,578: Apparatus for document annotation and manipulation using images from a window source, U.S. Patent 5,625,833: Document annotation & manipulation in a data processing system. [Based on filings in 1988.] Some of the Wang Freestyle patents.

So as you can see, the thinking 10 years ago was quite deep, with applications on par with anything being shown today.[9]

Why the machines are version 1 or 2

Looking at some of the machines, you can see that we still haven't learned all the tricks necessary to make a tablet without rough edges. For example, on the

---

[9] You can find a lot more material in the essay by Bill Buxton about multi-touch systems. I mention it in my next essay, and it's available on the Web at http://www.billbuxton.com/multitouchOverview.html.

Toshiba, which is supposed to have one of the better pen holders, when you put the pen back in its holder, the pen tip is close to the side of the screen and entices the mouse cursor to move over to it, away from where you left it. (This might be when you put the pen away in keyboard mode and use the touchpad, or in tablet mode to use just the arrow buttons for reading.) Worse yet, putting the pen in the holder often presses the tip, signaling a mouse click. If there are buttons or icons on that side of the screen, they sometimes get selected.

The screens vary in their feel and the pens in their weight. The perfect paper-like feel of drag for writing, without muddying up the image with ground glass, hasn't been perfected.

Some of the machines have built-in prop-up stands for reading on a desk in portrait mode, and others don't . . . yet. (I find that important.) We don't know enough about how many buttons are best, nor how to place them, though manufacturers are experimenting. I'm sure there are other physical attributes to be worked out.

As I pointed out in my "First Impressions" essay, the default values for things aren't always tuned to tablet use.

On top of all this, the weight and battery life still isn't down far enough, though the 4.25 lbs. of the Toshiba Tablet PC is much better than the 6 lbs. of the old GRiD Convertible. (Since both are normal convertibles with similar battery life, they are a good comparison.)

Why we'll see renewed advancement

In the early 1990s, innovation in tablet and pen computing moved at a rapid rate. Once the hardware and operating system companies stopped pushing it, though, independent software developers stopped. Without constant trying of new things, and testing them in the marketplace, it is hard to have advancement. The main "new" thing you hear from Microsoft has been about their book reading software, developed for other purposes. While functionally similar to Slate's old PenBook and other products, Microsoft persevered in the image quality area to solve various problems and get a nice improvement in the eyes of many people. This improvement shows what happens when you keep trying.

The big thing from my viewpoint, though, is Microsoft's trying again and going to the trouble of integrating basic tablet and pen functionality into the latest version of Windows, and simultaneously driving better hardware with some minimum requirements. In addition, they are spending the time and money to upgrade their Office products with tablet-specific features and to provide a complete set of APIs for developers of other products.

If developers learn about what was done in the past, they can move ahead and produce better solutions to the problems we were addressing, and discover new areas to be covered. Software development is a continuous process of building on what came before, and then testing with real use. By Microsoft starting with an advanced ink application of the last generation, they've set the bar high enough to give people a boost. If they really leave things open for outside development (from both a technical and business viewpoint), and continue innovating themselves, new ideas can be tested and evaluated by the market. The fact that we now have good hardware with lots of marketing behind it means there will be at least some market for new software.

Remember what happened with the Internet as developers experimented with HTML after the early browsers came out. Compare what web sites looked like in 1994 and 1996 to today. (For example, compare the early browser-based web site authoring systems to later ones like Trellix's, and you'll see huge improvement.) Now that we have a basis to build upon, that type of advancement, like we saw in tablet and pen computing in the early 1990s, can resume where it left off.

http://www.bricklin.com/tabletcomputing.htm

What Has Happened Since to Tablet PCs

As I write this in late 2008, Tablet PCs are still being produced, with new models released by many manufacturers along with traditional laptops.

However, no special general-purpose software seems to have caught people's attention to the extent of being a "killer application" that drives huge sales of Tablet PCs. (The spreadsheet, for example, was an early personal computer killer application.) At least one of Microsoft's products tuned to work well with Tablet PCs, OneNote, is quite popular.

What has happened, though, is that the Tablet PCs have become popular in various vertical applications, such as for data collection, medical-office use, etc. Microsoft continues to invest in the technology and has been maintaining the tablet-related capabilities of its general Windows operating system.

Part of the reason for the low amount of new innovation in the Tablet PC area, I believe, is related to the fact that most entrepreneurial software development money has been spent in the online and mobile areas. Browsing software does not, in general, have additional features for pen interaction, and there are not enough Tablet PCs to satisfy the "make it up in the volume" business plans of many Web 2.0 companies.

Another reason for the lack of adoption of Tablet PCs is that one of the initial driving uses for them was as computing devices we carry around. When sitting on a desk, with a vertical screen, for many applications touching a pen to the screen doesn't buy you that much over a traditional laptop. For email, word processing, and typing the exacting text needed for web browsing and searching, a keyboard is much more reliable. In order to compete functionally with a laptop, and have long enough battery life for untethered use, Tablet PCs have continued to be quite bulky and heavy.

It seems, instead, that a much smaller form factor has become popular for carrying around: the handheld. This has moved from the PDA (like the Palm Pilot and the related Microsoft-software-based machines), to the RIM Blackberry (for the dominant application for many people of doing email), to the Palm Treo and then Apple iPhone (general-purpose computing platforms that handle scheduling, email, web browsing, and "long-tail" applications).

We are seeing a surge in innovation in hand-on-computer interacting thanks mainly to the ubiquity of the iPhone and Apple's App Store software application distribution system, which give developers an easy way to make money with popular applications.

As usual, we see how it is hard to predict exactly how evolution will go with technology. Many factors come into play.

Gestures and No Pen

The keyboard still seems to win out over the pen for data input. Where the pen has always done well is for pointing and issuing commands. The fine control of the pen, though, is not needed for many applications. Even more importantly, in handheld devices, needing to use a cumbersome, easy-to-lose pen is at a disadvantage compared to systems where you can point and gesture with just your fingers directly on the screen.

Here is an essay about interacting with a computer screen that is sensitive to contact with a person's fingers.

October 24, 2007

GESTURES, THE IPHONE, AND STANDARDS: A DEVELOPER'S QUESTIONS

A discussion of the nature and use of gestures in a computer controlled by screen contact and some of the issues with regard to developing standards

The release of the Apple iPhone (and now the iPod Touch) has renewed interest in computing devices controlled by gestures. Over the years, I've been writing about different devices with direct hand input (either by touch and/or pen) and it's time to do it again.[10]

Introduction

This essay is going to address the issue of a gesture-based interface.

In the "real" world, a gesture is a motion of the limbs or an act made to express a thought or as a symbol of intent. You gesture to your waiter to come over and see the fly in your soup, or wave an oncoming car past your stopped car. You make hand gestures to express disgust and anger at others, or to signal approval and disapproval (thumbs up and thumbs down).

These gestures are often shortcuts or silent, nonverbal alternatives for expression. In other cases, especially when we want a richer vocabulary, we may use spoken or written language to express ourselves more explicitly.

These gestures and their meaning are usually learned. While they may have a relationship to the idea being expressed (waving a car around your stopped car), they often have more obscure symbolism and take longer to learn (handshaking, giving a "high-five"). They may be a bit ambiguous and very context dependent. For example, to order a hot dog from a vendor walking the aisles at a ball game, a variety of gestures and meanings are often necessary: You get the vendor's attention with the "choose me to start a conversation or transaction"

---

[10]This paragraph was included in the original essay:

Many have written about the iPhone, so why should you listen to what I have to say? In addition to my general experience with user interfaces and "tool" design, I have experience directly related to such systems. Back in the early 1990s, I worked on a variety of such systems at Slate Corporation and was heavily involved in the developments at that time. A few months ago I attended (and gave a presentation to) a small conference at Brown University about current pen computing research. In preparation, I looked over some of the old videos from my Slate days, and even played a bit with some of the old pen computers in my personal collection. More recently, I've spent some time with the Apple iPhone and have started doing a little experimental development with my newly acquired iPod Touch (which shares the same interface and programming environment). Here are some thoughts.

gesture (a raised hand with palm facing the other person); signal the desired action with a raised index finger ("one, please"); tell him to not put on relish with a "stop" gesture (the raised hand with facing palm gesture again); and then tell him to wait a minute while you borrow some money from the person next to you (the raised index finger, again).

In the realm of computing, we have other gestures. When using a mouse, we indicate position on the computer screen by sliding our hands over the desk in a relative (not absolute-positioned) motion. We use finger gestures, including some we call "pushing buttons," that are really more akin to the dexterity of playing a note on the clarinet than on a piano or pushing a button to choose something from a vending machine. The same gesture can have different meanings when we press a second button on the mouse or use our other hand to hold down a modifier key on the keyboard.

Again, the computer gestures are learned, sometimes with an obvious symbolic connection to the operation desired (clicking while "pointing" to an object displayed on the screen) and sometimes not (using the "control key" along with clicking to mean "also select this one"). Basic mouse use was helped by the addition to Microsoft Windows of the Solitaire program, a brilliant move (in terms of training).

The keyboard is an interesting situation. When entering text, the symbols printed on the keys make their meaning very clear. Pressing the "a" key enters the letter "a." Pressing the "Del" key deletes a character or selected item. Sometimes, we have additional meanings to learn and use, such as two-key combinations like pressing "control" along with the arrow keys for different types of cursor motion, or with the letter keys to format text (e.g., ctrl-B for bold). Again, these are gestures we make that the computer "understands." They are gestures that have varying levels of symbolic connection to the actual operation being performed. They are gestures that must be learned through experimentation, reading documentation, or other training.

Once you learn a gesture and its meaning, it becomes a "natural" way of expression. In your mind, you start thinking of waving a car around yours or stopping one approaching a crosswalk by using an upraised hand as directly "controlling" something else. You start to think of the gesture like a lever that is mechanically effecting what you want, and may think that is the only gesture that could have that meaning, just as in the physical world only that particular lever could actually control the thing to which it was connected.

However, without learning, many gestures probably have little intrinsic meaning. A gesture that might be common and "obvious" in one culture, perhaps being so offensive as to lead to fights for honor in that culture, might be completely ignored in another, or have another, polite and commonly used meaning. The "ctrl-" modifier of the Windows world (such as "ctrl-B" for bold) is used differently in other systems, where, for example, the Mac more commonly uses the Command/Apple key (such as "cmd-B" for bold).

I remember learning to hitchhike (that is, standing by the side of the road asking the passing motorists to give me a ride) by facing traffic, stretching out my arm, making a fist with the thumb sticking out, and pointing behind me in the direction traffic was going. That's the symbol in the United States, I guess meaning "I want to go that direction." One summer, I was in another country, and there the symbol was an outstretched arm with a closed hand and the index finger pointing to the road by my side. I guess that came from "please stop here for me." Who knows? In both cases, the effective message was the same, but the gesture was different and certainly needed to be learned. After using it for a while, it became second nature.

Touch-screen and pen gestures

In the area of computers with screen-contact interaction, such as those using a pen or a touch-sensitive display, we become very much dependent on gestures for communicating with the computer. Looking at systems that had widespread popular use, the first systems included "kiosk" style systems, such as banking machines and some control panels. These systems, as I recall, mainly used images of buttons which you could "press"—a very simple, somewhat obvious, and easy to learn gesture.

The first really popular (and long-lived) system for the general public was the Palm Pilot. In addition to "tapping" gestures for selection (using a finger, fingernail, or the included stylus) and operating some of the "controls" that functioned in the manner of the already-common mouse-based GUI systems, the device used a large set of special gestures for entering text, known as "Graffiti." From the Pilot Handbook: "Graffiti is a system where simple strokes you write with the stylus are instantly recognized as letters or numbers . . . The strokes recognized by Graffiti are designed to closely resemble those of the regular alphabet."

While the gestures for some characters may be almost the same as normally writing the letter, such as the letter "L," others required some learning, such as "A" (upside down "V") and "T" ("L" rotated 180 degrees). The space character was entered as a horizontal line written left to right, while backspace was one written right to left. Period was two periods (tapping twice). While most letters were related to their printed uppercase selves, "H" was a lowercase "h" and "Y" was a lowercase script "y." "V" was either a "V" with an additional horizontal tail or written right to left as a "V," distinguishing it from a "U."

After a time of practice, for many people (millions of Palm PDAs were sold) the gestures became associated in the mind with the characters and writing became natural.

Some gestures are "easy" for the computer to recognize reliably, such as tapping on a button image. Others, like handwritten characters, are much harder.

A very famous and extensive use of gestural control of a handheld computer was the PenPoint operating system from GO Corporation. PenPoint used "handwritten" gestures for all input and control, including text entry. It could deal with a wide variety of seemingly identical gestures, appropriately placing them in context. A drawn vertical line could alternately be interpreted as a drawn line, the letter "I," a "flick" gesture to control scrolling, and more.

PenPoint-based computers were, in many ways, on par with full traditional laptops of the time, with word processing, spreadsheet, drawing, scheduling, custom applications, program development, and more. I have posted a copy of a GO promotional video aimed at developers that includes a very extensive demonstration by PenPoint architect Robert Carr of the system and its use of gestures. The 59-minute video is available as "PenPoint Demonstration 1991" on Google Video.[11]

I've also written an essay about the state of pen-based computing in the 1990s: "About Tablet Computing Old and New."[12] It lists a variety of products and patents. The patents are especially valuable for their descriptions of the thinking of those days, no matter what actually ended up in the patent claims themselves or the validity of those claims in light of today's reading of the law. (Note from a layperson: In a patent, the long section called the description is written before it is clear exactly which claims will be allowed by the Patent Office. Only the claims are what is "patented," not everything in the description. The extra material in the description is often quite interesting for learning, and itself is one of the forms of prior art used by patent examiners.)

More specifics about gestures

Feedback to the user while making the gestures is important. Just the fact that their fingers or pen touch the screen is one type of feedback. With a pen,

---

[11]http://video.google.com/videoplay?docid=9140399149118885327

[12]This essay appears earlier in this chapter.

the "feel" of the stylus point against the screen matters. Visually, "touched" objects often respond by either highlighting, morphing, moving, etc. With added computing power, objects could be "dragged" and now, on the iPhone, even more "realistic" responses can be displayed making the operation even clearer once you learn the gesture and making the illusion of direct connection to a "machine" more complete.

Gestures on these screen-contact computers have a variety of variables to distinguish them from each other. One is the shape of the gesture, determined by the path the finger or stylus takes while in contact with the screen. Another is the position of the gesture and the parts of its path, if any. Finally, there is the timing, both within the gesture itself and relative to other events. Sometimes the operating system generically interprets the gesture and sometimes a particular application interprets the user input with varying degrees of common assistance from the system.

For example, a "tap" is usually just a brief contact of the screen in one position. The path is very small, if any, and the shape doesn't matter, since to the user it's supposed to be thought of as a single "dot." If the tap is over an image of a button, it often means to "press" the button and do whatever that would do. If the tap is over an object of some sort, it may mean to select that object, either for operation immediately or perhaps at a later time, such as selecting an image for display. If the tap is close in time to a previous tap, and within a specified distance from that first tap, it may be a different command, such as the iPhone browser's use of tap to click a link and double tap for zooming in and then zooming out. In the At-Hand spreadsheet, described in one of the patent descriptions, the relative position of the second tap in a double-tap gesture indicated which direction a cell range selection should be extended, akin to the End-key shortcuts in Lotus 1-2-3.

Another gesture is the "flick" gesture. This is basically a horizontal or vertical line of contact with the screen. In PenPoint, the direction you draw (left to right, top to bottom, etc.) determines whether or not the gesture is interpreted as a Page Up, Page Down, Page Left, or Page Right command, and then performed accordingly by the underlying program. Some programs may ignore the recognition, and just use the tracking of the pen motions to control the motion of something being displayed on the screen. Sometimes, holding down the pen in one position before moving it in a direction is used to turn a Page Down gesture into a "drag" operation. Again, location of the gesture (on something that may be dragged) and timing can determine exactly what the gesture does.

On the iPhone/iPod Touch browser, dragging horizontally or vertically on a page seems to enter a "flick" mode, where the screen scrolls in pretty much direct response to continued motion of the finger in that axis (and that axis only), with the speed of motion at release determining some visual "momentum" for a nice, smooth feel that sort of makes it feel like there is a direct connection to a physical object and that also gives you an ability to scroll with each flick a bit further than your finger actually moves. Motion that starts out on a diagonal, though, can continue in any direction until you stop touching the screen. Once zoomed in on a photo in the iPhone photo viewer application, finger motion works equally in all directions, except that scrolling sideward stops at a photo boundary (the photos are displayed horizontally in sequence) unless certain speed and sequencing criteria are met in a way that makes it feel like you have to coax it over the boundary.

As you can see, the set of gestures and the definition of their functionality can be quite extensive and detailed.

Choice of gestures

Both PenPoint and the iPhone use a flick gesture of some sort (they both assign the same name to it) for paging through data on the screen. Unlike a lock which requires a specific style of key turned a specific amount in a specific direction, there is nothing inherent in scrolling that requires that particular gesture. Other systems have used sliding scrollbars, and Page Up and Down "buttons." The mimicking of a physical object does not even require that gesture. While a scroll of paper may respond well to being slid, or the turning of a knob, pages of "real" paper are also advanced physically by turning the pages one at a time. The iPhone has an orientation sensor of some sort and could possibly respond to physical "turning" as page turns just as well as it responds to switching from portrait to landscape.

In a computer system, like hitchhiking, the choice of gestures often leaves a lot of room for variations. The gestures used for particular operations (the visual feedback) may be chosen from a range of options. While some may be easier to guess or learn than others, many will serve the task. As with any mapping of functions to input options, be they in choices of keys or menu locations, there is technically a lot of choice. For human interface design purposes, though, there are other factors that may dictate the choices.

Product developers have found that there are advantages when you keep in common the general operation within various genres of computing devices. The GUI interface of point-and-click, drop-down menus, scrollbars, etc., makes it easier to learn new applications and to switch between using multiple applications on traditional personal computers. To paraphrase Jakob Nieslen from his old essay "Do Interface Standards Stifle Design Creativity?":[13] "Users spend most of their time [using other applications and devices]. Thus, anything that is a convention and used on the majority of other [applications and devices] will be burned into the users' brains and you can only deviate from it on pain of major usability problems."

This style of product design, of using commonly accepted user interface conventions, has served us well repeatedly in the past. As Jakob points out, it makes it easier to go from web site to web site doing e-commerce, with familiar components and terminology. Once you learn how to buy from Amazon or eBay, buying from Lands' End or Joe's Cellular Accessories becomes straightforward. Once you learned Lotus 1-2-3's moving-cursor-style menu and "F1 for Help," many other nonspreadsheet applications that followed those conventions seemed "natural."

The world now that we have the iPhone

In today's world, we have graphic manipulation ability that greatly outstrips technology available even a decade ago, with larger handheld screens with multi-touch, motion and position sensors, increasingly inexpensive memory to hold photos, audio, video, and forms of media, high-resolution-but-tiny cameras, and various forms of wireless connectivity. The general public is accustomed to carrying a cell phone, digital camera, and perhaps an MP3 player. WiFi and other connectivity are becoming quite ubiquitous. These conditions are opening up new opportunities for the user interface.

The excitement around the iPhone for its dazzling interface and design polish, and the desirability for pocket-sized devices with as much screen area as possible, makes it highly likely that we will be deluged with applications (and devices) that use a contact-with-screen gestural interface. A question that arises then is: What should be the standard interface on such devices?

I'm running into this problem as I contemplate programming for the iPhone/iPod Touch. At present, the only non-Apple programming for these devices allowed by Apple is through the browser.[14] While in some senses the browser in the iPhone is the "same" as the Safari browser on a Mac or PC, in many ways it is quite different—much more different than Safari is from other browsers (like

---

[13]http://www.useit.com/alertbox/990822.html

[14]This was the case in 2007. Apple has since opened up more of the capabilities of the iPhone to developers, though not all as of this writing, as I understand it.

Firefox, Internet Explorer, or Opera). The relationship between the physical screen and the virtual page on which the HTML is rendered is different than in a traditional browser. For an optimal experience, this requires coding the HTML page with the characteristics of the iPhone browser specifically in mind.

While iPhone Safari's operation with a page like the *New York Times* homepage shown in the TV ads looks quite usable, in practice many web pages are much less smooth to use on the iPhone than you would want. For quick operation on the go, this can be a problem. Web developers are finding that they have to make major changes, perhaps with dedicated URLs, to give iPhone users the support they deserve.

There is nothing wrong with needing to program specifically for the iPhone, especially given the likelihood that this is great learning for tuning applications to similarly sized screens. We did it before for the more minimal screens of earlier mobile devices (such as the special mobile portals for Google, the airlines, some news sites, etc.). It would be helpful, though, if we didn't need different code for different manufacturers (remember the notices on web sites in the mid and late 1990s of "best viewed in Netscape" and later "best viewed in IE").

Another challenge is that the iPhone version of Safari does not fully implement all of the input functionality expected by JavaScript[15] in a browser. For example, the tracking of finger contact (which would correspond to mouse movements) is currently reserved for the operating system and not passed through to your program. Basically, only the tap gesture is provided to a non-Apple program, and then only at the time when the finger stops contact. The flicking and zooming gestures perform their operation without much coordination with the JavaScript. Any Web-based application that depends upon that missing functionality can have compatibility and usability issues.

This means that, for developers outside of Apple looking to develop compatible software, there is a much more limited repertoire of gestures from which to choose than you would expect, and you are likely to end up with an application whose operation seems foreign to the rest of the system. There is a lot that can be done with tapping, from multiple taps in various configurations to various pop-up button pads, but the "soul" of the iPhone includes the smooth animation of its response to drag gestures of various sorts.

---

[15]JavaScript is a programming language that controls the browser. Programs written in JavaScript are included as part of web pages. Effects such as drop-down menus, data checking, and even full applications like Google Docs are often created using JavaScript.

What do we do now? What are some of the issues?

To further my original question: What should an iPhone programmer do today?

Here are some factors to consider. We'll start with which gestures to use.

As I hope I've demonstrated, gestures are learned and any apparent direct connection between the gesture and the operation being accomplished is usually something we also learn and later internalize. There is usually not one "right" gesture for most operations. For example, the show-stopping "pinch" gesture used for zooming in and out on the iPhone could also have been a single-finger drag in or out to a corner, much like sizing images in many existing programs. Both types, two-fingered pinching/stretching and single-fingered corner-dragging, need to be learned and have mnemonic value.

Historically, users "vote" for various preferences by their purchases and feedback, and software developers try different approaches or mimic existing products as they see fit, sometimes getting people "trained" on their approach because of the desirability of other features of the product or its ubiquity for other reasons. Over time, commonly accepted standards seem to develop, often aided by explicitly documented style guides from the "winning" developers. Apple seems to be "campaigning" for its choices, and doing prepurchase training, through heavy television advertising.

There are also legal issues.

Historically, some vendors have sought to lock in their advantages by precluding others from "copying" their interface standards. There were "look-and-feel wars" in the 1990s using copyright law. There is now more and more use of patent law for trying to keep an interface style proprietary. In the early days of popular GUI, Apple, after "borrowing" a lot from Xerox, attempted to keep elements of their particular expression from Microsoft, but contract and other legal issues got in their way and common use by everybody of the mouse and GUI proliferated. Apple appears to be signaling a desire to have some user interface elements of the iPhone to themselves when they refer to the "revolutionary" multi-touch interface and through the reported filing of patent applications. Microsoft seems to be signaling its intention to dispute those claims with actions such as the posting by their researcher Bill Buxton of his very interesting essay *"Multi-Touch Systems that I Have Known and Loved"*.[16] (This essay is also a great introduction to some of the advantages and disadvantages of a variety of input means. As you will see, the "touch" interface is not a "perfect" solution.)

---

[16]http://www.billbuxton.com/multitouchOverview.html

Apple has released some very detailed and helpful documentation about the current state of the iPhone browser. This documentation looks like it will help a developer wring the most out of the capabilities Apple is providing. Apple has also stated that they will be providing a more extensive SDK (Software Development Kit) to give developers even more access to the device's capabilities, but, as of this writing, they have not stated exactly which capabilities.[17] The legal notice at the beginning of the released documentation states:

> *No licenses, express or implied, are granted with respect to any of the technology described in this document. Apple retains all intellectual property rights associated with the technology described in this document. This document is intended to assist application developers to develop applications only for Apple-labeled or Apple-licensed computers.*

Apple's documentation in October 2007

From what I've seen as a nonlawyer, over the past few years patents have become a major battleground and invalidating patents has been very difficult and expensive (see "Thoughts on Patent Litigation in 2006").[18] Also, proving to the patent office that your idea was "non-obvious" (and thereby patentable) was relatively easy compared to what many laypeople would think is the case because of the interpretation of the word "obvious" by the patent courts. "Prior art" that would disqualify an application needed to be much more explicitly descriptive of what was being patented than most laypeople appear to assume.

I am not a lawyer, but as a layperson, the recent U.S. Supreme Court ruling on patents in *KSR International Co. v. Teleflex Inc. et al.*[19] will narrow the definition of "non-obvious" and change the dynamics. Exactly how is yet to be seen. Here are some excerpts (and you can see how Buxton's essay fits in here):

> *Common sense teaches, however, that familiar items may have obvious uses beyond their primary purposes, and in many cases a person*

---

[17] It is now (late 2008) possible for developers to access many additional capabilities of the iPhone. This has unleashed a huge wave of new applications, many of which take advantage of special features of the device, such as the touch screen and the accelerometer (that detects movement and tilting).

[18] http://www.bricklin.com/patents2006.htm

[19] http://www.supremecourtus.gov/opinions/06pdf/04-1350.pdf

of ordinary skill will be able to fit the teachings of multiple patents [(DanB:) and/or existing known technology] together like pieces of a puzzle . . .

A person of ordinary skill is also a person of ordinary creativity, not an automaton.

[The] Court of Appeals [concluded in error] that a patent claim cannot be proved obvious merely by showing that the combination of elements was "obvious to try" . . . When there is a design need or market pressure to solve a problem and there are a finite number of identified, predictable solutions, a person of ordinary skill has good reason to pursue the known options within his or her technical grasp. If this leads to the anticipated success, it is likely the product not of innovation but of ordinary skill and common sense. In that instance the fact that a combination was obvious to try might show that it was obvious under §103 [and therefore not patentable] . . ,

We build and create by bringing to the tangible and palpable reality around us new works based on instinct, simple logic, ordinary inferences, extraordinary ideas, and sometimes even genius. These advances, once part of our shared knowledge, define a new threshold from which innovation starts once more. And as progress beginning from higher levels of achievement is expected in the normal course, the results of ordinary innovation are not the subject of exclusive rights under the patent laws. Were it otherwise patents might stifle, rather than promote, the progress of useful arts. See U. S. Const., Art. I, §8, cl. 8.

Supreme Court of the United States, *KSR International Co. v. Teleflex Inc. et al.*

From what we can see here, for the ordinary small developer with little money, the legal landscape is unclear and perhaps perilous.

Putting all this together, what we as developers need to do is figure out where we should standardize and how, and where we should encourage experimentation. As we start programming for the iPhone, we need to decide where we will follow Apple, where we will use more common or legally clear gestures, and where additional innovation is needed.

Leadership needed

The world of handheld screen-contact computing looks like it will continue to blossom. We need leadership that will help us proceed with the commonality we have used to advantage repeatedly in the past to benefit all.

Who will step forward with that leadership and be followed? Will Apple try to maintain a sole position as a platform or will it encourage the whole industry to follow its lead? Will Microsoft go the Open route, and follow its previous examples evangelizing XML and other very open standards, or will it try to create its own proprietary following? Will some members of the academic or Free and Open Source Software community do the legal legwork, interface design, and initial coding to mimic the success of the work of Berners-Lee[20] and later the W3C vs. proprietary systems such as those from AOL, CompuServe, and Microsoft? Who will fund that? Google? Nokia? Will there be inward-looking greed or industry leadership?

As Bill Buxton points out in his essay, the iPhone interface has some important drawbacks. Unlike physical button-based interfaces, it is hard to use in one hand or while not looking at the screen for feedback. For those who are visually impaired its operation is difficult. In the early GUI world, Microsoft (knowing that there were few computers with a mouse installed and the value of keeping your hands on the keyboard during data entry) made sure that there were keyboard equivalents for almost all operations and encouraged that as a standard. The original Mac didn't even have a full complement of cursor movement keys. Eventually good elements of both Mac and Windows became common.

As part of our "common" system, we will probably need some physical actuators (buttons and/or sliders?), maybe more than the very few on the iPhone or iPod Touch. (A Tablet PC usually has a few input buttons available when closed and they are quite useful, I've found.) We will need alternative

---

[20]Tim Berners-Lee invented the HTTP and HTML web protocols in 1989 and is generally credited as the "inventor of the World Wide Web." He made those specifications available as open standards for anybody to use. He later moved to MIT, where he has served as director of the World Wide Web Consortium (W3C), which helps develop protocols and guidelines that ensure long-term growth for the Web. The W3C web site states (www.w3.org/Consortium/):

In order for the Web to reach its full potential, the most fundamental Web technologies must be compatible with one another and allow any hardware and software used to access the Web to work together. W3C refers to this goal as "Web interoperability." By publishing open (non-proprietary) standards for Web languages and protocols, W3C seeks to avoid market fragmentation and thus Web fragmentation.

(but pretty complete) input means for people with disabilities or other special situations, perhaps through means such as wired or wireless connection to other input devices, and these means must be commonly supported without too much extra work on the part of developers. Continued use and experimentation with today's systems will lead us to understand what other additions should be "standard."

As a software developer, I await signals from those with the resources to make things happen. In the meantime, I'll experiment with what we have and continue to hone my skills on other platforms.

http://www.bricklin.com/gestures.htm

October 24, 2007

Since the release of the iPhone, Apple has added gestural, multi-touch capabilities to some of its other computers through upgrades to the touchpad. Touch-controlled displays have been highly visible through CNN's "Magic" map used during elections. Microsoft has released their Microsoft Surface device (a coffee-table-sized box with a touch screen taking up the entire top surface). Upcoming versions of Microsoft Windows are reported to support more touch and multi-touch features. Google has released the Open Source Android software, which is used on cell phones like the T-Mobile G1 that integrates touch, buttons, a trackball, and a keyboard.

It seems that handheld, desktop, and wall-sized computing are all moving to a touch, gesture-driven interface. Some of the dreams of common acceptance that have driven development in the pen and touch area for so long are finally coming true. In these environments, the use of gestures provides us flexibility and richness of control, which gives us reason to switch from older technologies.

What the Devices of the Future Will Be Like

These are a series of blog posts and other writings about the general form and architecture of computer-powered devices.

Wednesday, May 24, 2000
PCS VS. APPLIANCES

I attended another conference yesterday. (I'll write it up in a few days.) I was taking notes with my Palm PDA and external keyboard accessory as usual when I noticed a person in the row in front of me similarly typing, but with one of those neat, tiny, 2 lb. Sony Vaios with a 1024×480 pixel screen and built-in video camera (the C1XS model, I guess). So cool! Boy, I'd like one of those.

I started thinking: You know, maybe this PDA and appliance business is silly. Here she has something just a little bigger and heavier, but it's a *real* PC. You can take notes on it just like I do. You can run lots of programs. Why pay for all these pieces of hardware for each application, each with its own microprocessor and memory, when all you need to do is add software to the laptop?

Then I got brought back to reality. Still in the morning session, her machine went off. She took out another battery and swapped it. She rebooted and waited for ScanDisk (I guess it didn't shut down cleanly).

I had changed the two AAA batteries in my Palm before I started taking notes at a conference *last week*. I took notes all morning yesterday. It still has over 90% power left.

Then I thought about all those applications. We're used to PC applications costing $99–$895 each. Lotus 1-2-3 was $495. Photoshop is about $600 (street price). Dreamweaver is $295–$120 just to "upgrade." Quicken 2000 is $69, Lotus Organizer is $75.

Thanks to Moore's Law and consumer-volume economics, "appliances" like a Palm III or Visor are $149–$249. It's only $99–$199 for "applications" executed in hardware like a folding keyboard, GPS, or a plug-in camera. Even a good digital camera is not much more than Photoshop. You barely think of the price of cell phone hardware. Replacing your old PDA with a new one costs about the same as a Microsoft Office "upgrade." I'm really using these things productively, as are other people I know—this isn't futuristic anymore.

With the younger generations brought up on Walkmans, GameBoys, beepers, cell phones, and cargo pants, new applications are just as likely to be another thing to carry as a thing to download. Maybe Microsoft's hardware group will branch out of mice and keyboards and threaten the Office group . . .

Of course, there are some applications, like Trellix Web, Photoshop, programming, spreadsheets ([smiley face in the original]) and lots of specific business applications, that really do work better on a PC, so you really will need one at least once in a while. They aren't going away. And, they make great companions to your appliances.

http://danbricklin.com/log/2000_05_19.htm

Thursday, March 9, 2000
WIRELESS IS LIKE BATTERIES

Driving to work today I saw a small video camera attached to an overpass on I-95/128, probably used as a webcam. It had conduits going across the bridge frame and into the ground. It struck me that this was an example of what Judith Hurwitz was saying about wireless (see March 3, 2000, entry).[21] Wireless is not about cell phones people carry. It is about removing the need for wires for anything to "work."

Let me elaborate.

Mechanical power used to come from water. Mills had to be next to rivers. Steam and internal combustion engines removed that need. Factories could be anywhere. Railroads were possible. Cars were possible. Lawnmowers can be powerful.

In the electrical world, power came through wires, but batteries removed the necessity of being tethered.

The microprocessor removed the need to be connected to computing power. You could put computing power anywhere. Together with batteries, you could use it anywhere in anything, in almost any physical form.

In our new world, being "connected" (by Internet Protocol, IP) is as much a part of a device "working" as having electrical power or computational abilities. Wireless removes the requirement of being connected physically with an unbroken wire. Just as batteries and microprocessors let us create watches, calculators, cell phones, digital cameras, CD players, game machines, blood sugar testers, etc., wireless connectivity to IP will open up whole new possibilities. (IP is for communicating data; the Web is just one application built upon it.) Letting any device with computing power take advantage of being able to communicate with other devices and "applications" running on "servers," without building specific infrastructure for that application, will be the revolution. The applications that are mainly people reading screens will be in

---

[21]http://danbricklin.com/log/2000_03_03.htm

Judith Hurwitz, www.hurwitz.com, has been doing technology research and strategy consulting for more than 20 years. At a talk in 2000, she addressed many topics including this:

Wireless: This area will explode, but not the way it looks now. "It's not just your phone so you can make a reservation at your favorite hotel, or check to see if your airline is on time . . . [More important will be] companies that use this wireless technology to do business-to-business—transactions—to put these types of devices on manufacturing equipment to check on quality. There will be real industrial applications for wireless and sort of this idea of pervasive computing which is any device to any device connecting in real time."

the minority. (Already my cell phone probably communicates more frequently with base stations telling them where I am than I do making calls.) Wireless will not just be for browsing web sites anymore than internal combustion engines were just for giving us home grain mills.

(I have no pictures of the cameras I saw: I was driving alone.)

http://danbricklin.com/log/2000_03_09.htm

This vision of ubiquitous wireless devices is starting to come true but has a long way to go to include breaking the dominance of applications where people read on screens. (Of course, most devices of any sort interact through computer screens now, thanks to the drastic drop in cost of flat-panel displays since this blog post was written in 2000.) The notebook and handheld computers have become almost always connected to the Internet through WiFi or high-speed cellular data and there are many different applications that take advantage of that connectivity. The 10.3-oz., $359 Amazon Kindle book-reader, with its built-in cellular data connection, is another example. Cell phones are evolving to be heavily data driven, from the simplicity of SMS texting to web browsing, on-demand map data, and now much more with devices like the iPhone and Google Android phones.

On the nonreading side, it is becoming more common to find new printers, cameras, and even electronic picture frames that connect through WiFi. GPS is an interesting variant of "wireless," using the reception of multiple radio signals to pinpoint location. My new car unlocks itself when it wirelessly senses that my key is nearby. More and more cars automatically pay tolls through wireless transponders. People talk wirelessly to their cell phones with Bluetooth headsets.[22]

Speech at the FPA World Leadership Forum 2000

Early in the summer of 2000, I received a call from Jim Dougherty of Intralinks, Inc. We knew each other from some previous work. He asked me if I'd be willing to participate on a panel about the Internet at a conference being held in New York at the same time as the United Nations Millennium meeting. There would be heads of state and heads of industry there. He was on the board of the Foreign Policy Association, which was sponsoring the conference. I told him

---

[22]Note that in most of these applications the addition of distance and proximity sensing (that is, finding nearby devices) helps make them work and be easy to set up.

that if he thought I'd add anything useful, I'd be glad to. It sounded like fun. I pretty much forgot about it until I needed to schedule things for September.

Here is the final draft of the speech I gave. The people in the audience were not computer industry people.

September 7, 2000

DAN'S SPEECH AT THE WORLD LEADERSHIP FORUM 2000

Thanks, Jim!

For a living, I invent things that I hope will help other people. I live in this Internet world. For example, I posted drafts of this talk on my personal web site, danbricklin.com, and people emailed me suggestions from around the world which made it better.

Here is what I want to get across: You need to understand that what you see today with the Internet is not what will be tomorrow. The Internet is not like television. What TV was 20 years ago is basically what it is today with just a few more channels. You need to swim in this river of Internet change to understand what it is so you can apply it to your own concerns. I'd like to explain some things about that river.

There are devices and applications that will be invented soon that eventually you'll feel you couldn't live without. And it's likely many of these new applications will come from individual entrepreneurs without government help.

First, some history. Electronic communications used to need a separate system for each application, like TV and telephone. That led to such systems being heavily regulated and requiring massive amounts of capital and time to create new applications. Now, in contrast, most communications are moving to a single system, the Internet. The Internet can connect anything digital. It can take advantage of wires, wireless, and optics. In the old days new communications infrastructure only supported the applications for which it was built. The Internet already supports many different applications simultaneously, and will also support applications yet to be invented. Individual, entrepreneurial inventors can take advantage of the Internet to create applications that previously would have been stymied by regulators and monopolies.

Connected to each other through the Internet will be a wide variety of digital devices. Personal computers running web browsers are just one of the many types of these. Digital devices come in configurations other than a box on a desk with a keyboard, screen, and disk. Other common digital devices are handhelds like the Palm Pilot, game machines like Nintendo, and digital cell phones. In all cases, there are different physical configurations of components.

For example, the Palm may seem like a joke compared to a PC with its small screen and slow input, but it fits in a shirt pocket, runs for weeks on batteries, costs just a couple hundred dollars, and requires almost no thought to use. It's perfect for sporadic personal use, much better than a PC. It made up for its lack of keyboard and printer by being able to connect to a personal computer to provide those things. Being able to be temporarily connected elsewhere was good enough to provide what it needed.

Here are some other digital devices:

[Palm VII] This is a Palm with radio email. [Stowaway] This is a folding keyboard for the Palm and devices like it. [RIM] This is a wireless email and web-browsing device. You can type on it with your thumbs as fast as you can write with a pencil. This is a digital camera. This is a digital miniDisc recorder. [FastLane] This thing lets me pay tolls from inside my car in many states—wireless cash. These are all different digital devices that have shown their usefulness in my life, and I'm sure you can think of many others.

Not all of the attempts will become popular. The highly successful Palm was the third completely different pen computer attempt from one inventor, Jeff Hawkins, and his were just a few of the many other worthy attempts. Getting just the right combination of functionality and ease of use is hard. If you need to think in the long term, don't ignore technologies just because early attempts are flawed.

Let me talk about personal computers for a minute. Personal computers were an obvious early choice for connection to the Internet because of their versatile nature. The personal computer has always been a very fertile device for innovation. It was designed to have new components or software just plugged in or old ones changed. Almost nothing is fixed. It's an inventor's dream. As it evolved, many applications could be deployed on it that changed the world. For example, the spreadsheet first put on personal computers by my friend Bob Frankston and myself and basically written in an attic over a six-month period, brought sophisticated financial scenario planning to individuals. Later, as the PC got more memory and better printers, others built desktop publishing. Capabilities once available only to large, rich organizations were brought to smaller, poorer ones.

In the very near future, all of these devices [Pick up devices], not just the personal computers, will be connected to the Internet, either by wire or radio. Because of the Internet, all will be able to communicate with any other device you choose, be they other devices you or your friends own or centralized machines run by big companies. In the old days, telephones could only talk to telephones, TV transmitters to TVs, etc. You couldn't fax to a TV or listen to TV sound on your phone. On the Internet, any device can send information to any other device. This combination of digital devices and communications is a very fertile field for innovation. No one device will be enough. You'll always need the right combinations of tools to get things done.

The barriers to creating these new applications are quite low. Individuals or small groups can have enormous effect. Tim Berners-Lee used a personal computer and the early Internet to publish some specifications that led to the World Wide Web, some of it over a weekend. Napster with—what shall we call it?—"sharing," was created by a college student with a little money from an uncle. These were done with just the components of a PC, a keyboard, and screen. Think what millions of different connected devices can do. They won't all be keyboards and screens just showing text and pictures. Scandinavia is famous for cell phones. Who will be famous for each of the other devices?

What will we communicate with the Internet? Well, we'll continue to communicate hand-typed text and pictures. This includes email, and online publishing, like web sites.

But web sites are just a small piece of what we can do. We can send live dynamic data—such as voice and video, we can have GPS units giving the positions of vehicles, manufacturing machines and medical equipment sending out readings to other computers for processing, and more. Engineers at Georgia Tech have developed ways of connecting body sensors to the Internet with their "Wearable Motherboard"—an undershirt with a special weave of cotton fibers and fiber optics. This will be great for heart and blood pressure monitors.

We can use the Internet to control things at a distance, like milling machines, vending machines, motors to move the cameras we're watching or anything else, locks, valves, and medical equipment. We can connect to services that do computation, data retrieval, and e-commerce.

However, understand that e-commerce is not the only driving force behind the Internet. I think something that is missed in all the discussions of the Internet is how many of these applications will be very personal and mundane. Like web sites with wedding pictures, they will be part of life and relationships, not just commerce.

Look at how regular people use cell phones, especially if the cost is low like it is in many countries outside the United States. Listen to cab drivers, bus drivers, mothers, and children. They mainly talk to their friends and loved ones about very personal, mundane things. When they pick up a cell phone, they aren't like a commercial radio station. They don't say: [speak in deep, announcer-like voice] "This is Dan's Cellular! Two Million Microwatts of Power . . . " No, they say: "I finally left the office, but traffic is light," or "I've got a free minute and thought I'd say hi," or "Where are you?" or "Well, tell him Daddy says no, too."

Look at what people do when they go to an Internet "cafe" when traveling. You don't find them surfing to buy things. They do email to stay in touch with friends and loved ones. A huge percentage of America Online usage is Instant Messaging. They say hi, flirt, and chitchat about their day, especially with their "buddies" whom they know from the physical world.

The Internet and other technologies are allowing us to stay close to people we care about, sharing our ever more busy lives at a distance. These interactions are often simple, but personally very important. There is a huge demand for these relationship-enhancing devices and services, giving rise to home video cameras, digital photography, email, instant messaging, personal web sites, and cell phones. These are huge markets. Companies that think only professionally produced, broadcast-like uses of the Internet matter to regular people are doomed to be pushed aside by this demand for an "Electronic Hug."

So, I hope you see how the Internet will be more than just the Web and browsers, how fertile the combination of digital devices and the Internet is for innovation, how that innovation can come about even by small groups of individuals acting on their own, and finally how many of those applications will be very personal and mundane.

It is important that you understand this world of the Internet and technology yourself. Use the latest devices and applications, or at least those that become popular enough that some of your friends use them. Don't just read about them.

Now, of course, you can find a copy of this speech and more information on my web site, danbricklin.com. Thank you!

http://www.bricklin.com/speeches/wlforum2000/final.htm

Looking at the Usability Aspects of a Famous Situation

Usability refers to how easy something is to use, how comfortably it interfaces with the user, and how unlikely its operation is to result in errors. Usability plays a major role in the design, and ultimate success or failure, of pen-based and touch-controlled computers.

In determining the usability of a design, many techniques are employed. One of the most well-known is "usability testing." This refers to formal testing, often in a lab setting specifically designed for that purpose with recording devices and perhaps one-way mirrors, where users of a product are observed as they perform tasks, make mistakes, ask questions, etc.

This essay is about the usability of a stylus-based system used by millions of people that proved to be error prone: the so-called Florida Butterfly Ballot. The essay was written soon after the voting in the 2000 U.S. presidential election, after it was known that there were problems in Florida but before the final outcome of the election was decided. It gives a nice case history for thinking about the nuances involved in designing a product with a high level of usability.

BALLOT USABILITY IN FLORIDA

Jakob Nielsen[23] has been insisting for years that usability is real important. I've written on this web site about how important we feel it is at Trellix Corporation. Well, here we have a new, about-to-be-a-classic example in another domain.

What is the issue?

In the oh-so-close presidential race in Florida, a major issue is whether some of the votes that went to Pat Buchanan were really meant to be for Al Gore. Larger-than-expected Buchanan numbers in some areas known to have only elderly, Democratic-leaning voters, along with complaints about ballot usability by those people, brought this to national attention. I heard about it from a relative in Florida before the voting closed.

What was the ballot like?

In the West Palm Beach area, like many other localities, you cast your vote by punching a hole in a card with a stylus. There are paper ballots that indicate which hole corresponds to which candidate. (See this example[24] page from Missouri.) A 1998 Florida state law made it easier for minor-party candidates to get listed on the ballot (the last presidential election was 1996). Apparently, this led to there being 10 parties plus space for a write-in candidate for president. The names were listed alternating left and right on the presidential ballot, with a single column of punch-card holes down the middle between the rows. Al Gore was second on the left column, Pat Buchanan first on the right. Gore's voting hole was number three, Buchanan's number two. There were arrows which covered a certain fraction of the distance to the column of holes. On other parts

November 8–15, 2000

---

[23]http://www.useit.com/

[24]http://www.showme.net/CapeCounty/clerk/pcard.htm

of the ballot (for senator and other offices) there was only one column—the first name corresponded to the first hole, the second name to the second hole, etc.

This situation sounds like it is full of classic usability questions. I wonder what the usability testing for this was like, or even if there was any such testing.

You can see pictures of the ballot and instructions on the Palm Beach County Supervisor of Election's web site and on some of the sites listed below.[25]

What isn't obvious from these pictures is exactly how the ballots aligned with the holes in real machines. Boston.com has an AP picture that shows one situation with a real holder. The *Sun-Sentinel* has a "Virtual Ballot" with pictures that show the alignment. The artist's conception many others are showing doesn't look as realistic.

Another issue is the sample ballot that voters were supposed to use to prepare. I have a separate web page, The Sample Ballot,[26] with photographs of the pages of one of those booklets. You can see whether that was helpful or confusing in comparison to the actual voting situation. Here are some of those pages:

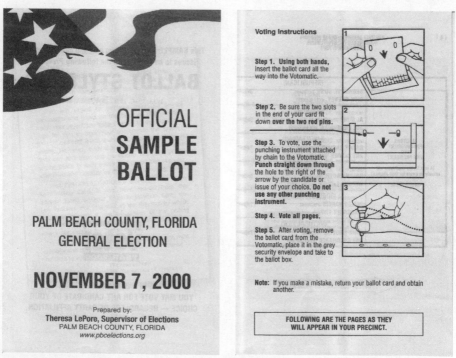

The cover and an instruction page from the sample ballot

---

[25]See the essay on my web site for these links. Many of them are no longer available.

[26]http://danbricklin.com/log/sampleballot.htm

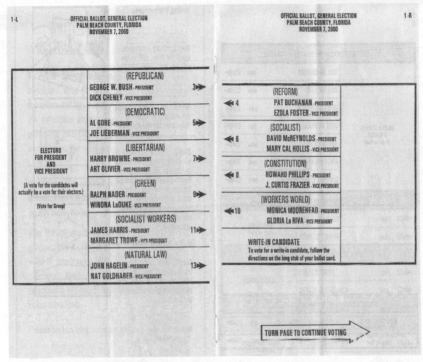

The two sides of the presidential candidate selection section

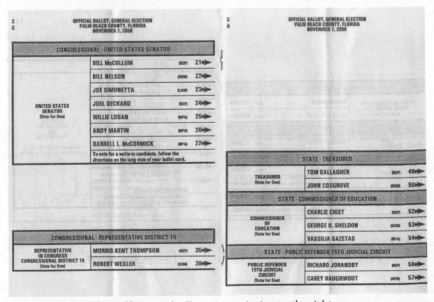

The section for other offices, with all arrows pointing to the right

Some obvious situations in which people could make mistakes

- Have poor eyesight (narrow field of view or can read large party name but not smaller number)
- Left-handed and use right hand to steady the vote recorder, covering list on right
- Are spatially challenged (can't read maps well) but can count
- Doing things by rote from last time (double column is new for presidential race)
- Cultural issues (don't understand the arrows)
- Thought arrows pointed to entire column, not specific hole, and are used to SAT-type tests with separate grid and ordered questions down the column
- Nervous or confused by new voting style (just moved to warmer climate)
- In a hurry because voting lines are long and you're unexpectedly late for an appointment

Kevin Fox shows how people could read the ballots different ways on his Basis for Alternate Interpretations[27] page (with illustrations). People interviewed have said some thought you needed two votes: one for president and one for vice president. Slate presents yet more analysis.

There is a question about how could people not know that punching two holes was a mistake. Well, most people are no longer familiar with punched cards like some of us were in the 1960s. A common thing where you push something in is a car radio. You can push as many times as you want. Only the last one counts. Wouldn't you expect a voting machine to let you change your mind or keep you from voting for too many? The old lever-operated ones do. Some people might have expected that.

Usability testing should have shown how common these situations were and whether or not they should have had any effect. Guessing what people might have thought isn't enough. That doesn't tell you how common that mistake would be.

There is some data to help determine what people may have intended and to help in understanding the usability issues. Palm Beach officials listed the combinations of multiple punches on a sampling of the precincts late Saturday night after the election (4,200 ballots were hand counted—about 1% of the total). There were only one or two instances of many combinations, but three specific

---

[27]http://fury.com/galleries/palmbeach/index.php

hole combinations stood out, with more than a few instances. (This data is from an email I received, but I saw the press conference on TV live and it seems OK by what I recall. Let me know if I'm wrong.) Holes 3 & 4 happened 11 times (Bush & Buchanan), holes 4 & 5 happened 80 times (Buchanan & Gore), and holes 5 & 6 happened 21 times (Gore & McReynolds). The ratio of Gore to Bush votes in the original count was about 1.8 to 1, similar to the ratio of the hole 5 & 6 ballots to the 3 & 4 ballots. (This could be people who mistakenly punched the holes next to both president and vice president candidates, voting for the "Group" as the instructions listed. One could argue that Gore supporters were just as prone to error as Bush supporters in making this mistake.)

The big picture

I have heard from a variety of people about voting instrument confusion in many states, not just near West Palm Beach, Florida. We know from lots of examples of usability studies that errors on tasks arising from "dumb mistakes" are very common, with rates of easily 5%, 10%, or more. Elections, even important ones like for president of the United States, are often decided by much slimmer margins than that. In our ever-mobile world, thorough testing of ballot techniques and standardization may be called for if we are to believe that we truly choose our elected officials rather than flip a coin.

We should address this problem not just for the current election in Florida. In some areas usability should be given as much concern as voter and official fraud because it probably has a greater effect.

Note that this instance was caught quickly because only one county had the problem ballot (take a look at a statistics teacher's scatter plot[28] where West Palm's data sticks out). When everybody uses the same flawed system you don't always see the anomaly so easily. For example, there is research[29] that says shorter people don't vote on ballot questions as frequently as taller people because the questions are displayed way above their eye level on voting machines. Who would ever suspect that?

Usability: my perspective as a software developer

Like many other computer software developers, I have had to deal with usability questions my whole career. Creating VisiCalc involved figuring out how to

---

[28]http://web.archive.org/web/20001217204600/http://cuwu.editthispage.com/ 2000/11/08 *and* http://web.archive.org/web/20030623205446/static.userland .com/sh4/images/cuwu/palmbeach.gif

[29]http://researchnews.osu.edu/archive/votedes.htm

make a calculating tool that was easier than the back of an envelope so people would do their first calculation on a *computer* spreadsheet so that their second one could be automatic. At Trellix, we have been using usability studies to ensure that our tools could be used by regular people to create great web sites by themselves. We have a lab with video cameras, one-way mirrors, etc.

I can tell you, regular people get tripped up by the simplest things. It is sobering to observe a test where a user repeatedly asks, "How do I go to the next step?" and you want to scream, "Click the 'Next' button!" that they just somehow can't see. You thought the button was obvious, but, as anyone who's missed a highway exit learns, in the real world what's obvious to one person who knows the answer is not always obvious to a newcomer. People who are making fun of the voters who made mistakes should think about the obvious mistakes they've made in their lives. If "most people" never have problems doing simple things why were there so many flashing 12:00s on old VCRs?

The difference in this case looks like it was an error of only 0.75%. However, there are reports that almost 20,000 Palm Beach ballots were disqualified because voters punched more than one hole, perhaps because they caught their mistake and then punched the one they really wanted (4.4%—an apparently high number). Would usability testing (which often only uses 5–20 people of each background) have caught it? I think so. People's confusion, false starts, questions to the person running the test, hesitations, etc., all can point out potential problems even if the actual final performance is without error. In this case, so many people complained afterwards (when such complaints would have been embarrassing before the closeness of the election was known) you know a test would have discovered it.

Usability is important in many areas. Read this letter[30] I received November 13, 2000, about its role in safety and environmental protection:[31]

> *Dan:*
>
> *I'm finding your discussions on usability quite interesting. I don't work in the software or computer hardware field, but instead work with safety and environmental protection. Usability is a _big_ issue with us in that field, too!*

---

[30]http://danbricklin.com/log/usabilityandsafety.htm

[31]I became acquainted with the author, John Palmer, through email correspondence about issues like this in response to my blogging. His comments, and sometimes photographs, appear at various points in my blog. We finally met in person in 2007 when I followed his suggestion and took a beautiful vacation in New Mexico.

If one looks at major industrial accidents in the world over the last fifty or so years, one finds that between 60% and 90% of the accidents are due to "human error." The range is due in part to the running debates on where designer errors fit into "human error." Having worked as a fire and explosion investigator in "another life," I can say that the stats are pretty accurate. Reviewing my old accident reports a few years back, I estimated that the error factor was right around 90%.

The issue of punching out the wrong ballot position ("hanging," "pregnant," and "dimpled" chad aside) is smaller than picking the wrong valve to open in an emergency, or to use a real world example, actuating an isolation valve in reverse during testing, and thereby releasing highly flammable materials. That case chalked up more than a score dead, close onto $1 billion in overall losses, and dropped out about 5% of the USA's capacity in a specific polymer's production. All from an "error."

The number of "smaller" accidents with fewer dead and smaller dollar losses is high. Arguably to some, although not me, a national election is more important than these cases, unless you're the woman or man who dies in the accident.

Usability is a complex issue that requires multidisciplinary approaches, a highly flexible mind to coordinate the approaches, and some old-fashioned hard nosed thinking about Murphy and Finagle. It's not something that one just happens into one day, and then produces marvel after marvel. As the level of consequences goes up for failure, the quality of usability must similarly rise in at least the same slope, and arguably proportionally higher. In the case of the federal election results in Florida where the form was poorly handled, or the results in New Mexico where a specific windowed box was not "clicked off," the consequences are pretty high right now— look at the stock market if nothing else . . . although again, I tend to consider people's deaths a higher issue.

Which then segues to the next point, most usability issues are decided at relatively low levels or by people without experience in the area. The placement of light switches in rooms, location of critical shutoffs, or simply where to sign one's name are typically determined by one of the most junior members of the project team. Some exceptions exist, to be sure, such as the relatively recent studies by software companies on usability, but even those packages fail the usability tests in less "important" areas like installation. The stories of installation failures are legion.

All this leads to the final lesson on usability. Usability only becomes important when a (relative) catastrophe occurs. It shouldn't be this way, but it is. The issues with Florida's election in terms of recounts are not new. The failures of New Mexico in the area of failures to deploy systems are not recent. Only when the failures reach a crisis level is any serious study made to the problems, and at that, is often a "band-aid" approach to pass through the periodic crisis.

Usability is and will continue to be a serious issue.

John Palmer

There are news reports about a simple ballot test with children, but not a real usability test. To learn more, read "A Ballot Usability Test" [reprinted next in this chapter].

http://danbricklin.com/log/ballotusability.htm

A BALLOT USABILITY TEST

There is a report going around about second-graders being asked to fill in a ballot "similar" to the Palm Beach one I discussed on "Ballot Usability in Florida." This report is being publicized with headlines like "Butterfly Ballot a Cinch for Ga. Second-Graders."[32]

A school psychologist asked 74 eight-year-old children to vote for their favorite Disney characters. Unlike the Palm Beach ballot, this one was on one page not two, with no split down the middle. The arrows were larger than the Palm Beach ones. The only instructions were "Check the box for the one you choose."

---

[32]http://web.archive.org/web/20010210142725/http://foxnews.com/election_
night/111000/ballotquiz.sml

Lo and behold, all of the kids (when asked to evaluate their own ballot) checked the one they "intended." None made a mistake. Of the 74 kids, 71 marked their ballot "correctly" by checking or filling in the box, and 3 circled their answers.

The story is written like it is making fun of the grown-ups in Florida, but what do we learn from it? How does it relate to the Palm Beach situation?

In Florida, there are statistics that could be interpreted as saying 0.75% of the ballots were marked for the wrong person. Here, with larger arrows and no alignment problems in relation to punch holes, you'd expect a lower error rate—let's guess about 10%—giving us around 0.1% expected error rate if it were related. Since we only have 74 kids, the chances of them making a similar mistake would be low. Anyway, we don't know if it was just the arrows, or if it was the lines or the alignment or who knows what else that caused any given error. We don't know if it was just the two columns and arrows.

In Florida, a little over 4% of the ballots were marked incorrectly. Here, also 4% marked them incorrectly. Pretty remarkable coincidence (or is that why the story was publicized?).

You can't really tell just from people's behavior why they make mistakes, though you can get some clues. By asking them why they do things and what they are thinking, you can understand more. Usability testing lets you do all that. You get to see things from their perspective. Watching them from behind a one-way mirror you see how reasonable mistakes can be and how hard it is to design something that everybody can use.

http://danbricklin.com/log/ballottest.htm

In this chapter we looked at some of the ongoing attempts to develop a use of a stylus or finger on a screen for computer input that becomes widespread. We saw how long it often takes for all of the technologies to come together so that something we've been dreaming about and perfecting for decades becomes mainstream. We also looked at a particular instance that illustrates the nuance that goes into ensuring the usability of such systems.

Next we'll look at some issues we'll have to deal with as computer technology is widely adopted and becomes an integral part of society's infrastructure.

9 The Long Term

Usability deals with errors that occur when a device or system is used. It is one source of failure. Another source of failure is when the device itself breaks. In the case of software and computer data, that is not just when the hardware on which it is running stops operation. It is also when the program does not function correctly in light of a new or changing environment or when previously accessible data cannot be read anymore.

I've written about this issue since the early days of my blog.

Wednesday, November 3, 1999
AFTER WE'RE GONE

My connections to the Internet have been quite flakey the last few days. My cable modem's been quite slow in the evening (I guess the loop I'm on is popular). Our email was out at work over the weekend a lot. And for hours at a time our main connection to the Internet at Trellix was out. Something about "routers in New York" having problems.

On the way to work yesterday, I passed by some digging in the street and stopped. Here's what I saw:

Water main from 1929

I asked what was going on. It was a water main, made of steel and originally built in 1929. They were doing periodic maintenance cleaning it out. Unlike a water main I remember in my town that broke a while back and that had outlived its intended life by many decades, they said this one was still OK.

What a contrast. Here we were building infrastructure for our electronic future and we're lucky if some parts last 6 months. We fight extending the IP address space from an artificial limit on number of servers yet we hope to wire everything with a clock tick (IPv4 vs. IPv6).[1] We're thinking about letting there be only one use for the word "fidelity," and the use will be for money (trademarks and domain names as I described November 1).

We should learn from the Y2K situation that computing has become the pervasive structure on which we are building more and more of society. Unlike the old days when we assumed everything we built out of computers would be continually replaced, we now have to live up to the fact that some things may have to be good enough to last for the rest of our lives and beyond. The people who built that water main 70 years ago are probably in their 90s or resting in peace knowing their work was done well.

http://danbricklin.com/log/1999_11_3.htm

The following year, on a visit to Jerusalem, I went on a tour through the excavation next to the Western Wall. One of the parts that you pass that especially impressed me because of its long-term survival was the Strouthion Pool.[2] This is a public pool created about 2,000 years ago under a public market and sealed until a little over 100 years ago. It still holds water. I stopped to take a photograph, which you can see here.

---

[1] The term "clock tick" is engineering slang I used to refer to computing power, micro-processors, etc. The IPv4 vs. IPv6 issue is a technical problem with dealing with the maximum number of device addresses available on the Internet that I covered in some of my other essays that are not included in this book.

[2] http://english.thekotel.org/today/article.asp?ArticleID=8

October 9, 2001

This issue of long-term survival of what we create continued in my writings with the following essay:

COPY PROTECTION ROBS THE FUTURE

Copy protection will break the chain of formal and informal archivists who are necessary to the long-term preservation of creative works.

Introduction

The other day I wanted to listen to a song I remember from my youth. I took the old vinyl record out of its sleeve and put it on my aging turntable. I gently dropped the needle onto the appropriate track, and out came the music, but it was way too fast. It seems my turntable broke, and now plays everything at exactly 45 rpm instead of 33. Bummer! It was a slow song and I wanted it slow. Luckily, I found I had another copy of the same song that the record company that owned the rights to the song had released (the CD was "Greatest Folksingers of the 'Sixties"). Much nicer. Unfortunately, they had only included that one song . . . I couldn't play any of the others I wanted from the original album. I'll have to try to fix my turntable.

This got me to thinking about preserving old works of composers, musicians, authors, and other creative individuals. How does that preserving come about and will today's works produced on digital media last into the future?

How are works preserved through the generations?

As human beings, we benefit greatly from the works of others. Artists, thinkers, scholars, and performers create works that we all enjoy, learn from, and are inspired by. Many works are timeless. Either standing alone or in the context of their time or other times, they are valuable periodically years after they are created. We often hear of authors, artists, or composers who only become popular or have their greatest impact after their death, sometimes many years later.

How are these works passed down through the generations? It usually isn't the direct result of the efforts of the original creator. Other people make it their job to preserve the works and pass them on. These jobs are either formal, like librarians and curators, or informal, like enthusiasts and hobbyists. There are additional other people who find interesting works and bring them to the attention of new generations. These may be scholars doing research, or a collector who develops a strong passion.

October 9, 2001

How are the actual works preserved? Sometimes just storing the work is sufficient, but in most cases a change in environment is needed. The artist's original location may be sold for another use. The work may be created in a material that is affected by air and water, and must be kept in a temperature- and humidity-controlled room. To preserve unique items, we often need to go to extremes, even to preserve them for just a few hundred years. According to a professional preserver,[3] the Archivist of the United States, the U.S. Constitution, Bill of Rights, and Declaration of Independence are stored in an encasement "made of pure titanium, high-strength glass, and specially treated aluminum to encapsulate these aging, fragile documents in argon, an inert gas, for their long-term preservation . . ."

For some works, it's enough to just preserve the words themselves. For these and others, copies are what we preserve, such as recordings of performances, or microfilm copies of newspapers. We produce the copies in more stable media, or ones that are easier from which to reproduce. (In a way, this is a form of "changing the environment.") The practice of constantly producing new copies before the old copies wear out has worked well. To increase the likelihood of long-term survival for a work, such as a religious text, producing many copies and keeping them in diverse places has also worked very well.

With ever-changing technology, in order to preserve many works we will need to constantly move them ahead, copying them to each new medium form before the previous one becomes obsolete. Also, as we create new media, we need to preserve the knowledge of the methods of converting from one medium to another, so we can still access the old works that have not yet been moved ahead. This is crucial. Without this information, even preserved works could be unreadable.

The most famous example of that type of translation information was an inscribed slab of rock from 196 BC found in 1799. It contained a decree written in Greek that was also written in two forms of Egyptian. It's called the Rosetta Stone. It let scholars finally read ancient works in hieroglyphics that they had physical possession of but whose language had been a mystery for 1,400 years (despite being common for the 3,500 years before being superseded). Cuneiform, a form of writing used by many ancient civilizations, was similarly opaque to scholars until they found a text in multiple languages carved into a cliff—the Behistun inscription.

---

[3] http://web.archive.org/web/20011019045107/http://www.nara.gov/nara/vision/unveil.html

October 9, 2001

A photograph I took in 2005 of the Rosetta Stone, and a closeup

Cuneiform writing that I photographed in 1966 at a NYC museum

A well-known example of preserving a work for many years is the Dead Sea Scrolls. These 2,000-year-old scrolls contain copies of Biblical and other writings. Thanks to the unusual environmental conditions of where they were stored (Qumran), they survived relatively intact. They were mainly written in the same Hebrew letters used today. I was fortunate to visit some of these at an exhibit in the United States in the mid-1960s. I took pictures of some of those that I saw at the request of one of my teachers for his research. I found those old negatives a few days ago, and, though you can't read such tiny negatives with your naked eye, my made-in-2001 film scanner can read them 35 years later. Looking at those images, I can read them now (I know modern Hebrew) and found that I photographed what looks like a variant of Psalm 136:

Dead Sea Scroll, still readable 35 and 2,000 years later. It starts:
". . . Key Tove, Key L'Olam Chasdoh (for He is good, for His mercy endures forever)."

This is an example of many types of preserving: repeated copying of the Psalms for hundreds of years from their original authoring until the days of the people at Qumran; good preservation of their copy for 2,000 years; independent preservation of the language; sharing of the work by the current preservers with the help of institutions like museums; having a copy made yet again for an enthusiast (by me for my teacher); preserving those copies (me and my parents who saved them at home for many years with my other negatives); today's film scanners being able to read the old film which was created before the idea of digital scanning; and finally, me being able to read it and then share yet another copy with you through the Internet. If you show it to someone who knows Hebrew, he or she should be able to read most of it. Quite a long, unbroken path. Let's hope we can continue to preserve things so well through so many steps.

Enter copy protection

There are things happening that make me worry that the future may not be bright for preserving many of the works we create today. For example, companies are preparing to produce music CDs that cannot be copied into many other formats (something allowed by law as "fair use").[4] Most new eBooks are

---

[4] http://web.archive.org/web/20011019234709/http://news.cnet.com/news/0-1005-200-7299321.html

copy protected. A new bill may be heading to Congress that will require all digital devices to enforce copy protection schemes for copyrightable material.[5] An existing law makes it a crime to tell people how to make copies of protected works.[6]

I believe that copy protection will break the chain necessary to preserve creative works. It will make them readable for a limited period of time and not be able to be preserved as media deteriorates or technologies change. Only those works that are thought to be profitable at any given time will be preserved by their "owners" (if they are still in business). We know from history that what's popular at any given time is no certain indication of what will be valuable in the future. Without not-copy-protected "originals," archivists, collectors, and preservers will be unable to maintain them the way they would if they weren't protected. (Many of these preservers ignore fashion as they do their job, because they see their role as preservers not filters.) We won't even be able to read media in obsolete formats, because the specifications of those formats will not be available. To create a "Rosetta Stone" of today's new formats will be asking to go to jail and having your work banned.

This is different from encryption or patent protection. With encryption, as long as the keys for reading survive, and a description of the method of decryption, you can recreate the unprotected original. It's even better—you can prove authenticity. Patent protection just keeps you from creating and using your own unlicensed reader for a limited period of time. After that, the legal duty of the patent is to teach you how it works so you can make your own. For long-term preservation of works (as opposed to short-term quick advancement in some fields), patented techniques are good because they discourage secrets and eventually put things in the public domain.

Let me give you another personal example, this time about copy protection.

One of the most popular parts of this web site is a copy of the original IBM PC version of VisiCalc.[7] Actually, that's not exactly true. It's not the same exact program you could buy. The original VisiCalc was only shipped on 5¼″ copy protected diskettes. Part of the program checked that the diskette it was loaded from had the special copy protection modifications. Despite the fact that I have an old computer with a 5¼″ diskette drive, I still couldn't make a copy that would run that I could distribute. I received permission from the current

---

[5] http://www.wired.com/politics/law/news/2001/09/46655

[6] http://web.archive.org/web/20011109023714/http://www.eff.org/IP/DMCA/

[7] http://www.bricklin.com/history/vcexecutable.htm

copyright holder to distribute the copies, but VisiCalc hadn't been produced for years and they lost track of any original masters they had owned.[8] (Companies usually don't have reason to maintain and catalog old, nonprofitable material for too long, especially through mergers and acquisitions.) Luckily for me, an employee of Software Arts, my company that created the original program, kept a "test" copy we had used internally that was created without the copy protection code. He was not one of the original authors, but is an informal "collector" of things. He ended up at Lotus, the next owner of the rights. He left Lotus years later, and gave me a copy he had moved ahead from system to system after that (he produced the copy for me on a Windows NT machine). Thanks to Lotus's permission (which I wouldn't need in the far future when the copyright expires), I was able to post a copy on the Web, and now many tens of thousands of people have their own copies. Thanks to those not-copy-protected copies, and the documentation available about the original IBM PC, it is much more likely now that future generations will be able to learn about early PC programs by running VisiCalc. If only the original diskettes could be passed down, then after they deteriorated they would not be useable, and until then, only people with special obsolete equipment could run them.

The IBM PC VisiCalc diskette with "Copy Protected" warning

Conclusion

Copy protection, like poor environment and chemical instability before it for books and works of art, looks to be a major impediment to preserving our cultural heritage. Works that are copy protected are less likely to survive into the future. The formal and informal world of archivists and preservers will be

---

[8] The VisiCalc story is covered in Chapter 12.

October 9, 2001

unable to do their job of moving what they keep from one medium to another newer one, nor will they be able to ensure survival and appreciation through wide dissemination, even when it is legal to do so.

If you are an artist or author who cares about more than the near-term value of your work, you should be worried and be careful about releasing your work only in copy-protected form. Like the days when "art" was only accessible to the rich, two classes will probably develop: copy protected and not copy protected, the "high art" and "folk art" of tomorrow.

Artists and authors need to create their works and still make a living. Copy protection is arising as a "simple fix" to preserve business models based upon the physical properties of old media and distribution. Our new media and distribution techniques need new business models (perhaps with different intermediate players) that don't shortchange the future. Trying to keep those old business models in place is as inappropriate as continuing to produce only 33 rpm vinyl records.

http://www.bricklin.com/robfuture.htm

The "Copy Protection Robs the Future" essay deals with data. A few years later, in response to things I heard from government officials, I wrote the following essay about a certain class of software programs, those that represent the software equivalent to the water mains and water pools of the past—the infrastructure upon which society depends.

July 14, 2004

SOFTWARE THAT LASTS 200 YEARS

The structure and culture of a typical prepackaged software company is not attuned to the long-term needs of society for software that is part of its infrastructure. This essay discusses the ecosystem needed for development that better meets those needs.

I've been following some of the writings and actions of the Massachusetts State Executive Office for Administration and Finance as it deals with its information technology needs. It was through listening to Secretary Kriss and reading the writings he and other Massachusetts government officials have produced, that I've come to look at software development from a whole new perspective. This essay tries to present that perspective and examine some of its implications.

Many things in society are long-term

In many human endeavors, we create infrastructure to support our lives which we then rely upon for a long period of time. We have always built shelters. Throughout most of recorded history, building or buying a home was a major starting step to growing up. This building would be maintained and used after that, often for the remainder of the builder's life span and in many instances beyond. Components would be replaced as they wore out, and the design often took the wear and tear of normal living into account. As needs changed, the house might be modified. In general, though, you thought of a house as having changes measured in decades.

Likewise, human societies also create infrastructure that is built once, then used and trusted for a long period of time. Such infrastructure includes roads, bridges, water and power distribution systems, sewers, seaports and airports, and public recreational areas. These also would be used and maintained without major modifications after they were built, often for many decades or even centuries.

Software has been short-term

By contrast, software has historically been built assuming that it will be replaced in the near future (remember the Y2K problem). Most developers observe the constant upgrading and replacement of software written before them and follow in those footsteps with their creations. In the early days of computer software, the software was intimately connected to the hardware on which it ran, and as that hardware was replaced by new, better hardware, new software was built to go with it. In the early days, many uses of computing power were new— they were the first application of software to problems that were previously done manually or not at all. The world got used to the fact that the computer version was an alternative and the special features and cost savings were what was special.

Today, hardware is capable enough that software can be written that will continue to run unmodified as hardware is changed. Computers are no longer new alternatives to other applications—they are the only alternative. Despite this, old thinking and methodologies have remained.

Computers and computer software have been viewed as being valuable for no longer than common short-term durable goods like an automobile or sometimes even tires. In accounting, common depreciation terms for software are 3 to 5 years, 10 at most. Contrast this to residential rental property which is depreciated over 27.5 years and water mains and brick walls which are depreciated over 60 years or more.

Records

Another aspect of human society is the keeping of records. Common records kept by governments include property ownership, citizenship and census information, and laws. Personal records include images (such as portraits) and birth, death, and genealogical information. General information kept by society includes knowledge and expression, and artifacts representative of culture. Again, the time frame for keeping such records is measured in decades or centuries. I can go to city hall and find out the details of ownership relating to my house going back to when it was built in the late 1800s. "Family bible" records go back generations. The Boston Public Library, like many city libraries, has newspapers from over 200 years ago available on microfilm, and many from the last 150 years in the original paper form.

Most of these societal records have been kept on paper. When computers were first introduced, they were an adjunct to the "real" paper records, and paper printouts were made. Computer-readable "backups" and transaction logs were produced and stored on removable media such as magnetic tapes, or even paper printouts. These were usually written and then rarely accessed, and even then accessed in a manner akin to the newspaper stacks of a library. Only the recent, working copies of data were actually available to the computers on an instantaneous basis. Much of the use of computers was for "transactions," and only the totals at the end of the time period of interest needed to be carried forward except in rare circumstances, such as disaster recovery or audits. Switching to a new computer system meant copying the totals and then switching the processing of new transactions to the new system instead of the old.

When it comes to moving ahead, most new software and hardware can only access the most recent or most popular old data. Old manuscripts created with old word processors, often archived on obsolete disk cartridges in obsolete backup formats, are almost impossible to retrieve, even though they are less than 25 years old. The companies that built the software and hardware are often long gone and the specifications lost. (If you are older than 30, contrast this to your own grade school compositions saved by your parents, or letters from their parents, still readable years later.)

Today's world and Societal Infrastructure Software

The world is different now than it was even just a decade or two ago. In more and more cases, there are no paper records. People expect all information to be available at all times and for new uses, just as they expect to drive the latest vehicle over an old bridge, or fill a new high-tech water bottle from an old well's pump. Applications need to have access to all of the records, not just summaries or the most recent. Computers are involved in, or even control, all aspects of running society, business, and much of our lives. What were once only bricks, pipes, and wires, now include silicon chips, disk drives, and software. The recent acquisition and operating cost and other advantages of computer-controlled systems over the manual, mechanical, or electrical designs of the past century and millennia have caused this switch.

I will call this software that forms a basis on which society and individuals build and run their lives "Societal Infrastructure Software." This is the software that keeps our societal records, controls and monitors our physical infrastructure (from traffic lights to generating plants), and directly provides necessary nonphysical aspects of society such as connectivity.

We need to start thinking about software in a way more like how we think about building bridges, dams, and sewers. What we build must last for generations without total rebuilding. This requires new thinking and new ways of organizing development. This is especially important for governments of all sizes as well as for established, ongoing businesses and institutions.

There is so much to be built and maintained. The number of applications for software is endless and continues to grow with every advance in hardware for sensors, actuators, communications, storage, and speed. Outages and switchovers are very disruptive. Having every part of society need to be upgraded on a yearly or even tri-yearly basis is not feasible. Imagine if every traffic light and city hall record of deeds and permits needed to be upgraded or "patched" like today's browsers or email programs. Needing every application to have a self-sustaining company with long-term management is not practical. How many of the software companies of 20 years ago are still around and maintaining their original products?

Software development culture

Traditional software development falls into two general categories: prepackaged and custom. Prepackaged software is written by application software companies (often called Independent Software Vendors, ISVs) who produce a program and then sell the same product to multiple customers. Custom software is written either by an independent company under contract or by in-house developers for a specific user. Common elements may be reused from project to project, but the overall program is unique.

Prepackaged software has the advantage of using the leverage one gets by spreading development costs over multiple users. Custom software has the advantage of being able to be tuned to very specific needs and circumstances

July 14, 2004

of each user. A challenge when developing prepackaged software is developing a product that appeals to a wide audience. A challenge when developing custom software is to take advantage of "generic" prepackaged components to lower development costs.

The most successful prepackaged software applications have been those that may be inexpensively customized to meet the needs of users by developers with less and less computer skills, most desirably by the users themselves, or that form a base on which other prepackaged or custom software is built. Examples of such software are the common "productivity" applications like word processors and spreadsheets, and "plumbing" software like operating systems, database engines, and web servers. The developers of prepackaged software are driven by a need to make their products appeal to today's potential users (and buyers), usually through features that distinguish them from competition.

A traditional prepackaged software company is organized as an ongoing enterprise, usually with a desire and plans for growth. An initial core of technical and product design people build the first version of the product. Marketing and sales people are added to sell the product and bring in revenues. Development continues and new, better versions are produced. New revenue comes from selling to existing customers, with each new version needing to give existing users a reason to replace the old product. The mentality, and the resulting major investments in corporate marketing, sales, and research activities, are focused on obsolescence and "upgrading," but only upgrading to products from that company. The potential for new customers and upgrade revenue is often a requirement to procure initial funding.

There are prepackaged software companies that are structured to make their profits from services and activities separate from the actual delivery of software code. The software itself may be available with no or little charge, but the organization is set up so that support of various sorts is provided by the company which has special knowledge of, and access to, the product. Again, there is a culture of obsolescence, to keep customers upgrading to new versions and paying for maintenance.

The needs of Societal Infrastructure Software

Let us look at the needs for societal infrastructure software. They include the following:

- Meet the functional requirements of the task
- Robustness and long-term stability and security

- Transparency to determine when changes are needed and that undesired functions are not being performed
- Verifiable trustworthiness of all three of the above
- Ease and low cost of training for effective use
- Ease and low cost of maintenance
- Minimization of maintenance
- Ease and low cost of modification
- Ease of replacement
- Compatibility and ease of integration with other applications
- Long-term availability of individuals able to train, maintain, modify, determine need for changes, etc.

The structure and culture of a typical prepackaged software company is not attuned to the needs of societal infrastructure software. The "ongoing business entity" and "new version" mentality downplay the value of the needs of societal infrastructure software and are sometimes at odds.

By contrast, custom software development can be tuned better to the needs of societal infrastructure software. The mentality is more around the one-time project leaving an ongoing result, and the cost structures are sometimes such that low maintenance is encouraged. The drivers of custom software are often the eventual users themselves, paying up front for development.

Some of the problems with custom development with regard to societal infrastructure software are the inability to spread the development and maintenance costs among a large number of customers and the narrow focus on the current requirements of the particular customer and their current stage of need (which often may change in ways visible to other customers but not yet to them).

A new style of development

What is needed is some hybrid combination of custom and prepackaged development that better meets the requirements of societal infrastructure software.

How should such development look? What is the "ecosystem" of entities that are needed to support it? Here are some thoughts:

- Funding for initial development should come from the users. Bridges and water systems are usually funded by governments, not by private entities that will run them for generations. The long-term needs of the funders must be more inline with the project requirements than the investment return needs of most private sources of capital.

- The projects need to be viewed as for more than one customer. A system for tracking parking tickets is needed by many municipalities. There is little need to have a different one for each. As a result, the funding should also be able to come from a combination of multiple sources. Funding or cost-sharing "cooperatives" need to exist.

- The requirements for the project must be set by the users, not the developers. The long-term aspects of the life of the results must be very explicit. Best practices must be established, tracked, and revisited.

- There is the whole issue of data storage and interchange standards that is critical to the long-term success and ability to do migration. Impediments such as intellectual property restrictions and "digital rights management" chokepoints must be avoided. (Lawmakers today must realize how important data interchange and migration are to the basic needs of society. They must be careful not to pollute the waters in an attempt to deal with perceived threats to a minor part of the economy.)

- Another critical issue is platform (hardware and software) independence. All development of long-term software needs to be created with the possibility of new hardware, operating systems, and other "computer infrastructure" in mind.

- The actual development may be done by business entities which are built around implementing such projects, and not around long-term upgrade revenue. Other entities are needed for providing the ongoing services with a mentality of keeping existing systems running. (The two entities may or may not be related.) Many such companies already exist.

- The attributes of open source software need to be exploited. This includes the transparency of the source code and the availability for modification and customization. Much has been written with regard to open source and its value for bug finding, security checking, etc., which is why this is needed. The added benefit here is that society as a whole may benefit in unforeseen ways as new applications are found for programs, be they in the private or public sector. The availability of the source code, as well as the multicustomer targeting and other aspects, enables a market for the various services needed for support, maintenance, and training as well as connected and adjunct products.

- The development may be done in-house if that is appropriate, but in many cases there are legal advantages as well as structural for using independent entities. Some governmental agencies may be precluded from licensing their results under licenses that are most appropriate for the long-term health of the projects. For example, they may be required to release the program code into the public domain where it may then be improved by others (and rereleased under restrictive licenses) without a return benefit to the original funders.

● Unlike much of the discussion about open source, serendipitous volunteer labor must not be a major required element. A very purposeful ecosystem of workers, doing their normal scheduled work, needs to be established to ensure quality, compatibility, modifications, testing, security, etc. Educational and other institutions may be employed with the appearance of volunteer labor as students and other interested parties are used, much as courts and other governmental agencies have used interns and volunteers for other activities. The health of the applications being performed by the software must not be dependent upon the hope that someone will be interested in it; like garbage collecting, sewer cleaning, and probate court judging, people must be paid.

The ecosystem of software development this envisions is different than that most common today. The details must be worked out. Certain entities that do not now exist need to be bootstrapped and perhaps subsidized. There must be a complete ecosystem, and as many aspects of a market economy as possible must be present.

Learning from civil engineering

My friend Peter Levin pointed out to me that the analogy between software engineering and civil engineering (the building of bridges, dams, and sewers) should be used to help flesh out a potential structure of the ecosystem. Here are some more thoughts inspired by that:

● Architects, civil engineers, and contractors as part of their training learn a set curriculum, pass tests, and are often licensed. They are supposed to share a body of knowledge and experience and demonstrate competence. What thrust should be part of the training of software engineers? For years we emphasized execution speed, memory constraints, data organization, flashy graphics, and algorithms for accomplishing this all. Curricula need to also emphasize robustness, testing, maintainability, ease of replacement, security, and verifiability.

- Standards bodies publish best practices (how high should a railing be above the stair tread, how thick should a concrete footing be under a supporting pillar, etc.). Even though a project might be novel (such as a new bridge or Boston's Big Dig), there are many standards that can (and must) be applied. By standards here we mean a conservative approach that is intended to minimize error, increase security, and lower maintenance costs, not just facilitate data interchange. Like all engineering, new software, as we know, commits old errors. We need to teach the right "war stories."

- Physical projects are subject to inspection by standards bodies. When you have electrical or plumbing work done, the town inspector comes to check the work before the job can be considered finished. Transparent societal infrastructural software needs inspection. This will raise the role of independent testing entities. There is much talk about such roles in the discussion about electronic voting and gambling machines, but it is also important for the software we are covering here. These jobs, part QA, part auditor, part private investigator, can be very high status because of the range and depth of knowledge and experience needed. For public projects, the transparency of open source is needed to allow multiple, independent inspections. There are also different inspection specialties, including standards compliance, security and other stresses, maintainability, and functionality.

- When physical projects fail (a suspension bridge twists in heavy winds, an elevated freeway falls down in an earthquake, an airplane crashes) public inquiries are performed, reports are published, and fixes are designed and retrofitted to existing projects. What we learn from failures enters the standards lexicon and is used for training and new design. We don't do this yet in the world of software. Access to the source code, the right to discuss it in detail, and the ability to search for similar code elsewhere are crucial to many such studies.

Further thoughts

The heart of this is some sort of open source software. The exact license requirements are not yet clear, and will probably vary depending upon the project. The depth of thinking that went into the GNU General Public License is needed, and it is a good start.

The role of open source software scares many traditional software developers. There is an image of a need for volunteer labor, and developers not getting paid.

This is far from the case. Developers and companies are still needed, and the best will be in high demand and well paid. Criteria of what is "good" may change. The ability to write clear, robust, maintainable code with an eye to the future, or do clean modifications, or explain how to use old software in new contexts, will become even more important. Documentation, training, servicing, testing, and more will still be paid for. In fact, the knowledge that such work has long-term consequences and may be amortized over longer periods of time raises its value. What does go away is the effort spent on making upgrading and replacement a desirable thing, both in development time and marketing dollars.

What about competition? There is nothing that says that there should only be one product for each application. Competition is very helpful for bringing out the best in product development. With that knowledge, funders should consider funding more than one project and keeping all promising ones alive even if, as is the tendency with software, one comes to dominate in deployments.

What does this say about the size of the development entities? There is no special requirement. Some may be very big, some may be very small. Smaller entities (and projects) have a better chance than today, because in such an ecosystem they would not be evaluated based on their own ability to provide long-term support (a major impediment today), but rather on their products' characteristics for fitting into the ecosystem.

The structure of the development may be concentrated mainly all in one entity, much as with a product like MySQL or Adobe Photoshop. Alternatively, it may instead be coordinated by a strong center, but distributed among many players, such as with Linux. The key skills will include the ability to manage such projects in the ecosystem. There is probably a separation between managing the initial development and the long-term maintenance and monitoring.

Is this "socialized software," with the government making all decisions? No. While funding and management cooperatives seem a likely part of the ecosystem, there is no need for a single such entity; in fact, that would be bad. Developers with promising ideas can still use risk capital for initial development, and would still be able to find single customers to provide the funding. Also, some projects may be worth funding solely because they are synergistic with existing products that are being supported by existing entities. So, for example, a training and support company may help fund a product that lowers maintenance costs and that will need training.

Remember, this is only for one part of the software world—that of social infrastructure software. There are many other uses of software, each with their own preferred ecosystem for development and support.

As part of this, buyers must get used to funding projects in advance. This is already the case in many areas, and the addition of cooperative funding with others can lower the costs or increase the scope of potential projects. Buyer funding lowers the requirement for potential "big hits" to incentivize development.

There is much talk about open source software in relation to existing software firms and lowering costs. What we are discussing here is opening up new types of firms, with huge potentials for revenues stemming from valuable services.

Open source essays often revolve around cost savings of acquisition and the use of volunteer labor for testing and maintenance. That is not the thrust here. In fact, the acquisition costs may actually be higher, and paid labor is assumed. The key is a model for long-term use, with a lowering of total cost of ownership, less disruption, and better integration. Open source discussion for government and business is often just in regards to existing open source applications, such as Linux and hoped-for desktop applications. There needs to be more discussion about projects of less general interest to the common software developer, such as EPA compliance monitoring systems, government record keeping, court workflow systems, and e-government components. Open source software discussion should be about keeping the trains running on time and not just saying it should run on Linux. The discussions should be about funding the companies needed in such an ecosystem and assuring their sources of healthy revenue. The code is not the only part of the equation, and leadership for all aspects of the ecosystem need to be addressed.

I hope that this essay is helpful to people that need to be involved in bringing about this needed ecosystem.

Related material:

Massachusetts Secretary of Administration and Finance Eric Kriss: "Open Mind on Open Source."[9] History and rationale for sharing source in government.

Dan Bricklin's Log reports of meetings with Secretary Kriss: October 8, 2003,[10] and January 12, 2004.[11]

---

[9] http://web.archive.org/web/20050513210235/http://www.mass.gov/eoaf/docs/OpenMindonOpenSource_June-23-2004.pdf

[10] http://danbricklin.com/log/2003_10_08.htm#kriss

[11] http://danbricklin.com/log/2004_01_12.htm#massit

GNU Project: "Philosophy of the GNU Project."[12] Links to essays about Free Software and free software licenses such as the GPL.

Peruvian letter about Open Source in government:[13] Reactions from a Peruvian lawmaker to statements about open source submitted by a Microsoft representative.

The *New York Times* article on why slot machines are more trustworthy than voting machines because of testing and enforcement: "Gambling on Voting."[14]

Books about the role of failure in engineering:

- Henry Petroski's *To Engineer is Human: The Role of Failure in Successful Design.*[15] This book, which has a picture of the Tacoma Narrows bridge collapsing and the Challenger in flight on its cover, discusses several well-known engineering failures. It goes into detail about how the failures were analyzed and what we can learn from them.

- Another Petroski book: *Design Paradigms: Case Histories of Error and Judgment in Engineering.*[16] Petroski presents several general paradigms of error, such as errors in conceptual design, errors related to scale in size, errors in logic, success masking failure, and others. To quote from the preface: "This book argues for a more pervasive use of historical case studies in the engineering curriculum."

- Charles Perrow's *Normal Accidents: Living with High-Risk Technologies.*[17] This book emphasizes learning about failures through detailed study of many "accidents" and especially "near-misses" and the systems around them. Don't say "Whew!" and ignore "almosts," or say "well, it was an accident"—learn from them both. There are about 5,000 people a year killed in U.S. industry. This book is covered in great depth in my "Learning From Accidents and a Terrorist Attack" essay [which follows this one in this chapter].

http://www.bricklin.com/200yearsoftware.htm

---

[12] http://www.gnu.org/philosophy/

[13] http://web.archive.org/web/20061013072653/http://www.opensource.org/docs/peru_and_ms.php

[14] http://www.nytimes.com/2004/06/13/opinion/13SUN1.html?ex=1402459200

[15] Vintage, 1992, ISBN: 0679734163

[16] Cambridge University Press, 1994, ISBN: 0521466490

[17] Princeton University Press, 1999, ISBN: 0691004129

As a continuation of examining the area of long-term software, I wrote another essay as part of a process of looking for design principles to follow. Here is "Learning From Accidents and a Terrorist Attack":

September 7, 2004

LEARNING FROM ACCIDENTS AND A TERRORIST ATTACK

There are principles that may be gleaned by looking at Normal Accident Theory and "The 9/11 Commission Report" that are helpful for software development.

Introduction

In my essay "Software That Lasts 200 Years," I list some needs for Societal Infrastructure Software. I point out generally that we can learn from other areas of engineering. I want to be more explicit and to list some principles to follow and examples from which to learn. To that end, I have been looking at fields other than software development to find material that may give us some guidance.

Part of my research has taken me to the study of major accidents and catastrophic situations involving societal infrastructure. I think these areas are fertile for learning about dealing with foreseen and unforeseen situations that stress a system. We can see what helps and what doesn't. In particular, I want to address the type of situations covered in Charles Perrow's *Normal Accidents* (such as at the Three Mile Island nuclear power plant as well as airline safety and nuclear defense) and "The 9/11 Commission Report"[18] (with regard to activities during the hijackings and rescue efforts).

Normal Accident Theory

Charles Perrow's book *Normal Accidents* was originally published in 1984 with an afterward added in 1999. It grew out of an examination of reports about accidents at nuclear power plants, initially driven by the famous major one that occurred on March 28, 1979, at the Three Mile Island nuclear plant in Pennsylvania. Perrow describes many different systems and accidents, some in great detail, including petrochemical plants, aircraft and air traffic control, marine transportation, dams, mines, spacecraft, weapons systems, and DNA research.

---

[18]W.W. Norton & Company Ltd. , ISBN: 0393326713, and http://www.9-11commission .gov/report/index.htm

Perrow starts the book with a detailed description of the Three Mile Island accident, taking up 15 pages to cover it step by step. You see the reality of component failure, systems that interact in unexpected ways, and the confusion of the operators.

To help you get the flavor of what goes on during the accidents he covers, here is a summary of the Three Mile Island accident as I understand it:

> Apparently a common failure of a seal caused moisture to get into the instrument air system which caused a change in pressure in the air system. The change in pressure triggered an automatic safety system on some valves to incorrectly think some pumps should be shut down, stopping the flow of water to a steam generator. That caused some turbines to automatically shut down. Stopping the turbines made an emergency pump need to come on which pumped water into pipes with valves that had accidentally been left closed during maintenance. The pipe valves had two indicators, but one was obscured by a repair tag hanging on the switch above it and they didn't check the other assuming all was well. When things started acting funny several minutes later, they checked but by then the steam generator boiled dry, causing heat not to be removed from the reactor core, which caused the control rods to drop in, stopping the reactor, but the reactor still generated enough heat to continue raising pressure in the vessel. The automatic safety device there, a relief valve, failed to reseat itself after relieving the pressure, letting core coolant be pushed out into a drain tank. The indicator for the relief valve failed, indicating that it was closed when it was not, so the draining continued for a long time without the operators knowing it was happening. Turning on some other pumps to fix a drop in pressure seemed to work for only a while, so they turned on another emergency source of water for the core, but only for a short time to avoid complications that it could cause if overused. Not knowing of the continued draining, the drop in reactor pressure didn't seem to match the increase in another gauge, and they had to choose which was giving a correct indication of what was going on. They were trying to figure out the level of coolant in the reactor (since too little would lead to a meltdown), but there were no direct measures of coolant level in this

type of reactor, only indirect. The indicators that could indirectly help one figure out what was going on weren't behaving as they were trained to expect. Some pumps started thumping and shaking and were shut down. The computer printing out status messages got far behind before they found out about the unseated valve. The alarms were ringing, but you couldn't shut down the noise without also shutting down other indicators.

The story goes on and on. This is just the beginning of that accident.

In addition to describing the many accidents and near accidents where good luck (or lack of bad luck) kept things safe, he also tries to figure out what makes some systems less prone to major accidents than others. It is, he believes, in the overall design.

Here are some quotes:

> *The main point of the book is to see . . . human constructions as systems, not as collections of individuals or representatives of ideologies. . . . [T]he theme has been that it is the way the parts fit together, interact, that is important. The dangerous accidents lie in the system, not in the components. [Page 351]*

> *. . . [Here is t]he major thesis of this book: systems that transform potentially explosive or toxic raw materials or that exist in hostile environments appear to require designs that entail a great many interactions which are not visible and in expected production sequence. Since nothing is perfect—neither designs, equipment, operating procedures, operators, materials, and supplies, nor the environment—there will be failures. If the complex interactions defeat designed-in safety devices or go around them, there will be failures that are unexpected and incomprehensible. If the system is also tightly coupled, leaving little time for recovery from failure, little slack in resources or fortuitous safety devices, then the failure cannot be limited to parts or units, but will bring down subsystems or systems. These accidents then are caused initially by component failures, but become accidents rather than incidents because of the nature of the system itself; they are system accidents, and are inevitable, or "normal" for these systems. [Page 330]*

Charles Perrow, *Normal Accidents*

This theory of two or more failures coming together in unexpected ways and defeating safety devices, cascading through coupling of subsystems into a system failure, is "Normal Accident Theory" (Perrow, pages 356–357). The role of the design of a system comes up over and over again. The more that subsystems are tightly coupled, the more accident prone they will be. The most problematic are couplings that are not that obvious to the original designers, such as physical proximity that couples subsystems. During a failure of one system (for example, a leak), a different system (the one it drips onto) is affected leading to an accident. (In computer systems this is very common, such as memory overruns in one area causing errors elsewhere.)

Another key point I found in the book is that in order to keep failures from growing into accidents the more an operator knows about what is happening in the system the better. Another point is that independent redundancy can be very helpful. However, back to coupling, redundancy and components that are interconnected in unexpected ways can lead to mysterious behavior, or incorrectly perceived correct behavior.

More examples from *Normal Accidents*

An example he gives of independent redundant systems providing operators much information is of the early warning systems for incoming missiles in North America at the time (early 1980s). He describes the false alarms, several every day, most of which are dismissed quickly. When an alarm comes into a command center, a telephone conference is started with duty officers at other command centers. If it looks serious (as it does every few days), higher-level officials are added to the conference call. If it still looks real, then a third-level conference is started, including the president of the U.S. (which hadn't happened so far at the time). The false alarms are usually from weather or birds that look to satellites or other sensors like a missile launch. By checking with other sensors that use independent technology or inputs, such as radar, they can see the lack of confirmation. They also look to intelligence of what the Soviets are doing (though the Soviets may be reacting to similar false alarms themselves or to their surveillance of the U.S.).

In one false alarm in November of 1979, many of the monitors reported what looked exactly like a massive Soviet attack. While they were checking it out, ten tactical fighters were sent aloft and U.S. missiles were put on low-level alert. It turned out that a training tape on an auxiliary system found its way into the real system. The alarm was suspected of being false in two minutes, but was certified false after six (preparing a counter strike takes ten minutes for a submarine-launched attack). In another false alarm, test messages had a bit stuck in the 1 position due to a hardware failure, indicating 2 missiles instead of zero. There was no loopback to help detect the error.

The examples relating to marine accidents are some of the most surprising and instructive. It seems that ships sometimes inexplicably turn suddenly and crash into each other much more than you would think. He sees this as relating to an organizational problem along with the tendency of people to decide upon a model of what is going on and then interpret information afterwards in that light. In ships, at the time, the captain had absolute authority and the rest of the crew usually just followed orders. (This is different than in airplanes where the copilot is free to question the pilot and there is air traffic control watching and in two-way radio contact.)

In one case, Perrow relates that a ship captain saw a different number of lights on another ship than the first mate. They didn't compare notes about the number of lights, especially after the captain indicated he had seen a ship. The captain thought the ship was traveling in the same direction as them (two lights), while the first mate correctly thought that it was coming at them (three). Misinterpreting what he was seeing, the captain thought it was getting closer because it was a slow, small fishing vessel, not because it was big and traveling towards him. Since passing is routine, they weren't contacted by the other ship. When he got close, he steered as if he was passing, and turned into the path of the oncoming vessel, killing eleven on his boat. In another case, apparent radar equipment errors made a ship think an oncoming ship was to its left when it was really to its right. Fog came in, and midcourse maneuvers by both ships were increasingly in a feedback loop that caused a collision.

Another book about failures

To get a feeling for how common and varied failures are, and to see how some people have attempted to classify them for learning, there are books such as Trevor Kletz's *What Went Wrong? Case Histories of Process Plant Disasters*,[19] which chronicles hundreds of them. Examining many failures and classifying them for learning is very important. You don't want to just prevent an exact duplicate of a failure in the future, but rather the entire class it represents. Failures of parts and procedures are the common, normal situation. Everything working as planned is not. Safety systems are no panacea. "Better" training or people, while often helpful, won't stop it all.

---

[19]Gulf Professional Publishing, 1999, ISBN: 0884159205

Like Perrow, Kletz believes that design is critical for preventing (or minimizing the effect of) accidents. Here are some guidelines he discusses that relate to process plants:

- Use processes with fewer dangerous intermediate products, and store as little dangerous product as possible. In Bhopal (where over 2,000 people were killed by a leaking chemical), "the material that leaked was not a product or raw material but an intermediate, and while it was convenient to store it, it was not essential to do so." "What you don't have can't leak." [page 369]
- Make incorrect assembly impossible, so that, for example, you can't put a pump in backwards.
- Try to minimize designs that use items that are easy to damage during installation, such as expansion joints.
- "Make the status of equipment clear. Thus, figure-8 plates are better than slip plates, as the position of the former is obvious at a glance, and valves with rising spindles are better than valves in which the spindle does not rise. Ball valves are [user] friendly if the handles cannot be replaced in the wrong position." [page 378]
- "Use equipment that can tolerate a degree of misuse." [page 378]

It is crucial that reports of encountered problems be made available to others for learning, especial those problems that result in accidents. There are many reasons for this. Kletz lists a few (on page 396) including our moral responsibility to prevent accidents if we can, and the fact that accident reports seem to have a greater impact on those reading them than just reciting principles.

The 9/11 Commission Report—a story of reaction to a forced change in a system

After reading *Normal Accidents*, and with its lessons in mind, I read the sections in "The 9/11 Commission Report" that relate to the events during the hijacking of the planes and at the World Trade Center until the second tower collapsed. I was looking to learn about how the "system" responded once a failure (the hijacking and the buildings being struck) started. I was looking most toward finding descriptions of communications, decision making, and the role of the general populace because of my interest in those areas. I looked for uses of redundancy and communications and real-time information by the "operators" (those closest to what was happening). I looked for unplanned activities. I mainly dealt with the descriptions of what happened, not with the recommendations in the report.

Why look at terrorism? It is different from normal failures.

Terrorism is an extreme form of "failure" and accident. The perpetrators and planners look for weak components in a system and try to cause unexpected failures with maximum destruction and impact. Many traditional books on engineering failure, such as Perrow's *Normal Accidents*, explicitly do not tackle it.

I see terrorism (for our purposes here) as being a form of change to a working system, with often purposeful, forced close coupling, and that has bad effects. We can learn from it about dealing with changes to a system that must be dealt with and that were not foreseen by the original designers. It is like a change in environment or a change in the system configuration.

The entire report is available online for free and in printed form for a nominal fee. I have put together excerpts that I found in the Commission Report that I think are instructive. They are on a separate page, with anchors on each excerpt so that they can be referred to. The page is "Some Excerpts From The 9/11 Commission Report."[20]

I think it is worth reading the actual, complete chapters, but in lieu of that, anybody interested in communications or dealing with disastrous situations like this should at least read the excerpts. I found it fascinating, horrifying, sad, and very real. As an engineer, I saw information from which to learn and then build systems that will better serve the needs of society. Such systems would be helpful in many trying situations, natural and man-made, foreseen and unforeseen, and could save lives and suffering. Let us learn from a bad situation to help society in the future. As Kletz points out, as engineers and designers, it is our duty.

Some key quotes from "The 9/11 Commission Report":

> . . . [T]he passengers and flight crew [of Flight 93] began a series of calls from GTE airphones and cellular phones. These calls between family, friends, and colleagues took place until the end of the flight and provided those on the ground with firsthand accounts. They enabled the passengers to gain critical information, including the news that two aircraft had slammed into the World Trade Center. [page 12]

---

[20]http://www.bricklin.com/911excerpts.htm

The defense of U.S. airspace on 9/11 was not conducted in accord with preexisting training and protocols. It was improvised by civilians who had never handled a hijacked aircraft that attempted to disappear, and by a military unprepared for the transformation of commercial aircraft into weapons of mass destruction. [page 31]

General David Wherley—the commander of the 113th Wing [of the District of Columbia Air National Guard at Andrews Air Force Base in Maryland]—reached out to the Secret Service after hearing secondhand reports that it wanted fighters airborne. A Secret Service agent had a phone in each ear, one connected to Wherley and the other to a fellow agent at the White House, relaying instructions that the White House agent said he was getting from the Vice President. [page 44]

We are sure that the nation owes a debt to the passengers of United 93. Their actions saved the lives of countless others, and may have saved either the Capitol or the White House from destruction. [page 45]

According to another chief present, "People watching on TV certainly had more knowledge of what was happening a hundred floors above us than we did in the lobby . . . [W]ithout critical information coming in . . . it's very difficult to make informed, critical decisions[.]" [page 298]

[Quoting a report about the Pentagon disaster:] "Almost all aspects of communications continue to be problematic, from initial notification to tactical operations. Cellular telephones were of little value . . . Radio channels were initially oversaturated . . . Pagers seemed to be the most reliable means of notification when available and used, but most firefighters are not issued pagers." [page 315]

The "first" first responders on 9/11, as in most catastrophes, were private-sector civilians. Because 85 percent of our nation's critical infrastructure is controlled not by government but by the private sector, private-sector civilians are likely to be the first responders in any future catastrophes. [page 317]

The NYPD's 911 operators and FDNY dispatch were not adequately integrated into the emergency response . . . In planning for future *disasters, it is important to integrate those taking 911 calls into the emergency response team and to involve them in providing up-to-date information and assistance to the public.* [page 318]

The 9/11 Commission Report

The Report strongly suggests that the billions of dollars spent on military infrastructure failed to stop any of the hijacked planes from hitting their targets. It was civilians, using everyday airphones and the unreliable cellular system, together with our civilian news gathering and disseminating system, and intuition and improvisation, that probably stopped one. Courage and bravery were shown by all, civilians and official personnel.

I thought the Report, in its analysis, paid too little attention to the important role of civilians and professionals acting out of their prepared roles. There is a lack of attention to societal communications, including TV, radio, Internet, cellular (voice, GPS, cell cameras, etc.), and too much just on those specific to officials. TV news was a crucial source for all, including the highest levels of government. While the phone network bogged down, it did provide crucial help, and civilian non-PSTN[21] systems, such as Nextel Direct Connect, the Internet, and message-based systems did work well. Even the president suffered from a version of what we all get when traveling with wireless. "[H]e was frustrated with the poor communications that morning. He could not reach key officials, including Secretary Rumsfeld, for a period of time. The line to the White House shelter conference room—and the vice president—kept cutting off." [page 40] The vice president learned of the first crash from an assistant who told him to turn on his television on which he then saw the second crash. [page 35]

There are other examples of the general populace being an important component of what is usually thought of as being the province of "law enforcement." The AMBER Alert system is apparently working, as is the "America's Most Wanted" TV show, both of which use the general populace as a means for information gathering in response to detailed descriptions and requests. In Israel, the general populace has been instrumental in detecting suspicious behavior and even taking action to thwart or minimize terrorist attacks. According to "The 9/11 Commission Report," a civilian passenger with years of experience in Israel apparently tried unsuccessfully to stop the hijackers on AA Flight 11. The fourth hijacked plane, UA 93, was stopped by civilians. An almost-catastrophe on an airplane was thwarted by attendants and passengers on AA Flight 63

---

[21]Public Switched Telephone Network (PSTN) refers to the normal telephone system.

when they restrained "shoe bomber" Richard Reid, now knowing that suicide terrorism on airplanes was a possibility.

What do we learn here with respect to reaction to disasters?

- Disasters like this and many forms of terrorism are characterized by unforeseen situations and the inclusion of everyday people.
- There is lots of happenstance going on, some of it good and some bad.
- Improvisation is used and often needed in unanticipated places. The coupling of systems may be changed by the terrorists through their actions and through the effects of those actions, changing the nature of the entire system.
- Procedures help if appropriate to the situation but may not if the situation is different than anticipated.
- People close to specific situations throughout the emergency need to decide what to do based upon information.
- The information needed is often available somewhere in the "system," if only it can be found.
- Regular people can use the information and are a crucial component (e.g., UA 93).
- Official people also use the information, and can be very helpful in additional ways, especially since they have equipment and training and "authority" to lead and comfort.
- A suboptimal response comes from lack of information at the right place in the situation as it unfolds (e.g., 911 operators not having timely evacuation instructions).
- People often will ask the right questions, or at least some do, and then share what they learn and decide with others.
- Outsiders will join if needed and asked (and sometimes will try to join even if not asked), and will need information. For example, General Wherley, commander of the 113th Wing, "reached out to the Secret Service after hearing secondhand reports that it wanted fighters airborne." Many first responders from nonassigned groups as well as off-duty personnel showed up in New York and at the Pentagon with both good and bad results.
- Multiple modes of communication and sources of information are necessary and help. Redundancy is good.
- It is hard to know in advance all of the people and groups that will need to be connected through communications.

The Secret Service, an organization whose mission involves working against the unexpected, shows up in places you wouldn't expect, such as air defense and even providing information at the World Trade Center. This shouldn't be surprising. In addition to planning and post-event analysis, they specialize in improvisation, and are trained[22] to be "prepared to respond to any eventuality."

Examination of "The 9/11 Commission Report" comes up with some of the same lessons as Perrow, namely the need for people nearest to what's happening to have access to detailed, real-time information relating to what is happening in many parts of the system that may not have been foreseen.

Here are some additional things that we learn about cases like this:

- There is a need for the ability to easily improvise to deal with new situations.
- The people involved in dealing with the situation now include the general populace instead of just "operators."
- Some of the information is coming from more generic sources as well as those participants themselves.
- The general populace, and even the "official" participants, are likely to seek information from everyday channels (TV, 911, cell phones, Internet).

What we can do

Here are some of my thoughts about reacting to catastrophes:

- I see a need for a source of coordination of information from afar. Being too close to the situation may cause those coordinators that are close to lose the wide perspective and get sucked into a growing situation. Multiple, independently redundant means of information acquisition, evaluation, and dissemination are important.
- We need ways for everyday people involved in a disastrous situation to both give and receive information. We need ways that they can query quickly for what they need. Telephone 911 has served some of this, but it is apparently not good in an unusual, widespread, unforeseen situation. The Internet could be used, and could serve as a resource to those 911 operators, too. In today's world, they pull out their cell phones and call

---

[22]http://web.archive.org/web/20041011102006/http://www.secretservice.gov/nsse.shtml

loved ones who look at the TV and could serve as gateways for sending and receiving information.

- The work that is going on in the blogging world in regard to seeking out, filtering, and disseminating information coming from a huge number of data sources for a diverse set of needs may be helpful for learning how to deal with such situations. Blogs, RSS, and the search engines are currently tuned for situations that unfold over many hours, days, or weeks. We need to look for principles that can be applied to minutes and seconds. The media forms of text, images, audio, and video are appropriate here, too.[23]

- We have a populace that is getting more and more comfortable with message-based forms of communications. Much of the information needed during 9/11 was relatively static: the fact that planes had been hijacked, that planes had hit buildings, where exactly they hit, that an evacuation had been called for, etc. Such information was of life and death importance. Even short text messages would have sufficed in some cases (though they shouldn't be the only means of communications, of course).

- Communications devices used by official first responders (and hopefully everyday people) need to handle message-based communications better. Stored messages in voice may be the best for some users. (I don't think we want to depend upon fire fighters reading tiny screens surrounded by smoke nor typing on keyboards while wearing heavy gloves.)

- Communications devices need to handle degrading connectivity situations better. For example, they should be able to move from two-way voice to real-time, during-the-call store-and-forward voice, to delayed voice (like auto-delivered voicemail), and even text delivered from speech-to-text (as text and perhaps as text-to-speech). This would handle intermittent connectivity and saturated bandwidth gracefully with little change in operation or training. Drop-outs and degradation should be flagged, perhaps with an appropriate sound indicating that there was a possible loss of information. Requests for retries should be possible, perhaps built into the system so the sender doesn't need to repeat themself but rather an ongoing real-time recording would be used (much as we playback voice mail) both on the sender and receiver side.

---

[23]Looking at this in light of our tools today, I would add social software tools such as wikis, SMS text messaging, Twitter-like systems, etc.

Storage requirements and processing power for such functions are well within the capabilities of multimedia-enabled handsets. User interfaces and standards need to be developed. Perhaps this is an area where new generic handsets and WiFi-enabled VoIP will take a leap forward.

- The ability to switch communications seamlessly or manually between many different types of carriers, be it normal Internet connections, hand-held point-to-point radios, or some sort of mesh system could be key. Rather than just pour more money into "beefing up" single agency-specific systems, find out how to take advantage of multiple systems, including civilian ones. Cell phones may have been overwhelmed, but they saved lives, people got through some of the time, and they were used by even the senior officials. Redundancy and the ability to impro-vise must be exploited. Packet-based communications can have advan-tages over circuit-based in terms of graceful degradation.[24]

- Traditionally, unusual situations are handled with "situation-specific conference calls" where interested parties share an open "line" and par-ticipate or just listen in. During 9/11 there were several and the right people were not always present. We are learning about "joining" mul-tiple simultaneous conversations with online "chat" as one style[25] and RSS aggregators as another. We need to move this further.

- I can imagine many "regular" people reacting to an emergency need for information by turning on the TV and/or radio, using their phone or cell phone, and using Google or their preferred search engine. (Many of my readers would probably check their RSS aggregators.) There should be a known way to specify to the search engines that they should return only real-time and situation-specific information.[26] There needs to be

---

[24]The traditional telephone technology uses a circuit architecture in which a dedicated connection is established between the two end points. A break or corruption at any point in that chain disrupts the call, with data lost.

The Internet uses what is called "packet-based" communication. The information being passed between the end points is broken down into small "packets" of hundreds or thousands of bytes each. The route each packet takes from sender to receiver can vary from packet to packet, and packets that are deemed "lost" because of communication or other errors may be retransmitted.

[25]See John Morgan's descriptions of the use of chat on ships in Chapter 5.

[26]In the photo sharing Flickr system and the Twitter system, among others, people have learned to decide early on a common tag to add to new posts to aid in aggregat-ing observations about a particular event. For example, during the November 2008 attacks in Mumbai, many Flickr users used tags like "attack, mumbai" and Twitter users used "#mumbai."

a way for "officials" to disseminate information to such feeds. There need to be ways to establish limited-access feeds and easily give access to such feeds to appropriate people, much as "talk groups" are used on "point-to-point" radio.

- We must guard against the attitude that only the authorities know best. In many cases, civilians are closest to details and may come up with the appropriate improvisation to an unforeseen situation. They must be part of the solution, and therefore must be used for getting information and must have access to it.

Summary and next steps

This essay covers a wide range of topics. It introduces "Normal Accident Theory," looks at some of the aspects of a major terrorist attack, and proposes some areas for design that are suggested by the results of that attack. The original goal, though, was to come up with some principles that could be applied to making software that fits with the long-term needs of society. Here are some of those principles:

- Instrument the subsystems and components so that failures can be detected and so that behavior can be monitored when there are changes. There is a need to know "what is going on."
- Examine failures and share what is found with others so that there is learning.
- Try to keep subsystems loosely coupled, the interfaces understandable, and the intermediate steps comprehensible.
- Allow for, and anticipate, improvisation. The design of instrumentation and the coupling of subsystems can make improvisation easier or harder.
- Those who deal with changes may not be the ones for whom the designers planned nor who were pretrained to deal with those changes. This affects the design of instrumentation, coupling, and documentation.
- Generic, "global" resources help and should be able to be used as part of instrumentation and improvisation.

The next step will be to put these together with other principles gleaned from other areas.

http://www.bricklin.com/learningfromaccidents.htm

Here we added the dimension of time to our consideration. Too often we don't think about how the environment changes over time and our duty to account for it in product design, or business model design.

In the next chapter we look back at the evolution of one product over a 25-year period.

10

The PC: Historical Information about an Important Tool

The personal computer, in particular the IBM PC and its descendents, is an important product that has successfully evolved over three decades. In this chapter, I look at the evolution of the PC, including source material from its introduction. Too often we think of tools as static entities, born fully formed and staying unchanged, with their use and potential fully understood at the outset. Looking at the evolution of important products can help us get a better feel for what really happens.

THE EVOLVING PERSONAL COMPUTER

The PC has stayed relevant by evolving its components.

I was interviewed by *PC Week* magazine for an "end of the millennium" Vision 2000 look at the PC (December 20/27 issue, page 66). I related to them my latest explanation of why the personal computer is a general-purpose platform for computing. At that point, on the phone, I realized that the original IBM PC design has really evolved and is continuing to evolve and that this evolution is part of its strength and staying power. This essay looks into that a little further.

The early personal computers, such as the S-100 bus machines and the Apple II, borrowed from minicomputers the concept of using plug-in parts. When Apple wanted to add diskette drives to the Apple II, Woz just had to design one (elegant) board to plug in and all Apple IIs could upgrade to include disk storage. Serial and printer adapters were added the same way.

The IBM PC followed the Apple II design, including using plug-in cards for major features. Copying the Apple II, IBM thought that 64KB was enough memory since they could find few Apple IIs with more than that. This was based

December 21, 1999

on market research without seeming to realize that the 6502 microprocessor in the Apple II could only address 64KB vs. the 640KB of the IBM PC's 8088-based design. (A true story: That's what they told us back then.) Luckily for IBM, Tecmar and others temporarily filled the gap with "add-in" boards with more memory so that products like Lotus 1-2-3 that needed more than 64KB could be developed.

Compaq Computer helped define what it meant to be an "IBM Compatible" when it released its first product. It had to run software unmodified, use the same add-in boards, have the same connectors, and have the same keyboard layout. The video-display adapter was improved, but was upwards compatible so that existing programs would function properly.

Over time, other peripherals became available. When a particular peripheral became popular, the PC manufacturers made it standard equipment, eventually integrated into the main design. Modems, higher-resolution display adapters, CD-ROM drives, sound cards, speakers, and more were added.

In each case, older applications and devices were supported until they weren't important to purchasers. For example, for a few years you could buy computers with both 5¼″ and 3½″ diskette drives and both size serial adapters were provided. Microsoft Windows didn't really catch on until it supported more memory and ran DOS programs at the same time.

The Apple Macintosh showed that a mouse and GUI were an important advance. The PC evolved, first by using an add-in mouse and add-in software, and later with the mouse standard and Windows preloaded. Apple products evolved, too, but with more quantum jumps.

PC laptops got expandability through PCMCIA cards. This proved that hardware interfaces other than the techie plug-in boards worked in the PC world. The Mac world had shown that a serial bus and the daisy-chained minicomputer SCSI system were also viable.

The internal plug-in boards have now evolved into the Universal Serial Bus (USB) system. You can add all sorts of devices, from cameras to disks to printers to scanners, all using one style of connector.

The PC has evolved from a simple machine for running BASIC programs and character-based spreadsheets and business forms to a machine for viewing, manipulating, and sharing formatted text, images, sounds, and more.

As we find new uses for computing power, the PC will continue to evolve to stay a platform we can use for general-purpose computing.

December 21, 1999

To drive home this point of the evolution, look at these pictures of the connectors on an original IBM PC:

Compare those parts to the ones on a new Gateway Profile 2 PC:

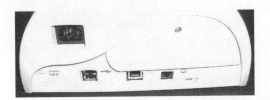

The screen is completely different (XGA color LCD vs. the old monochrome green-character display), the keyboard is somewhat different, and the 5¼″ floppies are replaced by a DVD drive and a 3½″ diskette. It adds integral speakers, microphone and sound card. The parallel printer adapter and serial ports (borrowed from minicomputers) have been replaced by USB ports. The keyboard is now USB and there is no extra game port. There is an RJ-11 (modem) and an RJ-45 (Ethernet) jack built in. It takes up much less space and has some nice curves.

The only connector these two machines still have in common is the power cord socket. The only "IBM PC specific" things are some funny keys like "PrtSc," and the fact that it can still run software like the original VisiCalc[1] (shown on the screen in front of a browser with my blog). Intel and Microsoft are still "inside," but quite evolved.

http://www.bricklin.com/pcevolution.htm

THOUGHTS ON THE 20TH ANNIVERSARY OF THE IBM PC

First encounters with the IBM PC in 1980 and 1981, why the PC has taken over the role of the desk in our lives, and why it will continue to be important

As part of a celebration of the 20th anniversary of the announcement of the IBM PC, Bill Gates and Andy Grove are hosting an event. They have asked many people to attend and contribute thoughts about the past and future of the PC. Here are some of my thoughts before the event.

First encounters with the IBM PC

At Software Arts,[2] we first heard of the IBM PC on October 22, 1980. Pat Harrington of IBM ISD in Boca Raton called, and, according to my notes from that day (labeled as "Confidential," of course), said that they were "interested (maybe)" and he was coming up to visit the following Monday, October 27th, at 9 a.m. I remember how secret they all tried to be, but still signed in at the guard desk of our office building as "IBM," which was a dead giveaway about what was happening. We told them that we'd love to do a deal with them, but that our publisher, Personal Software, had to do the actual licensing of VisiCalc to them.

---

[1] http://www.bricklin.com/history/vcexecutable.htm

[2] Software Arts, Inc., was the company Bob Frankston and I founded to develop VisiCalc. The story of VisiCalc and Software Arts appears in Chapter 12.

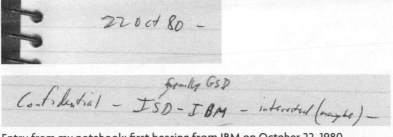

Entry from my notebook: first hearing from IBM on October 22, 1980

According to my notes, we went down for a meeting in Boca Raton, Florida, on December 15, 1980. They had given us the code name "Bridge" for the machine. They had us stay at the Bridge Hotel (now called the Radisson Bridge Resort, named for the drawbridge next door, I guess), so we assumed that's where they got the code name. Years later I learned that they gave different groups different code names to track leaks, and a more common name was "Chess," so "Bridge" was the game, not the hotel.

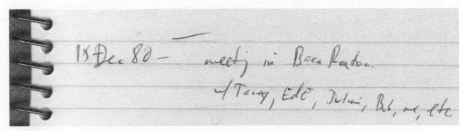

Entry from my notebook: meeting in Boca Raton, Florida, on December 15, 1980

The meeting was attended on our side by Bob Frankston, and me, as well as Julian Lange, senior executives at Software Arts, and Terry Opdendyk and Ed Esber, senior executives of our publisher, Personal Software.

At the meeting we had problems with IBM getting one of the confidentiality agreements to work with the fact that we did incremental magnetic tape back-ups of material on our timesharing system, causing meaningless "comingling" that they were restricting. While the lawyers did their things, we supposedly couldn't talk much. The IBM technical people were very anxious to tell us things and very proud of their machine. As Julian tells it, to get around the secrecy restrictions during the wait, what evolved was something like this: One of us would say, "Does it have slots for plugging in accessories?" and they would reply, "Well, a really good personal computer would have that, wouldn't it?" and we'd say, "Yes," and they'd say, "Well, this is a very good computer." It was very funny, but we ascertained what each side needed to know quite well. (We eventually did sign acceptable agreements.)

As Bob tells it, "the first time we got our hands on a machine was when Fritz [a technical person we knew] from the IBM Research office near us in Cambridge, Massachusetts, dropped off a plywood board with components on it and a listing of an operating system from Seattle Computer Products. The comments in the listings were the only documentation we had." As I recall, we thought that, given all the secrecy and code names, "Seattle Computer Products" was a pseudonym for Microsoft. In hindsight, it was more complicated.[3]

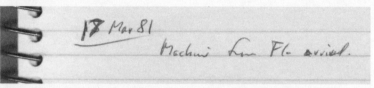

Entry from my notebook: We get our early machine on March 17, 1981.

Here's another entry in my notebook as we learned more and more about the system:

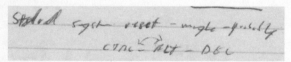

Entry from my notebook: Stdrd system reset—maybe—probably CTRL-ALT-DEL

On August 12, 1981, the day the IBM Personal Computer was announced, we made a videotape of the events at our company and I have a transcript[4] you can read with further notes about our prototype and how we did the translation.

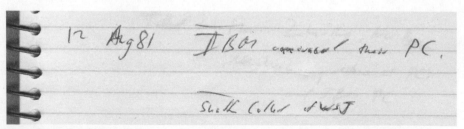

Entry from my notebook: IBM announced their PC, August 12, 1981; Dick Shaffer of the *Wall Street Journal* called.

---

[3] http://www.patersontech.com/Dos/

[4] See later in this chapter.

Futures

August 3, 2001

I commented about "The Evolving Personal Computer" back in December of 1999. Please read those comments [earlier in this chapter]. I still agree with my conclusion: "As we find new uses for computing power, the PC will continue to evolve to stay a platform we can use for general purpose computing." Another observation, that the main component that has stayed the same is the fact that the operating system is (usually) from Microsoft and the processor (usually) from Intel (and maybe the power cord plug is the same), shows us why Bill and Andy are the right ones to host the celebration. They were able to keep that evolution so smooth that programs like the original VisiCalc from 1981 still run despite a 1,000 times or more improvement in power and tremendous API advances.

I've been trying to come up with an analogy for the personal computer. Calling the PC a "platform for general-purpose computing" is not clear enough, nor specific enough. I finally came up with this metaphor (while walking my dog, as usual for such ideas):

The precursor to the personal computer is the desk. To understand how this relates to the PC, first let's think about the role of the desk in one's life. There were many types of tables in the old days, but one type evolved on which you did your correspondence, writing, some reading, record keeping and simple transactions, calculations, simple art, etc. It was where you did "work" that involved you devoting your entire attention and took some time to do it. The desk was a "platform" (literally) that held your tools, such as pencils and paper, straight edges, etc. It may have had local storage, such as drawers or openings, aids for the tools, such as inkwells and power outlets, and even simple security, such as roll tops or drawer locks. It evolved over time to meet the needs of the tools you used to do your work. Blotters for fountain and quill pens gave way to hard tops for ballpoint pens. If you do any of many types of work, you have a desk. A dorm room, the most basic of places to live and work, gives each student a bed, a place to keep clothes, a chair, and a desk.

The personal computer has taken over much of the role of the desk, with the desk being one of the places to hold a personal computer (keeping its role). The PC (in the generic sense) is where we do correspondence: first typing up and printing out letters for mailing and later faxing, now email and instant messaging. It's where we do writing, some reading, record keeping, calculating, analysis, creating, and more. It is the "platform" on which our software "tools" run, and the interface to our hardware "tools." Over time, the PC has evolved, just like the desk. Things that were optional, like CD drives and floating point processors, became standard when they became popular and expected.

The personal computer is not the only use of computing power. Other forms also exist, such as wearable and handheld devices to take our attention for small amounts of time or to use while doing other things (like walking, waiting, or driving), or dedicated powerful devices attended to by specialists. (Some of these dedicated devices may be built out of PCs or PC components to keep costs down, both for hardware and software development.) There are other types of tables, too, from butcher blocks to card tables. They each have their uses.

If you look at the personal computer this way, then the future is clear. The personal computer is not going away. We read more and more on-screen, and our "work" and communications involve connectivity like the Internet and LANs. The PC will stay something that is big enough to take up a reasonable amount of our field of view to interface with our eyes. It will have input/output devices that let us use it as a tool, probably a keyboard and other interfaces to our hands, mouths, ears, etc. We will want to take it with us wherever we do work. (The idea that there would be "terminals" everywhere that we'd use hasn't happened. Hotels were forced to put in outlets that let us bring our own PCs and connect them to power and communications, often replacing all of their old telephones just so we can connect a modem.) Wireless technology like 802.11 is freeing us from the need to work in any one fixed location in a building. Rather than using projectors or needing to print out copies of material we create on our PCs for sharing with others, we'll all have machines with us and do ad hoc sharing when we get together.

The desktop computer has evolved into the laptop, and the laptop will evolve further into some new form more appropriate for keeping with you and carrying around as you would a notebook or stack of papers. (The old GRiD Convertible was a great example of this direction.)[5] Almost everybody will have one, much as almost everybody has a desk or something that serves as one. This is distinct from the small personal device, the cell phone/PDA, used for short-attention purposes that you will carry most of the time just as you carry a watch, wallet, or purse today. This evolution in form factor will ensure a continued upgrading of PCs, as will new uses that come from combinations of new capabilities like higher processing power, "usually on" connectivity, new peripherals, and advances in software.

---

[5] The GRiD Convertible is discussed in Chapter 8.

The designers of the IBM Personal Computer learned as much as they could from the designs before it. They followed many things that worked well elsewhere, such as being expandable like the Apple II and S-100 machines, and using outside vendors for components and software. They even used the chip being designed into other 2nd or 3rd generation personal computers of the day (like the Victor from personal-computer-industry pioneer Chuck Peddle): the Intel 8088. It was branded by a strong, well-known company (IBM) for potential purchasers. It attracted many software developers. The defining by Compaq of "PC compatibility" and the ability to make compatible but different versions sealed its role as the design to become dominant. Others, most notably Apple, have helped give innovative direction, but descendants of the original IBM PC have held their own. The innovations of GRiD and Data General (the modern laptop), Compaq (distribution and compatibility while advancing), Dell (distribution and manufacturing), and others, have combined with IBM, Intel, and Microsoft's advancements to keep up the evolution.

Is the PC market over? No. The ability to evolve by including individual advancements in hardware, software, and usage styles is what makes the PC so successful. Those advancements will continue. The fact that users can mix and match applications and devices connected to the PC, and that these things can be made to coexist appropriately, sharing what they need to (screen, storage, data, CPU, whatever) is important. As long as the PC continues to have that forward-thinking, "we don't know everything that must be in the box and what you'd do with it" design, then its future is assured. Unlike an automobile, it doesn't "wear out" that quickly. It is additional value that gives us reason to upgrade. With a cost of much less than an automobile (or, for many homes, less than the yearly insurance, gas, and maintenance for the automobile), it will be at least as necessary to most individuals. If we can give people the value, they will pay for the device, applications, and services. They have already shown that they don't just buy the cheapest available. The desk was made all the more useful by the fact you could use anybody's book on it, anybody's pen and paper, anybody's ruler, anybody's lamp. If we can leverage the advances from all in the PC then it will always be advancing and we will always need one.

At the event I was able to present a few of these thoughts as part of the panel. I've posted pictures I took in my album "Celebration of the 20th Anniversary of the IBM PC."[6]

---

[6] http://www.bricklin.com/albums/ibmpc20th/

Essays for the anniversary from some other people

Dave Winer:[7]

> *I felt supremely powerful. I told my friends I thought of it as a "big blank machine," which is exactly how you get an ambitious young software developer excited . . . the PC was originally a revolutionary tool for individual empowerment.*
>
> Dave Winer, August 1, 2001

Bob Frankston: It was raw material waiting to be shaped and then shaped again and again . . . The success of the Internet has been due, in large part, because the PC serves its owner, rather than the network. Here is the full essay:[8]

> *The IBM PC: 1981 to . . .*
>
> *Introduction*
>
> *This essay is being written as part of the celebration of the 20th Anniversary of the IBM PC. You should also read Dan Bricklin's memories and thoughts for specifics about our first experience with the PC (officially, the IBM-5150).*
>
> *PC: Past And Future*
>
> *I first saw the IBM PC on a plywood board and I find that wonderful. This wasn't an overly polished office machine. It was raw material waiting to be shaped and then shaped again and again. It wasn't just a platform for VisiCalc. Anyone could write programs and make it into what they wanted. And as we did, we could learn. It didn't matter that this seemed a toy compared with the IBM 360, 370, and all the other systems we had used. You could open up the PC and replace boards, make any changes to any programs. Treat the screen like a terminal or like a video screen. You could use the keyboard as a typewriter or just watch as each key went up and down and turn it into a game control. It didn't matter that DOS 1.0 didn't even have much of a file system. That could all be changed. And those of us who were used to the ARPAnet and, later the Internet, knew that*

---

[7] http://www.scripting.com/davenet/2001/08/01/bigBlankMachine.html

[8] http://www.frankston.com/public/?name=ThePCFrom1981To

the question is when, not whether, the systems would be connected. At Software Arts we immediately connected our PCs to our Ethernet, albeit initially as terminals.

While there were variations on the PC that emulated more traditional computing devices and terminals, the general purpose PC thrived. The differences between corporate and personal computers were insignificant compared to the benefits of having a common system.

The PC is being joined by many other computing devices but it retains its importance as the place where one can experiment and innovate because of the richness of the environment. As we've seen, attempts to focus on one aspect of the PC to the exclusion of others as in so-called Internet Appliances and Network Computers have largely failed. The value of the PC has been in the personal ownership and the ability for the owner (not just as a "user") to experiment and fail. Typically a reboot is sufficient to get started again and those who take chances learn the value of backing up.

The PC has evolved and is still struggling to transition from standing alone to being a network participant. The success of the Internet has been due, in large part, because the PC serves its owner, rather than the network. In fact, by being distrustful of the network it allows the kind of experimentation and innovation that we've seen on the stand-alone PC to take place on the network where, once again, you can experiment without causing undue harm to others. Not because you have to be careful, but because others take the responsibility for protecting themselves thus leaving you free to innovate.

With the PC, many focused on the costs rather than the opportunities. Thus the fascination with network terminals. With our current concern about computer "viruses," we shouldn't lose sight of the tremendous potential as people learn to program their own computers using scripting languages and more powerful tools. Just as the connected PC has become central to the economy and our society, the ability to take control of the computer, not just use it, becomes part of what it means to be literate in this society.

Yet we are only seeing the earliest phase of what the Internet can be, just the prototype. And with Windows XP we are just getting the kind of industrial strength platform that is more important for consumer programming than industrial programming. And we will see these systems enhanced by a growing number of devices on the network that extend the reach and capabilities beyond nearby screens and keyboards.

As a society our challenge is in understanding the value of innovation. Rather than trying to limit the possible harm, we need to revel in creating opportunity.

As an industry we need to respect our users—they are us. Our future depends on the tools we give them to create their own solutions, not in our ability to do it all for them.

Bob Frankston, August 3, 2001

http://www.bricklin.com/ibmpc20thoughts.htm

This celebration of the IBM PC anniversary occurred soon after the peak of the "dotCom Bubble," when people had been writing about all the new ideas that would replace the old and how the old people "didn't get it" about e-commerce, building systems, etc. I am a firm believer in the value of experience or at least learning from the experience of others. (That's one reason I write all those history-centric essays.) Here is an essay on that topic related to the IBM PC.

THE VALUE OF EXPERIENCE

The IBM PC is an example of a system designed by people very experienced in the field—it was a revolution from within.

One thing that struck me during the panel during the celebration of the 20th anniversary of the announcement of the IBM PC was the depth of experience of the individuals involved with the PC at the time it was developed. This is in contrast to the image a couple of years ago of inexperienced "New Economy" people who could invent the new because they weren't "held back" by knowing the old.

The effect of the IBM PC was enormous, and has been well documented elsewhere. Its design in many ways was a base on which 20 years of industry prosperity was built. Those people must have done a pretty good job. I think one reason was that those people knew the past well, and used lessons learned to guide them. They had extensive experience with mainframes, minicomputers, and microcomputers, and with the structure of the industry. They were trained at leading institutions and knew all the theory.

Look at the backgrounds of some of the people involved in getting things going:

- Dave Bradley, who did the BIOS, was a veteran of the Series/1 and the Datamaster like many of his IBM peers. He had a doctorate in electrical engineering from Purdue. Other members of the IBM team were very familiar with the Apple II as users, and had years experience with designing (from scratch) various minicomputer and microcomputer systems.
- Bill Gates and Microsoft (founded 1975) were the most experienced microcomputer software developers, knowing the details of just about all the machines built up to that time. Bill had been programming on mainframes, minicomputers, and microcomputers since 1968 or so, most of it for sale to others.
- The operating system that MS-DOS was based upon (CP/M) was developed by Gary Kildall. Gary was extremely experienced in microcomputer development, and brought ideas from the products of minicomputer leader DEC and others to his design. At one point, before creating CP/M, he taught computer science at the Naval Postgraduate School, and knew classic mainframes like the Burroughs 5500.
- Rod Canion, who helped define the "standard" we followed, got his masters in EE/CS in 1975, and then went to Texas Instruments (at the time a dominant force in several fields), working on computers and hardware before founding Compaq.
- Mitch Kapor put together and led a "dream team" of experienced individuals to create and market Lotus 1-2-3. Ray Ozzie learned the promise of workgroup computing from one of the leading educational research projects, and then went on to work at a major minicomputer manufacturer before joining the microcomputer world at Software Arts and then Lotus before creating Notes.

- Bob Frankston and I had extensive experience with mainframes, mini-computers, and microcomputers, starting in the 1960s. I worked at minicomputer leader DEC as well as at a small company that used microprocessors before being trained by establishment-supporting Harvard Business School. Not only had I worked implementing inter-preter-based calculating languages on mainframes (APL, LISP), but I also helped develop early minicomputer-based word processing and editing systems.

As you can see, the IBM PC represented a revolution led by many of the old guard's troops and leaders. I believe that experience and knowledge of the past are very valuable and that the success of the IBM PC is an example of that.

http://www.bricklin.com/experiencevalue.htm

There is tension between the idea of industry people being unable to envision a quantum change with new technology and the idea that experience is helpful. You'll note that in Chapter 2 Claude Fischer quotes Alexander Graham Bell as foreseeing, and extolling, the social use of the telephone, even if others in the industry did not. I guess there are different mindsets, and some people sometimes give us the best of both worlds.

Here is a related humorous blog post:

Tuesday, May 2, 2000
IT'S COOL WHEN AN INSIDER LEADS A REBELLION

Passover was a couple of weeks ago. In listening to some commentary on the radio about the holiday, I started thinking about the timelessness and general interest of some of the themes in the Bible. In the Passover story, which we tell over and over again each year, we learn of Moses, who was born an Isra-elite slave but brought up as a free member of Pharaoh's court. It took him, a temporary Egyptian insider, to lead the people.

The story of a temporary insider who leads a rebellion is a timeless story that people like to pick up on, I thought. My mind looked for a computer example. Years ago, such a story was of the young Bill Gates, working with IBM to make their PC, going off on his own and helping create the PC industry that toppled much of IBM's dominance. Oh, my! Bill Gates as Moses! (Would it then be Steve

Ballmer as Aaron, the better talker?) That was how the story was portrayed. There must be other examples, I thought.

Well, there are, and we still hear of the insider leading a rebellion. Today, of course, Bill and his company are the dominant ones, and a story that comes up over and over is of Rob Glaser, once VP of Multimedia and Consumer Systems at Microsoft, now leading its competitor in multimedia, RealNetworks. Rarely do you hear a story about RealNetworks without hearing of "the man who founded RealNetworks after spending years as a Microsoft executive."[9]

Just some thoughts while driving home from work while listening to the radio . . .

http://danbricklin.com/log/2000_04_17.htm

Source Material

So far I've covered commentary about the IBM PC written in retrospect, with a few images of material from the early days. This next section consists of a transcript of a recording made the day the IBM PC was announced. You get to "hear" what we thought was important at the time, what IBM wrote in its marketing material, and more.

IBM PC ANNOUNCEMENT 1981

> *Transcript of Software Arts staff meeting on August 12, 1981, reading and reacting to the material from IBM announcing their new Personal Computer*

On August 12, 1981, the day the IBM PC was announced, VisiCalc's developers, Software Arts, held a staff meeting to go over what was happening. Like most of our full staff meetings, it was videotaped with home video equipment so employees who missed it could watch it later. Little did we realize that a segment of this tape would appear as part of PBS's *Triumph of the Nerds*[10] TV documentary 15 years later. PBS people told me that at the time they put the

---

[9] http://news.cnet.com/2009-1023-238221.html

[10] http://www.pbs.org/nerds/

show together it was the only appropriate video they could find from that day. Here's a picture from the tape:

The meeting was in our air-conditioned computer room and I do most of the talking for this part of the meeting. What follows is a transcript I made to commemorate the 20th anniversary. I've put some annotations that should help you understand the transcript better in "Notes About the IBM PC Announcement 1981."[11]

The transcript

Dan: We called this staff meeting for several reasons. One, so I can get laryngitis, yes . . . If we turn it [the air conditioner making so much noise] down . . . the temperature of the Prime [(the minicomputer used to run the company and do development)] has been rising over the last half hour. You have to watch it carefully. If you want to turn it off for a few minutes, you can, but if we can't do the whole meeting . . . [Comments] I'll move up.

Julian: The Prime is getting excited over the announcement.

Dan: Yeah . . . Here we go. Is that better? [adjusts lapel microphone] This is so that if you miss it, you can hear it again later. [Laughter][12]

We're calling this staff meeting for a couple of reasons. But the reason we're calling it right now is that it was the first time we felt that we could all get together after we got a package in the mail from the people down in Florida,

---

[11]See later in this chapter.

[12]It's always ironic to hear comments like this years later. Now we are used to seeing ourselves in old video, but in those days people would laugh when you implied that you'd want to hear something like this later.

which [noise of taking things out of an envelope] . . . has a picture like this on it [excitement]. Supposedly, maybe at this very moment, IBM is announcing their Personal Computer. We don't know that yet. Until we know that we can't tell anybody, but everybody here is supposed to know about it so we're allowed to tell you. They were nice enough to send us all their brochures, their press release, so we know everything that occurred, everything that they said. We're only allowed to tell people outside what they have publicly announced. They are not going to announce all the technical specs, which most people here don't know, so it doesn't affect you, and they are not going to announce some other things like that. Not all the prices have been announced. They announced quite a bit. Barbara right now is finishing collating a copy for everybody of the press release, the letter that came with it from them, and a few highlights of some of these brochures. Just to show you one of them, here's one that says VisiCalc on the front, and on the back it says VisiCalc is copyrighted by Software Arts [positive reaction from audience],[13] and there is some more on the hardware.

Me pointing out attribution on a brochure

There is only one place that I found where they mentioned what processor chip is being used, if people ask you that, but they did mention it on this and you are getting a copy of it so you'll know. OK?

---

[13]Attribution was considered important. Such notices were often the only way that most users were exposed to the names of the companies behind certain software that was distributed by other companies. Having people know who created software that they liked could help in the marketing of other products.

Me reading the material from IBM

The letter comes addressed to Bob. It says, "Dear Mr. Frankston: I am very pleased to share the IBM Personal Computer announcement information with you. I think you will agree our cooperative efforts have resulted in an outstanding product of which we all can be proud. Please note that the attached information is not to be disclosed prior to any public announcement."

[Voice from the back of the room]: It's on the ticker.

Dan: It's on the ticker? OK. So now you can tell people. [Laughter and excited sounds from the audience]

Part of a frame shown on the TV show[14]

---

[14]This little segment (with "It's on the ticker" and Julian Lange looking at his watch) is one of those included in the PBS documentary. It is followed by the narrator, Bob Cringely, saying, "What we are watching are the first few seconds of a one-hundred-billion-dollar industry." It is interesting how a chance happening (the sound of phones ringing and the news feed ticker mentioned) and a common gesture ended up getting us both on television years later.

"If this information should become available to the public prior to a coordinated public announcement, it could seriously detract from the overall success of our joint efforts. This information is furnished under the provisions of the existing confidential disclosure and other agreements between IBM and your company related to restrictions on disclosure," (which most of you have read). "Following the product announcement, you may wish to refer to the press release, fact sheet, and promotional brochures in answering any questions from the public concerning the product. Anyone with questions requiring more detailed technical information than provided by the announcement material should be referred to IBM. It is our intent not to provide a more detailed technical description until the product is made available to the public." (In other words, any more than is in here you are not supposed to tell people, you are not allowed to tell anybody.) "On behalf of all of us who have worked with you and your people, we would like to thank you for your efforts in making the announcement possible. Please pass on our sincere appreciation to your staff. If there are any questions that you may have about this information please feel free to contact me . " dah, dih, dah.

Bob: [something about an IBM employee in Yorktown calling to find out more about the machine]

Audience: [laughter] They called us?

Dan: I'll read just a little bit of the press release. You can read it in detail when we get them. It's datelined New York, August 12th. "IBM Corporation today announced its smallest lowest priced computer system, the IBM Personal Computer. Designed for business, school, and home, the easy to use system sells for as little as $1,565."

Audience: Whoa! [some clapping]

Dan: Dah, dah, dah, dih, dahtah, dah. "Sold through participating Computerland dealers and Sears Roebuck and Company's new Business Machines stores, beginning this fall." It's also going to be sold through IBM Product Centers and a special sales unit of their own division. It says here software for it, it has BASIC from Microsoft, it'll cover popular business and home applications, for example Easywriter will store letters, manuscripts, and other text for editing or rapid reproduction on the printer. Businesses can use an accounting system, it's Peachtree, it generates balance sheets, tracks accounts, and automatically prints checks. VisiCalc (trademark) is available for applications ranging from financial analysis to budget planning. Microsoft Adventure brings players into a fantasy world of caves and treasures. [Lots of laughter.] OK. They've also contracted with Digital Research and Softech Microsystems to put CP/M-86 and UCSD Pascal on the machine.

Here's the interesting part to a lot of people. "The IBM Personal Computer can be tailored to fit the user's needs. A basic system for home use attached to an audio tape cassette player and a television set, would sell for approximately $1,565 in IBM Product Centers," meaning it may be discounted elsewhere, "while a more typical system for home or school with a memory of 64K bytes, a single diskette drive and its own display would be priced around $3,005." [Audience: Whoa! Some talk. "$3,005?" "Around . . ."] "$3,005. An expanded system for business with color graphics, two diskette drives, and a printer," it appears to be the Epson printer, "would cost about $4,500." [Audience: Surprise.] Pretty competitive! "The IBM Personal Computer was developed at the Information Systems Division in Boca Raton, Florida," that's why nobody else knows about it, "facility, and first deliveries will be scheduled for October." OK, so that's, and it weighs this much, and it's this big, and whatever. [Bob: I need to see what is says about it . . .] Everybody is going to get a copy of this to see all this stuff.

"Applications Software: VisiCalc is a problem solving package for financial mathematical forecasting, computation, all data is arranged in a grid of 63," dah, dih, dah, "what-if, VisiCalc has vertical or horizontal scrolling, easy cursor and ability to vary formats." [Question: How much is VisiCalc going to cost?] It doesn't say. The other thing is that they released another press release that "IBM to publish user generated programs for personal computers." "Computer program authors who write applications for the IBM Personal Computer may have them considered for publication by the company's new Personal Computer Software Publishing Department. IBM employees, external authors, professional programmers to hobbyists, can submit programs for consideration." [Audience: DEC's had that for 15 years.] Rumors that we hear, not from IBM, that are not confirmed, are that they have reserved a goodly number of machines for internal use, so there will be machines around that people can play with. "Packets to tell you all about that will be available for outside authors about September 30th" and they give an address to write to. It says elsewhere in here that their people will write it on their free time. [Laughter]

So here's the VisiCalc brochure, which Jeff has already pointed out that the screen is a little strange. Some of the things have moved around from where they really are in VisiCalc, but it's good enough.

Hardware, shows the hardware, picture of VisiCalc, same one I think. [Audience: It was the only one they had running?] Well no, they have another one, but it's the best one they had though. [Looking through brochures] General

August 1, 2001

Ledger by Peachtree, you know, Accounts Payable by Peachtree. [Audience: They mention Peachtree?] Yes. All of them say copyright on the back by whoever copyrighted it, like Easywriter by Information Unlimited. Peachtree got them to put "by Peachtree Software Incorporated" in the front, it appears to be because everybody else has a name on the front that is their own trademark, but Peachtree Accounts Payable is not their paid trademark. They have Accounts Payable, General Ledger, Accounts Receivable. Communications, which is a way of using it as a terminal. [Question.] We don't know, it appears to be theirs, it doesn't have . . . "The modem shown is for illustration purposes only and does not constitute an endorsement by IBM," dah dih dah, get your own. [Audience comments.] On the back of the home one it says "the television set shown is for illustration purposes only and does not constitute an endorsement by IBM." Easywriter, Adventure, Software. When they show software, of course inside: VisiCalc picture . . . VisiCalc picture . . . On the front they have Easywriter, they have Easywriter on the front. [Audience: Dan, who did they credit Adventure with?] Adventure is credited to, Adventure is copyrighted by Microsoft. [Audience: Microsoft?] It's Microsoft Adventure, it says on the front. "At Work" [Going through the brochure.] VisiCalc on the front, VisiCalc in the middle, VisiCalc in the very middle. This picture you're going to get a copy of. And VisiCalc on the back.

"For Learning," this is for home use. No, this is for learning use, you see people here, it has a person sitting here answering questions. "Question: Question mark. Picasso was: (A) an engineer, (B) a musician, (C) a painter, (D) a computer programmer. Answer: (C). Excellent." [Laughter] Was "excellent" spelled right? [Julian: Looks like excellent is spelled "A N T."] So, here we go. You have to have this picture. The wife adoringly holding onto the husband who is challenged by it as the kid gets it to play music or something. Ah, VisiCalc, VisiCalc, VisiCalc, VisiCalc, um, Picasso, Picasso again over here, and a picture of the keyboard playing music again over here.

Don't take these, they are our only copies. The one of VisiCalc you'll get both sides of this, the one of the hardware where it lists all the details over here that includes the fact that it's an 8088, you'll get a copy of that. If you want copies of any others we can make them in the front.

That's it about the IBM announcement.

We have some other announcements. [Julian: Does everybody know that HP . . .?]

Oh, HP announced the Apogee, called the HP-125[15] yesterday officially. It was in the *Globe*. The *Globe* . . . it was also in *InfoWorld* who did notice that it was the first time we had a VisiCalc on CP/M. The *Globe*, good old Ron Rosenberg, he says that, you know, you can buy it for this much, and then if you do this it raises the price to $10,000, ah, $10,600, and if you buy it with VisiCalc that "jumps" the price to $10,800 or something, so it's $200 on the Apogee. That machine is now out, and has been shown around. If you would like to see the brochure on it, there is a one-page blurb on it that mentions VisiCalc. We have a copy of that. [Question: Where will this stuff be kept?] This? Julian will be keeper of it for now. Julian is the keeper of all this stuff. [Julian: There's going to be a locket that someone has made . . . it's going to carry it around with me . . . in a suitcase.] We will try to get more. They were nice enough to send us this. We got it, was it, Monday? It came Monday, afternoon.

[Julian: Anyone who wants copies of anything, just . . .] The full press release you are going to get and that letter telling you. Remember you are not allowed to say any more than what it says in the thing, but since it appears it has been, it has been announced, you can say whatever it says on the press release and stuff. [Julian: That's a good reason to read the press release fairly carefully at least once through so you know what you can say.]

The machine is still secret. It has to be, we are not to say we have a machine, we can't show anybody the machine until it's generally available, and we can't use it for anything except for VisiCalc, that's still is the way that it is. [Audience] Yeah. [Audience] Can we run Adventure on it? [Laughter] I think that after Lisa did so well at getting PSI to get our name on the front maybe can see if she can get us a copy of Easywriter and Adventure. It would be a good thing to try.

[End of that part of our meeting—the rest was about moving to a different building. In the middle of that part someone mentions that Dick Shaffer of the *Wall Street Journal* had called to ask questions.]

http://www.bricklin.com/ibmpcannouncement1981.htm

---

[15]The Hewlett-Packard HP-125, code-named "Apogee," that I was talking about was a personal computer that had a touch screen. Using invisible light beams in the bezel around the screen, it could detect touching the screen. Since then, HP has continued to make pen and touch-sensitive computers. For example, in 2008 HP announced a line of "TouchSmart" computers with touch-sensitive screens. In late 2008 they announced multi-touch systems that can detect gestures using more than one finger.

To better understand this transcript, read the companion commentary I provided in "Notes About the IBM PC Announcement 1981," which follows:

··

NOTES ABOUT THE IBM PC ANNOUNCEMENT 1981

What is "the Prime," "the ticker," etc., in the transcript?

Here is commentary about some of the items mentioned in the transcript "IBM PC Announcement 1981":

- Microsoft and Intel: Notice that the operating system was barely mentioned. (At the time, it was called the "IBM Personal Computer Disk Operating System (DOS).") There were optional other operating systems "contracted." "Software" referred to the applications. Microsoft was listed as the supplier of BASIC and Adventure. The processor used (the Intel 8088) was worthy of just a minor mention. Nobody knew what would be important years later. The decision IBM made to use their products nonexclusively helped Microsoft and Intel become dominant in their industries.
- The Prime: This was the large minicomputer from Prime Computer that we used as a timesharing system to run the company. Using "dumb" DEC VT-100 terminals connected by serial lines or dial-up modems, we edited programs and documents (using our own version of the EMACS text editor that Bob Frankston wrote), used our own email system, compiled programs, etc. The Prime, like most computers, was sensitive to heat and produced a lot of it, so we had an auxiliary air conditioner in the large room that housed it. That room was the only one that fit the whole company for such meetings.
- Florida: Since we were dealing with IBM in Boca Raton, Florida, we called it the "Florida machine."
- The Ticker: As part of our R&D, we had a UPI news wire feed to the company. The comment that the news about the IBM PC was on the ticker meant that we saw it on the news feed just like news organizations around the country. A normal person couldn't just point their browser to CNN.com and hit "refresh" in those days.
- Bob, Jeff, Julian, Lisa: These were other Software Arts employees other than Dan Bricklin (cofounder). Bob is Bob Frankston, cofounder, and cocreator of VisiCalc. Jeff Stephenson is a programmer who actually did

most of the work converting CP/M VisiCalc for the Zilog Z-80 micropro-cessor to run on the Intel 8088–based IBM PC. He used a special variant of our macro assembler that automatically did some of the conversion and flagged potential problems. The original assembler was written in PL/I by Bob, with the additions written by David Levin (my cousin). Julian Lange was our president, and ran the second part of the meeting. Lisa Underkoffler was VisiCalc product manager and interfaced with our publisher, Personal Software/VisiCorp.

- Copyright and other notices: With many author/publisher relationships going on in the industry, and many new manufacturers deciding which software to pay to migrate to their system, getting proper attribution was considered important.
- Our IBM PC prototype: The first prototype we received was literally a breadboard—it was a circuit board on a piece of plywood with sockets to plug in a keyboard, etc. It got better over time. We kept it secret by putting it in a locked room that you could only get to by going through another room. Jeff, who was the main person working with it, was a black-belt Zen swordsman, so we assured IBM it would be well protected.

http://www.bricklin.com/ibmpc1981notes.htm

Hopefully, you get a feel for the excitement of different developers at the introduction of the IBM PC and see how it has evolved and continues to evolve. I recently watched an old video recording I have of a walk-through of the huge 1983 Comdex personal computer tradeshow. It is almost shocking to see how primitive some of those systems seem today yet how excited we were about them and how many companies were making their own versions. Most of the systems being shown were character-based, with just a few demos of the unusual mouse-based GUI systems. The primitive Microsoft Windows demo on the tape took place two years before Windows 1.0 shipped in 1985, and the Apple Macintosh was still unreleased, awaiting the breathtaking "*1984*" Super Bowl television advertisement to start telling the world.

Looking back 25 years to that Comdex video and seeing what we have today, it's clear that in the next 25 years we'll have other quantum leaps in several areas that will make today's systems seem just as primitive.

Reading this and the previous chapter, I can see how one future evolutionary path will be towards very large screen sizes. One size will be used to watch entertainment and communications and to do large individual productivity work. Another size will be even larger for group collaboration. (Already you are finding early such systems in schools and some businesses with devices like the SMART Board interactive whiteboards.) These systems will use touch and pen input—they will be more interactive than the huge screen showing "Big Brother" in the Apple "*1984*" advertisement. I also think we'll soon see better microphones and better video input for communications and authoring.

The IBM PC is hardware, developed by a large company. In Chapters 11 and 12 we'll look at software, developed by a few individuals. First, we'll examine the genesis of the wiki, where the germ of the idea was developed by an individual within a large company but the first incarnation of the type of system we have today was created as a tool to help him when he was consulting on his own. Then we'll look at the electronic spreadsheet, where the idea was conceived in a business-school classroom and the code was developed in the attic of a rented two-family house.

11

The Wiki: An Interview with Its Inventor

Ward Cunningham is best known as the inventor of the wiki. That means he came up with the idea for, and the first implementations of, a particular form of tool behind Wikipedia and many other reader-modifiable web sites. It is a system that, among other things, lets you create, read, and edit web pages using only a browser. The wiki has become a major way for groups to build a common repository of knowledge and to interact. In addition to the value of the use of wiki software in enabling the creation of something as groundbreaking as Wikipedia, it is also used by companies and organizations to manage projects and provide support. Wikis have proven helpful to open source projects and other activities carried on at a distance and have inspired the development of other reader-modifiable systems.

I first met Ward at a conference in 2006 (about wikis), a little more than 11 years after his first wiki implementation, and immediately hit it off with him. We went out to dinner at the Grendel's Den restaurant in Harvard Square and talked about old times in the computer business. I asked him if I could call him on the phone sometime and record a podcast about how this tool came about. He readily agreed and a transcript of that long call appears in this chapter.

In the "Introduction" I wrote about how the case method, which this book reflects, is similar in some respects to immersion learning for teaching a

A photo I took of Ward Cunningham when we first met in August 2006

language. Here, as we get close to the end of the book, I present an interview carried on between two product-developing engineers, Ward and me, as a form of total immersion. The other interviews were with people who come from other fields, and we tried to talk in a more neutral language. That is much less the case here. You should see in this interview some of the themes that have come up before in this book, such as trying to understand in a deep way how things work, the joy of solving problems, and more. Hopefully it will help you better understand inventors and the process of invention.

As I stress in Chapter 5, I'm not a professional interviewer, and this transcript is pretty raw and true to the actual audio. Try to read this as a conversation, not a speech. You may also want to listen to the original recording by going to the web site (the appropriate URL is noted). The timecodes in the transcript should help you jump to a particular part. I put in topic headings every once in a while to help you keep track of the conversation.

Ward Cunningham, February 14, 2007[1]

Dan as Announcer: [0:00] This phone interview was recorded on February 14th, 2007. The noise you hear in the background is not typing on the keyboard, but it's snow blowing up against the window once in a while—it was a quite blustery day!

Dan Bricklin: [0:14] Hi! This is Dan Bricklin, and with me today is wiki inventor Ward Cunningham. Hi, Ward!

Ward Cunningham: [0:20] Hi, good morning, Dan!

Dan: [0:21] Hi, thanks for joining me. Let's start by having you talk about your background. Don't explain how it relates to wikis, at least not yet—but where did you work? What type of projects have you worked on? What technologies did you use? Where are you coming from?

Ward: [0:38] Oh, gosh! I fell in love with computers in the college days, and that was back when we worked on big mainframes. I worked for the university and got plenty of access to that mainframe, so I enjoyed the quick turnaround.

First we were exploring timesharing, and I would fiddle with the timesharing terminal always trying to find a new way to put a problem onto the computer. At one point, I wanted to know how everything about computers worked, and I think back then you stood a chance, of course it's a big deal now.

---

[1] http://danbricklin.com/podcast.html#danbcast-2007-02-14-23-07-30

Dan: [1:20] Were you a computer science major or something?

Ward: [1:22] No. I was an electrical engineer, and I had graduate work in computer science.

Dan: [1:26] Where?

Ward: [1:28] Both at Purdue. Yeah, I grew up in Indiana. I'm an Indiana boy, but after hanging around for 10 years, I decided that if I weren't a faculty member that didn't make sense, so I took a position at Tektronix[2] in Beaverton, Oregon. The thing that impressed me is it looked like a college campus.

I worked in their research labs, initially on human factors. In college, the microprocessor had come along, and I embraced them and figured out how to squeeze big problems onto little computers.

That's what I did for my first four years at Tektronix. We imagined new kinds of electronic instruments that would be available. I wrote the first windowing system at Tektronix, and had a touch panel in front of it.

Working at Tektronix

Dan: [2:21] They were making, like, oscilloscopes?

Ward: [2:22] It was heavy times back then, because there was so much was possible.

Dan: [2:27] They were building like oscilloscopes, and stuff?

Ward: [2:28] I got tired of working on those small machines, and when the integrated circuits came along, the VLSI[3] design, I wanted to get back to my electrical engineering roots. So, I said, "If I do a little circuit design, I'll get to have a big machine again."

Dan: [2:45] Weren't they making measurement equipment like oscilloscopes, and things like that?

Ward: [2:51] Oh, yeah. In fact Tektronix is a company full of electrical engineers,

An old Tektronix oscilloscope

---

2 Tektronix is a major manufacturer of electronic test and monitoring equipment, such as oscilloscopes and signal generators.

3 Very Large Scale Integration (VLSI) design—designing integrated circuits.

and not all that many of them were good at digital electronics,[4] and even fewer of them were good at computers.

My boss hired me and he said he wanted some of that big system experience applied to little systems.

The usability—of course that was the '70s. Xerox PARC stuff was leaking out from them of what they were doing, and we just dreamed of the days that we could paint anything we wanted on a screen and make it move. It's hard to remember back then that things didn't move around on a screen very easily.

I was attracted to the little machines, because you could do more with them. You got the full access to the processor; you didn't have to share it.

Dan: [3:50] Now, you were working on usability for engineers who were using this stuff?

Ward: [3:54] Oh, absolutely. I had this system where you could have a waveform on the display, and you could just put your finger on it and slide it back and forth.[5] The cool thing is you could put your two fingers on it, and you could stretch it, squeeze it, or stretch it. That went back and controlled all the acquisition electronics to reacquire the waveform.

Dan: [4:17] Oh, so you had a two-finger just like the new iPhone?

Ward: [4:19] I had a two-finger touch panel display. It turns out it was one-finger only vertically, but two-fingers horizontally, because that was easy to build at the time.

Dan: [4:30] What technologies were you using?

Ward: [4:33] Gosh, we did 8-bit microprocessors, and we used multiple microprocessors. I wrote a little operating system that would send messages back and forth.

In reality, just a faster processor would have been better, but it gave us bank switching. We would load up each microprocessor with full 16 bits of addressable memory. We would switch into different banks of memory by just sending a message to a different computer.

Dan: [5:11] What languages were you using, and stuff?

---

[4] Digital electronics, such as those used in computers, are designed around the idea of manipulating two voltage levels, symbolizing the 1 and 0 of binary numbers. Analog electronics, which was the traditional domain of test equipment such as that developed at Tektronix, is designed around more smoothly varying voltages, such as seen on the waveforms displayed on oscilloscope screens or found in the sound signals in a stereo amplifier. The way things are built, and the components you make them out of, are different for the two types of electronics.

[5] Notice how touching screens keeps coming up throughout this book. This is an area that has always been of interest to many people.

Ward: [5:14] That was when Tektronix at that time had some pretty smart people in their computer systems group, and they thought they needed a language designed for 8-bit microprocessors and they named it after Tesla, it was called "Tesla." It was kind of FORTRANish, and kind of C like—it sort of anticipated C, but it wasn't quite C. It didn't have a runtime stack, so it was hard to do recursion.

Dan: [5:48] Did you use . . . ?

Ward: [5:48] But [inaudible] wasn't very well supported by those 8-bit machines at the time, so that was OK.

Dan: [5:55] Did you use any other languages around that time?

Ward: [5:57] Well, of course, I had seen [the] UNIX [operating system]; I did a little bit of UNIX when I was back in college. It was just coming out of Bell Labs at the time, and when UNIX showed up inside of Tektronix, I was all over it.

In fact, we bought one of the first [DEC] VAX [minicomputer] systems to work on integrated circuits, and I called it "Tekchips." Got into a little trouble with the IC guys—they said, "Well, if anybody is going to have a computer named 'Tekchips' it would be us," but I had gotten there first and named it "Tekchips," and designed integrated circuits on it.

Of course, about that time, it was interesting, because we had this idea that if you kind of like understood everything from top to bottom; to understanding the problem at hand, to knowing how the transistors work. Carver Mead called that the "Tall, thin man," that you could design systems on a chip.

The people who were doing a lot of that were [at] MIT. I went out to MIT and spent a couple of weeks out there with the people who were making chips there and came back with a lot of ideas, but one of the ideas that impressed me the most was that they sure had the confidence to program anything.

Those graduate students; if they could understand what they wanted, they knew they could program it. I admired that level of . . . Well, I kind of felt that off and on myself. I said, "I want to feel that more," and so I studied as much as integrated circuits, I studied how they programmed, and that was really my introduction to Objects.

Computer Languages and Objects

Ward: [7:47] The system there was, I think, it was Flavors or some variation. It's easy to make an object system when you're working in LISP, and they worked in LISP.[6]

---

[6] LISP is a programming language favored by Artificial Intelligence programmers. It was originally developed at MIT. Flavors is related to LISP.

So, I studied LISP, I came back to Tektronix to my research lab and I said, "Well, we got to buy a LISP machine,[7] or I won't be able to do this integrated circuit work," and that didn't get a lot of traction.

But, it turns out, as I was looking through the code to this guy across the hall: he was working on something, and darned if it didn't have the same idioms that I had seen in this MIT code. The idiom is kind of . . .

Dan: [8:30] What do you mean? What do you mean by an idiom?

Ward: [8:32] Well, there was this thing . . . I mean, I worked for a graphics company and we had this notion, that "move" and "draw" is how you would draw on the screen. Whereas the MIT guys they would draw a figure by saying, "Make a figure at the origin, and then move it to where you want," and that idea. I said, "Why would you draw it in the wrong place, and then put it in the right place, instead of just draw it in the right place?"

They had this command called "Align With," so of course what we were drawing is transistors. So, they would say, "Draw a transistor at the origin," which is not where you want the transistor—but then you could say, "Align the input point at the center of the input path of this transistor, to the center of the output path of this other transistor," and it would move it to the right place.

So, I call that the "Align Width" idiom. I've never seen that before. It seems so strange.

Now, I later realized that what that's really doing is saying: I'm going to draw a complicated object. Instead of having me remember where all the input points are and all the output points are in this complicated object, how about the object itself remember them.

Even though I just drew the object, I'm not going to keep track of all that. Instead, I'm going to just simply, when I want to later, ask that object where those points are. And that's why it made sense to draw it at the origin, where it was easiest to draw. Then later, figure out where you really want it when you have that object created and you can let it help you while it could participate.

It was fully formed and it could participate in your calculation of where it should ultimately lie. It turns out that I saw that exact same idiom looking through what turned out to be Smalltalk.[8] It was both the design procedure

---

[7] A special computer tuned to running LISP programs.

[8] Smalltalk is another programming language. It is object-oriented—a style of software development that has become very popular.

language at MIT was a listing, we still had paper. It was about three or four inches thick.

And Smalltalk, at that time, was a listing that was three or four inches thick. I read them both. I said: Man, I'm going do integrated circuit design tools in Smalltalk. And I tell you, that was my introduction to Object.

Now, I'm in a lab at the time that has some usability work going on, some instrumentation work going on, but I also had an artificial intelligence group. I thought if I'm going to get to keep this Smalltalk thing, I've got to go convince other people to use it.

So, that's when I became an evangelist for Smalltalk. Just in my own little group we ended up getting about, I don't know, 20 or 30 people to program in Smalltalk. That was a pretty fun time. The guy across the hall was Allen Wirfs-Brock and he wrote the first good implementation of Smalltalk on a conventional computer. Before then, they had all been done on specialized hardware, with a specialized engine.

So, this was a powerful language, kind of coming into the performance range, where you could do practical work.

Dan: [11:56] So, you went from programming operating systems, working on user interface to working on building chips. That's about as high and low as you can go, and into objects.

Ward: [12:05] Well, I really believed in this tall, thin man thing, you know. Of course, I was never very good as an electrical engineer, because I couldn't remember all the part numbers. But, when you are designing the chips at the transistor levels, you've got P transistors and N transistors. I could remember that much.

So, I really liked that. Now, it turned out that isn't the way that industry evolved. Somewhere along the line, I did develop a little processor that would solve a graphics problem. I managed to make an array of those on the surface of the chip. The plan was to do about a ten-by-ten array. So, that would be 100 processors on one chip.

At that time, you could mail this off by email and have the chip fabricated. A few months later it comes back and there you got a surface made by email.

So, that was an interesting problem, because it really was a system. If I didn't understand the mathematics of how this graphics is going to work, I would have never been able to figure out how to lay out the transistors.

Dan: [13:21] How big were the projects? How many people on your team?

Ward: [13:25] Oh, I think, I was kind of the point of contact between two teams. There was one team that was interested in the graphics. They had the idea that there should be a universal graphics standard. This is before PostScript[9] filled in that role. So, they were looking for resolution-independent descriptions of graphics. And I think, they had about 10 people working on that.

Then, I had another group that was interested in integrated design tools, or integrated circuit design tools. That's what I was in, and there were probably five of us. But, I just said: Well, let's do a project and I'll go work with this other team. So, I think there were . . . It was really me and part-time one other fellow doing it.

It turns out that was interesting. Now, again, we had this, I think, it was a quarter-of-a-million-dollar CAD system[10] that would design an integrated circuit. It was kind of bumping up the limit of its capabilities, because of the way it represented designs. The 16-bit integers that it used were only so big.[11]

The fellow who helped me design this, he was a real zealot for Forth.[12] So, he just designed his own design system in Forth and I was his user.

Dan: [14:53] The closest thing to Forth nowadays is like PostScript or something?

Ward: [14:57] Oh, well PostScript uses a Forth-style language. It was a simple language, but I consider Smalltalk a very exotic language, but it's very good at expressing abstraction. And Forth is the same way. Forth is very good at expressing abstraction, but instead of using objects, it uses a stack. Instead of hiding the width of a number, it embraced it.

So, I considered them both very sophisticated languages, but in the opposite end of the spectrum, in terms of the difficulty of implementation. You have to be very smart to put together a good Smalltalk interpreter, but almost anybody can put together a good Forth interpreter. In fact, that's kind of how you learn Forth, by writing a Forth interpreter.

---

[9] PostScript is a computer language developed by Adobe Systems that is best known for its use as a way of controlling the creation of printed material. It helped usher in desktop publishing when it was used in the Apple LaserWriter printer. Aldus PageMaker and other programs produced PostScript "programs" as output.

[10] CAD stands for Computer-Aided Design, like the drafting systems used when creating buildings, airplanes, and, in this case, computer chips.

[11] Computers usually store numbers in binary in a fixed number of consecutive bytes (8 bits each) for use in calculations supported by the hardware (and therefore performed most quickly). In the older minicomputers and many microprocessors they used 2 bytes (16 bits) to store integer numeric values. Only about 65,536 different values could be represented in those 16 bits. Today's computers have hardware that can easily directly operate on a much larger range of values.

[12] Forth is another programming language.

But, the interesting thing was, so really my interaction with Tom is I would be designing this chip. Every time I had a little trouble expressing how this chip was going to be realized in transistors, I would just go in and tell Tom. Tom Almy was the guy who wrote the system.

I'd say: You know, your Forth system isn't very good for designing chips. And he would say, "Oh, well, what's the problem?" And I would tell what was difficult. He would go home that night and invent a new part of the language. The next day, it would be easy.

Dan: [16:25] Now LISP, Forth and all are very extensible languages.

Ward: [16:31] Yes, and Smalltalk. And so, what we are tapping into here is this ability to . . . All right, so here's an idea. Computing should be easy. I don't know how it got to be hard. But, whenever computing is hard, what you ought to stop and say, there is something wrong with my approach. Let me adjust my approach until it is easy again.

And that's what I was doing with Tom. I didn't want to stay up late working on the Forth system, but he loved it and so I just told him that it was hard for me to know. He said, "No, it shouldn't be hard. It should be easy." So, he would figure out what I needed to do my job the next day. Oh, it was great.

Dan: [17:08] So, you were working on . . .

Ward: [17:10] I was probably using half of him, so one and a half people built the CAD system that outperformed a quarter-million-dollar system. Oh, did I mention it ran on a Radio Shack TRS-80?[13]

Dan: [17:24] Oh, my God.

Ward: [17:25] Yes. So, we just designed this hundred processor VLSI chip on a TRS-80.

Dan: [17:33] Oh, wow.

Ward: [17:34] Because as long as he is building his own system, he was careful to make sure that he never cancelled out the precision of the 16-bit numbers and . . .

Dan: [17:49] That's like less powerful than a telephone today.

Ward: [17:52] Yeah, yeah. And it would compile up the whole chip. I would say, "OK, run all my code that makes the chip," and it would run in 15 seconds.

Dan: [18:02] So, what do you do after Tektronix? Is that when you came up with the wiki?

---

[13]An early personal computer, less powerful than the original IBM PC.

Ward: [18:09] I showed all this Smalltalk stuff to my friends and tried to get more funding for VLSI design with Smalltalk and they were more interested in the Smalltalk than the chip work. So, I ended up evangelizing Smalltalk off and on.

Finally, I decided, look, if I'm so good, instead of telling other people how they should write programs, I should just go write programs myself.

Dan: [18:35] So, what year is this?

Ward: [18:37] Oh, this must have been about 1987, 1988.

Dan: [18:46] OK.

Financial Software For Securities Trading

Ward: [18:47] And so I said, "Well, OK. I'm loving this Smalltalk stuff. I got to go find a real job, not a research job, where I am actually building software. I need a job where the stuff is complex. There has to be natural complexity. Otherwise, anybody could program it."

I wanted to come in and I wanted to solve problems with Smalltalk and its ability to, as you mentioned, extensibility of the language, I wanted to build the abstractions I need to solve a problem. And I ended up in finance writing software for trading fixed-income securities.

Dan: [19:28] At what company? Or at another company?

Ward: [19:30] The company was called West Coast Software. It was acquired about the time I joined by a consulting company called Wyatt, and so we called it Wyatt Software Group.

Dan: [19:44] So, you were working in the financial world with the millions of dollars changing hands . . .

Ward: [19:50] Actually billions.

Dan: [19:51] Billions?

Ward: [19:52] Yeah, so that 16-bit precision was not enough.

Dan: [19:56] And it has to be up[14] because when it goes down money falls on the floor.

Ward: [20:00] One of the interesting things was, again, working with abstractions, we just decided to use unlimited precision arithmetic. And in fact, if we divided two unlimited numbers, we saved the numerator and denominator, we didn't actually do the divide. And that meant that there was no place where we ever had to round because we had unlimited precision on the left or the right.

---

[14] "Up," meaning that the computer is working; the opposite of "the computer is down."

Of course, that didn't mean we didn't make a mistake every now and then. We'd be looking at a screen full of numbers and our business analyst would say, "Well, you know, if I looked at this report and this report, these numbers should be the same" and we'd look at them, and they're off in the fifth decimal place.

Dan: [20:46] And this was all in Smalltalk?

Ward: [20:48] Yeah, this was all in Smalltalk. And somebody would say, "Oh, well, it must be a rounding error," and I'd just look at them and say, "Well, it's not a rounding error, because we don't do any rounding."

I can't tell you how important that was for us finding a way to drive the last bug out of those calculations, and not be able to just pass it off as a rounding error. Now, of course, I was a little worried because, again, this was on fairly small machines—this was a PC at the time, but I think it was 286s or something, they weren't that powerful—to have a megabyte of memory was a big deal.

Dan: [21:28] How did you learn the financial world?

Ward: [21:31] Oh, that was interesting. I learned it by programming it. We had, again, some great consultants—I'm trying to remember the guy's name—again, another MIT guy came out and spent a few days with us and taught us in two days what he normally taught in a semester in fixed-income security trading.

He described that as equivalent to chicken processing; as you're chopping up the chicken and taking out the white meat, whatever's left you've got to find a way to chop that up and sell that, and whatever's left from that you find a way to chop that up and sell that. That's really what you do in fixed-income securities. If you have a little risk here, you find somebody who wants that risk and you sell it to them.

Dan: [22:16] How big was the group that you're working with?

Ward: [22:20] That was from four to eight, depending upon how you count. The funny thing is the fellow who recruited me into that group had already told his management that the program was 90% done and that was after working for a month or two on it. So, they thought, "Well, another few weeks and we'll have this program done," and it turns out it was another nine months.

So, right off the bat, within two weeks, I was late, so I just stopped worrying about that and started worrying about actually delivering value every day. To me, delivering value means understanding something that I didn't understand and getting it into the computer in the way I could wield it.

Dan: [23:08] So, how long were you there?

Ward: [23:10] I worked on that one program for almost four years and in the process, I developed a new distribution of responsibility; instead of focusing on promising dates and making them or not making them, we focused on what are we going to do week by week—how much effort do we think something is and when will we know when we're done? And when we've put that amount of effort in, if it isn't going well, we know that there's something that needs to change, but it wasn't like we were doing the wrong thing.

This, ultimately, became Agile software development.[15] What we did is we worked up financial models for everything that we were coding. We actually did them all on a spreadsheet. So, we would work them up on a spreadsheet from looking at the contract and then when we coded in Smalltalk, we compared the Smalltalk against the spreadsheet.

Now, the spreadsheets were for instance, we'd say, "Here's an example." So, we'd do examples on a spreadsheet and then we would code in the Smalltalk as systematically as possible where every kind of thing can hook with every other kind of thing. So, we were kind of system designing in Smalltalk, but we were putting financial instrument understanding in a spreadsheet.

Then, we just read the spreadsheets into Smalltalk and reported where they matched and where they didn't match. And where they didn't match, we knew we had more work to do. We had a little system where you could click on a number that was wrong and start single stepping immediately.[16] That was neat.

We had, at that time, they called them the Big Five, a Big Five Accounting Firm came out to audit what we were doing and they had never seen anything like that. We could browse . . .

Dan: [25:03] That's interesting, there you have a step by step . . . finding out . . . how to be able to find where errors were.

HyperCard

Dan: [25:14] Now you hadn't developed the wiki yet, at this point, I take it.

---

[15]Agile software development is a methodology for going about developing computer software. It is more of a management thing, like an organizational style, than a technical thing, like a particular computer language.

[16]Single stepping is a debugging technique where you slowly execute the computer program statement by statement to closely observe its operation as part of trying to find the cause of errors.

Ward: [25:17] No, no, although I had played with HyperCard.[17]

Dan: [25:23] Oh yeah, this is where you first did?

Ward: [25:25] I thought it was a fantastic program. That showed up while I was still in the research lab and I took the time to play with it, to understand what it wanted to be. I guess, when I was in college it was that period where whenever you had an idea, you invented a language to represent the idea, so you had to learn like a language a week. I was always just used to learning languages.

And with object-oriented programming, one language could kind of make all the different objects, so it may have had to only be an object a week instead of a language a week, or an API[18] a week, I guess is our modern terminology.

Dan: [26:05] So, it's kind of like the difference between a language and a different object written in that language. It's new things. It's all the same space.

Ward: [26:14] Yeah, I got tired of learning how to write arithmetic expressions in every different language, I just wanted arithmetic that worked. But, I wanted to know: what was the real semantic difference between this language and that language? And I love getting into how things worked underneath and what worked well in it.

Dan: [26:35] So, HyperCard was one that you learned.

Ward: [26:36] What was that?

Dan: [26:37] So, HyperCard was one that you got into.

Ward: [26:38] Let me go back to our testing. One of the interesting things is we had our—they're called quants—they're rocket scientists or physicists who would read the contracts and write formulas, and he would make some mistakes and I would make some mistakes.

So, when there was an error on the screen, when we were comparing our spreadsheet results to our Smalltalk results, the interesting thing is we would look at the pattern, this was all in a table, and we would highlight everything where they disagreed and if we saw scattered mistakes, like a little mistake

---

[17]Apple's HyperCard was a programming system that let you work with a series of screen displays that could contain text, images, etc., and navigate among those screens (or within "stacks" of "cards") with visual elements like buttons and clickable images. It was used to create educational applications, interactive games, data storage and retrieval systems, and more.

[18]Application Program Interface (API) is the specification of how a software system interfaces with other programs. It is like the instruction manual that lists all the ways to control the system, how to give it data, and how to get data from it. For example, Windows has a different API than the Mac OS operating system for drawing graphics and characters on the screen.

here or a little mistake there, he would say, "I bet I made a mistake in selecting it, probably just didn't set the formula right."

But, if we saw a whole column was wrong or a whole row was wrong, then we said, "Oh, it's got to be a systematic error," so that's probably a mistake I made in the Smalltalk because that's where we were being systematic.

And I would say, nine times out of ten, just by looking at the distribution of errors, we could guess correctly whether it was his mistake in setting up the problem or my mistake in coding the solution. And that's an example of how these different systems have a different semantic in figuring out how they want to be.

I say that kind of in prelude of going back to HyperCard. I had this HyperCard thing show up on my desk and people said, "Well, what's HyperCard? Is it a graphic system, is it a painting system, is it a database, whatever?" and I looked at that and I thought, "Well, I guess, it's a database for things that aren't in rows and columns," because, of course, we knew about SQL by then and how database management systems wanted everything in rows and columns and this seemed to be good at irregular data.

Building a Program for Irregular Data, and Learning That People Like Clicking from Page to Page

Ward: [28:37] So, I set out to write a program that would capture some irregular data, because I wanted to feel what it was like to really do an application, and I wanted an application that wasn't too important. So, that project was perfect.

I set up this application to take care of who knew whom and who shared ideas with whom inside of my research lab and, in fact, inside of my whole company. And I would ask people to come and use the program.

In fact, people kind of drifted over when they heard I had this cool thing from Apple called HyperCard, and I'd give them a demo. Then, they'd say, "Well, what's this good for?" And then I'd show them my application, and it turns out that they loved filling out hypertext.[19] So, I said, "OK. So, I found kind of a sweet spot on hypertext here."

---

[19]Hypertext is where you have multiple pieces of displayable data on a computer and you can jump from one piece to another through links of some sort. Web pages are a form of hypertext (including especially the pages of a wiki), as are the Help systems for many software applications. The term was coined by Ted Nelson (ted.hyperland.com).

Dan: [29:28] What do you mean? They liked to use it or they liked to fill it out? What do you mean?

Ward: [29:31] Well, they liked browsing it. Hypertext has this kind of nice sense. When you have it set up well, you're reading something and it says, "Well, if you're reading this, you'll probably want to go to one of these three other places."

Dan: [29:48] And on the Macintosh people played Manhole and Myst and stuff.[20]

Ward: [29:52] Yeah, that made a great game where they said, "Oh!" The hypertext is going to align with a physical place, like some island, and you would travel around the island.

Dan: [30:01] So, people like clicking.

People's Motivation to Build, and Early Wiki Principles

Ward: [30:03] In my thing, it was traveling around the project history of my company. People would be reading about a project, and they were probably imagining, "Oh yeah, I knew that project was over in Building 50," or "I knew that project was done down in Wilsonville." But, I didn't have a geographical metaphor, just everybody knew the project name if you worked at the company for a year or more.

They were moving around through this space of people and projects and even time. So, you'd get close to something that was important, and then you'd look at the links coming out of it and you'd say, "Oh yeah! This is even more interesting!" And you'd click on it, and maybe there isn't anything there. And they'd say, "Well?" and HyperCard made this easy, if there isn't anything there, why don't you type it? It was WYSIWYG.[21] So, when you got to some place where you wished there were something there, if you knew anything at all, you wrote it down. So, it had this nice two-way characteristic. It's like a blank slate, except that it doesn't have any bounds.

Dan: [31:12] We have engineers who when they see a problem they like to fix it. So, here, when they get to a page where they expect to see something, if it's not there, they like to build it.

---

[20]These were very popular computer games. Manhole was first written in HyperCard. It showed a scene and you had to guess where to click to get to another relevant scene.

[21]What You See Is What You Get (WYSIWIG) refers to systems where the users feel like they are directly manipulating the output, like most word processors, spreadsheets, drawing programs, etc.

Ward: [31:22] Yeah, they like to write it!

Dan: [31:23] OK.

Ward: [31:23] And the nice thing about it is they don't have to write an introduction or a conclusion, because it's a hypertext. It's right down to, "This is the page where you would explain about how this project interacted with those people on this idea," and you just write down what it was.

Dan: [31:39] They're engineers. They're not going to write a novel.

Ward: [31:42] Three sentences and you're done. So, it had this nice effect of . . . Well, the way I think about it now is it's kind of trading off the ease of reading—because I think hypertext is actually a little harder to read than a good novel—for ease in writing.

The ideas are all kind of jumbled together in our collective mind, so the hypertext kind of captures that jumble. And if you want to read it for some purpose, you have to forage through that hypertext. You have to go hunting for the gems that you want. So, there's this kind of sense of being lost, having to look.

I think, anybody who's ever searched for information on the Internet, you know, you go to Google and you say what you want, and they say, here's 10 places you might try or here's 30,000 places you might try, and then you start looking. That's the foraging feel. I don't think we'd ever really felt that much back in, I guess, this was around '85. It was cool to experience that for the first time. That was the heart and soul of hypertext.

Now, I've seen some demos where some author had cooked up his version of a hypertext, and all you got was the flair. If we assume that hypertext is a little harder to read than a good novel, then all I got was the hard part. But, when you make it writable too, I got the easy part. The hypertext makes it easier to write.

If we think about this blank slate, well how big is this slate? That's like a blank piece of paper. Well, the first thing you have to do is decide how you are going to divide up the page. How much space should I spend on this part? How many pages am I writing?

But, in hypertext, you just don't worry about that. You write your first page, and if you need a second page, you write your second page, if you need a third page, you write your third page, and pretty soon you've got 10,000 pages. And all that time it seemed like the right size.

Dan: [33:54] So, what year did you do this at that company? This hypertext, what all our projects are?

Ward: [34:01] It was within a year of HyperCard coming out.

Dan: [34:08] OK. When you were at Tektronix still?

Ward: [34:10] When I was at Tektronix. I had seen the prototype of it, because my friend Kent Beck had gone down to Apple, and it was floating around inside of Apple. I don't know if he was supposed to, but he showed me this thing and said, "Hey take a look at this." So, as soon as it was available, and that was on the Mac.

Dan: [34:34] Did you use this at the next company?

Ward: [34:36] I did! Actually, when we were doing the financial software, I took that same stack that was for tracking ideas, and I had this idea that our code should just be so carefully written that you could just read the code if you knew it. But, then every now and then people would come into my office and they'd say, "Ward, I'm having trouble. Can you explain how blah blah blah works?"

So, I had to explain how blah blah blah works, and then I'd turn around to that same HyperCard stack and I would say, "How blah blah blah works." And I would just write down what I had just told him. So, I had a HyperCard stack, which was all the questions that couldn't be answered by reading the code.

Dan: [35:19] So, you basically did a frequently or infrequently asked questions or documentation that you built over time through what was this primitive wiki thing.

Ward: [35:30] Yeah. It was wiki-like, and I think that grew to about 100 pages. Some of them were frequently solved bugs, recurring bugs. I think, we only had about three of them that we just kept falling into the same trap. Finally, I said, I'm going to write down the answers so I don't have to think so hard next time.

It's funny. I remember doing that. I can't remember what the bugs were, but that was when it was handy, and I would just turn to the computer and go look it up. You know, it actually did more for me than it did for anybody else.

Because I love computers and I developed this ability to kind of keep all the abstractions in my head, as programs get bigger and more complex, I was the last one to lose track of the whole picture.

And that's why people would come to me to ask questions, because they would be on some interaction between different parts of the program that didn't normally interact. They would know parts, but I would know the whole. So, I was trying to capture that sense of wholeness in the hypertext.

Dan: [36:43] But, it wasn't sharable. It was just . . .

Ward: [36:45] It wasn't sharable, no. In fact, HyperCard at that time had something where you could actually put the stack out on a file server or something, but it didn't really work. There wasn't any machinery for notification or anything. There wasn't enough there. So, I'd made this simple stack, and I'd used it a couple of times.

I used it a third time, before I left Tektronix, working with a design team. When they would design stuff in a "not object" model, I would say, "Let me write that in object terms." I'd go in again, and I'd just write it in the stack. I'd use the same stack three different times, capture three different connectedness things.

Incremental Construction

Ward: [37:31] And there were a few little tricks in my stack that I really liked. Like I could refer to a page before the page existed, and that wasn't built into HyperCard. So, that was the one idea that I carried forward between all these stacks is you could refer to pages that didn't exist, and they would automatically link up when the page finally did exist. And that engineer came by and said, "Oh! I know something about that. Let me write it in."

Dan: [37:55] So, they'd think it was there . . .

Ward: [37:58] Right. Because I would just make the page at the instant you went and clicked on it.

Dan: [38:03] Right. But, you already said you think there should be a link here. You just didn't have the thing . . .

Ward: [38:07] Yeah. I said, "Well, someday I'm going to have to write about this and this and this." I'd just write down that someday I would have to write about it.[22]

Dan: [38:12] Right.

Ward: [38:13] So, some visitor comes along, and he clicks on it thinking that I've written about it. No—lo and behold there's nothing there! I say, "Well, why don't you write about it?" "Well yeah, OK . . ." Bump, bump, bump, bump, bump. He will say, "But there's also this, and this, and this." I say, "Well, we'll just make note of that."

At the boundary, there's this kind of boundary between the known and the unknown. What's known and what you don't know—and making that transition graceful.

---

[22]This portion of our conversation is about the feature of a wiki where you can refer to another page by typing its name as a link, even if the page doesn't exist yet. When you click on that link, the wiki software creates a dummy blank page that you can edit to actually make a page there.

What's great about hypertext is you can have a description that's useful, even when it's half-done.

I know that there's so many hundred engineers, and so many ideas, and so many projects; I could predict how big that hypertext would be. It would probably be 4,000 pages, and I only had 100, but my 100 pages were useful.

So, I think, the same thing about a computer program. When you're writing a big program you can kind of figure it's going to be an 18-month effort, but you want to find a way that program is kind of alive after the first month.

Dan: [39:30] Yeah.

Ward: [39:30] You want that first month to be useful; you want it to grow.

Dan: [39:35] Yeah, that is scaffolding one path through to start. Frankston and I always, that's how we program.

Ward: [39:41] Yeah. A very, very important idea, and somehow that got lost in the last decade or two. The people who are used to finishing programs knew it, but the people who were just trying to follow a formula for writing a program got these crazy ideas about how you were supposed to write down everything you were going to write, and then go write it one at a time, and hope it all worked it together.

Dan: [40:05] So, that same idea goes into the wiki-like thing if you can start with something that sort of is a scaffolding.

Ward: [40:13] That's right. You'd make your first page, and when that page gets a little awkward then you say, "Well, why don't we cut this first part and make that another page, and cut this third part and make that another page, and I'll just add the middle of a page." In fact, maybe that first part, you've moved it on another page, maybe that's really the beginning.

One of the problems is, where do you enter a hypertext if you have this web of information? There's no preface or conclusion. That's kind of like life, isn't it?

The APL Programming Language

Dan: [40:42] Is this the days when you were working with APL?[23] Was that back in Tektronix or . . . ?

---

[23]APL (A Programming Language) is a terse programming language mainly used on interactive systems. It uses a special set of symbols, and the operations are very powerful. For example, there is a symbol for minimum, and it takes only the two characters "+/" to sum a list of numbers. Reading and understanding someone else's APL program is often very difficult. It was popular in the 1960s and 1970s.

Ward: [40:48] Oh, gosh! APL was a strange animal, too, and I loved mastering that.

Dan: [40:57] That's that language that operators were a single character, they had a special . . .

Ward: [41:03] Yeah, and it had hundreds of them.

Dan: [41:05] Hundreds of them, and it had all sorts of arrays. You actually used the version that I programmed if I'm not mistaken, the one on a Honeywell machine?

Ward: [41:14] I remember talking about that.[24]

Dan: [41:15] Yeah, on a Honeywell machine or something.

Ward: [41:18] That's right. That's when I was back at Purdue, before I left college. I heard about APL and it sounded so neat, and I'd heard about the Internet. Everybody was going to different computers, because we had the . . . It wasn't called the "Internet," it was called the "ARPANET" back then.

I just decided, "Oh, I want to go to Multics," where they had APL, and I wanted to learn APL. I learned enough about it, but I didn't actually solve any problems on that.

It wasn't until I got to Tektronix a year or two later, and Tektronix made a version of their graphics terminal that had the APL keyboard. On the keycaps it had all those strange little symbols on APL, that's the big difference.

The other thing is I really had a problem that was a great fit with APL, and that was signal processing.

I was working in an instrument company. They actually acquired a lot of signals; they looked at me for insight into digital. So, I said, "I'm going to build a model of new kinds of instruments by writing long strings of APL characters," and I could.

Of course, I wrote a few extra little [mathematical] functions like, fourier transform, and convolve, and all those things that I'd learned in signal processing back at Purdue. I just had all those functions, but I could string them together, so I could write it.

So, I could be talking to some engineer and he would say, "Well, we ought to do this and this and this and this and this." I could just write that as one line of APL, hit carriage return, and see what the output would look like on the screen.

Dan: [42:58] Yeah.

---

[24]To my surprise, when I first met Ward, I found out that he had used a version of APL that I had led the development of at the end of college 34 years before. He was the first person I remember running into who had used it.

Ward: [42:59] What a waveform would look like. In fact, a lot of what I would do is, you know they would say, "Well yeah, that's great for a sine wave. But, what about the junky signals I have to deal with? How are you going to see glitches?"

I would say, "Well, where do glitches come from?" So, I would compose up, say we got a sine wave and say we have got some noise and say we have got this—I would sometimes write a line or two of APL that would produce a signal that looked so real that they couldn't believe I didn't have a probe hooked into the back of that terminal.

Dan: [43:31] So, you became very fluent in a language that you used a few characters to do things. You could just look at it and read it to some extent.

Ward: [43:39] Yeah. Yeah. Of course, APL, what was neat about that was you would make big arrays and that was great for signal processing. Then, if you wanted to make that array times another array you could end up with a matrix. And then, you could make it a giant cubical matrix. Pretty soon you are up to six or seven dimensions and it was a real struggle.

It was cool that you could use the computer's memory so effectively because it was storing all those dimensions. It was managing that memory.

Then, you would build up this thing. Then, you would say, "OK, now slice it and turn it and twist it and get me out a waveform and plot it on the screen."

Dan: [44:22] Yeah. Well, I remember programming that stuff because I did the other side. [laughs]

Ward: [44:26] Oh, man.

Dan: [44:27] I was inner/outer product.

Ward: [44:30] Well, I tell you, I would sit there.

Dan: [44:32] It's nice to have somebody use my code.

Ward: [44:34] It had a CDC supercomputer on the other end of a timesharing line. I would sit there. I knew it was in the building, but behind glass walls and stuff. I would just sit there at my graphics terminal and I would type a line, hit carriage return and boom, it would just flash up on the screen.

Every now and then I would write something. I would go to so many dimensions and so many vectors and whatever, I would hit carriage return and nothing would happen. I would say, "Hmm. I wonder what happened."

I would be looking at my code. All of a sudden the answer would flash on there. Wow, that was 10 seconds of stupid computer time.

Dan: [45:12] Wow.

Ward: [45:13] It is hard to imagine now that we all have our own computers and we get to wait on them all the time. But, back then, to use 10 seconds of computer time was a big deal.

Dan: [45:24] It was a lot of money.

Ward: [45:25] That was real money.

Dan: [45:25] Yeah.

Ward: [45:26] Most of the things I would type it could solve in 400 milliseconds. So, I had better think twice about that.

Dan: [45:35] Yeah.

Creating the First Wiki System

Ward: [45:37] So, this idea that every system has kind of a soul and you have to find that soul—of course, I was attracted to the ones where that system wanted to give me answers before I had finished a question, where I had this conversation with the computer.

I could put part of the problem in that I know and see some answers and then put a little more of a problem in and feel my way to someplace. I'll tell you, I was thinking about that.

Really, the foundation of wiki was to take that conversation that I was having with my hypertext system, the HyperCard thing, and throw it on the Internet.

Dan: [46:29] So, after you worked at this financial place, what was the step that got you to wiki?

Ward: [46:36] So, it turns out when I was still at Tektronix, we were starting to realize that the way ideas flow among people is really pretty complicated and worthy of study. While I was doing the financial software, I told my research friends that I was really going out to do field research.

But, that meant that I kept in touch with them and we talked about this "how is Objects going to change the world and why is it people have trouble understanding?" We started a line of research.

It was actually after I had left the financial company and I was doing my own consulting basically. Basically, I had let the computer teach me something for four years about finance and then I was going and consulting on that.

But, that's when we had our first conference on the subject of Software Patterns.[25] That's really what we ended up calling these ideas that float around. We could have called them software meme. Meme is a modern term for that.

---

[25]This is the concept of describing commonly occurring problems and how to generally solve them.

But, we said, "Gee, we need to work as a group. We have got 500 people on a mailing list that all want to talk about this stuff." I said, "Let me see if I can set up a repository using hypertext to do that."

I tried to do it with me as the editor. That just didn't work. Then, I said, "Let me see if I can get that self-editing thing going that I saw on HyperCard." I just programmed it up. I kind of invented a baby version of HyperCard. I just sat there and I started typing stuff into it and it was just exactly the right feel.

Dan: [48:20] Yeah.

Ward: [48:21] I said, "I've got it. I can get people on here. We can stumble our way from the knowns working toward the unknowns." It worked just like anticipated only people didn't have to come to my desk anymore.

Dan: [48:35] That was in 19 _ _ ?

Ward: [48:38] That was '95.

Dan: [48:39] 1995. OK. You wrote it in Perl?[26]

Ward: [48:43] I wrote it in Perl.

Again, Perl was a new thing for me because I had been in object land for 15 years at that point. Somehow the Internet blossomed. When I got back into there I thought, "I've got to get back into UNIX."

UNIX isn't objects. UNIX is a hierarchical file system full of characters. So, I needed something that could read and write characters. I had been an AWK[27] programmer years before. Perl seemed to be the new AWK.

I looked and I said, "This is an amazing language." It is very fast. Of course, people think it looks kind of junkie. But, I was an APL programmer so that didn't bother me at all.

Dan: [49:26] Right, it was gorgeous.

Ward: [49:28] I just started writing. It turns out wiki was really my first substantial Perl program. I'm a little embarrassed about it now because I really only knew 10% of Perl. I had read one book on it.

Dan: [49:40] Mmm. Which book?

Ward: [49:42] I read Schwartz.

Dan: [49:51] Not the Camel book?[28]

Ward: [49:52] Yeah, I think, it was the Camel book.

Dan: [49:54] OK.

---

[26]Perl is a computer language that is popular for programs that run on web servers.

[27]AWK is a computer language especially suited for processing text. It is popular with users of the UNIX operating system.

[28]Many programming reference books from O'Reilly have animals on the cover. A major Perl book that I use has a camel.

Ward: [49:56] Randal Schwartz was one of the authors. He is a local guy here. So, it was a Randal Schwartz book. It was Christiansen and Schwartz, I think.

Dan: [50:05] So, how much of what we now think of as a wiki did you have within the first six months?

Ward: [50:12] I had within one week, I had 95%.

Dan: [50:15] Wow.

Ward: [50:16] Of what I have as wiki. In fact, over the first few years of operation, mostly I took features out that proved to be unneeded. I kind of misunderstood.

I had some complicated way to make a link to a remote site. Then, I realized, "Oh, you should just type the URL. If you had 'http' at the front, that is enough of a clue. I don't need some complicated way of doing that. Just recognize it for what it is."

Dan: [50:47] Huh.

Ward: [50:48] Also, it was the first time I had really run a program 24 hours a day, 24-7 as they say. I had problems related to scaling. So, I had to watch the system. When it was teetering I would go, "Oh yeah, OK. I had better do this to it now."

So, I learned a lot of systems administration. But, no, the basic idea, I feel it is a historical artifact now. I think, as wikis go, mine is pretty ugly and old. It looks like a 1995 website. You can imagine what they looked like back then. But, I left it the same old way.

Now, I'll tell you, I think the Wikipedians, they have volume and a community that is so much bigger than mine. They have done a lot of innovation that I wish I had thought of.[29]

How to Use the Word "Wiki"

Dan: [51:44] Mmm hmm. Well, let's go back to your stuff. First of all, how do you use the term wiki? Because I have heard you use it as, "Well, wiki has this," versus a wiki or my wiki. How do you use it?

Ward: [52:01] I am pretty sloppy, I guess. But, what I had always imagined is wiki naming the technology that I use to make the site. I actually called my site the Portland Pattern Repository or PPR.

So, I was hosting a site called the Portland Pattern Repository. But, if you looked at the URL it named the program that I was running, the CGI script

---

[29]The software used to run Wikipedia was written later.

and that was called wiki because that was the technology. So, everybody else just called it Ward's Wiki.

Dan: [52:36] OK.

Ward: [52:37] So, the world's usage called my site the wiki, whereas I thought of it as the technology.

Dan: [52:47] So, just like you would say, "Well, Forth has this," you would say, "Well, wiki has this."

Ward: [52:53] Yeah.

Dan: [52:54] But, you can then say, "On my wiki I have this."

Ward: [52:58] That's right. That would be like saying, "On my Forth," which is really talking about on my Forth program.

Dan: [53:03] An instance . . . on my Forth program. OK. So, that's how people can use it.

Ward: [53:07] Yeah. But, as people start incorporating the word into so many other things, I think it has become an adjective. It means I think something that is done, they have grown. It's this whole idea of starting small and growing something and being in a community. So, if you have a bunch of people working together to grow something with shared input, people say that's wiki-like.

Dan: [53:39] Yeah.

Ward: [53:40] I love that usage. So, I like to see the word float around. So, if you say the Wikipedia, well that would be the encyclopedia that is done in the wiki style.

Dan: [53:52] So, do you have to make sure we distinguish carefully between Wikipedia, which is an instance of using wiki and . . .

Ward: [53:59] Yes. And it is an encyclopedia plus some.

Wikipedia and Other Uses

Dan: [54:02] Right. And just using wiki yourself or having your own wiki. They are different because people confuse it. They think all wikis are Wikipedia or because Wikipedia does it a certain way and has a culture of doing it a certain way, then every wiki has to be that way.

Ward: [54:22] Oh yeah. Yeah. See the first few years, I had that problem. Whenever anybody would try to make a wiki, people would start talking about their wiki and my wiki and because I had all the eyeballs, people would say, "Well, to heck with his. Let's just do it over here on Ward's wiki, where all the people are." That was called the—I think I called that a "wiki suck" where I would suck people into my wiki.

I think Wikipedia has a little bit of that going now. But, if you really want to do something up on Wikipedia you really have to adhere to the social norms that they have developed, which are all about writing in that kind of dispassionate, encyclopedic style.

I think it's fantastic that it has been so successful and I just love it as a resource. But, that's not all a wiki could be.

Dan: [55:17] Yeah.

Ward: [55:18] I run 15 or 20 of them now. I don't want to do a project without creating a wiki there just to collect what we are doing on the project. I don't want us to have to match the conventions of the encyclopedia authors when we are just trying to get some work done.

Dan: [55:36] Right.

Ward: [55:40] Every wiki I run—of course this is because I am a programmer and I know this piece of code—I just make another version of my wiki. I will get in there and I will just adjust it a little bit because I know how to program. I just get in there and I make it do something that it never did before.

Dan: [56:05] What did you add recently?

Ward: [56:06] As long as I been in computing, we have talked about end-user programmability. I think, that is a very elusive concept.

Dan: [56:11] What is something you added recently?

Ward: [56:14] I was just having this conversation. I said, "We should really understand how a wiki behaves in the same way we understand how a company behaves." We can talk about the balance sheet and so forth of a company. There's just a lot of convention. We know about inventory and things like that.

I said, "Well, we should study wikis that way." So, I started writing statements about, oh, "How does a reader of a wiki become a writer of a wiki?" Thinking I could build a computer model where I would say, "Well, let's say that every month 2% of the readers become writers." I am model building.

I'm not even at the quantitative level. So, I started typing this stuff into a wiki. I said, "You know what? I would like to just check my usage of terms. I have got 40 statements now that are statements about how people behave on wikis."

So, I wrote a little script that just looks up all the terms, lists them out alphabetically, and then lists all the sentences that use that term. It's the smallest possible step towards a compiler of this language that I'm inventing.

But, it just echoed back to me what I had been writing in a different order. So, I would use the term "reader" and "writer" to refer to people interacting with a wiki. Then, on this other form, everywhere I use the word reader, it would just quote those sentences back to me under reader.

Under writer, it would quote those sentences back to me under writer. It just let me read my own. What it did is it stirred up my own writing, and my writing was being slightly computer-ish. I was using terms carefully. It would show me where I was making sense and where I wasn't.

Now, my goal is to actually turn this into formulae so that I can come up with a model, like anybody doing a profit and loss statement, I could do a reader and writer loss or something.

Dan: [58:31] But, what you are doing is you are mining the data in the wiki, in that particular thing.

Ward: [58:37] That's right.

Dan: [58:38] In the tool you have produced.

Ward: [58:40] And the way I happen to implement it is because I don't have end-user programmability in my wiki. So, I just did it by throwing a little more Perl code at it.

What Makes Something a Wiki?

Dan: [58:52] So, I had this product I was working on, which was going to be an online creating spreadsheet. Then, since I started seeing that multiple people will be editing it, so it is kind of wiki-like. The name wikiCalc came up.

Ward: [59:05] Yeah.

Dan: [59:06] Suddenly, I am stuck with, "Hmm, what is a wiki and how will I know when wikiCalc is wiki-ish enough?"

Ward: [59:14] Ah, good question.

Dan: [59:16] So, I have been looking at what makes something a wiki. What are the special things? Where is the line when it is or isn't? We know Microsoft Word is not a wiki.

Ward: [59:29] Yeah. If you get more people working on a Word document, it gets worse and worse instead of better and better.

Dan: [59:35] And it's just missing . . . So, I have come up with a handful of things . . .

Ward: [59:43] Let me just say a couple of things that I think are really important.

Dan: [59:46] OK.

Ward: [59:47] First of all, having more people should make the experience better instead of worse. There should be some way that you can have an impact without affecting too many people. It should be incremental. You should be able to add a new page or something.

There should be a way that you can watch other people work, this is the "Recent Changes" [aspect of a wiki]. So, if you are sharing, you can see what other people are doing and you can take your cues from them. Or you can correct them if they are misbehaving.

Finally, I think, it ought to look pretty good. It ought to have a presentation that makes sense. In my case, it was pretty simple. But, it was this hyperlinking and the way you could remember what the words meant. The regularity of the presentation on my wiki actually made reading it easier then reading random web pages.

Dan: [60:51] What do you mean, "the regularity"?

Ward: [60:53] Well, one thing I did is I said that if you are going to make a link to another page, that link will look the same on every place you encounter it.

Dan: [61:02] Ah.

Ward: [61:03] If I make the page named "Ward Cunningham," you can't call it "Ward" in one place and "Dad" in another.

Dan: [61:09] Ah!

Ward: [61:11] I mean Dad is a pretty good name if it is my son writing the page. This is something that is built into hypertext that you can have the name of the page, the URL and you can have the name as it appears in the document be different.

Dan: [61:27] Yes.

Ward: [61:28] And I just said, "No. For my internal pages, it ought to all be the same."

Dan: [61:32] So you decided not to do that and specifically to try to enforce it.

Ward: [61:37] Well, by not providing any way to do anything but, I guess I was enforcing it. Of course, that is one of those things that those Wikipedians reversed on me. I think, they live with it.

Dan: [61:50] So, that is four.

Ward: [61:53] Well, let's just say however you achieve it. Wikipedians have a very consistent look. There is a lot of stuff there. When you go to a page, if you went to a page and it looked completely different than Wikipedia, you would be disappointed with the variability.

It's not just the frame. A lot of websites will have very elaborate frames around the page that, see, the left column, the top margin, the bottom margin. But then, they will have what you are going to get is kind of lost down in the middle.

The stuff that you add ought to be front and center.

Dan: [62:40] Yeah, that's some of it.

Ward: [62:41] I think I'm drifting into style instead of not what the essence of wiki is. The essence of wiki is about . . . **But, there has to be this thing if you can read it, you ought to be close to being able to write it.**

Dan: [62:53] OK.

Ward: [62:55] That is what is important. It shouldn't be much harder to write than it is to read. Your skills in reading it ought to be equal to your skills in writing it.

If I dare go back to that naming thing, I wanted people moving through my wiki to see a name and know what page it was, by not having different names in every place and that learning those names was a very important part of learning what was the nature of the conversation.

Dan: [63:28] Right. Well, it is the unique identifier. But, it is also something that can be used in a sentence.[30]

Ward: [63:33] In a sentence, it is pronounceable.

Dan: [63:34] Right. Now, basically, it does have multiple linked pages. That's kind of key I take it. That goes without saying.

---

[30]In a traditional wiki, a link to a page is displayed as the name of the page in blue with an underline (like normal links). When editing the wiki, you just type that name as part of your text. The wiki software automatically displays that text as a link. Ward used the convention that if a word had an appropriate mixture of lowercase and uppercase characters (such as ThisIsMyPage) it was considered a page name. Other wiki systems, such as the one used for Wikipedia, use other methods to indicate a page name (for example, in Wikipedia you surround the name with double brackets: [[This is my page]]).

When instructing a computer, there is often the need to have a way to uniquely identify a particular thing, be it a variable, a page name, or a spreadsheet cell, so that, for example, you can unambiguously refer to it in a formula or link.

When developing the spreadsheet, the form for unique names for data values was one of the important design decisions I had to make. In a traditional computer language, the author makes up a name for each storage location, often words like "TOTAL" or short names like "I" and "N." I decided that requiring the user to name each value would be too tedious for my system to compete with "the back of an envelope." I wanted an automatically generated name that would be easy for people to find meaningful and perhaps even be able to figure out on their own in advance. I thought of giving them names that included the sequence number in which they were created (e.g., "V1," "V2," etc.), but rejected that idea. By going to a grid layout for the whole sheet, which was different than the page layout systems I was modeling VisiCalc on, and using the paper-map-like grid naming convention of letters and numbers, I had an intuitive way to name cells. The letter-number combinations (e.g., "A1" and "D12") were easy for both the software and users to distinguish from numbers (which have no initial letters) and function names (where the first few characters are always letters). Like Ward's wiki, you could also refer to a cell before you put something in it.

Ward: [63:42] That is just so the space can grow, so there is always room for what you need to do. So, what did you come up with?

Dan: [63:50] Multiple linked pages.

Ward: [63:52] Yeah.

Dan: [63:53] The ability to name the page, which causes it to be created.

Ward: [63:58] Yes.

Dan: [64:00] And one that I have fallen down on in wikiCalc, that there is, in your case, it is text on a page. In other words, it is something that people can understand.

Ward: [64:11] Yes.

Dan: [64:12] There can be lots of it.

Ward: [64:13] Yes.

Formatting Text in a Wiki

Dan: [64:14] It can be paragraphs and you can organize it as you see fit.

Ward: [64:20] Right. So, it will grow a natural structure.

Dan: [64:22] Natural structure. So, it is not built-in. But, it is a structure that people can express whatever they feel comfortable expressing, using carriage returns and stuff as they see fit.

Ward: [64:33] Yeah. Yeah. It is more open than, say, a tax form.

Dan: [64:39] That's right.

Ward: [64:39] Where every single thing you type has meaning and the meaning is actually in the form, not on what you type.

Dan: [64:46] It's not like Semantic Web, that everything has to be tagged and all that; it's like a spreadsheet, where every cell can be whatever you want it to be.

Ward: [64:57] Yeah. It's where things can have meaning. But, if you have something that steps out of the meaning that you have written so far, you can still write that too.

Dan: [65:07] You can still write that. So, that was an interesting thing of using text. The free-form text was key. But then, you put in markup, because, as you say, looking good, to help express yourself you need things like headings and list items and stuff like that. And you figured out in the days what we could do in those days and put a markup language in.[31]

---

[31] A markup language consists of special characters or a special way of typing that is translated into fonts, indents, and other instructions for the program displaying the text. An example, from Ward's wiki, would be using three single quotes to bracket something to be displayed in bold, so that '''bold''' would display as **bold**.

Ward: [65:29] Yeah. I tried to align my markup—I just wanted it to be better than email. And email at the time was very flat. Well, I liked the idea of being able to have stretchy text, so there was not an assumed column width. At that time, I think, we just always assumed email was 72 characters wide.

Dan: [65:58] Yeah. It's still biting us.[32]

Ward: [66:01] I thought I wanted to be able to squeeze the window narrower. I think, this was built-in in the way Web worked at the time. I think it has been subverted a little bit with too much CSS.[33]

That was important to me. I liked bullets because I thought that was an organizational element where we are listing things. But, I wasn't inventing. I honestly used horizontal rules and people told me that they were awful. Maybe, horizontal rules are a gratuitous nod to the way people formatted web pages in 1995.

Dan: [66:37] Yeah, they wouldn't have had very much then. But, you used a very simple markup language.

Ward: [66:42] No, there wasn't much. But, the thing is, I wanted people to . . . One thing that was important to me, if somebody is telling a story in say six paragraphs and there is something wrong with the second paragraph, I wanted somebody to be able to go back and correct the second paragraph, not to have to write a seventh paragraph down at the bottom that says, "Oh, so-and-so made a mistake back there in paragraph two."

Dan: [67:06] Mmm hmm.

Ward: [67:08] So, it's this idea that the organization of the page was not the chronology of its creation.

Dan: [67:18] I view it as opposed to a blog, where chronology is the whole thing in many cases, I mean, it is an important part. The wiki is the end result is what you see.

Ward: [67:31] That's right.

Dan: [67:32] You are maintaining an end result.

Ward: [67:33] That's right. Some people have called that the timeless nature of wikis.

Dan: [67:40] Yeah, because you are maintaining . . . it is the state of the knowledge that you are putting in there.

---

[32]There are some email programs that automatically put in explicit carriage returns when a line exceeds 72 characters in length. This often makes reply emails ugly or breaks up long web addresses inappropriately.

[33]The Cascading Style Sheets (CSS) language and functionality on web pages make it much easier for the designer to control the display of text in a browser.

Ward: [67:46] Right.

Dan: [67:47] This is the current state.

Dan: [67:49] Now, it turns out that if chronology is important, if that is what you are writing about, of course you organize the paragraphs chronologically.

Dan: [67:57] Right.

Ward: [67:58] But, if what you are talking about is geographical, then you organize them geographically.

Dan: [68:02] Right.

Ward: [68:03] Choosing how you organize your production is as important as actually producing it.

Dan: [68:12] Yeah. That is one of the reasons that having wikiCalc with a spreadsheet editing metaphor lets you lay it out in those type of things.

Ward: [68:20] And that's what's beautiful about a spreadsheet versus a database.

Dan: [68:24] Mmm hmm.

Ward: [68:25] In a database you have rows and columns. But, in a spreadsheet you have cells.

Dan: [68:29] Yeah!

Ward: [68:31] Yeah. That is like saying in a tax form you have fields, but on a wiki page you have text.

Dan: [68:42] That's great.

Ward: [68:46] Yeah. There is probably a reason to have databases and tax forms.

Dan: [68:52] Yeah. Oh yeah.

Ward: [68:54] And there is probably a reason to have a blank canvas and some paint brushes too.

Dan: [69:00] Yeah.

Ward: [69:02] We are talking about something that is kind of in the middle, not as structured as computers typically are but it is not completely blank either. There is a style that you can adopt and it is productive.

Dan: [69:17] Now, the markup you chose is little characters inside, which, coming from APL that was like second nature I guess.

Ward: [69:25] Yeah. I would have rather been WYSIWYG [style editing]. If I had WYSIWYG—because HyperCard was WYSIWYG and I just didn't have it.

So, I said, "Well, I want to just make a simple little markup language, where it looks kind of like what the output is going to be, but the rules are easy to remember."

Gosh, I would not have done it if I didn't have to. But, I had to at the time. It turns out that it takes some really great programming to make something WYSIWYG on the modern Web.

I can't remember. I think, you have done a pretty good job of it. You are using all the JavaScript power of the modern Web.

Dan: [70:11] Yeah.

Ward: [70:13] So, I didn't have that to work with. So, I said, "I'll send some text back to the server and see if it can make sense of it."

Dan: [70:19] But, the thing you learned is that people learn to just look at certain symbols and remember what the idiom is. You learned that from the APL days.

Ward: [70:27] Yes.

Dan: [70:27] Eventually enough people can deal with a funny markup language instead of WYSIWYG to start.

Ward: [70:34] Yeah. It is kind of like getting inducted into your fraternity. It's not something you want to do, but now that you have done it, you are kind of proud of it. It is a hazing in a sense.

Dan: [70:46] Yeah.

Ward: [70:47] I'm embarrassed that it is there. It surprises me that people defend it so . . .

More about Why Ward Did Things a Certain Way

Dan: [70:53] Well, there are certain things you want to do that don't express themselves as well WYSIWYG.

Ward: [71:00] Yeah.

Dan: [71:02] Because you had the primitives and stuff. Another area was having an ID.

Ward: [71:10] Yes.

Dan: [71:11] Or a name so people can own their comments or not.

Ward: [71:15] Yes.

Dan: [71:16] Depending on whether people know who the names are.

Ward: [71:20] Yeah, I decided not to keep track of names. I found that people wanted to. So, I said, "Well, OK. Here is a convention. How about you put your name at the end of your writing?"

I was thinking of letters to the editor, where I read the letter and at the end I see whose name it is. "Oh, gee! That was from the mayor. How about that?"

As opposed to like dialogue style where the actor is in a play it says, "So and so, says this. So and so, says that."

That's what we were doing in email, and I wanted to de-emphasize the role of a person. It's something where I think I turned out to just be wrong, that people really did want to know who was speaking. They wanted to know who was speaking, so you could judge what the words mean. In fact, Wikipedia is criticized a lot for kind of minimizing the speaking.

Dan: [72:29] So then, there's also you keep a history of all changes.

Ward: [72:35] I didn't to start with . . .

Dan: [72:36] Oh, no?

Ward: [72:37] . . . because computer people were pack rats, but I think that keeping that history turns out to be important.

Dan: [72:45] When did you add that? What made you add it or did somebody else add it?

Ward: [72:48] Well, I added first the history when a browser showed up on the Net that would only save the first 256 characters of any page it edited.

So, whenever anybody edited with that broken browser, it would just cut the bottom off of every page. I had to put something in to correct that error. It wasn't actually malicious.

Dan: [73:09] Oh, so you put the history in for rollback purposes?

Ward: [73:11] Yeah, for rollback when someone's crazy browser came and wrecked the page. In fact that's what, I think, as people say, "Well, if everybody can edit, what if somebody wrecks it?" You say, "Well, obviously now they can't wreck it. So that's that."

I don't actually think people want to go back and read a lot of history, but you just don't want to be afraid.[34]

Dan: [73:35] Right.

Ward: [73:38] And that not being afraid, I think is important. I think that different cultures are different. If what you're making is highly finished, like a beautiful Wikipedia page where you're arguing about every tense of every word, or maybe thinking more of in calculation the final proposal on something with all the numbers just right.

---

[34]This exchange was an eye-opener for me. I thought that the ability to undo changes, and see revision history, was a basic idea in a wiki system. From what I heard from Ward, it was an accidental addition, later found to be key, put in to defend the system from a bug in another product.

Dan: [74:09] Or a spreadsheet where you want to do Sarbanes-Oxley auditing[35] and stuff.

Ward: [74:14] Yeah, then I think, "Yeah," you would want your computer to keep track for you. I had this feeling that people got so caught up with the history, trying to save every last thing that they did, that it was actually muting them. So, I did it without history, but in any wiki I've ever made for anybody else I said, "OK, you can have history too."

Dan: [74:38] So, how long was it before you ended up adding history?

Ward: [74:41] I think it was in the first year I had that one level of backup. I think, on my own site, I still don't keep anything after a month, but that's only because I feel that I should be faithful to the historical thing, and what I've done on other versions of wiki, which I wrote probably two or three years into it, I just save everything.

Part of it is when computers went from kilobytes to megabytes, and then from megabytes to gigabytes, then it just became less of an issue, and it's cheaper to save everything!

Dan: [75:23] Yeah. So, let's see, we're not going to have too much more time, so let's do just a couple more things in this area. I think we may want to do another call to discuss maybe spreadsheets and wikis, I think that might be interesting.

Ward: [75:38] Yeah, I'd love to talk about modeling.

Dan: [75:40] Yeah.

Ward: [75:41] What I really feel like now that you've interviewed me, I'd love to spend some time building some models in your environment and talking about your work.

Dan: [75:51] OK, well, we can do . . . Let's finish up this one. So, you got what, like another 5 or 10 minutes?

Ward: [75:58] Yeah, yeah. Just someone's coming over that we're going to move some furniture.

Dan: [76:03] OK, so let's see. I got to watch the video that they made at the Computer History Museum,[36] where John Gage interviewed you, and it was really good—really good!

Ward: [76:18] Yeah, I hope I haven't told too many stories that match that.

---

[35]Sarbanes-Oxley refers to following the laws passed in the wake of the Enron affair and where you want to have internal corporate controls relating to who did what when performing financial calculations.

[36]http://video.google.com/videoplay?docid=-7739076742312910146

Wiki as an Embodiment of Ward's Philosophies

Dan: [76:20] No, I think, we were able to do some of it different. One of the things I see is that there's this whole thing between software development, and how wikis came out of your whole doing software development and doing projects.

Ward: [76:38] Yeah.

Dan: [76:39] That using a wiki to do a project is where your mindset came from, not to do an encyclopedia but to do a project or something.

Ward: [76:48] Yeah. I have a very strong attitude about how software should be written in a group, and it's this kind of growing the software with it always working.

I think that was different, and also not divvying up the pieces; that I can work on the software you wrote, and you can work on the software I wrote—that's sharing.

Dan: [77:13] And you can always drill down . . .

Ward: [77:14] See, I was having arguments with my colleagues in the Patterns community about the idea. So, I was working in patterns where we were talking about how software is written—what is the world's experience with software?

But, I also had my experience in this financial company and so forth with what was emerging as Agile software development, and that was still unresolved on making this site.

So, I know that people are going to write about their software experience on this site, and I said, "While I'm at it, I might as well make it as dynamic and flexible—I'll make it as agile as I can." It's me, and I'm kind of rubbing my hands together in a sinister way as I do this. I think, "I'm going to trick everybody. I'm going to make a site that's more agile than they've ever seen, and on it they're going to talk about programming."

This was quite a coup, because as it started out, we were all talking about patterns of this, and patterns of that. Then, when the Agile software development—Extreme Programming it was first called—as people started talking about that it was a natural fit and it just kind of slid in.

Some of the people who weren't into Agile, who thought that was all wrong at the time were shocked. They said, "Hey! This whole community has shifted from being about patterns of software, and to turning into the extreme programming methodology site."

Dan: [78:52] The wiki, while mirroring it also helped it. I mean, a lot of development . . . I mean, I hear, at IBM, they use wikis for development, because it worked for open source projects, they're using it for all projects.

Ward: [79:04] Yeah, it's that case, and of course you can see it, because it's got my fingerprints on both of those things, but it's really the same fingerprints. It's just this idea that you can't know everything at once; you can't keep it all in your head.

You have to kind of move around the system, and computer programs have always been hyper. There's always been this link; there's always you're calling from here to there, and so forth. Now that the modern IDEs[37] will follow those links for you, it feels like you're in a browser.

Dan: [79:42] Yeah. I like how you talk about when you're trying to figure out part of a program, you may just look a little bit about a particular object to look a little bit of its method to understand what's going on, and you can always go deeper and deeper. A wiki sort of mirrors that in the documentation of something, that you can go as deep as you want or as not deep as you want.

Ward: [80:03] Yes, right. So, I was hoping that a structure would evolve, would emerge in my wiki that was as beautiful as a well-structured program.

I don't think I quite got that, because it's not as important that a wiki be well structured. On the other hand, maybe there is—maybe it's just that it's hard to look at it all at once.

Dan: [80:35] You made a statement about, "Objects are not about hierarchy, but about sharing."

Ward: [80:41] That's right.

Dan: [80:42] So, when you think in a strict hierarchical view, they're problems, because the real world isn't strictly—it might be hierarchically locally, but not on a global sense.

Ward: [80:55] Yeah, and in the Agile, the Extreme Programming stuff, worked better in Smalltalk than it did in other languages, because Smalltalk had very little hierarchy.

Dan: [81:06] How so?

Ward: [81:07] Well, I say that it had very little hierarchy, of course it had a hierarchy, but it didn't feel hierarchical. You had this object talking to that object, and if they could understand each other, who cared what the hierarchy was? The hierarchy was really there just to save time programming.

---

[37]Integrated Development Environments (IDE) are software tools that facilitate some of the tedious aspects of editing program code, especially in large projects with many components.

Now, whereas in C++ and some other programming languages—boy! You can't talk to that object if he doesn't inherit from the right folks. Just because it knows how to add, and you need something to add, if it's not the right kind of add it's not going to let you call it—it's a strict hierarchy.

Dan: [81:44] So, that's where wikis versus a database, because it's like it's free-form within the page, it's free-form within the organization of the pages, but you keep this consistency as, you say, of the name.

Ward: [81:58] Yes.

Dan: [81:59] So, if it's called a "duck," it's always a duck—something like that.

Ward: [82:04] Yeah, yeah, right. I was thinking, in [the programming area of] typing, they call it "duck typing," meaning that this thing is a "collection" if you can add to it, and remove from it, and search it—it's a "collection," and who cares whether it inherits from the "collection" class?[38]

Well, in the same way, if you have a page and it describes a person, and it has that person's name at the top—it's a person page. Now, I didn't have to create a type called, "Person page."

In fact when somebody discovered that they like to write notes to other people on their page, everybody would look at the bottom of their own person page to see what notes people were leaving for them.

That emerged as a paradigm—I thought, "Oh, gosh! That's so cool!" Of course, you wouldn't leave a note for a person on some other page, because there's nobody there to read it.

Dan: [82:59] Cool. The other thing "duck" comes . . . I remember Carl Hewitt, back who did Planner, one of these early languages. His statement was, "If it walks like a duck and quacks like a duck, you can't tell that it's not a duck."

Ward: [83:15] That's right.

Dan: [83:16] So, that's why we use ducks and stuff a lot in computer languages, is that . . . ?

Ward: [83:20] I didn't know that history. I heard it first as an explanation of Ruby's system. I said, "Oh yeah, OK. Same as Smalltalk, and if you want to call that duck typing that's fine," but that's Hewitt-ism?

Dan: [83:32] I don't know, I just remember him saying that back in the early '80s.[39]

---

[38]This is a philosophical discussion that will be most interesting to a computer language designer.

[39]I heard it said when I was at MIT, which was mainly in the early 1970s (and when I spent the most time with Carl). As I recall, it was said by Carl or someone describing

Ward: [83:35] Yeah, I think, everything comes from MIT. [laughs] That's what I've learned.

Dan: [83:39] Well, hey! Some of us did, it was kind of fun there, I'll tell you! If you didn't one of your professors did, I think is the way it worked out.

One last thing, because I think we better go. If people want to get more information about you, you have a website C2.com. For example, they can watch that great video of what you did at the wonderful Computer History Museum.

Ward: [84:13] I've had a couple of great interviews, and I think this will be the third.

Dan: [84:17] Oh, thank you.

Ward: [84:17] The first two, I put links to them. One is text pages in kind of a blog style, and the other is a video at the Computer History Museum.

Dan: [84:27] Yeah, that was really good. It's an hour and forty-five minutes, but it was well worth it. We'll do another one of these, but how did you get C2.com? That's a two-letter domain name, wow!

Ward: [84:41] I tried to get Cunningham, and it was already taken.

Dan: [84:44] When was this?

Ward: [84:45] This is in 1994, when I got my first Internet setup. I thought, "Well, my company is called Cunningham & Cunningham, Inc.," it's my wife and I. I wanted to call it "Cunningham" or "C" and "C," or something like that.

I realized that shorter was better, and then I just thought, "I wonder if . . ." I was looking up names, and all the good and short names were taken. I thought, "I wonder if numbers work?" and I like numbers. So, I said "C2," it's for Cunningham & Cunningham.

Dan: [85:20] That's really cool!

Ward: [85:22] Possibly, who would have thought? I guess, it also stands for "Command and Control," and a few other things.

Dan: [85:26] Oh, yeah! [laughs]

Ward: [85:29] I judge the health of the industry by how many requests a month I get to sell that domain.

Dan: Well, thank you very much, and we'll do this again.

---

his work developing computer languages. Carl included a version of the sentence as an unattributed quote in a paper titled "A Universal Modular ACTOR Formalism for Artificial Intelligence" (Carl Hewitt, Peter Bishop, and Richard Steiger, 1973, http://dli.iiit.ac.in/ijcai/IJCAI-73/PDF/027B.pdf). Carl tells me that he thinks it may be an old aphorism.

For the listeners: If you want some more podcasts from me, Dan Bricklin, go to Bricklin.com, there's a podcast link on my blog page. Thank you very much!

This is Ward's story. The wiki has opened up a whole new way of creating cooperatively. The group-constructed Wikipedia has become one of the major "first look" sources of information for people on a huge number of topics. This was made possible by a conceptually simple tool that lets us tap into the information and power distributed throughout a group. Through the invention of the wiki, you can see how one person helped harness that knowledge and the drive to share it.

Finally, it's time to tell some of *my* story with the spreadsheet, a tool that helps leverage the individual. I cover that in Chapter 12.

12 VisiCalc

The complete story of VisiCalc, including the people and companies involved, is a long one, way too long for this book. However, I think it is worth including some of that story as an example of the development of a general-purpose tool. It shows how a few people can create something that can have a great effect on the world and in many ways is not atypical of other such products. I've also included some related things I wrote about VisiCalc.

The VisiCalc Story

Background

I have a bachelor's degree in Electrical Engineering/Computer Science from MIT, class of 1973. In 1970, I met Bob Frankston, then a recent MIT graduate, when we both worked on MIT's Multics project. Multics was a groundbreaking operating system that was a precursor to UNIX and other systems. (The Multics project included hundreds of people.[1]) I worked on parts of the user interface (the command system) and the computer languages for applications programmers (APL and LISP). Bob worked on various systems and also had a programming job at Interactive Data Corporation, a large computer timesharing firm catering to the financial industry, and did consulting. He soon thereafter started graduate school at MIT.

After MIT, I worked as a product developer and programmer at Digital Equipment Corporation (DEC) on computerized typesetting and word processing. Those were the early days of computer-screen-based word processing. (The plain electric typewriter was king at the time.) After DEC, I worked on

---

[1] http://www.multicians.org/

microprocessor-controlled cash registers for the fast-food industry. Finally, in 1977, I entered the Harvard Business School (HBS) to study for an MBA. I studied accounting, finance, marketing, production planning, logistics, business law, personnel policy, and more.

HBS teaches by the case method. The students prepare for a class by reading a "case" that comes as dozens of pages of prose and figures describing a business situation. From that experience I saw how important, and how varied, layouts of text and numbers were in business. I'd "run the numbers" at home, doing calculations to determine optimal prices, project cash flow, list options, and more.

Here is a sample of some of my actual homework pages:

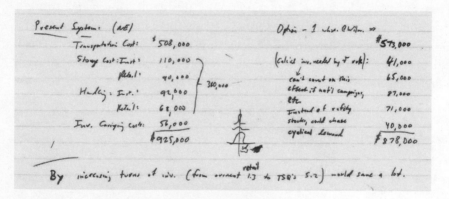

In class we would go over the work, comparing approaches, and discuss the issues. At home, I might have assumed a 5% advertising growth rate, but in class we might want to examine the effects of a 10% or 1% rate. All my figures would then be wrong. Thinking of how a word processing system "re-word wraps" text when you make an edit, of the interactive calculations of BASIC and the APL programming systems I had worked on, and of the two-dimensional layout capabilities of some computerized typesetting systems like the Harris 2200 that I was exposed to, I came up with the idea for "word processing with numbers." The idea was rough and needed lots of crafting to become what we now know as the electronic spreadsheet and to be practical with the limited power of desktop computers of the day.

In a private paper about an advertising issue required as part of a course on advertising at Harvard, I wrote in late 1978: "After hours of pushing numbers on pro-formas and production projections, [I] invariably found that one of [my] initial calculations was in error, invalidating all of the numbers that followed it. 'If only I had a magic piece of paper where I could change a number at the beginning of a set of calculations, and have all of the other numbers automatically recompute themselves . . . If only I had an electronic spreadsheet,' were some of the ideas that went through [my] head."

At the time, personal computers were in their infancy. The most popular ones when I conceived of VisiCalc were from Apple, Radio Shack, and Commodore. The Apple II, of which about 20,000 systems were sold in 1978, was just getting a diskette drive, and audio cassette storage was the most common. A personal computer with a lot of memory had 32K bytes (that's K, as in 1,024 bytes, not today's millions or billions). The IBM PC was three years away; the first Apple Macintosh, six.

In business, most "spreadsheeting" was done by hand, with paper, pencil, and perhaps a calculator. The calculations for production planning, I've been told, were often done on a blackboard, or a series of blackboards side by side. There were timesharing computer systems available for doing financial forecasting, such as those provided by companies such as Interactive Data Corporation where Bob worked or RapidData where my brother Jonathan worked, but these often cost hundreds or thousands of dollars a month to use.

Here's an example from the old days—it is part of a handwritten ledger sheet from my father's printing business:

31

	CUMULATIVE INCOME STATEMENTS 1960-61						
	7/1/60 to 8/31/60		7/1/59 to 9/30/60		7/1/60 to 11/31/60		7/1/60 to
	AMOUNT	%	AMOUNT	%	AMOUNT	%	AMOUNT
SALES - REGULAR	107474	471	1522555	408	2248888	421	3021734
MATERIAL	2525	—	8200	—	126	2	12600
OFFSET	1153394	506	2134687	572	2757889	560	3178729
LABOR ONLY	36950	16	49475	13	64225	12	102850
MATERIAL AT COST	15300	7	18725	5	24825	5	37550
TOTAL SALES	2282443	1000	3733642	1000	5108427	1000	6353463
PURCHASES: PAPER	408205	179	650642	175	894681	176	1107961
INK	27807	12	30257	8	43309	8	52309
BINDERY	67550	30	119615	32	210115	41	271210
OFFSET	242544	106	429550	115	508188	100	588055
ARTWORK	15832	7	30680	8	44689	8	57795
OTHER + OUTSIDE	102328	45	132948	36	186672	36	243140
TOTAL MATERIAL USED	864266	379	1393692	374	1887654	370	2320470
RENT	45000	20	67500	18	900	18	1125

Except where indicated, the next sections are based on the "History" section of my web site.[2] That section was first posted in early 1999. There has been substantial editing and additions to it at various times since.

The Idea

The idea for the electronic spreadsheet came to me while I was a student at the Harvard Business School, working on my MBA degree, in the spring of 1978. Sitting in Aldrich Hall, room 108, I would daydream. "Imagine if my calculator had a ball in its back, like a mouse . . ." (I had seen a computer mouse previously, I think in a demonstration at a conference by Doug Engelbart, and maybe Xerox PARC's Alto.) And "imagine if I had a heads-up display, like in a fighter plane, where I could see the virtual image hanging in the air in front of me. I could just move my mouse/keyboard calculator around on the table, punch in a few numbers, circle them to get a sum, do some calculations, and answer '10% will be fine!'" (Ten percent seemed to always be the answer in those days when we couldn't do very complicated calculations . . .)

During the summer of 1978, between first and second year of the MBA program, while riding a bike along a path on Martha's Vineyard, I decided that I wanted to pursue this idea and create a real product to sell after I graduated.

---

[2] http://www.bricklin.com/history/intro.htm

Here is a picture of me holding that calculator, a TI Business Analyst:

My calculator from business school

Eventually, my vision became more realistic, and the heads-up display gave way to a normal screen. I tried prototyping the product's display screen in BASIC on a video terminal connected to the Business School's timesharing system. (Prototyping is a great way to force you to work out design problems.) That's when the desire for general placement of numbers, formula results, and text turned into rows and columns, to give them human-friendly names. It also was when I decided upon the status line for displaying the formula and formatting behind the values being displayed.

The hope for using a mouse had to be replaced in the first personal computer prototype I wrote in the early fall of 1978 on an Apple II. The Apple II at that time did not have a mouse, but it did have game paddles. (These were dials you could turn to move game objects back and forth, for example in the game "Pong.") The game paddle was a very poor replacement for my original idea of using a mouse. Initially, you could move the cursor left or right by turning the dial. If you pushed the "fire" button, the paddle's effect on the cursor would change. Now, turning the paddle would move the cursor up and down. Pushing the "fire" button would switch back to horizontal movement. Through testing, I determined that the Apple II circuitry that interfaced with the paddle was too sluggish, and my pointing calculations were too slow and imprecise, to reliably and quickly position the spreadsheet cursor that way, so I switched to make use of the arrow keys of the Apple II keyboard. Since the Apple II keyboard had only two arrow keys (left and right), not the four we expect today, I modified my original paddle code and used the space bar in place of the paddle "fire" button to switch between horizontal and vertical movement.

I created that first personal computer prototype over a weekend on an Apple II I borrowed for the purpose from Dan Fylstra of Personal Software, later our publisher. I wrote it in Apple BASIC. It did not scroll, yet, but it had the columns and rows and some arithmetic.

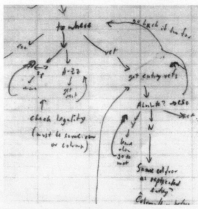

8 Oct 78 — Did Finance test program @ Personal Software.
Dan F. liked it.

12 Oct 78 — showed John Reese. He liked it — will comment.

13 Oct 78 — modified program. — Letter human interface.
Showing to Prof. Jackson wed. — Got Bob Frankston together w/ PS on
Basic program.

14 Oct 78 — did a bit more work @ PS.

Comments in my work journal which shows that first prototype done on an Apple II was October 8, 1978. I kept a work journal for most of the first few years of developing VisiCalc.

To design exactly how the program would work, I'd create state diagrams, showing what would happen when you pressed various keys. Here is one of those diagrams that included many features, such as replication, help, etc. It was written on the back of a sheet of spreadsheet paper, and has blue column and row lines showing through. It was about 17″ × 11″. (See following spread.)

Here is a detail, showing some of the steps in early replicate. Note that you could point with the arrow keys ("<->") and space bar ("sp"), since this was for the Apple II. "A-ZZ" referred to typing in the cell coordinate explicitly (e.g., "B14"). The Return key ("Ret") would get you some options for incrementing the value (one of several features specified that was not implemented in the first version of VisiCalc):

Detail of my state diagram

Dan Fylstra, who had graduated the year before from Harvard Business School with an MBA and ran a personal computer software company out of his rented apartment, made a deal with my friend Bob Frankston and me. The basic deal was worked out during dinner at Joyce Chen's Restaurant in Cambridge, Massachusetts, near Fresh Pond. Bob and I would create the program, as authors, and Dan's company, Personal Software, would publish it. This "author/publisher" arrangement became popular in the PC industry. Personal Software would pay us 35.7% of their net gross for normal sales, and 50% for OEM (computer manufacturer) sales. This was based, as I remember it, on an initial price for the product equivalent to the TI calculator (like the one shown on page 427) that was popular at Harvard ($35), less some costs, and then splitting the profit by some percentage. The OEM sale percentage reflected the difference in costs and other factors.

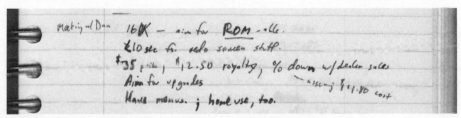

Notes from November 11, 1978, showing deal and requirements

These payment rates were high by publishing standards, but the founders of Personal Software were MBAs and computer people, and they saw the value of the product. Even with their sales of other products up to then of less than a million dollars, they were perhaps the largest publisher of software for personal computers at the time, helped by the popular MicroChess program written by one of their founders.

Bob and I decided to form a company under which to do business. Software Arts, Inc., was born, incorporating on January 2, 1979.

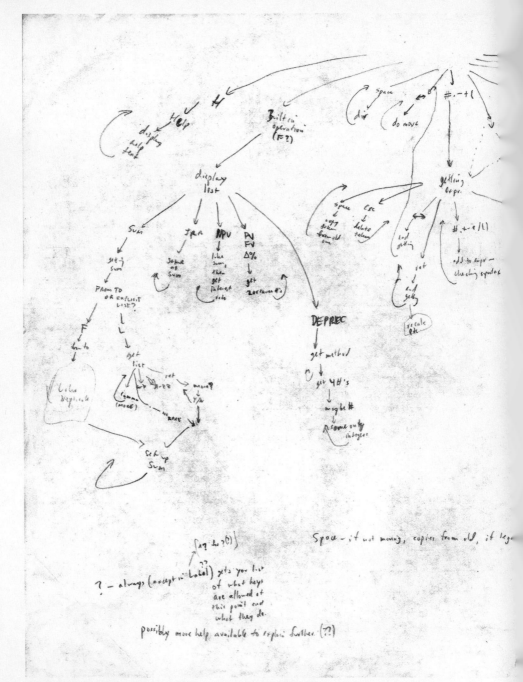

State diagram design for spreadsheet, from winter 1978-1979

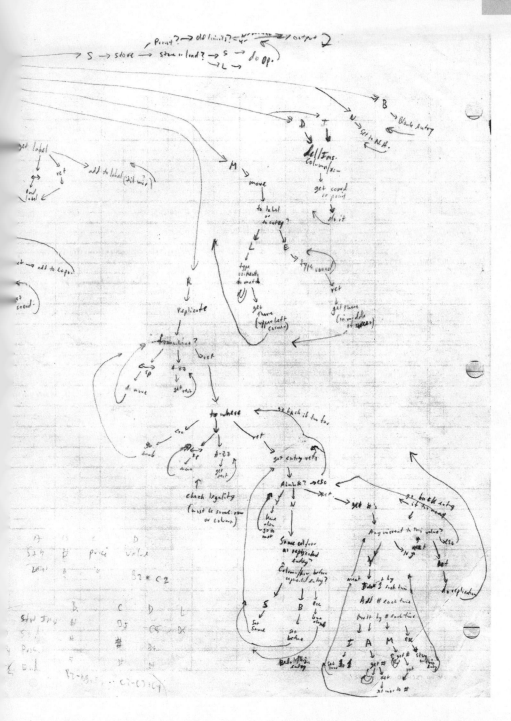

Patents

Here is the essay I posted when I first created my web site:

January 22, 1999

PATENTING VISICALC

We didn't patent VisiCalc at Software Arts because you really couldn't patent software prior to 1981, and VisiCalc was shown to the public in 1979.

Why didn't we patent the spreadsheet? Were we stupid?

This is a very common question, since, by the late 1990s, software inventions were routinely patented. Today, it seems negligent to ignore patents. However, in 1979, when VisiCalc was shown to the public for the first time, patents for software inventions were infrequently granted. Programs were thought to be mere mathematical algorithms, and mathematical algorithms, as laws of nature, were not patentable. The publishers of VisiCalc, Personal Software (their name at the time—later renamed VisiCorp), retained a patent attorney who met with executives from Software Arts and Personal Software. The patent attorney explained to us the difficulty of obtaining a patent on software, and estimated a 10% chance of success, even using various techniques for hiding the fact that it was really software (such as proposing it as a machine). Given such advice, and the costs involved, we decided not to pursue a patent. Copyright and trademark protection were used, and vigorously pursued. The enormous importance and value of the spreadsheet, and of protections in addition to copyright to keep others from copying our work, did not become apparent for at least two years, too late to file for patent protection.

At that time in history, and before, few fundamental programming concepts were patented. We all borrowed from each other. Just a few examples of concepts where patents played no role in those days: word wrapping, cut and paste, the word processing ruler, sorting and compression algorithms, hypertext linking, and compiler techniques.

Two years after VisiCalc was introduced, in 1981, the U.S. Supreme Court held, in *Diamond v. Diehr*, that: "a claim drawn to subject matter otherwise statutory does not become nonstatutory simply because it uses a mathematical formula, computer program, or digital computer." This, and other decisions around that time, changed the likelihood of receiving patents on software inventions, and eventually opened the floodgates of software patents. Unfortunately for the players in the VisiCalc story, it came too late to help us patent the spreadsheet.

Even after 1981, it was a long time before patents were routinely used in the PC software industry. Several years later, when Lotus sued the makers of products it claimed were too similar to 1-2-3, it used copyright, not patent, protection. Even then, using patents was not obvious to even the biggest players.

If I invented the spreadsheet today, of course I would file for a patent. That's the law of the land . . . today. The companies I have been involved with since Software Arts have filed for patents on many of their inventions. In 1979, almost nobody tried to patent software inventions.

Personally, I think that the fact that software patents started being granted so late in the history of programming (which was in full swing 30 years earlier in the 1950s) will cause all sorts of problems for the software industry. I have spoken publicly about this, and have even testified before Congress. Nevertheless, patenting software is encouraged by law, and I find it my duty to the shareholders of the companies I've been working for to take advantage of this protection.

For more on my views about patents, see my essay "Patents and Software."[3]

http://www.bricklin.com/patenting.htm

Here are my notes from that meeting where the attorney explained some of patent law to us and how it related to software:

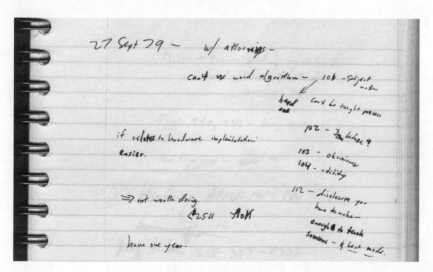

---

[3] http://www.bricklin.com/patentsandsoftware.htm

Writing VisiCalc

Software Arts was founded on January 2, 1979, by me and Bob Frankston. It was named by Bob while we were having dinner together in a fast-food restaurant we nicknamed "Kentucky Fried Fish." (It was an old KFC building reused by another restaurant.)

Our first location was in the apartment Bob rented in Arlington, Massachusetts. He worked in the attic:

Initial VisiCalc development in the attic

The inside of the attic looked like this:

The attic where Bob Frankston created VisiCalc, including Apple II and programming manual 12/21/78. Photo courtesy of Bob Frankston.

Bob wrote the vast majority of the program code for the original VisiCalc. I wrote drafts of a reference card and tutorial using a rented IBM Correcting Selectric typewriter. These acted as a specification of the product as Bob programmed. Here is an early copy of the reference card from February 27, 1979:

```
                         REFERENCE CARD    27 February 1979
What you can do at
MAIN LEVEL

←  →          - Moves the cursor.

space         - Changes the direction indicator.
;             - If screen is split, moves cursor from one window to the other.
!             - Forces a recalculation of all expressions.
                 manually
>             - Move command.  Requests coordinates of where you want to
                move the cursor;  you end coordinates with RETURN.

ESC           - Usually erases the last thing you typed;  used to recover
                from simple typing mistakes.

A-Z (letter)- Starts a label entry;  ended with ←, →, or RETURN.

"             - Starts a label entry;  ended with ←, →, or RETURN.

+             - Starts a value entry;  see Expressions below.

0-9 (number)- Starts a value entry;  see Expressions below.
- @ ( #

/             - Starts a command;  see Commands below.


Expressions

      A value entry display the result of evaluating the expression stored
      at the entry.  Expressions consist of numbers, arithmetic operations
      (+ - * /), builtin functions (such as SUM), and the values of other
      value entries (entry value references).  Evaluation is from left to
      right, except as modified by parenthesis.  Expressions are terminated
      by RETURN, ←, or →.                        (Has 5 levels)

Numbers

      12.34   - Normal numbers, with optional decimal point and/or sign.

      3.14E5  - Power of ten notation.  The number after the "E" tells you
                what power of ten you multiply the number before the E by
                to get the actual value (e.g. 314000, in this case).

Builtin Functions

      @SUM(   - Calculates the sum of the values in its range.  For example,
                @SUM(B4-B15) is the sum of the values in B4, B5,..., B15.

      @NA     - Results in a "not available" value that makes all expressions
                with that value result in "NA".
```

Reference Card -- page 2

Value Entry References

To use the value of another value entry in an expression, you
place a value entry reference in the expression anywhere where
a number would be allowed. You make the value entry reference by
either typing in the coordinates of the desired entry (such as "B5"),
or by "pointing" to the entry by using the cursor -- the coordinates
will be filled in automatically.

If you want to use the value of an entry as a number (i.e. you don't
want the value to change when the other entry is modified, you want
to use its current value), you use the #. Typing # after a value
entry reference will cause the reference to be erased and the number
that represents its current value to be put in the expression being
typed. If the # is used by itself (that is, not after a value
entry reference), then it will be replaced by the current value
of the entry whose expression you are changing.

Commands

/B   - Sets an entry to blank.

/C   - Clears the screen, sets all entries to blank. *It Waits for you to type Y* *to confirm that you indeed want to blank all entries.*

/D   - Deletes a row (R) or column (C).

/F   - Sets display format of entry to G (general), I (integer), $ (dollars and
            cents), or * (graph) format; or D to use global default.

/GC   - Sets column width (type number from 3 to 37, then RETURN). *[Per window]*

/GF   - Sets global default display format to G (general), I (integer),
            $ (dollars and cents), or * (graph) format. *[Per window]*

/GO   - Sets order of reevaluation to down the columns starting at A1 (C),
            or across the rows starting at A1 (R).

/GR   - Sets recalculation to be automatic (A) or manual (M).

/I   - Inserts a row (R) or column (C).

/T   - Sets a horizontal title area (H), a vertical title area (V),
            sets both a horizontal and vertical title area (B), or resets
            to no title areas (N).

/S   - Storage command, saves and loads memory. See Storage command below.

/R   - Replicates an entry. Needs entry to replicate (such as B5) *which will be pre-typed,* or entry
            range of what to replicate (such as B5-B15) followed by RETURN.
            Then needs entry range specifying where to place copies (such
            as C5-F5) followed by RETURN. If replicating an expression, it
            will ask for each value entry reference whether it should not
            be modified (N) or should always refer to the entry in the
            same relative position (R).

Reference Card -- page 3

/W   - Window control, sets split screen at cursor position (H for
            horizontal, V for vertical), or returns screen to one window (1).
            Windows may be synchronized (S), or returned to unsynchronized (U).

/M   - Move command. Asks for where to move current column or row to.

Storage Command

    Diskette System

    /SS   - Prompts for file name (end with RETURN) and then saves the
                current contents of all entries into the file.

    /SL   - Prompts for file name (end with RETURN) and then loads the
                contents of all entries that were saved in the file. This
                command does not blank all entries before doing the load --
                use the /C command to do that first.

    Cassette System

    /SS   - Saves the current contents of all entries on a cassette.

    /SL   - Blanks out all entries and then loads the contents of all
                entries that were saved on a cassette.

Here's another view of the attic, with me discussing the product with Bob
Frankston's father, Ben:

Me and Bob's father Ben in the attic 4/1/79.
Photo courtesy of Bob Frankston.

The VisiCalc screen looked like this:

VisiCalc Screen, early Alpha version, 1/4/79

This version of VisiCalc was from very early in the coding (Bob had been writing his version of the "real" computer code for about one week). You'll note that all of the numbers are left justified. There were no fixed decimals, yet, so we carefully typed in numbers that would all look good, with no zeros to be suppressed (e.g., "12.10" would have been "12.1"). VisiCalc used a variation of decimal arithmetic so all money values could be represented exactly, with no funny behavior common at the time from binary floating point (a method that was faster to compute, but that often led to answers with apparent rounding errors arising from converting between decimal and binary arithmetic).

In those days we got screen photos by taking pictures ourselves. I used my old, trusty 35mm camera with a telephoto lens to flatten the image as much as possible and long exposures to avoid the "TV photograph" look.

VisiCalc was coded in assembler (a low-level computer language that gives precise control), first for the MOS Technology 6502 microprocessor used in the Apple II. The assembler system Bob started with ran on the MIT Multics timesharing system. It was much less expensive to use it late at night than during the prime time of day, so Bob slept during the day, waking up when I came over after classes in the later afternoon. He dialed in using a modem and a DEC LA-120 printing terminal like this one:

DEC LA-120 terminal like the one Bob used to start coding VisiCalc

The assembler was a macro assembler, and Bob had it set up with structured programming (a technique that was gaining popularity at the time and is now taken for granted) and "IF-THEN-ELSE" type macros, so VisiCalc actually had only a couple of "GOTOs" in it, something novel (though not unique) for a program of its day written in assembler. It was heavily commented.

Here is an example of what some of the source code looked like. Each line represents no more than one CPU instruction. The "poll_keyboard" subroutine call was important. As Bob Frankston describes it: "There were no interrupts nor a clock [on the Apple II]. If the user typed a character before the keyboard input buffer was emptied it would be lost . . . To avoid [losing characters when the user typed fast during a CPU-intensive operation] I polled the keyboard in the middle of potentially long loops—keyboard checks were strewn throughout the code." (See Bob's "Implementing VisiCalc"[4] essay for a technical discussion of the implementation.)

```
zero_ptr  current.node          ; start in upper left.
copy_pointer_to_uid  himem,wsm_bottom_cell_uid  ; start out with this as high as possible
do                               ; and just dive in....
  poll_keyboard                  ; not to lose keystrokes...
  !         current.node.row     ; This gets stepped down at the bottom
  c         sheet_row_count      ; of the loop.
  until  larger_or_equal         ; at that point we're done.
  !#        0
```

This is an Apple II setup like Bob used to create VisiCalc (this is a later one with extra hardware for testing):

Apple II setup

[4] http://www.frankston.com/public/?name=implementingVisicalc

When shipped, the screen looked like this:

First version of VisiCalc screenshot

Naming a new product is always a challenge. I had originally proposed the name "Calcu-ledger" for the product. I wrote about the name in the paper for my course in advertising. I listed some of the traits of that name, such as that it sounded too much like something for a bookkeeper, and then explained, "Other names that I have thought of, such as 'electronic spreadsheet' or 'calcu-paper' don't sound right, or may not be understood by people, even after they know what it is (not everybody knows what a spreadsheet is, ledger is more common)."

The product's eventual name, VisiCalc, as I understand it, was coined at a meeting with Bob Frankston and Dan Fylstra (Personal Software) at Vic's EGG on ONE restaurant on Mass. Ave. in Cambridge, Massachusetts. Dan Fylstra, as head of Personal Software and in charge of the marketing for the product, made the decision to choose that name out of all of the others being considered. Vic's is no longer there, but this photo that I took ended up in *Popular Photography* magazine as an example of pictures people take themselves for speeches they give, fulfilling a childhood dream of mine to be recognized as a photographer (well, at least sort of recognized).

Where VisiCalc was named

I showed the product to various professors or asked them for advice. Before coding the prototype, I got my first encouragement in the spring of 1978 from Professor Roger Schmenner, who told me how huge blackboards were used for production calculations in real companies, and from Professor Jim Cash, who praised me for dealing with the user interface issues of computing. I spoke to Professor Barbara Jackson, who had consulted to CEOs of large companies, and she emphasized going after simple use and that I'd be competing with the back of an envelope (a major driver of the interface). Professor Jeff Miller, after seeing the prototype, encouraged showing users how to do applications, including master scheduling and budgeting for manufacturers. Professor Buchanan thought it could sell for $50 for home use, and "lots (thousands) for business." Professor Robert Glauber recommended adding net present value (with end-of-year for each step) and table lookup functions (which we did), as well as IRR and other financial functions (which were put in the product well after the first release). Professor Charles Kelso, in addition to teaching me introductory finance and the value of doing financial projections, first introduced me to Dan Fylstra. I brought Dan Fylstra in to Harvard twice to meet with Professor Michael Porter to discuss competitive strategy in the market. My classmates also helped me in many ways, including John Reese's suggestions that improved the formula editing user interface. The Harvard Business School was very helpful.

The first "business problem" for which VisiCalc was used was for a class assignment at Harvard Business School. I needed to analyze the "Pepsi-Cola" case. This involved the "Pepsi Challenge" marketing campaign. (Little did I know that a Pepsi executive involved in that campaign, John Sculley, would end up a part of the PC industry at Apple years later.) To analyze the case, I used a very early version of VisiCalc running over in Bob's attic. It couldn't print (so I had to copy the output by hand) and it couldn't save (so each time it crashed I had to type in everything again). I was able to get called on in class the next day and "present" the case. I talked about five-year financial projections, testing multiple possibilities, with all sorts of variables. For those days of hand calculators, it was very impressive. The professor asked me how I did it. Not wanting to reveal our secret product, I just said: "Well, I added this and multiplied by that and subtracted this and . . ." He asked back: "Why didn't you just use a ratio?" I replied: "That wouldn't have been as exact." What I didn't tell him was that the program code to do division wasn't working yet.

The first advertisement for VisiCalc appeared in the May 1979 issue of *Byte* magazine.

Dan Fylstra, head of our publisher Personal Software and one of the founding editors of *Byte* years before, decided to take out a brash teaser ad in the back section. VisiCalc was unannounced at the time, and not scheduled to ship for a while. I thought he was being a little strong, but he really was right on target for many people (accountants, business planners, etc.):

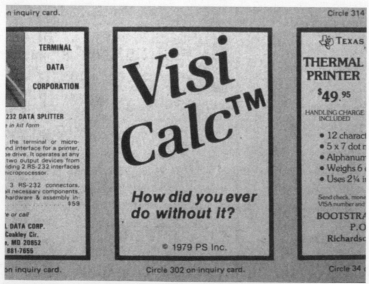

First VisiCalc ad in 1979: VisiCalc—How did you ever do without it?

VisiCalc was first shown to the regular personal computer press in a special room at the West Coast Computer Faire in San Francisco in May of 1979. Personal Software invited various people up to see it, as well as other products they were considering publishing. It was here that I first met Vern Raburn, who later went on to Microsoft, Symantec, and then to cofound Slate Corporation with me and others. I also met Dave Winer,[5] later of Userland, and saw his early outliner as he demonstrated to Ted Nelson, of hypertext (and *Dream Machines*[6]) fame.

Me demonstrating VisiCalc at the West Coast Computer Faire 5/12/79. Photo courtesy of Bob Frankston.

VisiCalc was announced to the public at the National Computer Conference in New York City in June of 1979. Personal computers were still very new, and

---

[5] Dave Winer, whose name comes up frequently in this book, went on to write the early personal computing outlining programs ThinkTank and More, helped popularize blogging, helped develop and popularize RSS, podcasting, and many other things.

[6] This was a book in 1974 that presented a lot of influential ideas about hypertext, a term he coined, and computer presentation and sharing of information. See http://www.digibarn.com/collections/books/computer-lib/.

typically viewed as toys for hobbyists by the makers and users of the larger mainframes and minicomputers.

Bob Frankston delivered a paper at the personal computer part of the conference (a small event in a hotel near the main show floor where the "real" computers were displayed) describing the new program he had just written.[7] Here are some excerpts:

> Many people justifiably ask what today's personal computers are good for, aside from playing games. Typically equipped with a BASIC Interpreter as the human interface, these machines either require extensive programming by the user or else require the purchase (when they are available) of restrictive canned programs for specific applications. Few people can be expected to be able or willing to expend the effort to write programs in BASIC (or PASCAL) for simple applications. Canned packages tend to be very specific, Procrustean beds to which the user's application must conform.

> This is not to say that there is no way to make effective use of the personal computer. As we can see by the acceptance of a primitive personal computer, the pocket calculator, a flexible aid will be used extensively. We would like to capture the convenience and familiarity of the calculator in a personal computer. Looking at the way most people use calculators—normally with the aid of a sheet of paper to plan their work and record intermediate results—we can see how the calculator plus a flexible video screen could be a powerful tool. This is the premise or starting point for VisiCalc . . .

> The benefits of VisiCalc go beyond its humble origins as calculating paper. It represents a way of using computers that allows the user to ask 'what if' questions that would be too tedious to carry out by hand. Not only are such questions important in planning, they can be vital to the user in learning and coming to understand his own application . . .

> As you can see, VisiCalc can take care of the details of calculations and keep track of what data is where. It is important that the user be able to construct a solution to his or her problem simply by laying out

---

[7] http://www.frankston.com/public/?name=VisiCalcPaper

the necessary information on the sheet. The user is then freed to work with the application. This work with an application is in contrast to the traditional model of programming which requires that the problem be essentially worked out before the program is written . . .

As personal computers become more common, the software problem becomes the limiting factor in the ability to use the personal computer. The current attempt to get everyone to learn and use BASIC is not the answer. Much of what is involved in programming is conceptualization and description—the hard parts of problem solving. Even the ultimate in general-purpose procedural languages will not remove the difficulties in programming. These languages are, of course, necessary for those people who do programming, such as the personal computer software engineers. But there are simply not enough programmers available to write all of the canned applications that can be anticipated . . .

Thus our task as professionals becomes one of finding the appropriate level of tools that correspond to the level at which the user deals with an application. On large computers this has been done with database languages such as IBM's Query By Example (QBE). At MIT, the Macsyma system provides a powerful tool for doing symbolic manipulation of mathematical expressions. For personal computers, VisiCalc presents an interface to the user which builds upon that with which he is already familiar. It is, of course, constrained by the memory and processing limits of the current generation of personal computers.

Bob Frankston, June 1979

In hindsight, it was a great paper for the time. However, it wasn't the well-received announcement you might expect. Lots of our relatives and our publishers attended. Almost nobody else cared. There were 20 friends and family and 2 "real" attendees, but as Bob recalls, the 2 people we didn't know walked out early, probably because it wasn't like the talk about the undocumented opcodes of the TI-59 calculator (a hot topic in those days). Afterwards, we went to a kosher restaurant nearby to celebrate the talk and Bob's upcoming

30th birthday. I returned to Massachusetts and graduated Harvard Business School soon after Bob's talk.

At that conference, Bob and I met Bill Gates and Ben Rosen for the first time. Bill was a young kid best known for his version of BASIC and speeding tickets. Ben was still an electronics analyst at Morgan Stanley. At Ben's conference a couple of months before, VisiCalc was shown privately to attendees by Dan Fylstra.

The *New York Times* ran a humorous article about the tradeshow: "A Layman's Trip into the Mega-Mega Land of Computers" by Francis X. Clines.[8] He saw a sign with a funny name being made for the Personal Software booth, and included a mention of it in the article:

> *An ignorant layman staggers away from a visit to the four floors of computer equipment on display at the Coliseum, and his heart leaps at the sight of the first fully comprehensible business tool he has seen all day—a set of sandwich boards worn by Sonny Monosson to advertise the used computers he is hawking on the sidewalk to the horde of passing conventioneers.*
>
> *. . . The machines perform what seem religious rites, telling their beads and chips, fueled by the sort of faith that built Babel.*
>
> *. . . Even as the believers gather, the painters in the Coliseum sign room are adding to the pantheon, carefully lettering "VISICALC" in giant black on yellow. All hail VISICALC.*
>
> Francis X. Clines, *New York Times*, June 7, 1979, page B1

Mr. Clines didn't fully understand the details of the products he mentioned (it was a "layman's trip"), but we sure appreciated the quote.

Interest in what it did, i.e., being an electronic spreadsheet, was low in the general business press. VisiCalc didn't appear in a major newspaper or business magazine for many months after that first mention. Technology often takes a while to be appreciated and catch on. Many business people who saw our demo in the booth, though, were enthusiastic.

Ben Rosen, one of the most major players in the PC world, who later went on, as a venture capitalist, to fund Lotus and Compaq, wrote this upon first using a sneak peek of VisiCalc in mid-1979:

---

[8] Mr. Clines was a reporter for the *New York Times* for 40 years and is now on their editorial board.

VISICALC: BREAKING THE PERSONAL COMPUTER
SOFTWARE BOTTLENECK

. . . it seems to be unique in the computer industry. Mainframe people I've shown Visicalc to claim there's nothing like it available on conventional machines.

So who knows? Visicalc could some day become the software tail that wags (and sells) the personal computer dog.

Ben Rosen, Morgan Stanley Electronics Letter, July 11, 1979

(The diskette he used, I believe, is in the Computer Museum collection, along with Bill Gates's papertape of BASIC and other artifacts.) Ben was working at the time at Morgan Stanley, were he was an analyst covering the semiconductor industry and later the PC industry. He ran a yearly conference. Sometime after this appeared, he left Morgan Stanley to found a small business to publish the *Letter* and run the conference. When he became a venture capitalist, he sold the business to Esther Dyson, who ran it for many years.

Using some of the early royalty prepayments from Personal Software, Bob and I were able to make the move to start being a "real" company to finish the coding. We sublet some space from another tiny software company, John Strayhorn's Renaissance Computing, in Central Square, Cambridge, Massachusetts, down the road from MIT. It was in the basement.

We borrowed money from a bank and bought a Prime minicomputer on which to run our development tools to finish the first release. The Prime had a good version of PL/I[9] in which to write the tools. Bob wrote a macro assembler and linker[10] for the 6502 microprocessor, and I wrote a simple visual editor and accounting system. We hired two employees, Steve Lawrence and Seth Steinberg, to help us get the product out the door and to create versions of VisiCalc for other computers, including those from Commodore and Radio Shack. Since the office was below ground, sometimes when it rained the drains would back up and the floor would get wet. We'd have to race to pump out the water to protect our expensive computer.

---

[9] PL/I is a computer language which was used in the development of Multics, among other systems.

[10] An assembler and linker are computer tools used to program a computer at the most basic level.

We first shipped about five copies of version 1.35 to some early customers in the late summer of 1979. I hand-typed the labels. The first "real" release, version 1.37, shipped in mid-October 1979.

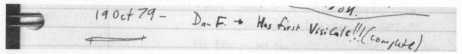

Entry in my journal: First complete VisiCalc in a package was October 19, 1979. I received a copy the next day as I recall.

Here is what the first VisiCalc packaging looked like:

The cover of the first VisiCalc packaging: "VisiCalc, Personal Software Inc." and the contents

It was a brown vinyl binder holding the manual, diskette (5¼" diskette), reference card, and registration card. The reference card was written by me. The production and volume printing of the card was done by my father, Baruch Bricklin. The diskette duplication and all other production of the product were done by Personal Software. The manual first shipped with VisiCalc was written by Dan Fylstra (the third in a series of attempts: first by me, then a freelance writer, and then Dan Fylstra until they got one acceptable to Personal Software). It included a combination of examples, including sales/cost projections to teach the basics, home budgeting to show more advanced commands and techniques, and scientific calculations to demonstrate the built-in functions.

The final Reference Card looked like this on the first two (of 10) panels:

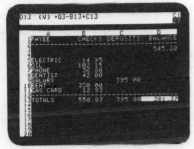

A Visible Calculator

For the

APPLE II

REFERENCE CARD

A Product of

Software Arts, Inc.

Distributed Exclusively By

PERSONAL SOFTWARE INC.

592 Weddell Drive
Sunnyvale, CA 94086
(408) 745-7841

© 1979 Software Arts, Inc.
9/79 V1.35

2

MOVING THE CURSOR

← →	Moves the cursor left, right, up or down.
space bar	Switches the direction indicator between horizontal (−) and vertical (!).
;	If two windows, moves the cursor from one window to the other.
>	Go To command. Type the coordinates of the entry where you want the cursor to go; end with RETURN.

THE ESC KEY

The ESC key is used to recover from simple typing mistakes. It usually erases the last thing that you typed. If you press ESC enough times, it will abort what you are doing and return VisiCalc to a blank prompt line.

SETTING A LABEL ENTRY

Label entries start with a letter (A–Z), or with the quote character ("). Terminate entering a label entry by pressing ←, →, or RETURN. Correct errors by pressing ESC. The prompt line will say LABEL while a label entry is being typed.

SETTING A VALUE ENTRY

A value entry displays the calculated value of the expression stored at the entry. Expressions consist of numbers, coordinates of other value entries (value references), functions (such as @SUM), arithmetic operators (+ − * / ^) and/or parentheses. Expressions are evaluated strictly from left to right except as modified by parentheses. You must start an expression with a +, a digit (0–9), or one of the symbols @ − (. or #. The prompt line will say VALUE while an expression is being typed. Terminate entering an expression by pressing ←, →, or RETURN. Errors can be corrected by pressing the ESC key. Examples of expressions are:

12.34	A normal number
.1234E2	A number in scientific notation
2+2	An arithmetic expression
+B4	A value reference
2*B4	An expression with a value reference
2*(3+4)	An expression with parentheses

VisiCalc Reference Card, 9/79 V.1.35, shipped with first release, panels 1 and 2

A scan of the entire Reference Card is reproduced on my web site.[11] The Reference Card serves as the specification of that original version of VisiCalc. The last panel,[12] which has a picture of the screen with the parts labeled, is probably the most interesting:

---

[11] http://www.bricklin.com/history/refcard1.htm

[12] http://www.bricklin.com/history/refcard5.htm

9

10

A *VISICALC*™ Screen:

Entry Type: V for value, L for label, /– for repeating label.

Recalculation Order Indicator: If R, across rows; if C, down columns.

Memory Indicator: How many K memory available. If flashing M, out of room.

Current Entry's coordinates

Explicit Format indication

Direction Indicator: If ↕, arrows keys will move cursor up and down; if –, arrow keys will move cursor left and right.

Entry Contents

Entry Contents Line

Prompt Line

Left Justified Format (/FL)

General Format (/FG)

Edit Line: flashing block means awaiting input.

Repeating Label (/–)

Row and Column labels

Dollars and Cents Format (/F$)

Label Entry

```
B9 /FI    (V) 1.2*B7               CI
VALUE                              25
+B8*B7
      A         B        K        L
1COST/SLS:  .8       1RATE:       .25
2OVHD INC:  10       2
3  SLS GRW: .29      3NPU        62.0151
4                    4
5YEAR           1979 5 TOTAL %/SALES
6                    6
7# SOLD         100  7   3066
8  PRICE        120  8
9SALES $        120  9   3680    100
10COST           80  10  2453     67
11OVHD           15  11   495     13
12PROFIT          5  12   118      3
13                   13
14                   14  1979 ***
15                   15  1980 **
16                   16  1981 *
17                   17  1982 *
18                   18  1983 **
19                   19  1984 ***
20                   20  1985 ******
```

Cursor

Two windows when the screen is split.

Right Justified Format (/FR)

Graph Format (/F*)

Integer Format (/FI)

Value Entry

"A VISICALC Screen" from panels 9 and 10

To get a feel for what VisiCalc was like to use, you can try a copy of the early IBM PC VisiCalc[13] from two years later in 1981. It still runs on many of today's PCs under MS-DOS in Windows. That version of VisiCalc was only 27K bytes in size. The original Apple II version from 1979 could run on a 32K byte Apple II. Those 32K bytes included the screen memory and the OS, as well as the VisiCalc program and the space for data.

After VisiCalc Shipped

We moved Software Arts on December 21, 1979, to good commercial quarters a few blocks away, also in Central Square, Cambridge, Massachusetts, eventually taking over the entire 12th floor of the building.

---

[13]http://www.bricklin.com/history/vcexecutable.htm

At this point, Personal Software had been working for many months introducing VisiCalc to the numerous computer stores around the country and was running large, color advertisements in the personal computer magazines. The program sold quite well compared to much of the other personal computer software in those days, selling on the order of a thousand copies a month for the first several months, at about $100 each.

The first award that we got for VisiCalc was months later. It was given by Adam Osborne, an important visionary, commentator, and entrepreneur in the early personal computer days. He founded a book publishing company (later sold to McGraw Hill) which published computer books. Some of those books were about accounting and included the source code of programs such as General Ledger. That "open source" helped start the use of microcomputers (especially CP/M machines) in small business. He also was an industry pundit, with a confident, British-accented voice, and gave a yearly "White Elephant" award to what he felt were the most important integrated circuit chips introduced in the previous year and to the people that changed the industry for the good.

In May of 1980, at the West Coast Computer Faire, Adam gave Bob and me the 1979 award for VisiCalc. I have a recording that was made by a member of the audience who held up a simple tape recorder and then kindly gave the tape to me. I ran some noise reduction on the recording back in 1999 to try to improve it (but it is still not very clear) and I posted it on my web site.[14] Listening to it helps you get a feel for the state of the personal computing industry at the time VisiCalc came out. Here is a transcription I made in 2008 that I hope is faithful to the original:

> So those are my choices for chip of the year.
>
> Now, what about people? Because that is the important part.
>
> Where is the industry today? When we began [inaudible] my first award we had a lot of silly little boxes being sold to enthusiasts and doing nothing. Then Kildall came along and gave us CP/M, an operating system that allowed these silly little boxes to start doing something useful. Even then we still had a neophyte industry that wasn't doing a great deal of [inaudible] and not many people were taking it seriously because it was so [inaudible]. Along came Apple Computer

---

[14] http://www.bricklin.com/adamosborne.htm

[inaudible] corporation, Radio Shack, Commodore; we began to see for the first [inaudible] time where [inaudible] some solid based companies.

And that brought us into 1979 where there is the beginning of a real industry with real system software and a total lack of any good applications programs. This was the area where I decided to look and [inaudible] my award for 1979, applications programs.

What will we need? We don't just need games. We don't just need a program that does a silly this or that. We have to look for something more solid—a real applications program, a product that is going to make this industry [inaudible] to sell the computer. I was looking for an application program that had proved itself to the point where people were going out and buying a ten-thousand-dollar computer system to run a one-hundred-dollar program. That is the economics of this business. [Applause] And that is what I found.

I'm sure you all agree with me, that if there is one shining example, a piece of superb software, a work of art, that has been designed by people who know software, for an industry that sorely needed their arrival, it has got to be Bob Frankston and Dan Bricklin for VisiCalc. [Long applause]

Unfortunately, one of these two gentlemen is getting married and isn't here. I believe the other one is here in the audience. Please come up and accept the award. [More applause as Dan Bricklin walks up to be handed the award.[15]]

I have used VisiCalc myself. VisiCalc is a program which essentially gives you a large matrix display. A matrix of numbers that you can formulate in almost any fashion making the data interdependent or [inaudible] dependent. You can put financial data on, scientific data, any form of data; I've used it extensively for such things as cash flow. And then as I was using some of those cash flow programs I had to say to myself, my God, if VisiCalc had been around perhaps Processor Technology wouldn't have gone under. [Laughter] Because you can set up an entire scenario on this program, change one number at

---

[15]I took the red-eye flight back that night to Massachusetts and made it in time to attend Bob's wedding with just a few minutes to spare.

the beginning and watch everything ripple right through to see what will happen in six months or [inaudible] because you didn't make quite the sales you thought you would now or that your growth isn't going to be 10% but 2%.

It is a fundamentally useful program that everybody should look at and see, not simply because of what it is capable of doing but because of the beauty with which that product has been designed and the timeliness of the product entering the industry now. Because now is the time that we are going to have to have solid, useful applications software, because people are no longer interested in simply buying a box and programming it. The industry has become too large, we have taken care of those enthusiasts. But if the industry is to continue to grow we are going to have to start selling to computer users who have no interest in programming, no interest in hardware, and the only reason they bought a computer is because they need the power, the capability of a VisiCalc and programs of that quality. That is what I wish to encourage.

For next year I only hope that I am able to choose something else of the same high level of achievement, because if you look through the products, if you look through from CP/M and Apple Computer and VisiCalc, you are looking at quality and integrity. I hope there is something of that level available to me next year.

Thank you very much.

Adam Osborne, May 15, 1980

The award consisted of a circuit board with the winning chips, some engraved words, and a tiny ivory white elephant (Adam lived much of his life in India).

We made versions of VisiCalc for many different computers, including the Apple III, TRS-80 model 3, Apple II, IBM PC, TRS-80 model 2, Commodore PET CBM-80, HP 125, and Atari 800. The IBM PC version became the most popular. The shipped version supported up to 512K of memory (the maximum we could test it on at the time). Over the years, hundreds of thousands of copies of VisiCalc (of all types) were sold.

We hired many programmers, managers, testers, and others. Here's a publicity shot of Bob and me from around that time:

Bob Frankston and me at Software Arts. © www.jimraycroft.com, 1982.

Over time, many other software companies developed and sold their own spreadsheet programs, including Sorcim's SuperCalc and Microsoft's Multiplan.

In January of 1982, publicity started to pick up. Bob and I appeared on the cover of *Inc.* magazine in an article written by Stewart Alsop. Stewart was new to computers (this was his first exposure) but he went on to be editor of *InfoWorld*, start his own publication and the Agenda conference, and later become a venture capitalist. In addition to the article about Software Arts, there was another one about "The Birth of a New Industry," which included Bill Gates, Mitch Kapor, Gary Kildall, Dan Fylstra, Tony Gold, and others, written by Steve Ditlea and Joanne Tangorra. Part of that article reads: "All five of their companies—whose combined revenues just missed $50 million in 1981 . . ."

We created an enhanced version of VisiCalc called VisiCalc Advanced Version, with features such as variable width columns, improved formatting, and keystroke macros. Unfortunately for us in hindsight, we implemented it first for the Apple III, releasing it in late 1982, and then the Apple IIe—the IBM

PC version wasn't until much later, and that was done in a higher-level language, to make it easier to produce versions for different computers, instead of fast assembly code. (This use of a higher-level language was a strategy similar to that taken by Microsoft with its Multiplan spreadsheet, and the developers of the Context MBA program.)

Lotus Development Corporation shipped their advanced spreadsheet 1-2-3 in early 1983. It was written in assembly code and was tuned very carefully to the IBM PC. For many reasons, 1-2-3 quickly replaced VisiCalc (and SuperCalc, and Multiplan, and every other spreadsheet of the day) as the dominant spreadsheet on the IBM PC just as the IBM PC was being widely adopted by large businesses (and probably helped that adoption along, too, of course).

In addition to VisiCalc, Software Arts produced the TK!Solver program (which facilitated engineering and scientific calculations) as well as other products.

If you are interested in additional details about the development of VisiCalc, there are some web postings you might find of interest. Bob Frankston posted some of his firsthand memories on his web site in 2003[16] in preparation for a panel we were on at the Computer History Museum. Spurred by that panel, Peter Jennings, who was one of Dan Fylstra's partners at Personal Software/VisiCorp and responsible for the MicroChess program that helped fund the early advance royalty payments for VisiCalc, then posted some of his recollections of the early days of VisiCalc on his web site.[17]

Afterwards

In addition to the product VisiCalc, there is the related saga of the relationship between the two companies most closely involved, Software Arts and Personal Software (later renamed VisiCorp). I won't cover that here (it is more of a business and legal story unrelated to most of what I cover in this book). For those who are interested, I found a history of Personal Software/VisiCorp in a business school case from the Anderson School of UCLA, which had access to material I hadn't seen before.[18]

---

[16]http://www.frankston.com/public/?name=implementingVisicalc

[17]http://www.benlo.com/visicalc/index.html

[18]"VISICORP 1978-1984 (Revised)," POL-2003-08, prepared by Professor Richard P. Rumelt with the assistance of Julia Watt: http://www.anderson.ucla.edu/faculty/dick.rumelt/Docs/Cases/Visicorp.pdf

In the spring of 1985, Software Arts's assets were sold to Lotus Development Corporation, the creators and publishers of the 1-2-3 spreadsheet, saving Software Arts from a looming bankruptcy. Lotus sold TK!Solver to another company and it continued to be sold for many years. Lotus also released Software Arts's Spotlight and Wildfire programs as Lotus Metro and Lotus Express.

Lotus decided not to continue publishing VisiCalc.

Bob went to work for Lotus, and I, after a brief time consulting to Lotus, founded a new company called Software Garden, Inc., to develop the Dan Bricklin's Demo Program (with Lotus's blessing).

For the players, it finished with a sad ending, but it was a fun ride while it lasted. The product we made was good and important enough that here, decades later, people like you take the time to read about it.

When I started work on VisiCalc, most regular people didn't know what a spreadsheet was. Now, thanks to the work of all the people involved then and since, what we built is so common that often people drop the modifying word "electronic."

I'm always interested in indications that technology has made a major leap in being accepted by everyday people. For me, I got a personal feeling about this on September 5, 1985, when the *Wall Street Journal* wrote in an editorial:

> *We've been reading stories this week about all the returning Members of Congress who say that virtually none of their constituents are interested in Ronald Reagan's tax reforms. Could be, but we doubt it. Our guess is that people everywhere have by now filled Visicalc spreadsheets, endless pages of eight-column accountant's paper, yellow legal pads, blank stationery and envelope backs with calculations of how they'd fare with the president's tax-revision proposals . . .*

> Wall Street Journal, September 5, 1985

Here they didn't go to the trouble to explain what VisiCalc was—it was assumed that *Wall Street Journal* readers knew what it meant and knowing what it meant was part of making a point about something else, not technology. And this was in an editorial, not an article in the technical section.

Finally, coming full circle, there is a plaque on the wall in room 108 in Aldrich Hall at the Harvard Business School commemorating the invention of

VisiCalc, dedicated in a ceremony in June 1999.[19] It includes a copy of a sketch I made as a student in early 1979 as I designed the reference card:

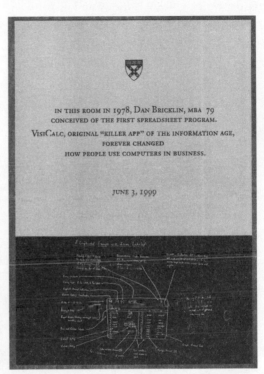

Plaque in Aldrich 108 at Harvard Business School: "In this room in 1978, Dan Bricklin, MBA '79, conceived of the first spreadsheet program. VisiCalc, original "Killer App" of the information age, forever changed how people use computers in business."

As I understand it, one of the reasons they put up the plaque in the classroom is to remind students that they, just like other students before them, could be inspired by something that they learn in school and go on to transform the lives of others.

Additional Material About VisiCalc

In addition to the VisiCalc "story," my web site has a few essays that answer some of the common questions I receive about VisiCalc or clear up some misconceptions. They don't fit well in the narrative, so I include them separately here at the end.

---

[19]http://www.alumni.hbs.edu/bulletin/1999/october/profile.html

WAS VISICALC THE "FIRST" SPREADSHEET?

It was the combination of many things including its "programming by example" user interface and its influence on others that made VisiCalc special.

Why am I writing this?

Every once in a while Bob Frankston or I get an email discussing something which they claim relates to "spreadsheets before VisiCalc" or saying that "Visi-Calc really wasn't first." This article is to address those type of issues and explain what I understand people to mean when they call VisiCalc the "first electronic spreadsheet."

Each of the writers usually has some valid point about a particular program that they or someone else created or proposed. Most of these were not something that Bob or I had seen. However, with the years of experience we had at the time we created VisiCalc, we were familiar with many row/column financial programs. In fact, Bob had worked since the 1960s at Interactive Data Corporation, a major timesharing utility that was used for some of them, and I was exposed to some at Harvard Business School in one of the classes.

First of all, we did not invent the word "spreadsheet." The name "spreadsheet," or more commonly in the early days, "electronic spreadsheet," was applied to VisiCalc precisely because it was like the paper spreadsheets, such as the ones I did as a student at Harvard Business School. (The command tree illustration earlier in this chapter was written on the back of such paper.)

The special thing about VisiCalc was not that it was the first row/column tabulation program. There were many such programs of various sorts prior to VisiCalc.

The things that are viewed as special about VisiCalc, as I understand it, include:

It was interactive in a WYSIWYG way:

- Point to change a value
- Instant automatic recalculation based on formulas stored in the cells referencing other cells

- Scroll left/right/up/down
- The input, definition, formatting, and output were all merged into a natural, program-by-example interface

The UI and design have stayed with us. For example, the combination of:

- Labels and formulas distinguished by first character typed
- Minimal-keystroke formula entry: type "1.1*" then move the cursor then type "-1" to enter a formula such as "1.1*B22-1." The goal here was to make it worth using the first time you needed an answer (instead of a calculator and paper) in a way that would let you benefit the next time by just changing a few values and recalculating. If the input style did not let you "teach" the computer by doing the calculation, people may not have used it.
- A1, B1, SUM(A1 . . A7)
- Real-time scrolling
- Numeric and text formatting
- Status and formula lines
- Replication of any range to any other range, with absolute and relative references

It ran on an affordable, personal machine, so it was accessible to all. (Most prior financial forecasting tools ran on timesharing systems and cost >$1000/month, or they used card input.)

It shipped and was successfully marketed to the right people and was widely used by them productively and was recommended by them to their friends.

It was a catalyst to the personal computer industry, by introducing personal computers to the financial and business communities and others. Many people cite VisiCalc as the thing that turned them on to the interactive possibilities of computers.

Most subsequent spreadsheets are directly descended from it; so much so that a user's VisiCalc data files could be moved ahead from product to product without much change or retyping.

It is the combination of all these things that made VisiCalc unique and special.

What others wrote

In his book *The Third Apple*,[20] Jean-Louis Gassée (then of Apple Computer) wrote about his February 1981 first encounter with VisiCalc. In the chapter "In the Bridal Suite at the Hilton" he says:

> *I don't know why, but I was assigned the bridal suite. . . It was in this inimitable decor that I married Visicalc . . . So Visicalc offered itself to me on the screen: a sheet of ruled paper with rows and columns . . . So Visicalc was the thing I had dreamed of making ten years earlier . . . That was the day I realized that you didn't have to be a programmer any more to use a computer. Visicalc was a phenomenal revolution . . . Approximations, trial and error, simulations—Visicalc is an intellectual modeling clay. It lets you program without knowing it.*

> *The Third Apple*, pages 23-29, translated from the original French

Bob Frankston, comparing VisiCalc to some early accounting programs, writes:

> *But VisiCalc was not an accounting program at all, it just made it possible for people to do accounting. Programs that were overly tuned for such function (Javelin, Lotus Improv, etc.) completely failed . . . What made VisiCalc novel was the ability to not only interact but have it learn by example. Again, VisiCalc doesn't summarize or do anything, it is just a tool to allow others to work out their ideas and reduce the tedium of repeating the same calculations.*

> Bob Frankston, 1999, private email

David Reed, in response to seeing a draft of this article, writes:

> *The metaphor presented by VisiCalc was not just a "user interface" in the sense of a display and a bunch of commands, but gave an enormous amount of expressive power in the visual structure and in the context of natural interaction when constructing a formula or a collection of related formulas . . . I think the two most powerful key*

---

[20]*The Third Apple*, Jean-Louis Gassée, 1987, Harcourt, ISBN: 0151898502

ideas that VisiCalc had were the following (and these did not appear in prior art, and were not properly understood by contemporary and even later systems like Target PlannerCalc, Analytica's Reflex, Multiplan, and Javelin):

Programming-by-example: typing in formulas where "variables" were indicated by pointing to and selecting other cells in the spreadsheet. These "cell references" were included in formulas and when they changed, the value of the formula would recalculate based on the new value. Since formulas could be defined in cycles, etc. a natural looping/iteration could be constructed.

The "Replicate" command, which allowed the construction of iterative calculations in a natural way by adjusting the formula cell references either to follow "relatively" to the displacement of the formula or "absolutely" to define a global parameter that affected all cells.

The nice thing about the "replicate" style of iteration construction is that it allows for regularity, while not requiring it (any individual formula in the repetitive structure could be overridden as a special case).

The financial modeling tools that constructed arrays with a separate formula definition language didn't have anywhere near the flexibility of the VisiCalc metaphor. And they didn't have "programming by example."

Also rather neat was the "range" concept, which allowed any rectangular subgrid to serve as the operand to a variety of aggregate functions. Range references, unlike traditional programming arrays, could overlap, and also followed the relative/absolute rules when formulas containing them were copied. This allowed for very interesting and powerful recurrence relations to be represented naturally and obviously in the programming-by-example metaphor.

David Reed, 1999, private email

The programs prior to VisiCalc, including the programs at RapidData and Interactive Data Corporation, were important, but it was the "personal computerness" of VisiCalc that seems to be what most people find important. The electronic spreadsheet, along with word processing (one of the product classes from which it was derived), helped define the "personal productivity" segment.

VisiCalc's User Interface influence has survived many years

Some screenshots may help show how much has survived. Here is a screen shot of VisiCalc on the IBM PC which was virtually identical to the version on the Apple II:

The screen has a command area at the top where the cursor location was displayed, as well as the formatting setting for the cell and its formula. The main area has rows and columns labeled A, B, C across the top and 1, 2, 3 down the side. The cursor highlights a cell which displays the calculated results. There are commands, including those to blank a cell, clear the sheet, delete, insert, and move rows/columns, edit the contents of a cell, format a cell for text or numbers as left/right justified, currency, etc., global settings for all cells for formatting, etc., printing, copying of cells with the copies modifying the references to be absolute or relative, save and load, locked titles synchronized with the scrolling, and multiple windows into the same data. The entire sheet was stored in a single file. To change a cell, you move the cursor to it with the arrow keys (the original design used a mouse, but the PCs of that day did not have a mouse) and then type the new value. The first character of what you type determines how the contents are interpreted.

Here is a screenshot of Microsoft Excel 97, shipped about 18 years after the first VisiCalc:

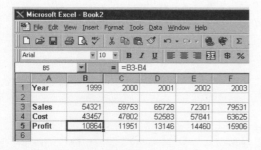

There is a command area at the top, with similar commands. In fact, the "/" key enters the command mode just like VisiCalc, and "/IR" inserts a row and "/WS" splits the window at the cursor, similar to VisiCalc. The format of the current cell is displayed, as are the location and the contents. The main area is labeled the same and works very similarly. To change a cell, you move the cursor to it with the arrow keys and then type a new value.

Much of the reason for this similarity comes from the strength of the design but also from the fact that Excel (the dominant spreadsheet of the late 1990s) needed to follow the conventions of 1-2-3, the spreadsheet that was most important during the major adoption years of PCs. (1-2-3 was actually one of the reasons for that major adoption, I believe. The relationship between 1-2-3 and VisiCalc is a whole other topic which I won't get into in this piece.) 1-2-3 followed, by choice where the developers felt it was best, many of the conventions of VisiCalc. (They didn't mindlessly follow them all, of course.)

To put this in perspective, here is the standard file listing program used in VisiCalc's day on the normal command environment (similar to many systems, like OS/8 from DEC, UNIX, etc.):

You typed something like "dir *.com" after a ">" command prompt, then got a simulated "printout" that scrolled, and then another ">" prompt. To rename a file, you type a new command, such as "rename oldname.ext newname.ext" (or is it "rename newname.ext oldname.ext"?).

Here is the common way today to find files:

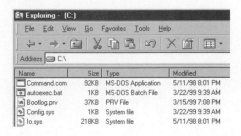

You can scroll through a hierarchy, sort by clicking on column headings, rename a file by pointing to it and typing, etc. Quite a change.

Hopefully this long discourse is helpful in putting VisiCalc in perspective.

http://www.bricklin.com/firstspreadsheetquestion.htm

WHY SHOULD A PRODUCT WANT TO BE "THE NEXT VISICALC"?

VisiCalc is an example of a pioneering product whose users could migrate their data forward to later products.

Periodically, writers refer to VisiCalc when they want to mention a well-known pioneering program, once the most popular, that was superseded and now is rarely used. While it's not the greatest feeling to have people think of one of your creations as an example of "what was and is no longer," it is nice to be remembered enough 20 years later to be used as a common example of something that was dominant. I like this better than not being remembered at all.

I received an email from Leonard Grossman[21] pointing out a story in *PC Week* that mentioned VisiCalc as something you may not have wanted to buy. Reading the article, I saw that I didn't agree with the reference. Actually, in this case, you do want to buy something that would be the next VisiCalc when it is superseded. Here's a copy of the email I sent to Michael Caton of *PC Week*, the author:

> *Michael,*
>
> *I noticed your mention of VisiCalc in your article "How do you pick an ASP that will last?"[22] on March 27, 2000:*
>
> *"Will a shakeout in the hosted application space happen, and if so, how do you keep yourself from picking tomorrow's VisiCalc today?"*
>
> *I believe you've got it backwards: It's "How do you pick the VisiCalc," not "How do you keep from picking the VisiCalc."*
>
> *Why is this so?*
>
> *VisiCalc was the dominant product of its time, and was the one from which the inevitable next dominant product, 1-2-3, could import data seamlessly. Lotus 1-2-3 is one you can seamlessly move ahead to the current dominant product, Excel. Most of VisiCalc's early competitors, the supposed "VisiClones and CalcAlikes" as they were once referred to, did not have such a smooth migration path.*

---

[21] http://www.lgrossman.com/

[22] http://web.archive.org/web/20010511042509/www.zdnet.com/eweek/stories/general/0,11011,2471902,00.html

April 25, 2000

In the long term, it is unlikely that any particular ASP will survive without you needing to migrate your data to something else.

I understand that you were trying to use VisiCalc as the name of a no longer used product that was superseded, which indeed it was (and for most purposes, Multiplan, SuperCalc, and even DOS 1-2-3 have become, too, along with the lesser known Sylk, ContextMBA, CalcPerfect, etc.). Its fame as a first product helps (what should we use for word processing? IBM MT/ST?) Unfortunately for your example of trusting your data with an ASP today, it is not a very good example.

The issue you bring up, of how do you deal with the fact that it is unlikely most ASPs will be around to maintain your data, is a good one. It should be discussed and careful attention should be paid to it. Your suggestion to go with ones that have the most partners and customers (VisiCalc's situation in its day) doesn't fit with your comparison to staying away from VisiCalc.

Thanks for your time and the article.

—Dan Bricklin

http://www.bricklin.com/nextvisicalc.htm

HOMEWORK QUESTIONS

December 9, 1999

Here are copies of email conversations with some students.

Every once in a while I receive email from a student doing a research paper for school who got me as the obscure technologist to write about. I rarely get to respond to these requests since they do take up a lot of time and the answers are already in some article somewhere or on my web site—or they are so difficult it would take me an hour to think and answer them well, or they are too personal for such a use.

This time was different. I received an email from the daughter of one of my cousins, a person I know. She had a college paper for a computer course and got permission to use an interview with me. Her email I'd answer. With her permission, I'm posting the questions and answers here in the hope that it might help someone else.

(Remember, these are quick, email answers for a paper, not heavily contemplated responses for a major historical work.)

1. How and when did you become interested in computers?

   I first got interested in computers as a child in the 1950s and 1960s. I was interested in electronics, and read *Popular Electronics* magazine (started by Ziff—of Ziff-Davis—who later owned *PC Magazine*, etc., and which in the 1970s had a cover that inspired Bill Gates and Paul Allen). I went from radios and stuff into wanting to make a computer, even making a punched card reader for a science fair in 6th grade. In the beginning of 10th grade (1966) I learned to program and stayed with that.

2. How much had you programmed before VisiCalc? How did you know where to begin? What made you decide to create VisiCalc?

   I was a self-taught programmer for the first year and then took a National Science Foundation summer course in computer programming at the Moore School of the University of Pennsylvania in 1967 (down the hall from where ENIAC was built). The following winter I got a job programming and helping students with their computer homework at the Wharton School at U of P from the head of the summer course, Dan Ashler. I kept that job until I graduated high school a year and a half later. The VisiCalc story is in the History section of my web site [and in this book].

3. What was the most challenging part of writing VisiCalc and why? (i.e., the existing technology, hardware, languages (what language was it written in?), etc.)

   I felt that I was competing with the back-of-an-envelope calculation. It had to be real easy to use and easy enough to use the first time you did a calculation, not just when you wanted a recalculation. So, the user interface was the challenge. Then specifying what features to leave out so it would fit on the computers available (the Apple II PC with only 48KB of memory and no swapping from diskette). My partner, Bob Frankston, who had been programming even longer than I had, did most of the actual coding. I wrote the prototype in BASIC, he wrote the final in assembler.

4. How have the challenges you faced in writing programs changed? Is it more difficult to write programs now that the technology is more advanced? Why?

    It used to be that computers were used to make impossible things possible (to quote David Liddle of Interval Research). Now we try to make things not just possible but even easy or almost invisible, so the user design is even more important. The stakes are higher financially and the business models behind what you do matter more. We always push whatever technology we have so advances don't buy you much—it's always hard work since you do more if you can.

5. I read an article that mentioned that VisiCalc takes up the same amount of memory as one line in a word processing document—why is that? Are programs really that more intricate now? What is the difference between the programs?

    VisiCalc took up as much space as a "picture" does today (less than 30KB).[23] The user interface and error checking and documentation functions make the programs so much larger today. We also do so many more functions. The code today's compilers produce is quite good, so you can't blame that (compiled code vs. hand assembler) for much of the size increase.

6. How do you feel VisiCalc changed the computer industry? I've read articles that call you and Bob Frankston the "fathers of the personal computer revolution." How do you feel about this? Do you feel that our society would depend on computers as much if it were not for VisiCalc's influence?

    As I understand it, various people were introduced to the possibilities of personal computers by VisiCalc. As such, it was a real catalyst to starting the PC revolution (or is it "the personal use of computers revolution?"). It's embarrassing to be called the "fathers," but it sure makes it easier when you wonder if you'll ever do anything useful with your life knowing that people feel you have. I leave it to historians to judge the impact.

7. How did the process of writing Textscape (and Dan Bricklin's Overall Viewer, and Dan Bricklin's Demo II . . .) differ from that of writing

---

[23]That was in 1999 and referred to a tiny image on a web page. A 3-megapixel photograph from a consumer digital camera can easily take up over 30 times that.

VisiCalc? Does writing programs such as these generally take longer now, or then, or does it take about the same time?

(You mean "Trellix"—Textscape was an early codename that appeared in one or two articles.) The difference today is that people already have personal computers. We don't have to give them reasons to buy. We can take advantage of new technologies and capabilities of PCs, like graphics, the Internet, and more. Programming takes whatever amount of time you schedule it for (though often a bit more). If you have more time, you can do more. VisiCalc took a year from prototype to ship. OverAll took a year. Demo II took a year. Trellix took a year or so. Not much change.

I found this question and answer to an email from another college student a while back:

In my computer class I was assigned to pick someone's name from a list of people that are related to the computer area. I picked your name . . . But, what was life like when you were developing this for the PC. Did other people get mad at you for what you were trying to create or were people okay with it. I just need some interesting facts and I saw that I could contact you so I thought that would look great on my BIB, and also I would like to have talked with the person I am doing a report about. Everyone else's people have already passed on and so I guess I am lucky that I can still talk with mine.

My answer in a quick email from the road (while covering the Digital Storytelling Festival):[24]

I'm glad I'm still around, too . . . Who were the dead people?

People were OK about it while I was developing it, but most didn't care. PCs were viewed as toys back then, and most stories about PCs were humorous (in hindsight, they were naive about what was about to happen, which is one reason the press has been all over Internet stuff to not miss this one, either, since the Web). Having been in computers for a while at that point, I was used to the indifference. My computer friends were supportive, as were most of my professors.

http://www.bricklin.com/homework.htm

---

[24]http://www.bricklin.com/webphotojournals/dstory/

This chapter, together with the one before, should have given you a feel for the early life of a new product. The early vision evolves through the reality of needing to implement the product using the computer systems available at the time. As the product comes together, sometimes new, genre-defining attributes emerge: for example, revision history in the wiki and a full grid in the spreadsheet. Some people see the product's benefits. Some people (usually most) don't—at least at first. The inventor's interactions with many people are influential. In the end, products have a life cycle, being superseded by better implementations and replacement products after they have served their purpose.

Summing It All Up

In this book I've explored a diverse collection of subjects. They range from the personal conversations of commuters returning from work to warriors guiding missiles; from music to gesture recognition; from the American Revolution to today's political conventions; and from nuclear power plants to simple tools used by millions.

Running through all this are a variety of themes. Let me highlight and summarize just a few of the important ones.

- The real world is a place rich in variation and complexity. On just about any topic, you can explore deeply and find nuance. There are many, many individuals in the world. Each of these people has a different set of skills and experiences and a different context in which he or she exists and relates to others. Technology-based tools need to address this diversity and depth.

- There is great value in designing for free-form use. To address the diversity in the world that no one person can comprehend, you need to build tools that give freedom of expression and facilitate that expression. A successful tool or system must be able to evolve, be used to improvise, and deal with the unforeseen. Innovators have a social responsibility to develop tools flexible enough to be built upon so that other people can figure out exactly what they should be used for. It is usually the users of technology, not the inventors, who determine how tools are applied.

- Developers and policy makers must understand how people and their motivations really work in everyday life to meet their personal, individual needs. As Professor Ariely points out, there is a difference in people's minds between the financial realm and the social realm. The importance of interactions in the social realm, even those that seem trivial to those uninvolved, should not be underestimated.

- Computer technology and the Internet have enhanced developers' ability to cater to these drives and skills, and to take advantage of people's innate adaptive creativity and social nature.
- The personal computer has evolved to be, in addition, the *inter*personal computer. Facts and figures are giving way to faces and feelings.

Inspiration

I'd like to expand a bit on the individual who builds the tools. It is not uncommon to find an early experience that sets an inventor in a direction that leads to the "invention" of which we all take advantage. One of the reasons I included the entire interview with Ward Cunningham in Chapter 11 was to show the thread of influences that led to the elegantly simple tool of the wiki. In my own history, you can see my early belief in the value of the computer as a tool for everyday people. To get to the spreadsheet, I started in the area of typesetting and word processing (stemming partially from being the son and grandson of printers and a newspaper editor) and then mixed in what I got from being formally exposed to the general needs of business.

Sometimes the driving vision stems from the ideas of others, even from works of fiction. Helen Greiner is cofounder of iRobot, a producer of robots for the military as well as the home. As a child, she was inspired by the vision of robots like R2D2 in the initial 1977 *Star Wars* movie. R2D2 was just a facade, but Helen and her workmates brought the vision to life, with some robots autonomously cleaning living room floors and others with human guidance defusing very real, deadly bombs.

There is another vision that I distinctly remember from that first *Star Wars* film. It is in the scene in which the Death Star has just destroyed a planet. The Jedi Knight played by Alec Guinness is suddenly distracted and seems ill. He says that he feels, "a great disturbance in the Force, as if millions of voices cried out in terror and were suddenly silenced." This really struck me. Here, in a science fiction film, with robots and fantastic weapons, was a strong spiritual metaphor: All living things were interconnected for good and for bad. It was their own voices that traveled, not a report from some observer distant from the event. It was so cosmic, personal, and all encompassing, trivializing the simple tools being shown on the screen at the time.

When we first saw that scene, the people of the world were very loosely connected. Few mobile phones, and no cell phones, were in public use. The ARPANET, the precursor to the Internet, was still pretty tiny. Here's a photo I took in 2002 at the Computer History Museum of a diagram of the state of the ARPANET in 1979 that shows how few systems were involved at the time:

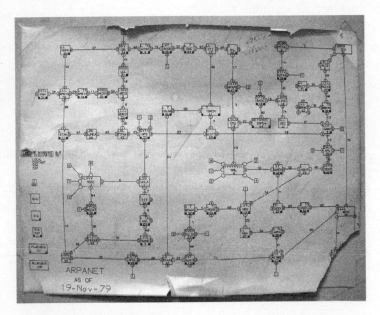

ARPANET as of 11/19/79

When the planes struck the towers on Tuesday morning, September 11, 2001, most people found out the details by watching network television or visiting news web sites like CNN.com. A few had a more personal connection, as the *New York Times* observed:[1]

> *Since cell-phone technology first came into common use in the past few years, there have been instances where someone trapped, nearing death, was able to call home and say goodbye. But there has been no instance like that on Tuesday, when so many doomed people called the most meaningful number they knew from wherever they happened to be and prayed that someone would pick up on the other end.*
>
> "The Call," *New York Times*, September 14, 2001

---

[1] http://query.nytimes.com/gst/fullpage.html?res=9C01E2D91138F937A2575AC0A96 79C8B63

When the tsunami struck on December 26, 2004, the world was able to get some idea of how sudden and horrible it all was through the widespread dissemination on the Internet of amateur video. That sharing in a realization of what it was like surely helped spur some of the surge of support sent to the victims. The BBC pointed out the importance of the video and reports of everyday people in an article by Clark Boyd titled "Tsunami disaster spurs video blogs." Quoting professor Siva Vaidhyanathan, he wrote, "There was just no way to have enough professionals, in enough corners of the earth, on enough beaches, to have made sense of this."[2]

To me, the idea that we were moving into the actualization of a fabric connecting humanity came at the beginning of the November 2008 attacks in Mumbai. I was checking my list of posts of people I follow on the Twitter "microblogging" web site. I saw reference to horrible things happening in Mumbai and a note that I could follow along by searching on the tag "#mumbai." I had a strange feeling reminiscent of other tragedies, but this time it came not through a call from a friend or relative but while participating in a worldwide conversation. Within seconds, I was seeing a flow of reports from people in the city, and information passed from person to person. As Charles Arthur wrote in the *Guardian*, "The effectiveness of the web showed itself once more with the terrorist attacks in Mumbai—with the photo-sharing site Flickr and the microblogging system Twitter both providing a kaleidoscope of what was going on within minutes of the attacks beginning."[3]

Finally, in December 2008, my Twitter stream pointed me to a set of unusual "Tweets" from Mike Wilson, a person I did not know or follow on Twitter. As Robert Mackey later reported in the *New York Times*, after assuring that he was safely out of harm's way, Mr. Wilson sent out (typo included), "I wasbjust in a plane crash!"[4] It was followed by very intimate, first-person accounts about the airplane that crashed during takeoff in Denver and how he was treated in the aftermath.

These are all stories of bad things happening to people. But, as I point out in Chapter 9, since the bad times are so stressful on systems, we often learn a lot from bad situations that can help us in better ones.

---

[2] http://news.bbc.co.uk/2/hi/technology/4173787.stm

[3] http://www.guardian.co.uk/technology/2008/nov/27/mumbai-terror-attacks-twitter-flickr

[4] http://thelede.blogs.nytimes.com/2008/12/22/plane-crash-survivor-tweets-from-denver/?partner=rss&emc=rsshttp://twitter.com/2drinksbehind

The new interconnectedness in the real world is different from the vision in the movie. In the world we have been building, *all* can participate, not just a special few. That is how we are molding technology into a force with which we all can be creative and connect with what is really meaningful to us.

Index